Anandibai Joshi: A Torchbearer

Inspiring Biography of India's First Woman Doctor

ANJALI KIRTANE

Popular Prakashan
www.popularprakashan.com

Published by
Harsha Bhatkal for
POPULAR PRAKASHAN PVT. LTD.
301, Mahalaxmi Chambers
22, Bhulabhai Desai Road
Mumbai - 400 026

First Published 2022

(4543)
ISBN: 978-81-950882-3-2

Disclaimer: The views and opinions expressed in this work are the author's own and the facts are as reported by the author, and the publisher is in no way liable for the same.

Cover design and layout: Anjali Sawant
Typesetting: Satyawan Rane

PRINTED IN INDIA
by Print Plus Private Limited
212, Swastik Chambers, ST Road
Chembur, Mumbai 400071

"Dedicated to my dear husband
Satish Kirtane
who is the constant source of inspiration to me,
all my life."

– **Anjali Kirtane**

"In the pursuit of medicine, the advancement of women's cause… pioneers - both men and women – suffered chill and utter loneliness in the performance of a duty upon which the world looked coldly. For us they were misunderstood and despised and calumniated; for us they went on the forlorn hope of truth in the service of peril to their own happiness and we cannot afford to forget them."

– **Dr. Anna Fullerton** (1893)

Physician in charge of the Woman's Hospital, Philadelphia, U. S. A

Contents

PART II - In America

Foreword

Anjali in Search of Anandi

Anandibai Joshi is a manifestation of a certain phenomenon. Not just a person or a character in the saga of fascinating family history. It is not easy to comprehend this phenomenon unless one pays close attention to the cultural and social milieu in which the epoch-making story of her life and death is carved. Anjali Kirtane has ventured into this complex territory with tremendous research and social analysis.

Though Anandibai appears at the end of the 19th century like a dazzling meteor that illuminates the sky for a while and disappears in the cloud at the early age of 21, she is not the only one in the firmament. There were quite a few others who were like guiding stars. That is what makes it a social phenomenon. Indeed, each of them has been a subject of biography and research. And yet Anjali's Anandi makes a mark on the biographical literature. Incidentally, all of them are from the same period — after 1850, which was the period of socio-cultural churning in the Marathi community. Her contemporaries interestingly were all born in almost the same decade: Rakhmabai Raut 1864; Kashibai Kanitkar 1861; Krupabai Khisty 1862; Pandita Ramabai 1858: Tarabai Shinde 1850. Rakhmabai became obsessed with the idea of becoming a doctor. Fighting all odds, she went to England, became a full-fledged doctor and devoted her life to the service of her natives, particularly women. When women were not allowed to learn, Kashibai Kanitkar, the first Marathi biographer of Anandibai, took her lessons from her husband at home and progressed so well that she became a well-known author in a short period of time. Krupabai Khisty who belonged to a progressive family and was encouraged to learn, dreamed of becoming a doctor. She was admitted to the Madras Medical College, but due to her poor health, she had to leave the course in between. Pandita Ramabai, an exceptionally brilliant woman, was such a great scholar of Sanskrit that Sanskrit pandits felicitated her with the title 'Saraswati' which is the name of the goddess of knowledge. Tarabai Shinde was so outspoken an author that she dared to write about the autonomy and independence of women. She expressed her views with such conviction and candidness that her book 'Stree-Purush Tulana' (Comparison of Man and Woman) could pass off even today as a manifesto of the women's movement.

In the late 19th century, Maharashtra was on the threshold of cultural transformation. But that transformation was not linear. Multiple contradictory forces were influencing its course. The pull of the tradition was strong, but the push for breaking out of the conservative trap was no less inviting. Indeed, often the same individual would simultaneously be pulled back and in equal strength pushed forward. This paradox affected many Brahmins, particularly the Chitpavan community, among the Marathi-speaking people. There was no 'State of Maharashtra,' in the political and geographical form. So here the term 'Maharashtra' is used in a sociological sense. Maharashtra had begun to take geopolitical shape in the 17th century, under Chhatrapati Shivaji Maharaj. However, the modern history of Marathi-speaking people (which became a political entity as 'Maharashtra' in 1960) begins after the British established their hegemony by overthrowing the Peshwas in 1818. The Peshwas represented the Marathi empire. Peshwas were quintessentially Chitpavan Brahmins. For over a century, they had almost a total sway — political and cultural. After the British took over the reins in this rocky belt of Sahyadri ranges, the Brahmins who had ruled the region, began to introspect as to why they lost the power. It is in this context that emerged the new thinking and even the appreciation of the British rule.

The new thinking essentially means the new awareness that there should be spread of education, including vocational and the knowledge of the English language. The social reformers thought that even the girls should be educated and their early marriages should be discouraged.

They strongly believed that unless there is such social reform, society will not undergo internal transformation. Even as the progressive Brahmins began to practise what they had begun to preach, there was another social movement started by Mahatma Jyotiba Phule, for eradication of the caste system, ousting 'Manusmruti ideas' from social ethos, promoting education of women of all castes and fighting the exploitation of peasants.

Though there was not much exchange of ideas between the progressive Brahmins and the Phule-led backward castes, all this was a reflection of a social convulsion and subterranean desire for change. It is necessary to place the 'Anandi phenomenon' in the socio-cultural history of the Marathi community. The epicentre of the social reform was Pune. A commercial cosmopolitan culture dominated the landscape of Bombay (now Mumbai.) Anandibai did not belong to both these cities. Though born in Pune, she was brought up in Kalyan, which was an emerging town. It was about 120 kilometres from Pune and some 70 km from Mumbai. But social mobility was evolving.

Railway had started in Hindustan or India in the mid-19th century. The Bombay-Thana (now Thane) train service started in 1853 and Kalyan station was inaugurated in 1854. Kalyan is not far from Thane. Social mobility had started influencing the new pattern of behaviour. Some people like Anandi's husband Gopal were seeking to shift their jobs and residences. For him, moving from Kalyan to Alibag, then to Kolhapur or Mumbai and even far away to Bhuj was not a geographical or cultural shock. In those days, that is 140 years ago, such mobility demanded openness of character and adaptability in lifestyle. He did this with a certain aplomb. Anjali Kirtane has been able to recreate Kalyan where Anandi grew, in a vivid picturesque manner. Moreover, she has done Maharashtra trotting by taking the readers to Bombay, Alibag, Kolhapur and even Bhuj in Kutch and finally Calcutta. The pictures of all these places in that era are depicted by Anjali, taking into consideration their history, geography and culture.

The atmosphere in Gopal's family was favourable to women's education. Living in a traditional environment where the marriageable age of a girl was to be below 9 and yet advocating girls' education, was being modern in those days. But there were people who went beyond this. Though surrounded by a patriarchal world, there was a fascination for equality between the husband and the wife. Anandi Gopal straddled this contradictory path but worked out a synthesis magnificently, sometimes with design, sometimes with intuition and occasionally, with contradiction.

It is a job of a cultural historian with insight into human behaviour, which is a complex bundle of contradictions, to write this kind of biography. Anjali Kirtane has shown that she has that talent though she is a Ph. D in literature, and not history or sociology. Originally written in Marathi and now for the first time appearing in English, it is a monumental work. It requires tenacity, eye for detail and felicity in Marathi as well as English for undertaking such a project. Anjali had to psychologically (and spiritually too) travel back in time to the late 19th century. The book is divided into two parts: 'In Hindustan' and 'In America.' Anjali had written two chapters in each part to study the period and environment thoroughly. In the 'In Hindustan' part, there are two chapters: 'Heartbeats of the 19th Century' and 'Women's Health: A Neglected Problem.' In the first chapter of 'In Hindustan', Anjali has analysed the many-sided conflict between the conqueror and conquered in the British era: conflict of ideas, ways of life, socio-political and cultural changes, religious debates, the onset of new inventions like railway, tram, post and telegraph, etc. Efforts of reformers to enlighten people, particularly women, are discussed against the background of the poor educational environment and lack of a proper educational system. Anjali has rightly devoted a full chapter, 'Women's Health: A Neglected Problem,' to the thorough study of dire medical needs and problems of Hindustani women and the role of European and American women doctors and the Missionary ladies in providing medical help to them.

Anjali graphically describes the life of the girls and women in patriarchal families, constrained by very strict norms. Luckily, Anandi's life took a different turn. Anjali had to enter into the soul of Anandibai to understand the convulsions and conflicts that must have been part of her material world. The most difficult part is to internalise the multiple layers of relationships that Anandi had to live through. A maverick husband like Gopal who had his rather complicated character, inexplicable whims and fantasies, surely tested her tolerance and tenacity. The only common bond was education. Her intense aspiration to learn and study various subjects and Gopal's ambition of educating Anandi.

But two crucial questions remain. Anandi (alias Yamuna before marriage) was married when she was just 10 years old and Gopal was 21 years older than her with an extremely volatile behaviour pattern. She was married on 31st March 1874. The marriage itself is fascinating and even frustrating drama. He used to beat or even torture Anandi; just as her mother used to flog her as a punishment when she was a child of five years of age. Only because her grandmother and her loving father were there to support, sympathise with and protect her, the cruel mother could not completely suppress her. Moreover, Anandi's willpower, grit and what is known as 'Life Force' was such that she survived all troubles, physical and mental. It must be read in details in the book to understand the turns and twists that took place before they actually married. For a 10-year-old girl, it was an ordeal. How could she handle such tensions at that stage of life? The second intriguing question is what made her choose a medical career? Anjali has investigated these two crucial questions and given convincing motives. Since it is a mystery story, I don't want to reveal all the mystery elements. Let those come to readers as a surprise.

Just to put the date and period in perspective, it is interesting to note that two great socio-political leaders — Lokamanya Bal Gangadhar Tilak and Gopal Ganesh Agarkar (both born in 1856) — were only nine years older than Anandi. Or take another fascinating contextual detail. Mahatma Gandhi left the Bombay port for England in 1888, five years after Anandi left for America. Gandhiji was under 20, Anandi was under 18. Swami Vivekanand was only two years older than her, born in 1863 and Anandibai in 1865. Vivekanand left India for America at the age of 30, in 1893, to deliver his famous speech in Chicago. If the political reference is to be seen, the Indian National Congress was founded in 1885, two years after Anandi's advent.

As a young girl of 7 or 8, Anandi had closely seen some very disturbing things and tragedies. Young girls getting married, not knowing what consummation of marriage means or what is the relevance of physical relations, young girls getting pregnant, delivering children, many a time the child dying and the little mother getting into a trauma, the household getting into turmoil. All these events played an important role in shaping Anandi's personality.

Anandi was not conventionally beautiful, either by face or by features. But she had an attractive persona. She was bold, basically playful, highly receptive and sharp in intellect. By the time Anandi and her reformer husband Gopal came to Calcutta, they had lived a married life of nearly eight years. It was at his tremendous initiative and her girt that she was educated up to a point to seek admission in an American medical college. In short, she had all the makings of a 'celebrity' which indeed she became while in America and even after returning to Hindustan. Of course, 'celebrity' in the context of that era, when the term did not have today's connotation. If she did not have that upfront, even somewhat aggressive demeanour, she could not have dealt with the people and strange circumstances she encountered.

It was the time when Missionary institutes had imported from America, women doctors who were trained in Medical colleges. They opened women's hospitals as well as organised Medical training courses for Hindustani women. Nuns and those women doctors were trying to educate and enlighten Indian women about the urgency of health and medicine issues. The Missionaries' contribution to philanthropic and educational work (albeit with the subtle purpose of influencing Indians by Christian faith) proved to be a significant impact on Anandi and even Gopal. Whatever be the (hidden or otherwise) motives of the Missionaries, they did empower women in general, and in health and Medical education in particular.

Most of the pioneering women mentioned earlier were trained in Missionary schools. Barring a few exceptions, generally, these schools had very warm, compassionate and encouraging teachers and guides. This involvement of Christian institutes had raised a storm of sorts. When young girls began getting the education and in turn started becoming independent, bold and competent, there was talk in conservative families about asking the Church authorities, government authorities or Rajas of States to stop their activities. But the traditionalists could not succeed.

I must write about two biographies of Anandibai written by her contemporaries. The one written by Caroline Dall in America is her first biography. The second one was written in Hindustan by Kashibai Kanitkar. While Anjali draws a lot on Kashibai's and Caroline's books, she does not accept their versions, facts, sequences and interpretations. Anjali has often corrected the earlier books and monographs on facts, making the account truthful. She has collected vintage material from various sources in India and America. Secondly, to get the feel of that period and the places, she visited (or even discovered) many places and buildings connected with Anandibai. To name a few, she discovered the old railway station of Roselle, which was not in use in 1991 and had become invisible when Anjali went there. She wandered on the roads of Roselle, observed many well-preserved old houses, including the house of the Carpenters, just for understanding the personality of the town, where Anandi once lived. Anjali's greatest achievement is that she discovered Anandi's grave which had remained unknown so far. According to her last wish, Anandibai's ashes were buried here. Even after her death, she wanted to remain near her American family. All these things make Anjali a profound researcher in history. A historiographer in the role of a biographer. And a literary writer who has converted the biography into an intriguing piece of creative writing.

History is a humongous mystery. Every individual also creates his or her own history. Here, we see an otherwise nondescript adolescent girl of 17 from a colonial country and underdeveloped small town of Kalyan, carving her own history that vibrates even today. She not only transformed her own life but also inspired one American and several Indian biographers and writers to re-explore her short life of 21 years. Such individuals are enveloped in deep, dark dormant mystery. What were the inner driving forces that shaped Anandi? Anandi broke the wall of tradition and fate facilitated her struggle.

A biographer in this case, must delve into the broad forces of psychology, culture and history. For that, one requires a broad canvas, vision and approach. However, understanding those forces is not enough. A biography writer has to be an author of mystery too. Only then the story becomes thrilling, romantic and full of suspense. Anjali Kirtane excels in these attributes. The writer has to recreate and bring to the surface the hidden relationships. That requires the skill of a psychoanalyst and the rigour of a researcher. With these skills and insights, the characters acquire LIFE! The mystery gets resolved and it enlightens too. It is a challenging task, a long journey into the mysterious history of the individual as well as the social environment. In today's idioms, we should say, the biographer must create the ecosystem of the period.

Kirtane has written a panoramic and three-dimensional volume of Anandibai Joshi. Anandibai was the first Indian woman who dared to migrate for some years into a foreign land like America, to study Medicine, over 140 years ago, when she was just 17 years old. Except for a few American Missionary ladies who hated her and felt free to exhibit their hatred, Anandi was almost alone in her two month-long journey by boat, from Calcutta (now Kolkata) to New York. Her first-ever journey beyond the borders of her native country, beyond the sea and beyond the socio-cultural boundaries that governed her life. One can imagine how difficult it might have been for Anandi to make this long journey, with totally unknown passengers, mostly men, with complex daily routines on the sea. It surely must not have been easy to adjust to the utterly strange surroundings.

Anandi completed the journey with gusto and reached an alien land for learning Medicine. While she lived there for three years, she picked up American English, the local slang and manners. She did not live merely like a 'paying guest' or a foreign student but virtually became a member of the family of her host. In no time, Anandi became popular among her neighbours. This clearly shows that Anandi was able to transcend the language, religion and culture barriers, perhaps not with ease but with effort. And soon, they ceased to be barriers. Caroline Dall, a feminist writer, was so infatuated by the young Marathi girl that she wrote a biography of hers.

Anjali Kirtane has not only travelled with Anandi in the boat but also stayed with her, in a kind of invisible form and observed closely all the persons who interacted with Anandi on a day-to-day basis. In a sort of occultist manner, Anjali has entered the body and soul of Anandibai. This biography also gives mini biographies of the Carpenters, Caroline Dall and so many others. At the beginning of the second part 'In America',

Anjali has thoughtfully established the feminist movement as well as the American women doctors' great struggle for their right to Medical education, as the backdrop for Anandi's life in America. This wider perspective underlines the significance of the struggle of a girl like Anandi who belonged to an underdeveloped country like India. This magnificent work of biography is also a sociological treatise on life in the 19th century, particularly the Marathi socio ethos and its changing values.

It is difficult to write in the preface, the fantastic experiences that the biographer has had while unravelling extremely complicated relationship issues, finding extremely minor-looking events, collecting photographs and so on. Kirtane's search for the memorial of Anandi where her ashes have been buried in Poughkeepsie is like an adventure film. Anjali made a research film on Anandibai when she was writing the book in Marathi. She worked on both projects simultaneously and completed them successfully. After having published 4 Marathi editions, with detailed introductions, now comes this English version, translated by Anjali herself. That in itself is a separate achievement. The book gives in the Appendix some valuable documents. For example, Anandibai's lecture delivered at Srirampur, Bengal, before she left for America which shows her excellent expression in English, her style and her confidence. There is also her thesis on Obstetrics and some informative letters. Anandibai's tragic death at the age of 21 in Pune and the entire episode of her last days bring tears to the reader's eyes.

But the book does not close at the tragedy of Anandi's life. The last chapter deals with the equally exciting accounts of other Indian women doctors of the 19th century and their magnificent work in the Medical field. Some of them were inspired by the enchanting story of Dr Anandibai Joshi. This chapter gives a new hope that life goes on. There is always somebody who rushes forward to hold the flag before it falls.

Biographies with historical and contextual research require deep exploration into the subject's environment. This is common to most European and American biographers. Anjali Kirtane has done the similar rigorous research and penetrating analysis one finds in the works published by Oxford-Cambridge or Stanford-Harvard scholars.

Sometimes such scholarship constrains the author. The biography could then compromise on style and get jarred by the huge data. The focus on the person and the period may get lost. But it does not happen in this case. There are not many biographies written in Marathi with such elaborate research into the period and personality, Anjali's Anandi acquires the same quality and standard of Euro-American writers and researchers.

I wish this biography a grand success. I am sure, this English version will contribute to the studies on Indology across the world, and also serve as a major reference for the studies on the century that changed the world. Anandi will remain a spirit of idealism and hope of liberation to the coming generations.

– **Kumar Ketkar**
Senior Journalist, Thinker, Editor, Writer
and International Speaker

Acknowledgements

I am deeply grateful to those organisations and persons who supported this project and helped me in various ways.

- Mumbai Marathi Grantha Sangrahalay Dadar, Mumbai
- Archives of the Medical College of Pennsylvania, Philadelphia, U.S.A. (Ms. Jennet Millar and her colleagues.)
- Rural Cemetery of Poughkeepsie, New York State.
- National Archives New York, U.S.A.
- Government's Archives at Kolhapur, Maharashtra State, India. (Mr.Vilas Kamble, Mr. Prashant Shirolikar)
- Pandita Ramabai Mukti Mission Kedgaon, Pune District, Maharashtra, India (Ms. Heather Johnstone)
- Tilak Smarak Mandir: Microfilm section, Pune, Maharashtra, India (Mr. Ketkar, Mrs. Patwardhan)
- Raja Kelkar Vastusangrahalay, Pune, Maharashtra, India (Mr. Hari Ranade, Mrs. Rekha Ranade)
- Kesari Grantha Sangrahalay, Pune, Maharashtra, India (Mr. Phansalkar, Mr. Alhad Godbole)
- Kalyan Nagarik Periodical (Editor Mr.Deodhar)
- Mr. Suresh Bhatia – Photographer

Nancy Cob Stone, Shyamsunder Adhav, Prabhakar Kelovkar, Ashok and Manisha Gore, Ajit and Vidula Gore, Ashok Tilak, Ashok Amberdekar, Dr. Shubha Pandya, Pro. M. V. Dhond, Dr. Usha Saraiya, Viraj Sardesai, Shashi-Sushma Rane, Suniti Ganpule, Bhagwanrao Oak, Ram Deshpande, Ratnakar Vashikar, S. N. Barve, Pratibha Deodhar, Vishwas Joshi,

Sindhu Oak, Damodar Joshi, Sushila Joshi, Rev. Bedekar, Pro. D. B. Wagh, Dr. Purnima Kirtane, Pro. Kusum Deshpande, Atul Joshi.

Very special thanks to my friendly publisher, Harsha Bhatkal. Thanks to Armaity, Editor Vrunda Juwale, typesetter Satyawan Rane, designer Anjali Sawant, Megha Bhagat from the Marathi Division of Popular Prakashan. Thanks to Swapna Bhagat and Swati Padwal who typed my manuscript efficiently.

Last but not least, my sincere thanks to my dear friend Kumar Ketkar, who introduced my book in a superb way.

Preface

A Letter to Dr. Anandibai Joshi

Mumbai, India

4th May 2022

Dear Anandi,

You have been living in my mind for years and I feel very happy in your company. But do you know when we met for the first time? My mind travels way back to the year 1965. It was your birth centenary year. *Satyakatha*, a prestigious Marathi magazine, had printed a close-up of your face on the cover. I was a schoolgirl then. While curiously observing your photograph, I asked my mother, "Who is Anandibai Joshi?" She briefly told me that you were the first Indian woman doctor who went to America to learn Medicine and received the degree of M.D. She further emphasised that in the 19th century, it was not customary to educate a girl; rather, it was considered to be a horrible sin. Child marriages were very common and a small girl of 6 or 7 years was given in marriage even to a 60-year-old man. I was shocked to hear this. I was watching your serene face and thinking, 'Could people be so cruel to girls? And why? What was wrong in learning?' I was lost in my thoughts when my mother asked me, "Like her, would you go to a foreign land to learn something?" Without any serious consideration, I said, "Yes!" But the truth is that I was not thinking about myself. I was fascinated by your expressive face which looked a bit sad to me. No one knew at that point in time, that in my distant future, I was to go to America, in search of you.

After a year or so, I read *Anandi Gopal*, a novel written in Marathi by S.J. Joshi which was based on your life story. But the novel left an odd impression of your personality on my mind. It depicted you as a girl who became a doctor just because her husband wished so; a girl who was very intelligent, but not really interested in learning. I was troubled by a question, 'Then what was Anandi's own dream?' I didn't know the answer and the novel didn't provide me with any. So, I lost interest in your story though your serene face on the magazine cover stayed with me. I was not ready to accept the author's interpretation. My mind declared, 'This girl can't be so stupid!'

Years passed. I was a married woman now and was pursuing my career as an author. It was 1987, the year of your death centenary, when you came into my life to live forever. Thinking that I would be interested in the subject, my relatives in America, Ashok and Manisha Gore gave me a photocopy of your biography written by a feminist American author, Caroline Dall. Though Caroline was 40 years older than you, a warm friendship had developed between you both, because Caroline was sympathetic towards the problems of Hindustani women and she had a good knowledge of your country.

While reading this interesting book, I was thrilled to know that to become a doctor was your dream and not an idea imposed on you by your husband Gopal. When Caroline interviewed you, you told her the real story behind your wish to become a doctor. You had become a mother at the tender age of 12 and your son died on the 10th day as he could not get medical help in time. This grievous incident broke your heart. But at the same time, you started thinking about the pathetic state of Hindustani women and children who badly needed well-qualified women doctors. Going one step ahead, you thought, 'What if I become a doctor?' And your answer was, 'Yes, I will! I will become a doctor.' When even primary education was denied to girls, you were thinking of becoming a doctor! How great was that! You simply enchanted me. I was eager to know more about your life story.

I found that Kashibai Kanitkar, who was your contemporary, had written your biography in Marathi. In those days, Indian women had just begun to write short stories or small articles in magazines. But Kashibai took the responsibility of writing a biography of a well-known person like you. It required research. She was a sensitive, frank and truthful biographer. She tried her best to understand a unique person like you who was rebellious and traditional at the same time. Though Kashibai had read Caroline's book, she gave the credit for your magnificent dream not to you, but to your husband. She had had some correspondence with Theodosia Carpenter, who had provided you accommodation in her house in America and had treated you like her own daughter. Kashibai could have checked with Theodosia Carpenter if the incident of your taking inspiration from the child's death was true or not. But surprisingly she overlooked the incident and didn't give you the due credit. Moreover, neither Caroline nor Kashibai wrote much about your professors, friends, your curriculum, your thesis; in short, your college life which was the most meaningful period in your life. In spite of being a feminist, Caroline chose not to speak about the American and European women doctors' magnificent struggle for their right to Medical education and about the feminist movement in general. Dear Anandi, I really felt sorry for you that the due credit was not given to you by your own people and knowingly or unknowingly, your personality was dwarfed by your husband's. They had done injustice to you. Hence, I felt an inner urge to do research on your life and write your biography with a fresh outlook, based on truths and facts. I knew very well that it was not at all an easy task. But accepting the challenge, I was ready to devote some years of my life to this project. My revered Guru and a great critic late Prof. M. V. Dhond used to tell me, "A biographer must study the period first, for the better understanding of any person. The reason is that every human being is a product of his time and place as well." Remembering his wise words, I decided to focus my attention on the 19th century Hindustan and study the period from various angles. In that era, Hindustan was conquered by the British. I wanted to probe into the relationship between the conqueror and the conquered, the socio-political atmosphere, the reforms brought here by the British which changed the lives of the people of this country forever; the system of education, the condition of women and the contribution of Indian reformers in the emancipation of women, so on and so forth. Hence, I prepared a list of more than 100 books, magazines, newspapers and other periodicals which would throw light on that period. Some biographies were of persons connected directly with your life, so those were valuable while seeking answers to some yet unanswered questions. One of your relatives, Damodar Joshi, generously gave me a copy of your family history which helped me analyse the nature of your joint family, depict the characteristics of your family members, their relations with each other and your family life in general.

After devoting 2 years to the period study, I asked myself, 'Am I fit to write the biography?' But denying me the permission, my mind said, "No! Your period study is not yet complete. You do not know anything about Anandi's college life in America which you are keen to understand. You will have to discover somebody from the Carpenter family also. You must know more about Theodosia Carpenter, her husband Benjamin and their two daughters, Eighmie and Helena, because these are important characters in the biography. Go and find out various places associated with Anandi. Old buildings would talk a lot about that period." My inner voice told me that something wonderful was waiting for me in America. I would be able to discover if I go there, vast research material, letters, documents, photographs, etc. Dear Anandi, you were calling me from American shores. A fascinating dream took shape in my mind. I told myself, 'Come what may, I must go to America. I must study in the archives of your college at Philadelphia.'

By the way, I would like to tell you something very interesting about your college. Now your college is not in the area where you studied; in your college days, it was behind the Girard College where North College Avenue and the 22nd Road meet. But when I went there in 1991 it was shifted to 3300 Henry Avenue. I wished to visit the place where once your college was; where you lived and studied. Hence, I went there with my acquaintance Dr. Meena Nerurkar. But I saw that the old building was demolished long back and a residential building had come up there. The place was very deserted. Hence, Meena thought that it was not safe to get down from the car and roam around. Otherwise, I wanted to walk on those roads and take photographs. I wanted to find out about Dean

Bodley's house where you lived for some years. Anyway, the image of that corner is imprinted on my mind. You would love to know that in the course of time, Girard College has changed for the better. In those days, it admitted only White orphans, but now it is open for *any* orphan. I remembered that even you wanted to organise an orphanage in Hindustan.

There is one more interesting story about your college. When you studied there, the name of the institute was, 'Woman's Medical College of Pennsylvania.' But now it is known as the 'Medical College of Pennsylvania' because now it admits male students too. And, yet the old name has miraculously survived. In front of the building on Henry Avenue, there are four huge white pillars and the old name 'Woman's Medical College of Pennsylvania' is carved on its beams. This name is connected with the history of women doctors' struggle to get entry into Medical colleges. Because women were denied permission to learn Medicine, some broad-minded, progressive people founded the 'Woman's Medical College of Pennsylvania' in Philadelphia. It was the first of its kind in the world.

To make my long story short, I decided to go to America, and went there in September 1991. In the course of my biography, you would know how and what I discovered. But I must tell you about a beautiful moment which changed the course of my life. On 28th September 1991, I visited the Rural Cemetery at Poughkeepsie, along with my relatives Ashok and Manisha Gore and their friend Viraj Sardesai, who helped us find your grave. It was a wonderful discovery for me — your last resting place. But I was told that for decades nobody had visited the grave and there was no caretaker of it. No one knew what happened to the Carpenters and where they had gone. In the office of the cemetery, a lady was giving us the information about your grave.

"Who is the caretaker of the Eighmie lot where Anandibai's ashes are buried?" I enquired.

"Nobody,' she said.

"Okay, but if some day, someone belonging to the Carpenter family visits, please tell the person that I am writing a biography of

Dr. Anandibai Joshi and I would like to communicate with him or her. Here is my visiting card."

"Yes, sure," she replied.

I knew that it was a shot in the dark, but there was no other way. When I saw your grave, I remembered your ancestral house in Kalyan, a town near Mumbai. I had discovered the house a few months ago with the help of our acquaintance Ratnakar Vashikar. So now, I had seen both the ends of your life. Even after your death, you wanted to be with your American family. That was your last wish. So, you requested your husband Gopal to send the vessel of your ashes to the Carpenters. They had given you a place in their hearts, so they fondly buried it in their private lot at the Rural Cemetery of Poughkeepsie.

With deep satisfaction, I touched your gravestone with both hands and felt as if I was touching you! It was a hair-raising experience that I will never forget. The grave was more than a hundred years old. No wonder, the letters engraved on the stone had faded. Though I was thrilled to discover your last resting place; as a researcher, I thought that I must make sure that it was your grave only. So, I put my finger on the engraved letters and read them like the Brail script. When I completed sensing the words with touch, I realised with joy, that it *was* your grave. They used to call you '*Anandabai*' and not '*Anandibai.*' Hence, they had spelt your name in the same way.

We had brought red and white roses to offer you because the rose was your favourite flower. When I put those flowers on your grave, I was very sad. How lonely your grave looked! I wondered, who might have visited it the last and when? On behalf of all your countrywomen, I saluted you and whispered, "It was *you* who opened the doors of higher education to Indian women, despite the staunch opposition from the Indian society. You were extremely courageous. Hats off to you! *We are because you were.*"

On that day, we spent a few hours with you, wandering and taking photographs of that place. I wrote down the names of the other members of the Carpenter family who were buried there. The small gravestones told us the touching story of Theodosia and Benjamin Carpenter's children who died very young. As the bright summer day turned into a warm evening, we had to start our homeward journey. When we were stepping down the small hillock, I suddenly felt an intense urge to turn back and look at your grave for the last time. You know what happened? I turned back, not knowing that it was going to be a turning point in my life. A wonderful thought sprang in my mind at that particular moment: 'What if I make a short film on Anandi's struggle story!' The next moment, I wondered, 'A short film? Was I dreaming? Or was I mad?' But I was fascinated by this idea. I could not forget it even when I came back to Mumbai. Filmmaking was a totally new and unknown road for me, but you motivated me to take it. I confidently made a new beginning. I need not tell you how I made the film, because this is not the place to go into those details. That is another story. But one thing that I must tell you is that I took your story to the masses. Even today, after 30 years, I screen the film at various places in India and abroad. Now I have made research films on different subjects. You know, *you* made me a filmmaker, a screenplay writer and a director. I have no words to thank you. The friendship between my pen and camera made my life enchanting.

You would enjoy the last part of this story the most. My film became instrumental in discovering Mrs. Nancy Cobb Stone, who is the great granddaughter of your American Aunt Theodosia Carpenter and granddaughter of your little sister Helena Carpenter. I completed my research film in March 1992. It won the best documentary award that year and was selected in the American-Marathi Convention to be held on 3rd July 1993 at Baltimore. Ashok and Manisha Gore organised the screening of my film at the Convention and invited Nancy as a special guest. Nancy talked very sweetly and naturally. She narrated your story to the viewers which she had heard in childhood, sitting comfortably in the lap of grandmama Helena. When you were living with the Carpenters, Helena was a small girl. You were there only for 3 years but she could never forget you. I have Nancy's speech with me. She kindly gave me a copy. See what she says about you and your relationship with the Carpenter family. "This history was told to me by my grandmother who in 1883 was nine years old. She lived the normal life of a middleclass girl in small town America. She went to school, attended church, played with her friends, took piano lessons, helped her mother in the kitchen and enjoyed a happy family life. In June of that year, her life changed forever. A young woman named Anandabai Joshi became a member of her family.... Anandabai lived in my grandmother's heart all her life. When I was 9 or 10 years old, she began to tell me of Anandabai she had known so many years before.... She told me of a shy, sweet girl—very solemn—but with a wonderful sense of humour. A tiny, delicate, dark-skinned girl with great liquid eyes and a slow beautiful smile. A girl who loved her country and loved to share it with her friends. My grandmother told of sitting for hours listening to Anandabai describe her country, the Indian people in all their diversity and the great legends of the Hindu religion, weaving a tapestry of Indian life and lore that she carried with her all her life. A girl who loved to play for though she was a young married woman, she was still a child, because she had lost so many years of her childhood to study and struggle.... Mostly she would tell me of a gentle girl with foreign but perfect manners and quiet dignity, alone in a strange land who approached her new life with immense courage.... Her courage and strength were manifest in her every action of every day.... She endured pain, loss, loneliness and illness without complaint.... My family said goodbye to her on a fall day at the New York dock. They knew they would never see her again. But she lived on in their hearts. My family has revered her and loved her over 100 years.... And how proud you must be that she is yours." Nancy's speech is so touching, isn't it? Your little darling sister Helena cherished your memories and passed them to the next generations. Because of her we could know you better. Nancy struck the right chord with the viewers who were gathered for the screening of my film.

Dear Anandi, I cannot tell you sufficiently how delighted I was to meet Nancy and her husband Jim. At last, my wish was fulfilled. Nancy had already handed over to Ashok Gore the photocopies of the correspondence between you and Aunt Theo and some other important letters. He gave those to me. This valuable treasure had been lovingly preserved by the Carpenter family. Helena was the only child of Theodosia Carpenter, who lived long. So, the correspondence might have come to her which she passed on to her daughter that is Nancy's mother. After the screening at Baltimore, sitting in a small corner, Aunt Nancy and I talked a lot even in the commotion around us. She told me that for many years, she was out of

America because her husband worked in the Foreign Service department. "When I returned," she said, "I do not know why but I was feeling an urgent need to visit our family graves at Poughkeepsie. There was no caretaker of our Eighmie lot; so, the authorities of the cemetery made me the caretaker. When I went there, I came to know about your research on Anandibai and the girl in the office told me that you wished to meet me. I was equally thrilled that day, as you are thrilled today to meet me. Do you know Anjali, why we met? This is our *karma*!" I was surprised to hear her utter the word *karma* from Indian philosophy. Then smiling through her blue eyes, she took out a small brass icon from her purse and asked me,

"Who is this?"

"Why, it is an icon of Lord Ganapati."

"Yes. I purchased it somewhere in America. When I went to India, I took it to Varanasi. Went on the shore of the Ganges, washed it with the sacred water and told him, 'Now you are pure.' You know your Ganapati bappa is my friend. He shows me the right way," Nancy said.

With her pleasing face and curious eyes, she was intently watching me. Dear Anandi, that moment I realised for the first time, how attached you might have been to the wonderful family of the Carpenters who always respected other people's culture and religion. Before meeting her in Baltimore, I had written a letter to her and had expressed my wish to visit her house. When we met, the first thing she did was to invite me to her house. After a few days, on 9th July 1993, I went to her house with my relative Ashok Ambardekar. Her house was near a lake which was covered with greenish shadows of various trees. There were other houses also. But the atmosphere was extremely silent and peaceful. I could clearly hear the chirping of birds and the song of the wind.

The day spent with Aunt Nancy and Uncle Jim was the most wonderful day in my research-journey. Spreading photo frames on the floor, she had prepared the family tree of the Carpenters for my better understanding. Putting her arm around me, she showed me her house. The glass windows of her house were very large; as if they were not windows but doors. The trees and shrubs outside the house looked as if they were painted on the window panes. Nancy's house was just like her —

open-minded and joyful. It was not divided into formal and informal parlours. Everything was informal and natural. The fireplace was fixed between two rooms, so that it could heat both rooms at a time. Her house was decorated with the choicest paintings, wall-hangings and show-pieces from all over the world. There was a beautiful painting from Rajasthan, India adorning a wall. A traditional water-heater of copper from Pakistan was standing in a corner. Near the fireplace a metallic mortar-pestle was kept artistically. Near one window stood a huge Egyptian King's chair and a tall, colourful cock. I wondered how she and Uncle Jim brought home those heavy things from all over the world. Forgetting the mutual hatred or hostility, various countries in the world were happily sitting side by side in her house. While wandering from one room to another, she said, "My house is not a typical American house."

"Even you are not a typical American woman!" I exclaimed. She pressed my hand with delight. At Baltimore, I had asked her, "You know that Anandi had organised an Indian feast for her friends at Roselle. That day all American women had appeared in saris which Anandi had provided them to wear for the occasion. Today, I have brought my mother's silk sari and blouse for you to wear. Would you please do that?" She was looking curiously at me. You know why I did that? I wanted to enjoy on a smaller scale, that beautiful moment in your life.

"Oh yes! Why not," she exclaimed enthusiastically.

In the afternoon I helped her to drape the sari. She found it very exciting. Then I fixed a broach on her shoulder to set the sari perfectly. Like Indian women, I applied a round red spot of kumkum on her forehead. With pearl tops and a neckless, she looked very beautiful. After her dressing was over, she looked confused. She asked me, "O my God! How to walk?" I took her hand in my hand and catching the flowing material of the sari by the other hand, she descended the staircase very carefully. She was smiling at her own confusion. It was such fun! She sat on a chair when I interviewed her and didn't get up even once. But I succeeded in getting a few photographs of Nancy in the sari.

I wanted to present Aunt Nancy and Uncle Jim something typically Indian. So, I had brought the famous 3 Monkeys of Mahatma Gandhi who tell the world, 'Do not speak bad, do not see bad and do not hear bad.' When she opened the parcel, she saw what it contained. She laughed heartily and looking at Uncle Jim, said mischievously, "Oh! I know the meaning of it! Jim needs it. So, I will keep it on his table."

Uncle Jim, who was working in the kitchen, gave her a big smile. He was tall and hefty. Aunt Nancy looked like a tiny doll before him. "Come on, let's have lunch friends! Aren't you hungry Anjali?" He called us into the dining room. On the smooth black tabletop, she had arranged pots, pans, glasses, spoons and dishes. While keeping an ice-cold bottle of Champaign in a silver pot, Uncle Jim smiled and said, "Anjali this is especially for you." When we were dining at a Chinese hotel in Baltimore, we were discussing something and I casually mentioned that I like Champaign the most. It was so nice of him to remember that! The large dishes on the table were bordered with two golden lines and a design of flowers in between. In the corner, there was a tall triangular cupboard wherein she had kept a silver kettle, sugar-pot and a cream-pot. Pointing at those things, she told us, "Those things and the dishes on the dining table belong to Theodosia Carpenter. Anjali, your Anandi ate from these dishes. I never use them. But today you have come from Anandi's country. We feel as if Anandi has visited our house, in your form. So, I am using them to welcome you."

Dear Anandi, I was speechless. I didn't know what to say. I was about to touch my dish when Aunt Nancy told me this. But now my fingers were trembling. I could not eat for a while and was just staring at the dish. Was I eating from the dishes which were used by *you*? I had never imagined this pleasure. Though I was very happy, my eyes were moist with emotions. The idea of comparing myself with you had never crossed my mind. Your dreams, your ambitions were only yours. You lived that wonderful life. I was only researching and writing about you. But of course, I could understand the delicate emotions and love that surged in the minds of Aunt Nancy and Uncle Jim.

Aunt Nancy was lost in her own thoughts and was staring at nothing in particular. But very slowly she said, "Anandi is really unsung. Please do write her biography Anjali." My book on your life was published in Marathi in the year 1997 and was very well received. Now 4 editions are sold out and the 5th edition will come out soon. But I had always wished to write it in English as well. So that the story of your struggle would be read by a wider audience. Ultimately, after such a long period, my dream is turning into reality. I have completed writing the English biography. I know it is very late. But better late than never. I am sure that your life story would continue inspiring the generations to come.

With love and respect,

Yours,

– **Anjali Kirtane**

PART - I
In Hindustan

1

Heartbeats of the 19th Century

When the British defeated Peshwa Bajirao II in 1818, no other ruler had the strength to stand up against the foreign invader and challenge his supremacy. In the beginning, the seafaring European merchants and Christian Missionaries had arrived in this country in the hope of expanding their trade and spreading the message of God among the heathens. But over time, they became aware of the political instability, the rivalry among the rulers and the wretched economic conditions of the ignorant masses. So, their simple hope gradually turned into a lust for conquest. They were shrewd enough to perceive that with some tactics, disciplined moves and the organised military forces, they could subjugate the Hindustani monarchs and rule over them.

When the British rose to power, Hindustan was a huge subcontinent fragmented into various kingdoms which were ruled by different Kings and noblemen in their own way; with no strong central power to bind them together. It was only when the British Raj prevailed over the country that Hindustan started evolving as one nation. Before the rise of the British, interstate wars constantly threatened the peace and normalcy of life. Rulers who were more interested in warfare than in the welfare of their subjects, always needed money for the fulfilment of their political ambitions, for the maintenance of the armies and also for their own luxuries. Therefore, soldiers and commanders were set free to extract money, not only from the people of the enemy countries but also from their own subjects. Killing and looting had become a way of life. Those who opposed, bluffed or hid their wealth, were exposed to the most brutal punishments like making them stand on hot iron plates, cramming their mouths with hot ashes, throwing boiling oil on small children or even violating the modesty of women. The protectors had turned into tyrants. In this dreadful atmosphere, the subjects had nowhere to turn for peace, safety, justice, hope and happiness.

No wonder many people fell into a lethargy or lost their will to shape their lives and future, and became fatalists. Another reason why despite the widespread unrest, dissatisfaction and potential anger, people did not rise in revolt was that there was a lack of intellectual leadership. Injustice, poverty and grief are not the sufficient conditions for a revolution. People need thinkers and philosophers to ignite the moral anger suppressed within them and motivate them to act. But such leaders were not born then in the pre-British period. People were so tired of the tyrant Kings and war maniacs that when the British conquered them, they felt relieved and looked at the foreign ruler with a new hope.

It was a challenge to rule over such a vast and unknown country. To meet this challenge, the British wanted to establish a communication network and an excellent administrative machinery. They desperately needed educated people who could keep the machinery rolling. The need was so acute that even those who had an elementary knowledge of English were invited by the British and palanquins were sent for them. In order to communicate with the natives and to understand them in a better way, it was made compulsory for the Britishers working in India to learn the regional language of their territory as well as Hindi, the commonly understood language in Hindustan. The British were not the conquerors who plundered, looted, destroyed and went away. On the contrary, they handled the looters and criminals with an iron hand and established law and order in the country. They brought everything under the British Law. A judiciary system was so badly needed in the country that people took time to realise that they were being conquered by a foreign invader.

Dr. N. G. Kalelkar has rightly acknowledged the debt of gratitude that Indians owe to the British. Says he, "They had a genuine desire to know and understand India. The vast multiplicity of its cultures and differences did not deter them. They explored it bit by bit. That is how we find among them scholars and investigators who pursued a single subject, wrote articles, published books, organised learned societies and brought forth an amazing mass of information which we ourselves did not possess. Works like the gazetteers, projects like the monumental Linguistic Survey of India or the ethnographical studies of the various parts of India, the comprehensive census operations are but a few examples of the valuable store of factual knowledge which they placed at our disposal and but for which we would be still groping in darkness regarding our own cultures, religions, history, customs and manners, languages, geography, etc. They were the pioneers in almost every branch of the studies a native is more naturally qualified to undertake."[1]

It's no surprise that slowly but steadily, the political victory of the British started deeply affecting the cultural fibre of Indian life. The Indians who learnt English, were enchanted to know the kind of knowledge that was stored in that language. They felt an inner urge to acquire that knowledge and bring it into their vernacular languages. The British were enlightened rulers who had political thinkers, philosophers, philanthropists, writers, investigators and scientists back home. In the 19th century, great European minds influenced the educated class in India in many ways and opened for them the door to a new world. The tree of education, which was planted here by the British, soon started flowering. Balshastri Jambhekar, a scholarly youth was the first among them who bloomed quite early. Being far ahead of his time, Balshastri realised that the print media was going to play an important role in awakening and educating the masses. He is known as the Father of Marathi newspaper because he launched the first Marathi newspaper named *Darpan* in the early days of the British Raj. The first issue of *Darpan* was published on 6th January 1832 which was Balshashtri's 20th birthday. The newspaper was printed both in English and Marathi, using two separate columns.

Balshastri had not only mastered Marathi, Sanskrit, Hindi and English but he also had a good understanding of Greek, Latin, French, Gujarati and Bengali. Through his newspaper, the reformer strongly supported remarriage of widows and generated debates about such sensitive issues. He died very young, at the age of 34 years. But within that short span, he pioneered many things. In October 1834, he was appointed as an Assistant Professor in Elphinstone College in Mumbai (then Bombay) and was the first Indian member of this new academic faculty. Dadabhai Naoroji, who later turned out to be a scholar and great political leader, was a student of Balshastri in the Elphinstone College.

Realising the value of a public library, Balshastri founded 'The Bombay Native General Library.' He founded the 'Native Improvement Society', a social service organisation, which inspired intellectual giants like Dadabhai Naoroji and Bhau Daji Lad. In 1840, he published the first Marathi magazine *Digdarshan* (meaning Direction) in which he published articles on Physics, Chemistry, Geography and History, to make people curious about these branches of knowledge. He was a prolific writer who constructed moral stories as well as wrote books on various subjects like History of India, English Grammar, and Mathematics — based on zero. He was the first Indian who published research papers in the quarterly journal of the Asiatic Society. In short, Balshastri was the founder of modern Maharashtra.

English, the language of the ruler, was a window to an unknown world. Hence, many of the youth who learnt English, looked at the British not as their enemy but as their benefactor. Gopal Hari Deshmukh, alias Lokahitawadi[F1] was one of them. He was an activist and a brilliant writer from Pune. At the age of 25, he began to write essays about social reforms, in a weekly named *Prabhakar* under the pen name 'Lokahitawadi'. In the first two years, he penned 108 articles about various social issues like women's education, child marriage, dowry and polygamy. In these articles, he analysed and compared the conditions prevalent in the pre-British and post-British India. He was of the opinion that God had sent this mighty ruler to improve the miserable lot of Hindustan. He advised people to understand the changing times and make use of the new knowledge brought in by the British. This group of articles became famous as *Shata-Patre* or 100 open letters to society. As a young man, he had started working as a translator for the government. In 1867, he was appointed as a small cause judge. He also worked as a Diwan in the Ratlam state. The government bestowed on him honorifics like 'Justice of Peace' and 'Raobahadur'.

When the British came to India, the barter system was prevalent in its villages and 12 service providers called Balutedar, like the milkman, barber, blacksmith, goldsmith, carpenter, painter, potter, tailor, shoemaker and so on, fulfilled the daily needs of the people. They worked in their small spheres, without bothering much about who ruled over them. Their main concerns were, how to master a particular skill and how to earn a living. In the social hierarchy, the Brahmans were at the top who enjoyed the position of religious leaders. They performed religious duties and interpreted the old Sanskrit scripts. Reading, writing and learning the Sanskrit language was traditionally their prerogative. A village was ruled

---

F1 Lokahitawadi – One who cares for the public welfare

by Gram Panchayat, the local system of justice, where a small group of chosen people listened to the complaints of villagers and pronounced their verdicts. There was no written law. For villagers, the members of Gram Panchayat were lawgivers and the Panchayat's was the last word. The Indian society was divided into small islands of castes. Due to the strong notions about castes, the various religious customs, the prohibition of intercaste marriages, and the lack of a common education system, on no ground could the people come together. Moreover, the concept of nation was so young and unknown, that the people were not prepared to unite for a national cause.

The sense of equality began to develop gradually, and reluctantly, when various unheard-of systems like the railway, tram, hospital, post and telegraph department, and newspapers were introduced by the British. They were available for everybody, regardless of their castes. A person of any caste could travel by a tram or a train. From a shoemaker to a sweetmeat seller, anyone could advertise their products in any newspaper. There were no separate post boxes for different castes. Water stored in a dam was for everybody's consumption whereas, in the period before that, the best parts of a river were kept reserved for the upper classes. In a way, these innovations challenged the unjustifiable custom of untouchability.

The advent of printing technology brought about a revolution in mass communication. Before this, knowledge had to be stored in handwritten manuscripts called *Pothy*. Making copies of a manuscript was a very time-consuming, tedious and an expensive job. The printing technology gave an easy access to knowledge and information in the form of books, magazines and newspapers at lower prices. Before the advent of the British Raj, there was no uniformity in the coins because every King had his own currency. For the first time, the British Rupee became the common Indian currency.

All such amazing developments expanded the horizon of people's experience, though, at the outset, they found it difficult to accept them. It would be amusing to note their reactions to the new systems. Their minds were flooded with questions, "How come a steam engine pulls the cars of a train without a bull?" They thought, it might be either the British God or some sort of witchcraft. Being scared to climb a train, they offered it flowers and coconuts and prayed for their safe journey before entering it. In those days, not only was the train travel free but to attract people, money was also offered to those who dared to travel by train. Wide-eyed villagers whispered that a telegram was nothing but a magic doll that slid over a wire at night, from city to city, for delivering messages. It was believed that if one read a printed book, one would go mad. The ignorance and fear of the natives made them suspicious of every reform and invention that the British introduced. Along the way of advancement, the colours of fantasy and magic surrounding the innovations faded away and they became a part of the common man's life.

Far-sighted Indian leaders like Jagannath Shankershet, Dadabhai Naoroji, Dr. Bhau Daji Lad were the valuable links between the British government and the Indian subjects. For understanding people's minds in advance, the governor of Bombay used to seek Jagannath Shankershet's advice before introducing any reform. It was Jagannath Shankershet who, along with his pro-reform friends, appealed to the British government to introduce a railway in India. Surprisingly, the government was not very enthusiastic. But Jagannath Shankershet pursued the matter with the British government and motivated his friends also. The railway had a humble beginning but it shows the farsightedness of Jagannath Shankershet. He is rightly called the 'Father of Indian Railway.' The railway track from the Bori Bunder of Bombay to Thane, a nearby town, which was inaugurated on 16th April 1853, was the first railway track in Asia.

In 19th century India, educational reform was the most important and urgent of all the reforms. Before the British regime, a well-developed education system did not exist. Rich landlords and money-lenders used to appoint teachers for their children at home. Others used to send their children to indigenous schools which did not have any definite curriculum. Generally, it was believed that the basic knowledge of reading, writing and arithmetic was more than enough to earn a livelihood. People were so indifferent to learning that the role of knowledge in self-development and in the progress of society was not thought of.

The indigenous schools were organised in temples or verandas of mansions where students of different standards were crammed together and a single teacher used to teach all the subjects to all the standards.

On an auspicious day, parents would ceremoniously take their child to a school. It was a custom to call a Brahman for selecting a holy day and time, known as *muhurta.* Guests were invited to a feast. The child going to the school was decked with rich clothes and ornaments. Family members and guests walked in a procession from their home to the school. After distributing sweets and gifts among teachers and students, the procession went back along with the child. This was how the first day of a child at school was celebrated. Despite the pomp that marked the initiation of children into school, they were often removed from schools at any time of the year, without a second thought. If a child's family needed him for some work at home or farm, his education was abruptly interrupted.

In 1849, a renowned Indian grammarian Dadoba Pandurang Tarkhadkar discussed this issue in his report on schools. "The people of this country are not yet prepared to appreciate the sort of education which is afforded by our schools to their children, their idea of school learning amounting to no more than mere reading and writing, the current hand in which business is transacted…They are...not very punctual in sending their children to the school. The ignorance added to their poverty, makes parents overanxious to remove their children from their schools, as they can read and write a little Modi[F2] character"[2].

Teachers themselves were unaware of the real significance of education. Teachers' training was an unheard-of concept. Learning meant nothing but mugging up information. It did not matter whether the students understood a subject or not. Students had no freedom to ask questions or argue with their teachers. An inquisitive student was often labelled as an arrogant boy and cruel punishments were inflicted upon him. The only way to maintain discipline in a classroom was to thrash students.

When education itself was in such a sorry state, it's not surprising that serious thought was not given to women's education. If a girl knew how to cook food, keep her house in good shape and rear children, she was considered to be a well-educated person. Women were looked down on as inferior beings having no intellectual capacity and hence were not allowed to learn. Their lives whirled in the ruts of housekeeping,

F2 Modi – The running hand in Marathi.

conjugal obligations, maternal responsibilities, and religious duties. Except for their daily visits to temples or the occasional visits to their relatives, women rarely crossed thresholds of their houses and mostly spent their lives in the secluded women's quarters. It was impossible for them even to think of going to school for gaining knowledge. Ideas like self-development, financial independence, ambitions and freedom did not apply to women. In fact, fundamental human rights were denied to women for centuries and so it was not considered as an injustice, but as their normal lot. The impact of tradition was so strong that women themselves opposed the women who tried to get out of the rut. [F3]Tarabai Shinde was an exceptional woman who didn't fit in the traditional image of an Indian woman.

Tarabai was an educated woman who developed her career as an author. She was lucky to be born in a progressive family. Her father Bapuji Hari Shinde, from Buldhana, was a radical who acted on his own opinions. He had four sons and Tarabai was his only daughter. There was no girls' school in their village but Bapuji taught his daughter Marathi, Sanskrit and English. According to the custom, Tarabai was married when quite young. But a few years after the marriage, her husband moved to his parents' house. So, Tarabai was free to do whatever she wished. Tarabai was also an associate of a social activist Jyotiba Phule and his wife Savitribai, and was a founder member of their *Satya Shodhak Samaj* or the Truth Finding Community. She was known for her fearless attitude, frankness and the sharp tongue. She gave voice to the injustice done to women. While comparing the lives of men and women in her book, [F4]*Stree-Purush Tulana*, she boldly criticised the then prevailing male chauvinism. This small, pamphlet-like book could be called the first feminist text in Marathi, which was published in 1882. She attacked the caste system and the patriarchy. Anger boiled in her mind to see what men had made of women. Through her writing, she relentlessly lashed out at men for treating women like inferior and sinful beings, treating them like slaves or the objects of pleasure, and denying them the opportunity to learn and the freedom of self-development. She

F3 Bai – In Maharashtra, this is a term of respectful mention used for a woman. But in North India, the same word has a different connotation. There, though Bai indicates respect, the word is used for artists who entertain men by singing and dancing.

F4 Stree Purush Tulana – Comparison of men and women

was exhilarated by the defeat of the mighty Peshwa because she regarded it as the defeat of Indian males and respected the British for opening the door to knowledge for native women.

In 1882, the English Education Commission presided over by Dr. W. W. Hunter visited India to inspect the conditions of educational institutions and to study the problem of women's education. The Commission examined some of the noteworthy persons like Jyotiba Phule, a native reformer fighting for the emancipation of women and low castes. In 1848, Jyotiba Phule had opened a girls' school in Pune, a town in the Bombay Presidency. His efforts were not supported by any institute, but he himself was an institution. He had trained his illiterate wife Savitri and carved a teacher out of her. For this benevolent work, he received nothing but abuse and stones from the orthodox townsmen. Before the English Education Commission, Jyotiba Phule analysed the drawbacks of indigenous schools. "Indigenous schools ... are conducted on the old village system.... The teachers as a rule are not initiated in the art of teaching.... The teachers generally come from the dregs of Brahmanical society. Their qualifications hardly go beyond reading and writing Marathi very indifferently and casting accounts up to the rule of three or so. They set up as teachers as the last resource of getting a livelihood. Their failure or unfitness in other callings of life obliges them to open schools. No arrangements exist in the country to train up teachers for indigenous schools. The indigenous schools could not be turned to any good account, unless the present teachers are replaced by men from the training colleges and by those who pass the 6th standard in the vernaculars."[3]

Pandita Ramabai Dongare, a Sanskrit scholar and the pioneer Indian woman reformer, was also called before the English Education Commission and was questioned by Dr. Hunter. Ramabai succeeded in impressing upon the Commission the acute need for women's educational institutes and lady doctors in India. She said, "I am a child of a man who had to suffer a great deal on account of advocating female education.... I consider it my duty to the very end of my life, to maintain this cause and to advocate the proper position of women in this land.... It appears to me evident that the women who are to become teachers of others should have a special training for that work. Besides having a correct knowledge of their own language, they ought to acquire English....There ought to be female inspectors over female schools. In ninety-nine cases out of hundred, the educated men of this country, are opposed to female education and the proper position of women. Male and female should be treated with equal justice.... women...are oppressed, are cruelly treated.... To put a stop to this anomaly is worthy of a good government. Another suggestion, I would make is, with regard to lady doctors. Though in Hindustan there are number of gentlemen doctors, there are no ladies of that profession. The women of this country are much more reserved than in other countries; and most of them would rather die, than speak of their ailments to a man. The want of lady doctor is therefore, the cause of hundreds of, thousands of women dying premature death."[4] Dr. Hunter regarded Pandita Ramabai's evidence so valuable that he made her the subject of his lecture in Edinburgh. "When I spoke," says Dr. Hunter about the reaction of the Edinburgh audience, "of, a high caste Indian lady being thus employed, that great English audience rose as one man and applauded the efforts which Pandita Ramabai was making on behalf of her countrymen."[5]

A woman's place in society, in various religions, and even in her own house, was always subordinate to that of a man. 'Independence should not be given to a woman' was an order of a religious script, which was proudly quoted and strictly observed by people. A husband had absolute power over his wife, whose status was no better than a bonded labourer. She had no choice but to be submissive and suffer, without a word of protest. The practice of child marriage was the biggest obstacle in the development of Indian women. Girls got married at the age of 7, 6, or even 5. These marriages ended their childhood and whatever little maiden freedom that they had. Moreover, many times, small girls were given in marriages to aged men. This inhuman custom was the root cause of a large number of child-widows in Indian society. There was no end to the evils and horrors which women had to face on every step of life.

The life of a widow was nothing but hell! Void of all hopes, love, joy or kindness! She was treated as if she was responsible for her husband's death. So, she was deprived of everything. She was prohibited from taking part in any religious ceremony or a festival. She was not allowed to wear anything but a single long garment of white, red, or brown colour. All the privileges of a married woman were denied to a widow. After her husband's death, the mangalsutra or the marriage-string, bangles and all other ornaments were removed from her body. She was not allowed even to apply the red pigment or kumkum upon her forehead. A poor widow had no right to happiness, no right to decorate herself, no right to enjoy womanly pleasures. She had no right on her own body either. Long hair used to be a mark of beauty and pride for Indian women. They loved to arrange their hair in different styles. They used to decorate their hairdos with flowers and head-ornaments. But to make a widow unattractive, a barbarous custom of shaving her head was followed religiously. Widows were threatened that if they did not shave their heads, their husbands would not get a place in heaven. Many a time, these ill-fated women were subjected to sexual harassment by their male relatives or even barbers, who had freedom to go into the inner courts. If women became pregnant with a child, the burden of guilt was loaded on the helpless shoulders of the poor women and they were thrown out of their houses. A pregnant widow had no other choice but to commit suicide, while those guilty men who harassed women could live happily. A widow had no right to remarry; no chance to turn her grief-ridden, burdensome life into a happy one. In contrast, if a woman died, her husband had full right to remarry, nay, he was urged to marry by his parents and relatives. Naturally, some widows preferred self-immolation upon the pyre of their deceased husbands, over the dreadful widowhood, the lifelong torture, and insults. It was very tragic that circumstances compelled them to observe this formidable custom of Sati.

Widowhood was the gravest punishment that life could inflict upon a woman. A mere utterance of this word struck terror in their minds. Knowing this, it was impressed upon their minds that if they chose to learn to read and write, their husbands would die. No surprise that to run away from learning was their reflex action. Thus, they remained unaware of the joy of learning and the intellectual satisfaction that knowledge could offer. Pandita Ramabai says, "Where conjugal relation is brightened by mutual love, the happy wife has nothing to complain of, except the absence of freedom of thought and action; but since wives have never known...what freedom is, they are generally well content to remain in bondage."[6]

Raja Ram Mohan Roy, an apostle from Calcutta (Kolkata now) was the first person to give a thought to women's education, when there had been no girls' schools run by either Christian Missionaries or the British government. Women's education was considered as an anti-religious activity and not to interfere in the religious matters of their subjects as far as possible, was the policy of the British government in those days. Hence, the issue of woman's education had remained untouched. Even Mount Stuart Elphinstone, a benevolent Governor of the Bombay Presidency never thought over this. But in 1821, Raja Ram Mohan Roy requested Margaret Cook, a Missionary lady in Calcutta, to open a girls' school and the financial responsibility of this school was shouldered by Raja Ram Mohan Roy himself. Three years later, in 1824, the American Mission established a girls' school in Bombay, with 5 branches in various parts of the city. When Margaret Cook married Rev. Wilson of Bombay, the couple also started a girls' school there in 1829-30. Though the main purpose of those Missionary schools was to propagate Christianity and motivate conversion, one cannot forget that because of them, Indian girls could get an opportunity to learn. Reading, writing, Arithmetic as well as sewing and knitting were taught to them. Not only the education was free, but allowances were also given to pupils as an added attraction.

Mary Carpenter, a philanthropic woman from England had heartfelt sympathy for Indian women and she earnestly desired to emancipate them. In 1867, she visited India for the first time, on the invitation of Raja Ram Mohan Roy. She travelled all over the country studying thoroughly the conditions of girls' schools and the impact of child marriage on their education. After discussing the multiple aspects of this issue with Indian reformers, she propounded some valuable suggestions to the British government, one of those being urgent training of women teachers. Since people were reluctant to send their daughters to an institute where there were male teachers, the need for women teachers was acute. When a girl came of age, she was removed from the school and was confined to her house. Naturally, there was always a noticeable drop-out in girls' schools.

In this land of secluded women, Mary Carpenter was taken by surprise to meet the well-educated daughters of a native doctor, Dr. Atmaram Tarkhadkar. The smart girls conversed with her in English with fluency. This was the fruit of Dr. Tarkhadkar's progressive views. But India needed many such Tarkhadkars for changing the future of women. In 1848, the students and alumni of the Elphinstone College came forward to form 'The Students' Literary and Scientific Society' for imparting knowledge to native girls. With the help of other reformers, this organisation promoted many girls' schools in Bombay, which were not Missionary in nature and imparted education in vernacular languages.

Understanding people's dislike for the Missionary schools and their fear about the possible conversion of their daughters to Christianity, the organisers founded those schools. The idea was that at least those who were ready to do this experiment of educating their daughters, sisters or wives, should feel motivated to take advantage of this facility.

To organise a girls' school was a thankless, uphill task. The organisers had to convince parents, attract students, raise funds, search for a convenient place for their school, and many a time, even perform the duty of today's school bus driver. The staunch supporters of women's education like Jagannath Shankershet, Dr. Bhau Daji Lad, Dadabhai Naoroji, Mangaldas Nathubhai, Bhagvandas Purushottamdas zealously took this responsibility on their strong shoulders, without worrying about the financial problems or opposition from society. Gradually, the seedling of women's education took roots and the opposition faded away. Ultimately, people began to understand that a mother plays an important role in the development of her children. So, if she is educated, she would bring up her children in a better way.

Raja-Maharajas bestowed grants and some of the British also donated generously for founding girls' schools. A noteworthy name among them was Sir William Wedderburn, who donated Rs.10,000, for the first government's girls' high school in Pune, in memory of his late brother David. On 19th July 1884, a meeting of respectable citizens and representatives of progressive Kings was called by Justice Mahadeo Govind Ranade and Sir William Weddernburn, for discussing various issues regarding this school, the most important one being financial assistance. Hon. Jaysingrao A. Ghatge of the State of Kolhapur and Hon. Hariprasad Desai, the Justice of Peace of the State of Bhavnagar, donated large sums. On 9th August 1884, the school got official recognition from the government. Completing all the formalities, the school opened on 29th September 1884. Though it was named as 'The High School for Native Girls,' it was popularly known as the 'Female High school.' The founders like V. M. Bhide, S.P. Pandit and R. G. Bhandarkar set examples by sending their daughters and daughters-in-law to this school. On the first day, there were only 18 students, but within a fortnight, the number increased to 45. Here, girls could complete the curriculum for the Matriculation examination. Before this, the only option to matriculate a girl was to send her to a Missionary high school, which people avoided.

The traditionalists couldn't turn a blind eye to such major happenings. The birth of a girls' high school immediately produced bitter reactions among the anti-reformists. Just to teach a lesson to the progressives, they started troubling the school-going girls. Though bullock carts were arranged to bring the students safely from their houses to the school, the ruffians had the effrontery to pull flowers from the hair-does of the girls in bullock carts. Their loose tongues showered a torrent of abusive words too. But giving no heed to them, the girls stood their ground and continued to go to school. After 6 years, the first student, Dwarkabai Kelavkar, passed the Matriculation examination with flying colours and brought honour to the school.

The traditionalists were not ready to accept the reality. So they tried in vain to reverse the time wheel. To save themselves from the changing times, they had constructed a castle of conventions around them. They believed that their values were perpetual and the reforms were nothing but passing fancies. But the rising generation was not ready to blindly accept the value system of the old generation. The youth bravely faced intellectual conflicts and tried to seek answers to the questions troubling their minds like, 'Should one stick to the old convictions and miss the opportunity of enlightenment or should one be open-minded and try to understand the new ways of life?' 'Should one run away from knowledge and be happy in ignorance and lethargy or should one acquire new knowledge, develop one's capacities, be industrious and raise the standard of one's living?' Those who could read the writing on the wall rebelled and tried to demolish the false fortification.

Krushnashastri Chiplunkar, a Sanskrit scholar could be mentioned as a brilliant, open-minded representative of the progressives. Krushnashastri started learning English in his late twenties and yet he could master the foreign language so well as to translate in Marathi, John Stuart Mills' voluminous book, *The Principles of Political Economy*. In 1882, [F5]'Sarvajanik Sabha', an institute in Pune, raised funds to send a scholar, Keshav Guruji Bhat, to the USA for mastering the techniques of making glass, colours, rubber and tar. The scheme was also supported by the Maharaja of Darbhanga State, who granted Rs. 2000/- per annum. In this atmosphere of enlightenment, people were motivated to study even the traditional branches of knowledge with a fresh, analytical outlook. In 1873, Bhalachandra Bhatawdekar, an intelligent native

F5 Sarvajanik Sabha – Public assembly

student of the 'Grant Medical College', stood first in the examination of 'Licentiate in Medicine' and secured the prestigious Jamshetji Jeejibhoy Gold Medal and many other prizes. This young doctor was grieved to observe that the traditional Indian branches of Medicine were not able to withstand the competition from European Medicine. Dr. Bhatawdekar carried on their comparative study and sought harmony between the two. When Sir T. Madhava Rao, the Diwan of Baroda State founded an institute for the enlightenment of the Indian Medical Science, Dr. Bhatawdekar was appointed as the principal. Here the facility to learn Medicine in a vernacular language like Marathi was offered to students and Dr. Bhatawdekar wrote Marathi textbooks for them. In Bombay, Dr. Sakharam Arjun Raut requested the authorities of the Bombay University to allow students to learn Medicine in vernacular languages. His request was granted and he was appointed as the professor in charge.

There was one more thing that disturbed the older generation but motivated the youth to evaluate the traditional concepts which were generally accepted without scrutiny. Rigorously attacking customs like child marriage, Sati and untouchability, the Christian Missionaries were raising fundamental questions: 'Why should women not learn?', 'Why is the right to education denied to women?', 'Aren't they human beings?', 'Why should widows not remarry?', 'Why are people belonging to certain castes considered untouchables?' Never before in history was the Hindu religion thus discussed or dissected. This was not a battle that could be won with the help of swords and soldiers; the only useful weapon was rational thinking. Gone were the days of authoritative commands like, 'Do this because old scriptures say so!' or 'Do this because your elders say so'. In that era of awakening, rationalists expected that every 'Why' had to be answered with a reasonable, convincing argument. It was not easy to silence the voice of reason, as blind faith had started losing its charm.

But when the Christian Missionaries tried to prove that their religion was superior to the Hindu religion in every respect and ridiculed Hindus as idol-worshipping heathens, Hindus fought back with zeal and refuted their arguments giving proper reasons. This battle interested people so much that newspapers were launched by different native groups to refute the religious attacks. One of them was [F6]*Vichar Lahari* which was edited by the same Krushnashastri Chiplunkar, who had translated

F6 Vichar Lahari – Waves of thoughts

The Principles of Political Economy. Vishnushastri, the son of Krushnashastri, forcefully depicted the brighter side of the Hindu religion through his essays and strongly advocated good principles in it. He was able to regenerate self-esteem, confidence and fighting spirit among the Hindus. Newspapers and magazines became the new battlefields where the regiments of words combated. This was a unique feature of this era. The awakened Indians were fighting without an order from their King and on their own. They were fighting for their values, thoughts and principles. There was no blood shedding, no killing, no destruction of human lives. On the contrary, these constructive battles enriched the minds of people and widened the horizons of their experiences.

Even the first Indian war of independence waged in 1857, which the British waved aside as a mere mutiny of soldiers, was not the product of war-mongers' whims and caprice. It was the first revolt of patriots against the foreign ruler. In fact, it was much more than that. It was the first sprout of the love of freedom. At last, people had identified their enemy and had revolted against him. While seeking leadership, people turned to the Indian rulers like the Badshah of Delhi, Rani Lakshmibai of Jhansi and Nanasaheb Peshwa of Pune. Though the British had already clipped the wings of these Indian rulers, Indians voluntarily accepted them as their own leaders. These Rajas became the symbol of the old Indian glory. The dissatisfaction of this once ruling class had remained dormant so far, as they were not strong enough to revolt against the foreign invaders. But now, with the support of the people, their unrest gave rise to the first war of independence. Though this attempt to gain freedom ultimately came to grief, one cannot undervalue its significance as the first outburst of the national spirit. People were ready to die for the noble values like freedom and the honour of their motherland.

The year 1857 is remembered as a turning point in the history of India for one more reason. In the same year, three major universities were founded to impart higher education to the Indians. On 24th January, the first university was founded in Calcutta. Immediately after that on 18th June and on 5th September, Bombay and Madras universities were founded, respectively. The first batch of students graduated from the Bombay University on 28th April, 1862, in the presence of Sir Bartle Frere, the chancellor of the University and the Governor of Bombay. On this memorable day, members of the Senate, professors, examiners and respectable citizens of Bombay had happily gathered in the Town Hall to witness the First Convocation. Mahadev Govind Ranade, who in his later life became famous as Justice

Ranade, was the first graduate of the University of Bombay. The degree of Bachelor of Arts was conferred upon him and his batch-mates like R. G. Bhandarkar, Bal Mangesh Lad and Waman Abaji Modak. Sir Bartle Frere addressed the newly graduated young men and urged them to work for the upliftment of their people. He said, "Your standard must henceforth be, not that of your masters or even of the Government to whose service some of you may devote yourselves; but of the whole educated world.... I trust that one of your great objects will always be to enrich your own vernacular literature. ... Remember, I pray you, that what is taught here is a sacred trust confided to you for the benefit of your countrymen....The learning which can here be imparted to... a few thousands of scholars, must by you be made available through your vernacular tongues to the many millions of Hindustan. The great majority of your countrymen can only learn through the language which is taught them at their mother's knee and it must be through such language mainly that you can impart to them all that you would communicate of European learning and science....Remember too that not only the character of the University, but the character of your whole people also is to a great extent in your hands." [7] Later, those graduates of the first batch proved that they were worthy of the trust that the chancellor had placed in them.

The foundation of universities opened the door to the world of fascinating goals. Thereafter, an increasing number of youngsters took advantage of this facility. There, young minds started cherishing wonderful dreams like becoming a doctor, engineer, lawyer or founding a school or launching a newspaper, and they pursued those with determination. The British viewed the higher education of the natives in two different ways. Thinking that once awakened, the educated class would try to overthrow the foreign ruler, some of the British were against imparting higher education to Indians. They argued that the British realm was safe in the ignorance of these people. They were not afraid of the educated people who preferred to remain loyal to the British throne and had no patriotic aspirations. Blind followers and 'obedient government servants' never posed any threat to the British. Mahadeo Govind Ranade and a few other government servants were true patriots and always had their sympathies with their own people, but they were exceptions.

The threat to the British Empire was from the free thinkers like Gopal Ganesh Agarkar who was neither afraid of society nor the government. The British were worried about a lion-hearted leader like Bal Gangadhar Tilak, who made people aware that the British had enslaved their beloved country and the prime duty of the people was to free her from their clutches. The threat to the British Empire was from the brave freedom fighters like Vinayak Damodar Savarkar whom the British put in a torture chamber for years. The threat was from the dauntless Subhash Chandra Bose who shook hands with the Germans, an enemy of the British, and organised his own army, 'Azad Hind Sena'. Those who ruled over the hearts of the people and flared patriotic wrath, posed a real danger to the British power. Since education nurtured such minds, some of the British officers advocated anti-educational policy from the very beginning. They insisted that Indians should not be made so much wise as to revolt against the government. Against this backdrop, the educational policy of Lord Mount Stuart Elphinstone, the Governor of the Bombay Presidency (1819-1827) stands out as a unique policy. In a letter to his friend Mackintosh, he says, "The belief that our Indian empire will not be long-lived is reason and not prejudice. It is difficult to guess the death it may die....The most desirable death to die of should be the improvements of the natives reaching such a pitch as would render it impossible for a foreign nation to retain the government....A time of separation must come and it is for our interest to have an early separation from a civilised people."[8]

The existence of such a civilised, freedom-loving generation was soon felt through their actions and reactions, words and deeds. To resolve the question of an inferior medical diploma offered to Indian doctors, Dr. Bhalachandra Bhatawdekar fought for 12 years with the University of Bombay. Since the medical diploma 'Licentiate to Medicine' indicated not the quality but just the permission to practise Medicine, it had no value in the outside world. The Medical education offered to Indians was in no way inferior to that of the English universities. Native doctors like Atmaram Pandurang Tarkhadkar, Bhau Daji Lad, Burjorji Dorabji had proved their brilliance since their salad days. Authorities of the Grant Medical College were so pleased with these students of the first batch that they specially mentioned their names in the annual report of 1846-1847. It says, "Bhawo Daji... Burjorji Dorabji...Atmaram Pandurang have advanced beyond what is usually expected of the students in the first year of their studies." Hence, there was no reason to deny the degrees like 'Bachelor of Medicine' and 'Bachelor of Surgery' to native doctors. It was very unfair because, on the ground of substandard degrees, various benefits as well as prestigious posts were denied to them. Secondly, many a time, European doctors looked down upon native doctors as mere licence-holders and even ill-treated them, despite their ability. Dr. Bhatawdekar stood up and rebelled against this injustice. Along with the Indian newspapers, a prestigious periodical like the *British Medical Journal* supported Dr. Bhatawdekar's demand. His long fight for equality in the field of Medicine carved a special place for him in the history of Medicine.

During the period when Dr. Bhatawdekar was fighting for a proper Medical degree, many expert native doctors had proved the validity of his argument, by their own good work. In Bombay, Dr. Bhatawdekar himself had set up a large practice. He had also worked in the states like Baroda and Palanpur where he was respected equally by the poor and the rich. It is interesting to note what Behramji M. Malabari, a well-known Parsi reformer, said about Dr. Bhatawdekar. He said, "One of the most useful agencies of the Administration is the medical department, virtually I presume under the control of Dr. Bhalchandra the hero of the Caesarean section. He has performed sixteen operations known by that name. It is curious to see how Hindus have of late been taking to the medical profession.... There are six medical officers in the Baroda territory, among whom Dr. Bhal, stands pre-eminent for his rare ability and tact. 'He is especially conspicuous for popularity and his earned confidence at the Palace,' says the Diwan and this is saying a good deal."[9]

In 1893, Dr. Bhatawdekar had raised this issue of the inferior degree to Indian doctors in the Senate of the University of Bombay and the members offered strong resistance. The demand particularly drove Dr. Grey to distraction, who was a professor of standing in the Grant Medical College. Being unable to refute the argument of Dr. Bhatawdekar and his supporters, Dr. Grey wrote malicious letters to him, so that he might keep quiet. But Dr. Bhatawdekar was resolute in his intention. The long fight put up by him had formed the public opinion in favour of the noble cause. Ultimately, on 15th December 1905, the resolution was passed in the Senate in favour of the native doctors. The grand victory of Dr. Bhatawdekar was an indication of the emergence of 'civilised people', who dared to fight for their rights even with the British government.

The subtly changing psyche of Indian people was reflected in their outlooks, reactions and attitudes. The urgent need for women's education was felt by the newly educated young men. They taught their wives to read and write and impressed upon their minds the importance of knowledge in human life. Education helped the youth to form a fresh concept of their life-partners. Feeling ridiculous to marry a child of 5 years, they preferred a mature wife belonging to their age group, with whom they could share their thoughts, dreams, goals and aspirations. They wished to discuss with their life partner literature, drama, poems, reforms, future and many other issues which they had at heart. Marriage was no more just an outlet to sexual desires but an intimate relationship; an emotional attachment based on mutual respect and understanding. This civilised attitude of the youth caused a real setback to the custom of child marriage.

Big talks and little actions never help any reform. Miraculous changes can take place only if reform begins at home and if examples are set before society. Here are some such examples of active reformers. Ganesh Vasudev Joshi alias [F7]Sarvajanik Kaka founded 'Sarvajanik Sabha', an association of activists on 2nd April, 1870. He urged his wife to take the lead and organise a similar association for women, to which she responded enthusiastically. For encouraging women to learn, she organised [F8]'Stree Vicharvati Sabha' in 1873. Rakhmabai, the wife of Dr. Krushnaji Kelavkar, was so illiterate that when her little daughter told her, "Mother, I scored 5 out of 5 marks in my exam," she opened her daughter's tiny palms to see what it contained and was surprised to see nothing. But Dr. Kelavkar educated Rakhmabai so thoroughly and she too worked so hard that within a few years, she could complete the teachers' training course in Pune and became the first native lady superintendent of the Education Department of the Kolhapur State. Avantikabai Gokhale, a biographer of Mahatma Gandhi, was encouraged to learn by her in-laws. Her husband, who was then in England, was so pleased to hear about her genuine interest in gaining knowledge that he sent her 300 books as a gift. Rebecca Simian was taught by her husband Benjamin at home. Since Rebecca wished to become a nurse, Benjamin enrolled her name in the Grant Medical College. Their own people gave a threat to outcast them. But dauntless Rebecca and Benjamin were not shaken. Later on, the kind-hearted nurse proved to be a boon for ailing women. The husband was so much impressed by the benevolent work of his wife that he enrolled his name in the Grant Medical College and became a doctor.

This might be the only example in that period where a wife inspired her husband. A young girl who later became famous as Dr. Rakhmabai

---

F7 Sarvajanik Kaka - Uncle of everybody or Public Uncle

F8 Stree Vicharvati Sabha -The Association of thoughtful women.

Raut, could muster up the courage to disown her unworthy husband to whom she was married in her childhood. Her decision was firmly backed up by her step-father Dr. Sakharam Arjun Raut.

In this atmosphere, a woman's relationship with her own self also changed. The search for identity had begun. Now she was no more a faceless non-entity. No doubt, she still thought of herself as somebody's daughter, sister, wife or mother and gave preference to her relations with others. Yet a thin sense of belonging to one's own self had begun to grow subconsciously. For the first time in history, she treated herself as an individual having her own sorrows, joys, wishes and dreams. The women who could cross the thresholds of their houses to fulfil their ambitions were overjoyed to breathe the fresh air of freedom. They could not ignore the calls of their minds any more. They wanted to become 'somebody' — teachers, nurses, doctors, lawyers, authors or artists and for that matter, they were ready to overcome any hurdles that might come in their way. The pioneer Indian lady doctor Dr. Anandibai Joshi represents this class of awakened women of the 19th century.

The intellectual conflicts of the 19th century Indian people remind me of the golden era of the European Renaissance or the glorious revival of knowledge which began way back in the 14th century. In that period, faith and reason crossed swords in every field of life, like literature, art, philosophy, science, politics and religion. For centuries, reason was defeated by faith and faith was favoured and encouraged by politicians and religious leaders. In the kingdom of blind faith, there was no place for a truth-seeker or a free thinker or a scientist. Science had no scope in the Dark Ages. Scientific statements like 'The Earth is round' or 'The Earth rotates around the Sun' were treated as sinful utterances of a profane person or a wizard. Scientists were burnt alive for their pursuit of knowledge. God and King were unchallengeable entities towards whom nothing but an unflinching devotion was expected. Ghastly punishments were inflicted on those who tried to challenge their authority.

In the 19th century India, though there was no such revival of knowledge; it was the discovery of a new world of knowledge. Moreover, the battle between faith and reason was the same. In spite of the dominance of faith, reason survived deep down in the minds of people, waiting for an opportunity to spring out. Ultimately, it could gain ground with increasing momentum in the 14th century Europe and the 19th century

India. Basically, Renaissance was the revival of reason. After the grand rebirth of reason, no concept or idea was to be accepted without analysis, evaluation, critical study and the application of the Law of Causality. No wonder, the very existence of God was challenged. In the atmosphere of free thinking, faith began to lose its charm. The Industrial Revolution was a triumph of science and technology which changed the face of the whole world. In England, the British challenged their own King and advocated democracy. The coalition of dictatorial political leaders and religious leaders was challenged by thinkers and the common people and it gave birth to the French Revolution. The Americans rebelled against the power lust of England and freed 13 of their colonies from the British control. By and large, all these revolutions were expressions of the same basic conflict between faith and reason. The Indian revolution unfolded itself in two steps. First the Indians freed themselves from the shackles of tradition with the help of new knowledge that the British had brought with them in Hindustan. Then under the guidance of their own native leaders, they freed their country from the bondage of the British rulers. This two-fold freedom fight makes the 19th century very interesting. This is a golden page in the world history of revolutions, written by the Indians.

References:

1. *Molesworth's Marathi – English Dictionary* – Preface to reprint – by Dr. N. G. Kalelkar. Shubhada Saraswat Prakashan, Pune. 6th Reprint July 1996. Page, Nine.
2. *Raobahadur Dadoba Pandurang Tarkhadkar* Editor and Author – Anant Kakba Priyolkar. First Edition 1947.Page 207 (Marathi Book)
3. Memorial Address to the Education Commission – Round Table India website. Taken from the book *Selected Writings of Jyotiba Phule*, 2002 (Pages 140- 145)
4. A Reprint of the *High Caste Hindu Woman – Pandita Ramabai Saraswati*. Introduction by R. L. Bodley. 1981 pages – Introduction xiii, xiv
5 Ibid, Page Introduction xii
6. A Reprint of the *High Caste Hindu Woman – Pandita Ramabai Saraswati* 1981 Page25
7. *Cloister's Pale – A Biography of the University of Bombay* – Aroon Tikekar 1984 Page 20
8. Ibid Page 11

2

Women's Health: A Neglected Problem

A 19th century newcomer to India was struck by the singular absence of women on roads, in markets or in any other public places. He was more puzzled to know that women equated the overflowing population of men but the Indian etiquettes prohibited them from mixing with men. The seclusion of women was supposed to be a mark of social standing. Particularly if a high caste woman was seen on a street, people raised their eyebrows and craned their necks with surprise. Once when Dr. Atmaram Tarkhadkar, a reputed doctor of progressive views, visited the mint in Bombay along with his wife and two friendly couples, the 'wonder' was reported in 'Bombay Times'.

A woman's place was inside her house, the threshold being the boundary of her existence. Her life was stuck in the ruts of household work, child-rearing and religious duties. For centuries it was taken for granted that the very purpose of her existence was to bear many children. The custom of child marriage imposed premature motherhood upon little girls. It injured their physical and mental development and caused gravest health problems which generally remained neglected through ignorance. The young mothers suffered the agonies of child-birth, mostly without any medical help, except that of uneducated, native midwives. Dr. Ida Scudder, who worked in India for years observed, "Probably there is not a practitioner here who has not stood by one of the little child wives in labour and felt that it was time something desperately should be done to save the little girls of India from the suffering forced upon them. Only a few weeks ago a little girl of 13 was brought in labour. She hardly realised what was happening and everyone present in that operation room rebelled against the custom of child wives. The day has come when a stop should be put to it."[1]

How to reach those secluded women and make them aware of the benefits of Western medicine, was a problem that vexed Western Medical people working in Hindustan. Hindustani women's idea of modesty and womanliness forbade them from accepting Medical help from male doctors. Their bashfulness was so deep-rooted that they preferred to suffer than discuss their physical problems with a male doctor. The help of European women doctors was accepted gladly but they were very few, compared to the dire need of the country. Dr. F.M. Smith, who had worked among native women, superbly analysed the situation, "The [F1]Zenana hospitals of the great Missionary bodies are far more useful than the Dufferin Institutes as they are worked entirely by women and to those the women of India flock, as they know that they can depend on not being examined medically by strange men, but by one of their own sex. I have practical experience of this; for at the station where I lived, I opened a free dispensary and although there were five large hospitals in the neighbourhood, admirably administered but run by men, the women from forty miles around would come to my small place, rather than the large hospitals simply because these were worked by men."[2]

The number of women dying in childbirth was extremely large. Those who survived the ordeal of childbirth, succumbed many a time to chronic diseases. Even the rate of infant mortality was abnormally high. The causes were many, the conspicuous among them being the physical immaturity of mothers, the disparity in ages of parents, and the ignorance of untrained midwives who overlooked even the simple hygienic rules. To quote Dr. Ida Scudder again, "Here again every one of us present could give instances of the horrible tortures women are constantly subjected to by the ignorant [F2]daiees. Our sympathies have been taxed by the poor sufferer who has been brought to the hospital in such a condition that her life cannot be saved and our hearts are often touched by the appeals from such a woman to save her life for the sake of little group of children waiting for her at home."[3] Though such sad events touched the hearts of Western doctors, they hardly had any effect on husbands or family members of the sufferers. If a wife died, another young girl was sought for the dear son by his parents and relatives.

To do away with the ignorant Medical practitioners like midwives, and to create awareness about women's health problems, Dr. Anna Kugler and many others persistently demanded the compulsory training of midwives. Dr. Kugler insisted, "It is possible to train the indigenous

F1 Zenana – Woman. A curtained area of women in the house was called Zenankhana

F2 Daiees – Midwives.

daiees so that she no longer carries poison under her fingernails; to teach her to wash her hands before she touches her patient, instead of deferring all cleaning up until the case is over; to teach her to recognise when she ought to call in help, more skilled than herself….it is possible to do all this and thereby save many lives."[4] These remarks were passed in the second decade of the 20th century. So, one can imagine how grave the situation might have been in the 19th century and before.

The Zenana Bible and the Medical Mission to India was founded in 1852 to reach the secluded Hindustani women. But it was not an easy task. The [F3]purdah system was rampant, and women were confined to the inner courts of their houses. As they seldom crossed the thresholds of their houses, there was no way to meet them outside. Due to the fear of conversion to Christianity, people used to keep Missionaries at a distance. Naturally, it was difficult to get entry into native houses. Sometimes, driven by curiosity, women would welcome a foreign lady; but after knowing about her unmarried status, they shrunk from her. As women in India were married at an early stage of their lives, they became suspicious about the character of young, unmarried, foreign ladies. It took a deal of explanation to make them understand that neither a custom nor their religion compelled them to marry and by choice they could remain unmarried.

Overcoming all such difficulties, the Missionary women and Western lady doctors entered into women's secluded wings and helped them in times of difficulty. There they could witness how motherhood was forced on young girls, time and again, without giving thought to their agonies. When lady doctors were not available, Missionary ladies acted as a go-between. Reporting patients' problems to male doctors, they brought back bottles of medicines for women. Some of them trained themselves in nursing, with the help of doctors and available books. Finding out ways to help native women, male doctors also rose to the demand of time and shared the responsibility. For example, in 1867, in a small town of Bareilly, Dr. Corbyn opened a Medical class for girls. He taught them first-aid, common rules of hygiene and nursing. His efforts were backed up by a wealthy native person. Dr. Corbyn's class proved to be quite beneficial to women. The situation in Bareilly further improved when in 1870 Dr. Clara Swain, the first qualified lady doctor to come to India, settled in Bareilly. She was a graduate of

---

F3 Purdah – A veil. Women used to draw a semi-transparent covering over their faces.

the 'Woman's Medical College of Pennsylvania' and a member of the Methodist Mission. While teaching Medicine, Nursing and Compounding, she observed that though native women were uneducated, they were not dull or disinterested in learning. In the beginning, Dr. Clara Swain opened a small dispensary and within 6 weeks, 180 women plucked up courage to visit it, which was quite heartening. In recognition of her benevolent service to native women, the Nawab of Rampur donated to her 40 acres of land and a huge bungalow. Here, she opened a women's hospital on 1st January 1874, which was the first of its kind in Hindustan. The beautiful landscape with a splendid house attracted women so much that even after their recovery, they urged Dr. Swain to extend their stay. Dr. Swain was followed by many other lady doctors like Dr. Sara Seward, Dr. Mary Seelye, Dr. Anna Kugler, Dr. Anna Thorburn and Dr. Ida Scudder.

In the 19th century, British and American women were fighting vigorously for establishing women's right to Medical education, but many intellectuals and professionals were trying to thwart the movement. The Medical profession was monopolised by male doctors and women had only a few sympathisers. While looking for new avenues for women doctors, the 'Woman's Medical college of Pennsylvania' became aware of India as a land of opportunity where they could have wider Medical experience. They decided to encourage their students to practise medicine in Hindustan, where women doctors were needed, welcomed and respected as life-savers. Considering the shocking rate of infant mortality and complicated gynaecological problems, even from a humanitarian point of view, it was essential to send women doctors to Hindustan. Since Hindustani women did not accept medical help from male doctors, the Medical field was completely open to women doctors. There was no question of male dominance.

Naturally, in spite of the strangeness of the remote land, the unhygienic sanitary conditions, unfriendly climate and the linguistic problem, the lure of India was irresistible to ambitious women doctors. With tremendous zeal, they opened dispensaries, founded hospitals, trained midwives and nurses, promoted women's institutes, formed the associations of Medical women and advanced their own career as well. Sky was the limit in Hindustan. They loved this alien country as their homeland and got involved into various problems of the native women. When Dr. Anna Kugler took ill, she was removed to America for Medical treatment. But as soon as she was a little better, she returned to Hindustan, for she wished to die on the Indian soil among the people she loved. In 1887, she had written, "The condition of women in India, is an argument for women's work…. Ignorant, superstitious, caste-bound, the slave of man's passions, the victim of child-marriage and enforced widowhood — this is the condition of the vast majority of women of India… Only by the elevation of her mothers and daughters can India hope to attain to the lights of true civilisation which recognises woman as an equal not as an inferior."[5]

Mary Scharlieb, the wife of Barrister William Scharlieb, had no connection with the Medical field. She had accompanied her husband to India and they lived in Madras (now Chennai). Leaving aside some exceptions, the wives of British officers generally, had little contact with native people. They lived in their closed circuits, being engrossed in nothing but their family life and small friend circles. As they had no affinity with this country, they were either unaware of the social issues or were indifferent to them. They always remained and behaved like outsiders. But Mary Scharlieb was different. The lady with a golden heart, befriended many native women around her and they too talked freely with her about the pathetic conditions in which they had to live. Mary heard the frightening stories of women who preferred to embrace death than to accept help from male doctors in their illness or pregnancy. She was pained to observe how helpless and lonely they were in the time of calamity. Her inner voice urged her to do something urgently for her native sisters. But not knowing what to do, she became restless.

Ultimately it occurred to her that she should become a doctor, since that was what they really needed. But in that period, no Medical college in India was open to women. Even in England, young women like Sophia Jex-Blake and her friends were fighting with the establishment for the Medical qualification of women. So, to begin with, Mary enrolled her name in the Maternity Hospital of Madras in 1871, for learning midwifery. Though she completed the training successfully, she was not satisfied with such a minor course. Therefore, she discussed this issue with Surgeon-General Dr. Balfour, head of the Medical Service in Madras. She succeeded in convincing him why it was essential for women to gain Medical knowledge. The sympathetic doctor Balfour wrote a letter to the Madras Government and put up the case of the Medical women before authorities. But the demand was considered premature by the government and no action was taken on it for 4 years. Only after the strong recommendation of the Principal of the Medical College of Madras, it was sanctioned in 1875. The University of Madras was the first in India to open its gates to women for Medical education. Overjoyed by this news, Mary Scharlieb enrolled her name in the College. In 1878, she received the 'Medical Practitioner's Certificate' and went to England for higher education, because by then, the situation in England had improved. There she took admission into the 'London School of Medicine for women' in 1879. In 1882, she received the degree of Bachelor of Medicine and Surgery, with Honours in all subjects and the Gold Medal and the scholarship in Obstetrics. In 1883, she returned to India and became a lecturer in Midwifery and Gynaecology at the Madras Medical College. With the help of the government, she established 'Queen Victoria Hospital for Caste and Gosha Women,' which was exclusively for women. At last, her heart's desire was satisfied.

Both Dr. Mary Scharlieb and Dr. Elizabeth Beilby were instrumental in revealing the medical needs of Hindustani women to Queen Victoria. When a lady in Pune who was referred to as the [F4]Maharani in Pune, was seriously ill, she was cured by Dr. Beilby. Due to her expertise and kind nature, Dr. Beilby had won Maharani's confidence. Being well-aware of the Medical needs of her countrywomen, the Maharani made a unique request to Dr. Beilby. She said, "I want you to tell the Queen and the Prince and Princess of Wales and the men and women of England what the women of India suffer when they are sick. Write it down, write it small, …for I want you to put it into a locket and you are to wear the locket round your neck till you see our great Queen and give it to her yourself. You are not to send it through another person."[6] Dr. Beilby kept her word by delivering the message to the Queen Victoria personally. The Queen lent an ear to Dr. Beilby's narration and was moved by the distress of Indian women. After a year, Mary Scharlieb, now, a qualified doctor was also received by the Queen. Once again, the sufferings of Indian women were described before her. The Queen was moved so much that she sent a message for her Indian daughters through Dr. Scharlieb, "Tell them their Queen sympathizes with them and how glad she is that they should have medical women to help them in their time of trouble."[7]

In 1883, when Lord Dufferin became the Viceroy of India, Lady Dufferin was ordered by the Queen to organise a relief-fund, for providing Medical help to Indian women. Lady Dufferin thoroughly studied the problem and acted on the advice of doctors, Missionaries and the organisers of Medical institutes. Finally, in 1885 she initiated the Countess of Dufferin fund, with the help of which she wanted to invite European women doctors to India. The provision was also made for women's hospitals and Medical

F4 Maharani in Pune - Her name is not known

training. Thus, having laid the foundation of Medical work, Lady Dufferin hoped it to flourish. But after her departure in 1888, the motivational force behind the scheme vanished and without much progress, her scheme died young. It was found that the Dufferin Hospitals were inferior to the Zenana Hospitals of Missions which were popular among women. The most important difference between the two institutes was that the Zenana Hospitals of Missions were entirely run by women, while in the Dufferin Hospitals, the controlling officers were always men. This factor influenced the choice of Hindustani women.

Even before the Dufferin scheme, another project was born out of one man's imagination and it could succeed without the help of the government. No one would have thought that an article by a lady doctor about the Medical needs of Indian women would so inspire an American citizen that he would devote some precious years of his life to the cause. In an article that appeared in the 'Contemporary Review' of August 1882, Dr. Frances Elizabeth Hoggan of London had remarked, "What is needed is a new Medical Department, as a part of the public service of India, managed by women and responsible only to some high officer of State working in harmony with the existing civil Medical service." Though the Government of India was unmoved by this innovative suggestion, it captured the attention of George A. Kittredge, an American businessman residing in Bombay. He was a Director of the Trombe Company of Bombay. He strongly felt that suffering women of India badly needed women doctors and something had to be done for them. He felt for certain that the Government of India would never give its consent for a separate women's department. But if the citizens themselves would undertake this project; it could be carried out successfully. He worked out a scheme for providing Medical help to India. He thought of inviting an expert woman doctor from Europe or America to Bombay in whose able hands could be placed the Medical education of native women as well as the relief work. Kittredge acknowledged the efforts of Dr. Balfour by saying, "Surgeon-General Balfour had obtained the sanction of Government to the education of women in Medicine at the Medical College of Madras and though not pursuing the full course of study and not obtaining the full degree, they promised to be of immense service to their sex." [8] But he was convinced that it would be a gross mistake to give partial education and an inferior degree to women. He consulted with the native leaders like Sorabji Shapoorji Bengali, Cummoo Sultan, Javerilal Umiyashankar

Yajnik who responded to the scheme with great enthusiasm. Particularly Sorabji Shapoorji proved to be very helpful in professing the significance of the project and veering the public opinion. To begin with, these activists undertook the fund-raising programme and within two months, a fund of Rs.40, 238 was raised, which was sufficient only to start a dispensary. But in March 1883, Pestonji Hormasji Cama expressed his wish to donate Rs.1 Lakh for this noble cause. The unexpected but timely magnanimity changed the whole picture. With such a large donation, it was possible even to establish a hospital. Thus, the original moderate plan got expanded beyond expectation. Here was a great project for which the citizens of Bombay were working hand in hand. With absolute care, they perfected the scheme and worked in various directions.

They requested the Government to allot a suitable plot for the hospital, corresponded with the authorities of the University of Bombay for women's entry into the Medical colleges and wrote to the Principal of the Grant Medical College urging that diplomas be given to women as a hospital assistant and an apothecary. Kittredge had realised that the appointment of a European lady doctor was a temporary solution. It was just not possible to import enough lady doctors for the millions of native women. It was essential to impart Medical education to Indian women and give them proper training. The country needed her own women doctors. Kittredge being a far-sighted person could look into the distant future. He wrote, "Not the least important part of our scheme and what may ultimately prove the most important was the admission of female students to the privilege of the University Medical degrees. This with the opening of the Grant Medical College to women was the beginning of a work, the benefits of which will extend long beyond the lifetime of the youngest amongst us. … It was in August 1883 that the Bombay University in reply to the letter of Mr. Sorabjee and myself offered its Medical degrees to matriculated female students who passed satisfactorily the usual five years' course of study; in the same year the Grant Medical College also at our request offered college certificates to non-matriculated students who would pursue a three years' course of study…. Now there are eight or ten ladies with Medical degrees here in Bombay." [9]

While the theme was taking shape, Kittredge sailed to England to search for a woman doctor who could be interested in working in India. He was not sure if an experienced and established woman doctor would willingly throw away her good practice at home for anything he could offer in India. He placed himself in communication with the East India Association and through them advertised in newspapers. But only 2-3 replies were received which did not satisfy him. He tried his best to inform Medical women about the scheme and the purpose behind it. Yet he could get no response at all. He was almost in despair when a thin hope flickered due to Dr. Garrett-Anderson's suggestion. Dr. Garrett-Anderson told him that Dr. Edith Peachey, a leader of the movement of British women doctors and a talented, dashing young doctor having experience of 8 years at Leeds, would be the right person and would perfectly fit in his scheme. But she had then gone to Vienna for surgical practice, as London hospitals were closed to women surgeons.

Dr. Edith Peachey met George Kittredge in Paris and after hearing all that he wished to say, she promised to consider his project. Ultimately, to his great delight, she accepted the post of Senior Medical Officer to the Fund, on a salary of Rs. 500 per month and quarters to live in, with the first-class passage out and home. Dr. Edith Peachey arrived in Bombay on 12th December 1883. This great event of her arrival was noted by the *Times of India* and she was referred to as 'The Pioneer Practitioner of Medical Women of India Fund Movement.' In the beginning, Miss Dewar, who had accompanied Dr. Edith Peachey to Bombay, assisted her. But in November 1884, another English doctor Miss Charlotte Ellaby was appointed as a Junior officer to Dr. Peachey. Until the completion of the Cama Hospital in 1886, Dr. Peachey developed her own private practice and also administered a temporary Medical dispensary for poor women. She learnt the Hindi language for communicating with native women. This reduced the distance between her and her patients. Soon she got involved in native women's problems and campaigned against the social evil of child marriage. In 1884, Lord Dufferin became the Viceroy of India. In 1885, Lady Dufferin founded the Dufferin Fund for giving Medical help to native women. In March 1889, Edith married Herbert Phipson, the Secretory to the Dufferin Fund and they worked together for the same cause. In 1889, George Kittredge wrote an article reviewing the movement of 'Medical women for India Fund of Bombay.' There this 'American Bombaite' said with due pride, "India would have waited many years for women doctors, had she depended on the Government.... the success of our scheme in Bombay was owing to the fact that it... was carried by private efforts.... To Bombay belongs the credit of first introducing non-official, non-sectarian female medical relief into India."[10] In memory of this loveable person, his name was given to the road from Colaba to Cuffe Parade.

This is the background of the struggle story of the pioneer Indian woman doctor Anandibai Joshi. When all over the world, women were fighting for their right to Medical education; when Indian reformers were desperately hunting in Europe a woman doctor who would agree to work in Bombay, a young girl, living in a small town; married at the age of 10; was fired with the idea of becoming a doctor. The social conditions around her were not at all in favour of such a magnificent dream. On the contrary, her goal was thought to be a castle in the air. No one but her far-sighted husband Gopal believed in her dream. But before beginning Anandibai's life story, it is essential to take cognizance of another woman who tried to become a doctor before Anandi. Though she could not succeed, her efforts were praise-worthy.

References:

1. *The Southern Medical College for Women* – Dr. Ida Scudder. *The Journal of the Association of the Medical women of India.*1916 Volume V No 10 Page 5
2. *Medical Aid for the Women of India* – Dr. F. M. Smith. *The Journal of the Association of the Medical women of India.* November 1913Volume IV No 12 Page 2
3. Ibid Page 5
4. *Some of the Problems which the Association Hopes to Help us to solve* – by Dr. Anna Kugler. *The Journal of the Association of Medical Women in India.* Volume VI- February 1918 page 4
5. *Medical Missionaries* – An article by Ellen J. Smith; from the book *Send Us A Lady Physician: Women Doctors in America* Edited by Ruth J Abram 1985 Page 200, 201
6. *Storming the Citadel – The Rise of the women Doctors* – E. Moberly Bell 1953 Chapter 7: *A new Field India* Chapter 7 Page
7. Ibid, Page 116
8. Reprint of *A Sketch of The Beginning and Working of The Medical women For Indian Fund of Bombay* – George A Kittredge, Esq. (Originally published in 1889) *The Journal of The A M W I* February1908 Volume I No 2 Page 20.
9. Reprint of *A Sketch of The Beginning and Working of The Medical women For Indian Fund of Bombay* – George A Kittredge, Esq. (Originally published in 1889) *The Journal of The A M W I* May1908 Volume I No3 Page 24, 25,26
10. Ibid Page 26.

3

A Footprint in Oblivion

"I would now throw aside the fetters that bound one and be independent. I had chafed under the restraints and ties which formed the common lot of women and I longed for an opportunity to show that a woman is in no way inferior to a man. How hard it seemed to my mind that marriage should be the goal of woman's ambition and that she should spent her days in the light trifles of a home life, live to dress, to look pretty and never know the joy of independence and intellectual work."[1] This is how Saguna, the heroine of the novel bearing the same name, reflects upon women of her era. It is the fictionalised autobiography of Krupabai Khisti-Satthianadhan, with changed names of places and persons.

As the autobiography is written in the form of a novel, the reality is veiled by giving it some colours of imagination. But at the same time the firstperson singular storyteller narrates the story. As a result, the novel takes the shape of an autobiography. Thus, Krupabai beautifully veils and unveils reality. Since the autobiographical nature of the novel was an open secret, it was treated then as her own story. *The Indian Evangelist Review* commented, "The reality of the book gives the impression that it is more historical or biographical than imaginative" whereas *Progress* stated, "This book is professedly a work of fiction intended to depict the home-life of a native Christian. From internal evidence however, we are compelled to see in it a virtual autobiography." The first edition of *Saguna* was published in 1892 and the second one appeared in 1895, after her death which occurred on 3rd August 1894. On 30th January 1895, the first meeting of the 'Krupabai Memorial' was held under the presidency of Lady Wenlock. In this meeting A. T. Arundel, a member of the committee, briefly but vividly described for the members, Krupa's life story. In the appendix of the second edition of *Saguna*, the proceedings of this meeting as well as some excerpts from the reviews of the first edition of *Saguna* and *Kamla*, her second novel, are included. *Kamla* was published in December 1894. Krupabai's health completely collapsed after giving birth to a child and the child too died as an infant. Racing against the time, she completed *Kamla* in the shadows of her death, the creative urge being uncontrollable. In the introduction of *Kamla*, Elis Grigg, a friend of Krupabai, had briefly depicted her life story. From these sources, biographical information about Krupabai became available.

Krupa was the youngest daughter of [F1]Haripant Khisti who was an early convert in the Bombay Presidency. Haripant, a Brahmin by birth, embraced Christianity not by force but by choice. If a person was converted by force, people had some sympathy for him. But the conversion by choice was treated as the most treacherous act, which ruined blood relations, friendship and emotional ties. Such people angered society beyond measures. Yet, in the case of some people like Haripant, the urge to embrace Christianity was so overwhelming that at any cost they remained loyal to their conviction.

Krupa, the 13th child of Haripant, was born on 14th February 1862, in a small town of Ahmednagar, in the Bombay Presidency. Haripant died when Krupa was just 2 years old. But with this youngest child, he had left behind his independent nature, determination and the wealth of his intelligence. The little girl grew like a boy among her brothers, to whom she followed everywhere. Her eldest brother Bhaskar had a soft spot for his little sister. He took good care of her education and she responded eagerly. Not only did he teach her reading, writing and counting but also enriched her mind with inspiring historical stories and fascinating tales of distant countries like Rome and Greece. In the portrayal of Kamla, the heroine of Krupa's second novel, the shades of little Krupa subtly linger. Kamla's Grandmother says, "He (Kamla's father) lets Kamla grow up like a boy and the girl is no better than the father. She will tell you the contents of many books though picked up; you know from her father."[2]

The sight of the little sister sitting close to Bhaskar with a book, too heavy for her small hands, made Krupa's other brothers laugh. Not

---

F1 Pant – A term of respectful mention used at the end of a male's name. There are some more terms like this – Rao, Anna, Appa, Dada, etc.

wishing to have a 'girl' around them while they studied, they asked her to go away and teased her for her 'madness' over books. Even her mother thought it foolish of a girl to study so much. She tried to engage Krupa in the kitchen, which was supposed to be the right place for a woman. But knowing Krupa's profuse interest in learning, Bhaskar always stood by her. Though Krupa was the youngest child, she was the cleverest. Finishing her lessons before others, she would point out the mistakes of her 'Big Brothers.'

While wandering together in the cool green silence of woods, Bhaskar revealed his innermost thoughts to little Krupa, as if she were a grown-up girl. He talked dreamily about freeing India from the clutches of the British, about becoming a great man and doing noble deeds. In an excited mood, he asked her if she would be his fellow traveller and though a mere child, Krupa tried to go beyond herself to grasp those profound thoughts. These talks developed in her a sense of longing for the unexplored expanse of the future. At the same time, an intense desire to become somebody, quivered in her tender mind. Unfortunately, Bhaskar died young, when he was about to graduate. His sudden death broke Krupa's heart and shattered all her beautiful dreams. Unprepared to accept the truth, her depressed mind used to weave a web of illusions in which she housed her lone self. In the world of fantasy, her dear brother was still alive and was always by her side. Feeling alienated from everything, she buried herself in books. Her health began to fail, which worried her mother very much. Realising that her daughter needed some change, the mother decided to put Krupa in the Girls' School of Zenana Mission of Bombay, so that among friends, Krupa might forget her grief, her loneliness and be happy. At the parting, her mother urged a teacher, "My daughter is alone at home. She learns a little too much. So, I have brought her here to become more like other girls, to learn a little and to play a little. But let her be free from the strict rules at first, for she is too delicate." The teacher smiled and said, "Discipline is for those who need it, not for the girls who are women from their childhood."

But Krupa posed a strange problem for her teachers. She was far advanced even for the highest class in the school. They asked her if she would like to be a teacher or would prefer to learn a new language for the mission work. But being more interested in learning than in teaching, Krupa murmured, "Let me learn something. Surely there is enough to learn in this world." In the same room, an old American lady doctor was sitting quietly, listening to the conversation. Suddenly she exclaimed, "Better learn Medicine!" Krupa was taken aback. She only said, "Medicine? Oh, I wish I could."

This small event was a turning point in Krupa's life. After her brother's death, Krupa just did not know what to do with herself and her mind could settle on nothing. Now the American doctor had shown a new path to the meaningful life. Krupa began to learn Medicine under her guidance. Though the doctor was known as an eccentric person, she was quite different with Krupa. She was a kind-hearted teacher, deeply interested in the well-being of her student. In *Saguna*, Krupa had described the first day at her Medical class, as if a tribute to her most revered teacher. It is amusing and very emotional at the same time. "On the day of my first lesson, I was in a great state of excitement. I trembled as I knocked at her door. She came out abruptly with some huge volumes under her arms and ordered me into her consulting room. My steps faltered as she made me walk in front, while she followed behind much as a warden follows a prisoner. I paused near the door, but she came up quickly, opened it and shoved me into the room, which I had not entered before. I had seen people entering and emerging with subdued steps and whispers and now I expected to find something dreadful, staring at me.... I saw a cheerful room, decorated with flowers and ferns and its windows looking out on the garden. In it stood a cupboard full of curiosities, a table and two chairs. The lady placed the big volumes on the table and when I went to fetch a chair for her she said abruptly, 'Stand!' and herself went and brought two chairs. She questioned me in a firm, distinct tone and expected me to answer briefly and to the point. The ordeal lasted for an hour and then she shut the book and opened the door for me, without a word. I hurried away as fast as possible. But as days passed, the overwhelming sense of her strong personality failed to oppress me.... On several occasions, especially when she had put on an unusually difficult question, I caught a look of anticipation on her face, which was followed by a look of relief and a shadow of smile when the question was answered. Ah! How I valued that little mark of approval." [3]

The doctor was always keen upon removing any inconvenience that might have hindered Krupa's study. As the school premises were full of noise, she told Krupa to use her consulting room for studies. There she placed a sitting chair and an easy chair. But shyness and an unknown fear prevented Krupa from using them. She used to sit on a box near the window. But nothing escaped from the doctor's observant eyes. One day, the mischievous doctor attached tags on both the chairs, with the same short sentence on them — 'FOR USE.' Thus, she expressed silently her affection for her dear student. Krupa disguised as Saguna in her novel remarks, "I began to love this strange lady, who was an enigma to others. Her influence upon me was unbound. It was a strange, silent influence. Her interest and love were shown not in words, nor in the display of emotion of any kind. They were only felt — felt in the firm grasp of the hands, in the flashing look of inquiry, in the abrupt unceremonious way in which she gave me books to read and in the unlimited freedom which she allowed me in the choice of subjects and books. Her grasp of the subject was thorough. A strange power seemed to emanate from her."[4] I wish Krupa had mentioned somewhere the name of this doctor. The benevolent lady had remained anonymous.

Thus, one year passed and the doctor was thoroughly satisfied with Krupa's studies. Soon she was to leave India but before that, she wished to do something about Krupa's further studies. As she was in no habit of expressing herself vocally, she wrote a letter to Krupa, informing that she had made the engagements for Krupa's study in England. A rich English lady had agreed to bear half of the expenses if Krupa could get a Medical certificate about her health and the Mission was ready to share the remaining expenses. The kind teacher promised Krupa to take her to America after the completion of her Medical course in England. Everything was so sudden and unexpected that hours later, Krupa asked herself, 'Is it true or is it a work of my fertile imagination?' The whole institute was stirred up by the unbelievable news. Some began to give Krupa special attention, while others turned up their noses at the news. Some thought that it was a quixotic project whereas others advised her to marry instead. But not responding to either flattery or hatred, Krupa patiently waited for her doctor's permission.

Though she got a doctor's certificate, the Missionary in charge of Krupa, whose discretion the Mission trusted the most, was not satisfied. He firmly said that Krupa's constitution was not strong enough to bear hardships, strenuous studies and the trying climate of England. Being a family friend of the Khistis, Krupa was like a sister to him. Unwilling to take any risk, the Missionary candidly denied the permission. Krupa tried to convince him that she was fit to study Medicine in England but in vain. Neither her words nor tears had any effect on him. His firm decision was a death blow to all her ambitions. He was very sorry to disappoint her but could not help it. At the most, he promised to make arrangements for her Medical study in the Madras Medical College, the only institute where women were permitted to study Medicine. Even there, women were offered a partial course and an inferior degree. Krupa had no other option but to accept this proposal.

Thus in 1878, Krupa joined the college. She became a boarder at the house of Rev. W. T. Satthianadhan. In the first meeting of 'Krupabai Memorial', A. T. Arundel, a member of the committee narrated a unique incidence in the history of the Madras Medical College. He said, "The students of the college to their credit be it told, at her first appearance rose and cheered the delicate looking girl, who was the first Indian lady to join a Medical school."[5] Soon her intellectual endowments were felt by her teachers as well as fellow students. At the end of the year, Krupa was at the top of the ladder, winning several prizes. She stood first in every subject, except Chemistry. In Anatomy, she scored 95% marks, which was supposed to be the most difficult subject and even a brilliant student usually scored 50 to 60% marks. In this meeting, Surgeon-General Sibthorpe, who knew Krupa as a student, also talked about her with great respect, "I have met very few students who have the same power as she had."[6] Thus, Krupa was head and shoulders above the rest.

However, due to her failing health, she could not finish even this short course. After the First-Year annual exam, she went home to enjoy her holidays, but could not join the college the following year as she fell ill. Hence, she left the course in 1879. That means the Missionary was right in refusing her the permission to go to England. With a heavy heart, she said goodbye to her dream. Yet, the fact remains that Krupa was the first Indian woman to join a Medical college. Incidentally, though she could not become the pioneer Indian lady doctor, she became the pioneer Indian woman-novelist who expressed herself in English. In the introduction to Saguna, R.S. Benson wrote, "It is the pioneer volume. We do not know of any other work of fiction written by a [F2]Hindu lady in English."[7] Lady Wenlock was the first to recognise her literary merits. She brought *Saguna* to the notice of Queen Victoria, who read it with interest and asked to send to her the other books of Krupa, if any. Krupa expressed her heartfelt gratitude by dedicating her second novel *Kamla* to Lady Wenlock.

In 1881, Krupa was introduced to Samuel Satthianadhan, who was the son of her host in Madras. He had returned from England after completing his graduation from the Cambridge University. Krupa married him soon after. The couple settled in Utakmand where Samuel was the headmaster of the Breek's Memorial School. Krupa began to teach in the Hobart School for native girls. She organised a small school for Muslim girls which soon developed into a remarkable institute. Krupa was also planning to establish a home for Hindu widows. But due to her untimely death at the age of 32, this idea was not realised. But as a novelist, she achieved name and fame. In the introduction to *Kamla*, Elis Grigg says, "Her writing seems even better known to English than to Indian readers. Her Majesty the Queen Empress had recently accepted a copy of *Saguna* and was graciously pleased to request that any other work by the authoress should be sent to her."[8]

In her short span of life, Krupa cherished wonderful dreams and tried to do her best. Once her heroine Saguna had exclaimed, "There on those heights, should like to be, there above those clouds, in the midst of the lights, or nowhere at all." In fact, this sentence reflects Krupa's beautiful mind. Krupa's lifelong pursuit of her high aims exemplifies the fact that the zeniths of aspirations were calling native women and they had courageously begun to tread the path of unbound progress.

F2 Hindu lady – Though Krupa was a Christian, R. S. Benson referred to her as a 'Hindu' lady, because in that period, the word 'Hindu' did not necessary indicate the Hindu religion. Particularly the British used this word to denote a Hindustani or an Indian person.

References:

1. *Saguna – A story of native Christian Life* – Krupabai Satthianadhan. Second Edition 1895. Page 178

2. *Kamla* – Krupabai Satthianadhan. Introduction by Elis L. Grigg. First Edition December 1894.

3. *Saguna – A story of native Christian Life* – Krupabai Satthianadhan. Second Edition 1895. Page

4. Ibid. Page 191-192

5. Ibid. Appendix

6. Ibid. Appendix

7. Ibid. Preface to the first edition. By R. S. Benson Page XI

8. *Kamla* – Krupabai Satthianadhan. Introduction by Elis L. Grigg. First Edition December 1894. Page i.

4

A Backward Journey in Time

A visit to a historical place is a stimulating experience. Out of the ruins, one has to reconstruct the past in the mind's eye. My visit to Dr. Anandibai Joshi's old paternal mansion at Kalyan, a town near Mumbai, was one such experience. I started walking from the Kalyan railway station and after crossing a number of roads and lanes, reached Paar Naka where the house was situated. Anandi was the daughter of Ganpatrao Amruteshwar Joshi, the Inamdar or chief of Kalyan and the master of this house, before which I was standing on a warm summer morning. On the threshold of this house, I was forced to stop by the upsurge of thoughts….

In the 19th century, a threshold was not only the boundary line of a house but also the limit of a woman's existence. The threshold symbolised tradition and time-honoured customs which no woman dared to transgress. But taking a bold step ahead, Anandi crossed the very threshold in pursuit of knowledge and ultimately her ambition to become a doctor led her to an alien land. She was the first Indian woman who succeeded in becoming a doctor, when even primary education was denied to women. She was the one who opened the door to the world of knowledge for Indian women. Feeling enchanted, I crossed the threshold and entered the premises.

The grand entrance door of the house which once upon a time closed majestically at dusk and opened at the crack of dawn, was now removed from its hinges, because it was too heavy for the old house. The only sign of the old glory was a small decorative border of flowers and leaves carved on the wooden door frame. As I silently walked into the yard, I saw the house with caved-in roofs, tumbled-down walls, broken beams, a small room with an arch and a window with vertical bars. The room was filled with dry yellow grass, fallen bricks and stones. Only the three pillars at the centre of the house stood erect to uphold the collapsing roof. In the glorious days of this house, those empty niches in the walls might have been used to keep combs, snoods, silver caskets of [F1]kumkum and [F2]kajal and many other fancy articles dear to women. Anandi alias Yamuna might have played games with other children like hide and seek, [F3]Zimma and Fugdi in this house yard.

As I stood there staring at the ruins, someone whispered behind me, "I had lived in this house, when it was in good condition." Turning around in wonder, I saw a woman in her early sixties, standing at my elbow, with a pleasant, smiling face. She was late Mrs. Sushilabai Joshi, the mother of Mr. Vishwas Joshi who lived on the upper storey of the house, right above the entrance which was in a better condition than the ruined house. Soon I found myself cheerfully engaged in a conversation with Sushilabai. She pictured before my eyes, the house in its glorious days, "It was known in the neighbourhood as the three pillared mansion. At the centre of the house there was a long flight of stairs, leading to the upper floor. The central apartment on the ground floor was so large that 75 persons could be accommodated there for a sit-down dinner. Do you see that flowering shrub?" She asked me pointing at it. "A small fountain stood there. Then there was a well near the Coral tree. The garden looked colourful and lively when peacocks danced in the rain. The upper storey where my son Vishwas lives, was used in the old times as [F4]Nagarkhana. The room was so large that we ladies were afraid to go there alone at dusk." Her vivid description breathed life into the ruins and suddenly the majestic mansion became a reality for me. With this as an anchoring point, my mind journeyed back in time….

In the 19th century, the appearance of Kalyan was totally different from today's crowded, noisy and congested city with electrified houses and tar roads. It was a peaceful little town and life was tranquil and slow-paced. The wooded paths, crystal-clear lakes with beautiful temples on

---

F1 Kumkum – Red powder or pigment. A round mark of it is applied on the forehead by Hindu women.

F2 Kajal – A sort of soot, used as a cosmetic. It is applied to the eyes.

F3 Zimma and Fugdi – Zimma is a dance like game and in Fugdi, 2 girls hold each other's hands in a particular crossed way and move together in a circle, with speed. These games are accompanied by songs.

F4 Nagarkhana – A special room which is built on top of the entrance of a palatial building or a temple where kettle drum, shehnai and other musical instruments are kept and the band is played at stated hours.

their shores, white mosques with huge domes; houses with tilted red roofs, small gardens and pedestals of sacred Basil or Tulsi in house yards presented a picturesque landscape. As the town had a long history of centuries, popular legends, folktales and historical stories savoured with fantasy, lingered around various places. The quietude of the little town was occasionally broken by rattling carriages, bullock-carts, galloping horses or by the jingling rhyme of palanquin-runners. Activities of the town came to a standstill after sunset, as roads were not lighted and hence people preferred to be at home. Even houses with their flickering lamps casting long shadows looked mysterious and lonely at night. In thickets, twinkling fireflies alighted and disappeared like magic lamps and the monotonous songs of crickets heightened the melancholy of nights. Ambernath and Dombivali, today's over-populated and chaotic towns were desolate suburbs of Kalyan. Dombivali with its overgrown thick cactus, was a convenient hide-out of robbers, where no one dared to go late in the evening. Kalyan was a good place to live. It was located at the centre of four important passes: 'Thal Ghat', 'Bor Ghat', 'Nane Ghat' and 'Malshej Ghat'. It was also a port of consequence, on the river Ulhas. Though the town was quiet, the hubbub was felt in the port area where wood, bricks and mortar were traded.

The Bombay-Thane railway line was expanded up to Kalyan in May 1854, after which Kalyan began to grow fast. On 1st November 1855, the Municipality of Kalyan was founded. This was the first step towards urbanisation. Municipality fixed up oil-lamps on streets and it offered some solace to lone wayfarers. In the beginning, the municipality office was in the neighbourhood of the Joshi Mansion. But in 1870, it was shifted in the mansion itself and remained there for 2 years. To provide prompt medical help, dispensaries were set up in various parts of the town. A special doctor was appointed for the inoculation of smallpox, as it was a serious contagious disease with a high death toll. Sheth Mangaldas Nathubhai Baronate generously donated Rs.22,000 to a municipal dispensary in memory of his wife late Mrs. Rukhminibai. In short, Anandi and her family lived in a town that had caught up early with urbanisation.

The family of Inamdar Joshi was respected in Kalyan, because it had its own history. As it was a family of brave warriors, Ganpatrao was considered a man of exalted origin. Anandi grew in a large family, so it is essential to know about the family members. Ganpatrao, Anandi's father had married thrice. His first wife who died in 1839, had no child. He married again in 1840. Damodar, his first son, was born in 1845. Ganpatrao's second wife died after giving birth to their second son Narasimha, who too died in 1861. In 1853, Ganpatrao married for the third time, to Gangabai alias Durga Barve. Gangabai gave birth to her first daughter Varanasi, eight years after her marriage, that was in 1861. The long wait for a child had become unbearable to Ganga. In those days, a childless woman was held in contempt. The birth of a child was regarded as the proof of her fertility. The ceremony of consummating a marriage was performed when a girl reached the age of puberty, after which people waited expectantly for the 'good news' of her conceiving. To give birth to a boy was the greatest joy for women. It was considered to be a victory of womanhood. Though Ganga also wanted a son, she didn't mind the birth of a daughter – Varanasi, because it was better to have a girl than to remain childless. In 1863, another girl was born. The birth of the second daughter depressed Ganga, but the poor girl did not survive to flare up her mother's anger. In those days, a son was supposed to be the glory of a family. A son meant continuity of the family; heir to the property and the pillar of support in the old age of parents. It was believed that a man without a son had no place in heaven. When a boy was born, his arrival was celebrated like a festival.

Now Ganga urgently wanted to have a son. She had grown so impatient because she was at variance with her stepson Damodar and mutual hatred had deepened between them. Damodar had a feeling that his hot-tempered, young step-mother Ganga was leading his old, soft-natured father by the nose. So in 1863, he had demanded his share in the property and got separated from the family. Thereafter, he and his wife occupied half the portion of the ancestral mansion. The room with an arch which I noticed among the ruins, belonged to Damodar. In short, before Anandi alias Yamuna was born, the family was divided. There was a disparity in the ages of Ganpat and Ganga. Ganga was worried that if she had no son all her life, Damodar would be the sole heir to the property after her old husband's death. In that case, the stepson who despised her, would become the Master of the house and her status would be that of a lone, dependent widow. The thought of such a hopeless future cast gloomy shadows on her mind. The problem of having a son bulked large, considering the age of her husband. So, when she was pregnant for the third time, she prayed to God and worshipped the nearby holy Pimpal tree as was the custom, for getting a son. The tension mounted over her mind because of the expectations of her relatives.

Everybody was eagerly waiting for the arrival of Ganga's son, when Yamuna alias Anandi was born. Yamuna, the third daughter of Ganpat and Ganga, was born in Pune on 31st March 1865, in the mansion of Balshastri Maate, who was Ganga's maternal uncle. Ganga lost her peace of mind and was extremely disappointed to have a daughter for the third time. It worried her deeply that though she was married for 12 years, she was not yet called [F5]'Putrawati'. Yamuna's birth shattered all her hopes, once more making her insecure. Thus, the root cause of her hatred for Yamuna was the deep-rooted fear about her own future. Eleven years after Yamuna was born, that is in 1876, Ganga, at last gave birth to her son, Vinayak. Immediately after him, her last child Sundari, a daughter again, was born. Ganpat died in 1877 when Vinayak was just one year old and Sundari was a suckling.

Thus, Yamuna was the most disliked daughter of her mother from day one. On top of it, Yamuna was very naughty. She was always up to some kind of mischief and Ganga had no patience with her. She battered the little hoyden with blind cruelty, using a lash, stones or even burning coals and was not moved by the pitiful screams of her own daughter. She could not understand that it was not the fault of her daughter that she was not a boy. Being a slave to her brittle temper, the frustrated lady vented her wrath upon her unwanted daughter and made her innocent childhood miserable. The ghastly experience of her mother's cruelty left a sad trail in Yamuna's mind. When she grew up, she vowed that she would never treat her children the way her mother did. Like a crowned queen, Ganga exercised uncontrolled authority over everybody in the house, including her husband. Generally, a mother-in-law had an upper hand in an Indian household. But Amba, Ganga's mother-in-law had died long before her marriage and her aged husband was unable to control his young wife. There was nobody in the house who would dare to challenge her authority. In effect, Yamuna became her soft target. Ganga's own mother

F5 Putrawati – Mother of a son

lived with them but her position in the house of her married daughter was rather subordinate and she had little voice in any matter. Yet she tried her best to protect her darling granddaughter from Ganga. Had Ganga given birth to a son when Yamuna was a small child, she might have received some affection from her mother. Unfortunately, Ganga's son was born only after Yamuna's marriage. But Yamuna's father made up for the lack of motherly affection and showered profuse love on Yamuna who was the apple of his eye.

Both the father and the daughter were in the habit of walking down together in the garden after lunch. They would sit for a while under the spreading branches of a huge tree, enjoying the peaceful atmosphere. Sitting in her father's lap, Yamuna chirped like a little bird and shared joyously her childish secrets and fantasies with her father. She could ask him any question, without fear. When Yamuna was just 4 years old, she asked a strange question to her father. Every day a priest came to their house to clean the shrines and idols of Gods and to offer prayers. One day, Yamuna was sitting there and playing with her dolls. As usual, the priest washed various idols of Gods and before setting them back on their shrines, carefully oiled them. Suddenly it flashed through Yamuna's mind that there was no difference between the idols of Gods and her dolls, as both remained passive in the hands of a man. Though the priest rubbed the Gods hard and she rubbed her dolls, they didn't cry. Neither did they rejoice when they were left alone. She did not say anything to the priest. But the thought remained in her mind. In the afternoon, she eagerly took her father in the garden after their lunch. Settling herself comfortably near her father, on their favourite bench under the tree, she asked him, "Father, how come the Gods don't mind to have their faces washed by a man?" Without waiting for his answer, Yamuna narrated the whole incident and surprised her father by asking, "Are the Gods nothing but dolls?"

Impressed by Yamuna's power of observation, the father explained, "Those idols are not Gods! They are meant to hold the thoughts of human beings to Him, when they pray. The idols represent the justice of God, his love and the creative power. Could you pray to God, my darling, without them?" With confidence, the little girl replied, "Yes, indeed!" This astonished him further. He told her fondly, "If that is so, you need not think about them again. They will be of no use to you."

Ganpat's admiration for Yamuna soon turned into reverence because of a mysterious incident. One night, Yamuna had gone to bed as usual. She dreamt of a handsome man dressed like a warrior who carried curious weapons on him. He was silently staring at her with his sharp eyes. The frightened child asked, "Who are you?" In turn, the man gravely asked her, "Don't you know me?"

"No, I don't." Yamuna answered.

"Then go to your father," ordered the man, "and tell him to make you acquainted with my life, for it is you who are to tread in my footsteps. It is ungrateful to be ignorant of him whose blood flows in your veins."

At this point, she woke up trembling and perspiring. She was so small that she could not even understand the meaning of his words. But next day, she went to her father and narrated the incident. She told him exactly what she had seen and repeated the words of the man in her dream. Curiously she asked, "Father, who was that God?" Ganpat was puzzled by her narration, but he thought over it and felt that one of their ancestors might have visited Yamuna in her dream. The glorious history of the family began with the valorous ancestor Krushnajipant Joshi, who was a General of the great Maratha Emperor Shivaji. Another brave warrior in the family was Ramachandra Joshi who had conquered the Fort of Durgadi and freed Kalyan from the clutches of the Mughals, way back in 1719. The Joshi Mansion was built by Ramchandra's son Naro Ramchandra. Balajipant, a brother of Ramachandra, had also settled in Kalyan in 1750, because the First Bajirao Peshwa had rewarded him with 2 villages — Mauje Moshe and Bhatne, in the Kalyan province for his bravery. Anandi's father was the grandson of Balajipant.

Ganpat had the genealogical records of his family, which were preserved through generations by family heads. The history of each generation was written briefly on a special paper from which no word could be effaced. The story was illustrated with colourful pictures of heroes and warriors, wearing their special costumes. These records were always kept under lock and key and guarded like a treasure. Nobody except the family head was allowed to go into the secret room. But after knowing about Yamuna's dream, Ganpat kept aside the family rule and took her there. He respectfully opened the [F6]sacred records and together they went through the pages to find out the God in Yamuna's dream. They saw many pictures but not a single figure matched Yamuna's dream figure. They arrived almost at the end of the record when Yamuna recognised at once 'the God.' It was a picture of the valorous ancestor of whom the family was very proud. Though the name of the ancestor is not mentioned by Caroline Dall who included this event in Anandi's biography, the person could be Krushnajipant Joshi, the founder of the family. Ganpat, who was deeply touched by this incident, grew tenderer towards Yamuna. He decided to pay special attention to her education. He had already organised a small school in his own house where he began to send Yamuna, though it was against the custom.

Her mother's view regarding Yamuna's education was totally different. She did not mind Yamuna's schooling just because it kept the naughty girl busy and out of her way and she could have some peace for a while. In the beginning, Yamuna disliked the school because she could not play there. Games, friends and a swing or [F7]Zopala were the temptations too strong to resist. Hence Yamuna played many tricks to avoid school. Crying piteously and at the same time rolling on the floor, she tried to convince her Mother and Granny that she had acute stomach pain. She felt sure that at least dear old Granny would be moved by her acting and she was absolutely right. The Granny was so fond of Yamuna that she permitted her to remain at home which angered Anandi's mother Ganga very much.

One day, eluding her Mother, Yamuna went to her friend's house instead of school. After a few hours, the school was closed and the teacher went away but Yamuna did not return. When Ganga asked a servant about Yamuna, he told her that Yamuna was playing with her friend in the neighbourhood. Livid with rage, Ganga went there in a breath and brought Yamuna back beating her and shouting at her. She

F6. Sacred Records – Generally, such records were written on broad papers which were compiled in a manuscript called 'Pothi.' A Pothi which was wrapped in a large red cloth, was preserved with reverence.

F7 Zopala – Huge wooden square swing hanging from a ceiling with the help of 4 metallic bars. Big houses always had a zopala in those days. It was a favourite pastime of women to swing high on zopala singing melodious songs.

was annoyed not because Yamuna avoided school but because the unruly child challenged her authority. Later in the future, when Yamuna took a profound interest in learning, the same mother opposed her with all her might. Since there was no love lost between the mother and the daughter, the Granny spontaneously shouldered the responsibility of upbringing Yamuna. She particularly saw to it that the child got good, nutritious food and grew healthy. Therefore despite Ganga's thrashing, Yamuna grew into a sturdy girl. Once just for fun, her maternal aunt provoked Yamuna to wrestle with a cousin brother, who was older than Yamuna. She defeated him with ease. Feeling insulted, the brother shouted, "No wonder she could win. Grandma nourishes her with bowls of milk and butter. A fat cat that she is!" There onwards, her aunt started calling her *malla* or a wrestler. For her mother, she was an unwanted child. According to her relatives, she was an unmanageable girl of a haughty woman, and their neighbours had a notion that Yamuna who studied like a boy, was too bold. Barring her father, no one realised that she was an intelligent girl.

Once Yamuna saw a Missionary in front of her house preaching Christianity in Marathi, which was Anandi's mother tongue. His Marathi was peculiarly flavoured with an English accent and his talk was a queer mixture of English and Marathi. This attracted Yamuna's attention. Standing in the front gate, Yamuna watched him with amusement. In the afternoon, she entertained her friends with a perfect mimicry of the Missionary. Though Yamuna could not understand the meaning of his lecture, her memory was sharp enough to reproduce it, along with his gestures, facial expressions, intonation and accents. Soon it became a popular entertainment of the children and they urged Yamuna to mimic the Missionary. Someone asked her, "How come you know these English words?" She smartly replied, "Why? Didn't you hear the Missionary that day? Remember, this is how he spoke!" Not appreciating her singular memory, observation or wit, Yamuna's mother asked her sarcastically, "Eh, do you want to be a nun and give sermons? Better play the usual games! Why can't you be like other girls?"

According to Ganga's notion, girls were not supposed to behave the way her odd daughter did. She was worried about Yamuna's marriage as she thought that Yamuna was not beautiful. Except for her fine jet-black, long and curly hair, Yamuna had no mark of beauty. When she was 5 years old, she had badly suffered from smallpox. Her condition was very serious. Fortunately, she was saved, but her pinkish white complexion darkened and her face was pockmarked. The scars were visible even when she grew up. So, Ganga thought, "Who would marry my overgrown, over smart, pockmarked and not really beautiful daughter of an unusual nature?"

The mother struck fear in Yamuna's heart, but the father touched the right chord. He understood his daughter better than anybody else. In her garden, Yamuna often planted some plants or shrubs which attracted her attention. But most of the time, cows ate them. Every two days, she would go to her father complaining that the cowherd was not mindful of his duty and so cows ate her plants. Her elders advised Yamuna not to plant, but the father admired her persistence. He tried in vain to make his wife understand that their daughter was a brilliant child. On the contrary, Ganga thought that her husband was too indulgent, too lenient with Yamuna who was nothing but a pampered daughter. Ganpat had noted that despite her dislike for school, Yamuna had learnt a lot because she was gifted with superb grasping power and a graphic memory. He felt for certain that gradually she would develop an interest in her studies.

When there were guests at home, Ganpat asked Yamuna to read out something for them. He was delighted to see how zealously Yamuna responded and how fluently she read. Guests used to be stupefied to see such a queer girl who appeared before the guests and read without the slightest of fear. They could not understand how a wise man like Ganpat could encourage his daughter to learn, instead of engaging her in the kitchen for mastering womanly things. They thought that no one would marry a girl who could read. Yamuna's future development proved that her intelligence was not a fancy of her loving father but a reality. Her only fault was that she was not like other girls. She was like an ugly duckling who grew into a swan.

5

An Off-beat Marriage

The person who was instrumental in changing the course of Yamuna's life, was her husband Gopal Vinayak Joshi. Not much information is available about his early life. He was 20 years older than Yamuna, hence he was born somewhere in 1845. When he was a child, his family lived in Sangamner, a town in the Bombay Presidency. He had an elder sister Mathura, a younger sister Yamuna and two younger brothers Ravji and Appa. As a child, Gopal had no liking for studies. He could not master even the Marathi alphabet till he was eight years old. His father did not mind offering elementary education to women, so along with Gopal, he taught Mathura, who was cleverer than Gopal. She prepared her lessons very sincerely while Gopal lagged behind. He became so jealous of Mathura that one day he tore her books when she was having lunch.

His childish jealousy was a negative way of appreciating Mathura's merits. Deep down in his mind, he was impressed by his clever sister. When he matured, he came to the conclusion that it was unjust to deny education to women. Given an opportunity, they too would cherish serious aspirations like men. Gopal grew up amid social upheavals when reformative ideas like women's education, widow remarriage and abolition of child marriage were heatedly discussed in various strata. The jealous little boy who had turned into an avant-gardist youth, was sorry to observe that people seldom practised what they preached. So, to give active support to women's education, he vowed to set an example, by educating at least one woman.

As better educational facilities were available in Nashik, Gopal was sent there when he was in high school. As per the prevalent custom, the young boy was married by his parents to Savitri alias Mai Oak who was a cousin sister of Gopal's friend Gangadhar Narasimha Ketkar. The bride was just six years old at the time of marriage. Gopal looked at this marriage as an opportunity to carry out his vow to educate a woman.

Till then, he had only heard of the sufferings of child wives, but now he saw with his own eyes how difficult it was for a small girl to live among strangers. A girl who hardly understood her own needs like hunger, thirst or sleep was expected to behave like a grown-up woman and hard disciplines were enforced upon her. Moreover, if she made any mistakes in her household duties, she had to endure taunts, bitter remarks about her parents and punishments as well. The poor girl had no other choice but to shed tears in silence. Gopal decided not to allow such things in his house. So, he exhorted his mother to treat Savitri with love and consideration. Savitri represented all those suffering girls who were victims of the custom of child marriage and Gopal was determined to change his wife's fate by giving her good education.

He discussed this issue with his friend Gangadhar and expressed his wish to educate Savitri and the idea was heartily welcomed by Gangadhar. With great enthusiasm, Gopal slipped a slate in Savitri's hands and set to carry out his vow. He was delighted to see that Savitri took an interest in learning. Soon he got a job at a Post office in Pune, therefore the responsibility of teaching Savitri was placed in the able hands of Gangadhar. To the satisfaction of Gopal and Gangadhar, Savitri was soon able to write letters to Gopal. In the meanwhile, Savitri had given birth to a boy, Krushna. Very soon the family was to unite in Pune but unfortunately, Savitri fell ill and could never recover. Her untimely death was a sudden blow to Gopal who was thrown into the abyss of despair. The frustrated young widower lived alone in Pune. Little Krushna was with Gangadhar at Nashik, who took good care of him. Gopal's father urged him to remarry but he had no wish to have a child-wife. Instead, he wanted to marry a widow of his age.

In 1865, a few like-minded people had united under the leadership of Vishnu Parshuramshastri Pandit to set up an institute for encouraging widow marriages. The movement had the firm support of the law because the legislation of widow marriage had been passed by the Government in 1856 itself. Yet it had gained little momentum because people lacked the courage to act against time-honoured customs. The first widow marriage took place on 15th June 1869 when Pandurang Vinayak Karmarkar, a dashing young man mustered up his courage to marry a widow, Venu Paranjape. It was arranged by the organisation of Vishnushastri Pandit and was regarded as a great victory of the movement. Wishing to marry a widow, Gopal had corresponded with Vishnushastri. The only thing that he expected from his wife was an honest desire to learn. He went to the extreme and said, "I would marry even a fallen woman, if she is ready to learn." By marrying a widow and educating her, Gopal aimed to bring about two reforms at a time. Thus, he looked at his marriage not only as a joyous event in his personal life but also as a means to reform.

Such noble thoughts were brewing in his mind when in 1870, he was transferred to the General Post Office of Bombay which was situated in the Fort area. Afterwards, he was promoted to the Thane Post Office as the Postmaster. This transfer was instrumental in uniting him with his second wife Yamuna alias Anandi Joshi. Two versions of the event of Yamuna's marriage with Gopal are available which are based on two different sources of information.

A) The version of Kashibai Kanitkar, a Marathi biographer: The main source of her information was Gopal.

B) The version of Caroline Dall, an American author: The main source of her information was Anandi, with whom she interacted when she was in America.

According to Kashibai Kanitkar, Yamuna's parents were worried about her marriage. Her mother Ganga had a feeling that no well-to-do youth would marry her daughter who was not beautiful, was a bit hard of hearing in one ear and was pockmarked. Plus, she had crossed the normal age of marriage. So, she thought that only a poor man or a widower might accept her. Secondly, they were not in a position to give large dowry which parents of a well-to-do youth might have demanded. One day, a matchmaker informed Ganpat about Gopal Joshi, the new Postmaster at Thane. As he was a widower and 20 years older than Yamuna, she stood a good chance. One afternoon, the matchmaker hastened to the Joshi Mansion and asked the ladies to get ready immediately if they wished to see Gopal Joshi, the would-be husband of Yamuna, who had come to the Kalyan Post Office. He was ready to take them there secretly, so that they could look at him without being observed. The ladies decided to snatch this golden opportunity and were thrilled to take part in this 'adventure.' Hastily preparing themselves, they rushed behind the matchmaker. Varanasi, the married sister of Yamuna, her maternal aunt and the grandmother went with him. Entering unnoticed by the back door, they curiously watched Gopal and were glad to see that though a government servant and a man of good position, he was not dressed like an Englishman. He seemed to be a simple man in his native dress of dhoti-kurta and a turban. Feeling satisfied, the ladies returned home. Only a day before, Ganga had asked Yamuna to pray to Lord Shiva for getting a good husband. So, they felt that Yamuna's prayer was heard. Having the women's approval, Ganpat approached Gopal and arranged a meeting in his house so that Gopal could meet Yamuna. He came to see his would-be wife and the meeting was successful.

Considering that period, this dramatic account sounds fictitious. Ladies never visited public places. So, it was just not possible that the highborn ladies of a well-known family could go unnoticed, in a crowded place like the post office. A young married woman like Varansi and an old widow like Grandma could never have gone so smartly to a post office, without creating havoc. The 'scandalous news' would have spread through the town like fire. Instead of the ladies observing Gopal, he would have noticed them instantly with a shock. This information was provided to Kashibai by no one else but Gopal himself, who was notorious for his mischievousness, frivolity and sensationalism all through his life. He did not mind weaving a web of lies just to amuse himself or to confuse people. It is very likely that he had deliberately misled Kashibai for the sake of dramatisation of his life story. The falsification of the story would be clear after going through the other version of Caroline Dall.

According to Caroline, Gopal was transferred to Bombay and then to Thane in 1870. He was a stranger in this part. Therefore, he sought the acquaintance of Ganpat Joshi, the Inamdar of Kalyan as they belonged to the same community. Yamuna was then 5 years old and had just begun to attend the school in the Joshi Mansion, started by her father. Ganpat who was quite impressed by the scholarly young man of progressive outlook, thought that Gopal alone would properly guide Yamuna. Caroline says, "Ganpatrao was an educated man. He … saw at once that Gopal's knowledge of Sanskrit would be of great advantage to Yamuna."[1] Since the towns of Kalyan and Thane were connected by the railway, it was not difficult for Gopal to spare some time for Yamuna. How and when

Gopal taught Yamuna, Caroline did not know; but she was certain that under his able guidance, Yamuna gradually developed a keen interest in learning. In short, according to Caroline, Gopal knew Yamuna and her family at least for a few years before their marriage. In this case, the tale of ladies going to the post office to have a look at Gopal does not stand. As Caroline's source of information was Anandi herself who was known for her sincerity and truthfulness, it could be considered reliable.

Then how was Yamuna alias Anandi married to Gopal who had no interest in marrying a small girl? Caroline does not provide a satisfactory answer to this question. Her account of Yamuna's marriage is rather confused because many of her questions had remained unanswered due to Anandi's untimely death and Gopal did not help her much. Caroline had stated that by the time Gopal was promoted to Alibag, Anandi's interest in learning was developed so much that she thought if Gopal went away, who would teach her? She went to her father and asked his permission to go with Gopal. Caroline thought that as they were not married then, her father was puzzled by his daughter's request. He could not send his unmarried daughter with a young man like Gopal. "In this emergency," says Caroline, "the grandmother…. came to Yamuna's aid. 'I will go with her' she said, 'and I will shield her as if she were my own."[2]

When Caroline wrote this account, she herself was not sure of it. Moreover, Pandita Ramabai, a kinswoman of Anandi, who was then in America, emphatically told Caroline that it was just not possible that in India, parents would thus send their daughter with a man, without marrying them. So for certain, Gopal and Yamuna were married before they went to Alibag. But not giving due credence to this valuable information and not correcting her mistake, Caroline just mentioned this in the preface and preserved her confusion in the biography and hence misplaced in time many other important events. To give another example of her incorrect account, she could not decide whether Gopal went to Kolhapur before marriage or after. "From Alibag, Gopal had been transferred to Kolhapur and it was probably there that the grandmother parted with the child, who was soon to be married to Gopal."[3] This means Gopal went to Kolhapur before marriage which took place on 31st March 1874. Why did the grandma part with Yamuna before marriage, when she had promised Ganga that she would protect Yamuna all the time? Then further Caroline stated, "Anandabai's only child was born in her 14th year, probably at Kolhapur sometime early in 1878." [4] Was she sure that Gopal was at Kolhapur for four years? If so, she was wrong. Not knowing the exact order of the events, Caroline was proceeding with uncertainly. First of all, when she interviewed Anandi, not caring much for details, she jotted down some points, which it seems, were insufficient for writing a biography. Secondly, even after Pandita Ramabai's affirmation about the Indian custom, Caroline did not realise that something was drastically wrong in assuming that Gopal and Yamuna lived together before their marriage. And yet with undue confidence she says, "In a memoir prepared as this has been, there must be more than the usual liability to errors in details. I have done all that I could to prevent such errors and I hope that no serious error is likely to appear."[5]

In the course of the narration, I have arranged the misplaced events in proper chronological order. But at present, it is essential to discover the truth about Yamuna's marriage, which lies between the two versions. Since Gopal had canalised Yamuna's intellectual energies and made her interested in learning, and since he was a champion of women's education, Ganpat thought him to be an excellent match for his promising daughter. Though Gopal was a widower and 20 years older than Yamuna, he was not an old man. He was in his late twenties when he visited the Joshi Mansion and taught Yamuna. In those days, the disparity of ages between a husband and a wife was considered normal. Hence, through a middleman, Yamuna's father conveyed his wish to Gopal. Of course, Gopal could not have thought of marrying his little pupil, as he wished to marry a widow of his age. But his mind was in turmoil then because his efforts to marry a widow did not meet with success. No correspondence between Gopal and Vishnushastri Pandit, an advocate of widow marriage, is available, which would have thrown light on the reasons behind this. But for sure, Gopal had lost all hopes of marrying a widow. And yet, when Ganpat offered Yamuna's hand in marriage, Gopal accepted it rather undecidedly, not knowing if he should still wait for a widow or at least further the cause of women's education by marrying his clever pupil.

An auspicious day was chosen by the family priest of Inamdar Joshi. Preparations for the delightful occasion had begun with enthusiasm. Yet Gopal was in two minds. To marry or not to marry! He was suffering from the agonies of remorse, as he had accepted little Yamuna's hand half-heartedly. Being unable to share his thoughts with anybody, he needed some time to brood over. Therefore, he told Ganpat that he would go to Sangamner to meet his parents before marriage. His parents were delighted to hear the news, as they were urging him for a long time to remarry. His elder sister Mathura had come to her parents' house for her pregnancy. Using this situation to his benefit, Gopal cautiously requested his father and mother to stay with Mathura and promised that he would manage everything about his marriage single-handedly. He did all this because he was still unsettled. Gopal started for Kalyan but went to Nashik. He told himself that he was not really interested in this marriage and would avoid it by remaining absent. He decided to tell Ganpat that due to some domestic problems, the marriage had been postponed.

Having no idea of Gopal's conflict, the Joshis were getting things ready for the marriage ceremony. Ornaments were chosen and marriage dresses were purchased. Invitations were distributed. The menu and some special dishes for the marriage feast were decided. The mansion was decorated. There were pre-marriage lunch and dinner parties given by friends and relatives. Now they were eagerly waiting for Gopal to return. Days passed but he did not come. Due to his mysterious disappearance, tension mounted in the house. When the chosen day ended without the marriage ceremony, everyone blamed the middleman, who could not find Gopal anywhere. Feeling guilty, he set out to Sangamner, in search of Gopal.

To his great surprise, he saw Gopal wandering on a platform at the Nashik railway station. Instantly he caught hold of Gopal and gave vent to his wrath. Gopal had no choice but to listen silently to the volley of angry words. The middleman approached Gangadhar Ketkar, the respectable friend of Gopal, who then took the situation in his hand. Accompanied by some relatives, Gopal was sent back to Kalyan. At last, Yamuna was married to Gopal on 31st March 1874, which was her 10th birthday. According to the custom, Yamuna's maiden name was changed. Hereafter she was to be known as Anandibai Gopalrao Joshi.

Anandi was so dear to her father that as her marriage present, he generously gave her precious ornaments like the anklets of solid gold, which were part of the heirloom and were generally preserved in the family. Being convinced about her bright future, he thought it wise to make some provision for her education. By allowing her to carry away some of the family Gods and relics, he placed complete trust in her. Generally, girls went to their husband's house after marriage, but Anandi's in-laws lived in Sangamner and Gopal lived in Thane. Anandi being too young to shoulder alone the responsibilities of a wife, it was decided that Anandi-Gopal would live in her father's house. Gopal went to his office at Thane in the morning and returned to Kalyan in the evening. Hence, Anandi's daily routine remained the same, even after marriage. But her nights changed and that was a shock to a girl of 9 years. Though Gopal showed no inclination to spend nights with his child-wife, the grown-up women in the house pushed her into Gopal's room and closed the door from outside. This gave rise to fear of Gopal which Anandi had never experienced before.

Generally, even after marriage, underage girls were supposed to sleep in the women's chamber till they reached the age of puberty. A religious ceremony known as 'Garbhadhan Vidhi' was performed after the first menstruation for the purification of the womb and the facilitation of conception. By convention, the sexual relation between a husband and a wife was supposed to begin only after this ceremony. In spite of this rule, many women entertained themselves by sending newly married, bashful girls into their husbands' rooms. They enjoyed their 'game' more, if a girl resisted, cried or shrieked in fear. Filled with perverse curiosity, they stationed themselves near the door of a couple's chamber; giggling, whispering and peeping through cracks, if possible. The scene became more pathetic when a small girl of five or six was married to an old man in his sixties, who looked more like her grandfather than a husband. Having no idea of higher pleasures that life could offer, those ignorant women indulged in such obscenities. Another reason was psychological. Widows who were deprived of sexual pleasures at an early age, never knew what it meant. Therefore, they took an excessive interest in other people's sex lives and sought indirect pleasure in watching their sexual acts. This compulsion of sex increased the agonies of innocent child-wives.

Having lost their innocence and privacy, the poor little victims could never get enough time to bloom naturally. Their girlish emotions, a dreamy sense of life and bewitching adolescent fantasies were cruelly crushed by the barbarous sexual compulsion. Sex came to them not as a beautiful relationship between a man and a woman, but as a right of the husband. On the other hand, women had no right even to raise their voice against any injustice. Anandi also fell prey to this perversity. Her relationship with Gopal whom she had held in high esteem as her Guru, changed completely after marriage. Women around her tried to make her accept that he had become the master of her body and mind, which disturbed her deeply.

Being wise enough to understand her state of mind, Gopal never forced her to stay with him at night. On the contrary, he allowed her to run away. But this unusual tenderness of the newly married son-in-law perplexed the women in the house. They could not understand why he would not act like a man and make his wife obey his orders. According to them, it was foolish of a man to show so much concern for the feelings of his wife. Even the loving, old grandmother warned Gopal that if he did not handle the situation properly and be strict with Anandi, she would turn into an unruly woman. The women had placed Gopal in a strange dilemma. On one hand, his prestige as a man was at stake and on the other, his little wife was just uncontrollable.

He was neither able to teach Anandi to his heart's content nor able to take any decision independently. His every action was closely watched and criticised by the whole household. Fade up with the criticism, one night he decided that he would not allow Anandi to go out of the room. So, he ordered her to stay but she would not listen. Her childish obstinacy was so unbearable to him, that in a fit of anger, he flogged her cruelly. The next morning, the women were grieved to see that Anandi's arms were swollen and blue-black. Even for Gopal, it was hard to continue like this in the house of his in-laws. To get out of this uncomfortable situation, he decided to go somewhere else and stay independently. He asked for his transfer and it was granted.

He was transferred to Alibag, a small town, not very far off from Kalyan. But the women were not ready to send little Anandi with Gopal. This grieved her very much, as she knew that without him, she would not be able to learn anything. She went to her father and requested him to send her with Gopal. Caroline Dall misunderstood this event when she wrote, "Forgetting her love for her father and mother, indifferent to brothers and sisters, she begged permission to go away with Gopal. Her father was sorely puzzled. Although only eight years of age, Yamuna was now marriageable."[6] She wrongly thought that the event took place before marriage. And hence, felt that Anandi wished to go with Gopal, forgetting her love for father and mother. Anandi was not asking to let her go away with a stranger but with her own husband, which was quite natural. There was no question of forgetting her love for her father and mother. A married Hindu girl was expected to do so and follow her husband wherever he went. A married daughter was treated as 'the wealth of another man.' But the misplacement of the event done by Caroline Dall culminated in its misinterpretation. The uniqueness of Anandi's request to let her follow Gopal, lies in the fact that the reason behind it was not conventional. She did not want to follow her husband because it was supposed to be the duty of a married girl. Her quenchless thirst for knowledge motivated her to go with Gopal, despite the fear of spending nights with him.

While talking about this event, Anandi told Caroline that she thought, if Gopal went away, she would not be able to learn anything, "I should never learn anymore… and I would rather have died." [7] This bitter cry was repeated again and again when she narrated those memories to Caroline Dall. 'How come Ananadi thought of death?' Thought Caroline. Considering the condition of Hindustani women in the 19th century, it was not unnatural. To prefer death to agony, was a typical reaction of those women, for whom abundant suffering was in store, from their childhood to the end of their lives. Anandi reacted in a similar way, when her grief knew no bounds. She had heard this expression hundreds of times and it drifted in her memory. She had tasted the luscious fruit of knowledge, so her biggest grief was to live without learning. Thus, the reaction was common but the reason behind it was uncommon. In the future, she dedicated herself to the quest for knowledge and this reaction was the first tender sprout of her passion for knowledge.

References:

1. *The Life of Dr. Anandabai Joshi* - Caroline Healey Dall. 1888. Page, 26
2. Ibid Page, 27
3. Ibid Page, 27
4. Ibid Page, 32
5. Ibid Preface Page, vii
6. Ibid Page, 26
7. Ibid Page, 26

6

The Beginning of a New Life

Saying goodbye to Kalyan, Anandi-Gopal and Anandi's grandmother went to Alibag at the end of 1874. A dwelling was allotted to Gopal in the post office building itself. Now that Gopal was the master of his house, he was free to bring his ideas into practice. The grandmother did not oppose him but her idea of a good wife certainly clashed with that of Gopal. Feeling strongly that a married girl had to be an expert cook and a perfect housekeeper, she tried to give Anandi some lessons in the kitchen, behind Gopal's back. Nonetheless, Gopal found it out and stopped her intervention. Occasionally they both argued over it and the little wife did not know what she was supposed to do. As the grandmother had no authority in the house of her grandson-in-law, gradually she learnt to keep herself out of Gopal's way. So now he could teach Anandi as much as he wished, without any hindrance. Gopal's passion for women's education was so intense that, had the grandmother shown some interest in learning, he would have taught her as well.

Gopal was an unconventional person in many ways. He was a simple man having few needs. Never did he expect Anandi to wait on him hand and foot or prepare for him square meals. He was content with plain food and if the situation demanded, he didn't mind eating parched rice and gram to fill his stomach. In that period, a married girl was supposed to devote her life to the welfare of her family, without giving a thought to her own joys and wishes. As women were mentally prepared for this kind of life since childhood, nobody looked at it as an injustice. But the marriage with Gopal offered Anandi the freedom and opportunity of self-development. As Gopal's service was transferable, Anandi did not have to live with her in-laws in the joint family at Sangamner. This was also an important reason why the marriage didn't impose strict rules on her.

Anandi had already learnt to read and write Marathi. Now Gopal introduced to her various subjects like History, Geography, Grammar and Mathematics. There was no girls' school in Alibag, but Anandi's sweet home became her school. Gopal's only expectation was that Anandi should give her mind to learning. To motivate her to study hard, he once brought her a pair of nice shoes, after the fashion of the English women. As women didn't use footwear in those days, and always walked barefoot, Anandi was excited to get such an unobtainable thing. Many a time, Gopal took Anandi for an evening stroll on the seashore of Alibag. In that era, men didn't even talk with their wives in the presence of a stranger. No wonder, the villagers thought it shameless on the part of the couple to wander together on the seashore. Naturally, the new Postmaster became an object of ridicule. Whenever they saw Anandi-Gopal walking together on the roads, people made fun of them. But in spite of this, Gopal had his own ways. He wanted his wife to enjoy life and experience the breath of freedom.

That did not mean that everything in their life went smoothly. Gopal was a grown-up man and Anandi was a mere child, having her own innocent wishes and interests. Games and playmates were irresistible temptations for her. It was her psychological need and her right too. She preferred to be left alone in her own world where she was nobody's wife, but just a small, playful girl. The grandmother lovingly advised Anandi to complete her lessons first and then play with her friends, so that she would not make her husband angry. Gopal admired Anandi's intellectual capacity but failed to understand her mental needs as a child. Her natural desire to play was misinterpreted as negligence of her study. The age difference between them reflected in their responses, reactions, wishes and choices. Another thing that Gopal hated was the way Anandi dressed. Anandi who was very particular about her appearance, disliked old-fashioned, loosely fitting blouses or dull coloured saris. She always selected colourful and gorgeous brocades and loved to put on exuberant ornaments. She took good care of her long beautiful hair. She washed, oiled and neatly arranged it in style. As Gopal preferred his wife to be plainly dressed, her style provoked his anger. Neither could he control his anger nor could he tame her with love. He inflicted severe punishment to force her into discipline. He was brutal enough to beat her with firewood sticks, thick books or the broken leg of a chair. A prey to his own anger, Gopal made Anandi's youthful days miserable. No wonder, she could never forget the bitter taste of this experience.

Gopal went to the limit of threatening Anandi that her disobedience would compel him to desert her and that he would send her back to her parent's house. Anandi was afraid of it the most. If a married girl was sent back, it was taken for granted that her parents were to blame and something was wrong with her upbringing. A mere thought of people accusing her father and mother broke Anandi's spirit. Not wishing to stain her father's reputation, she urged Gopal to kill her instead. Thus, he compelled Anandi to obey him and she lived under tremendous pressure of his anger and threats. To her credit, may it be said that even then she succeeded in preserving her mental strength and self-reliance. If she were an ordinary girl with lesser strength of mind, the fear might have crippled her mentally or she might have developed an inferiority complex. But that did not happen. On the contrary, gradually she took to learning as a duck takes to water and then she never looked back.

In Alibag, Anandi reached the age of puberty. As per the custom, the rite of 'Garbhadhan Vidhi' was performed for which Gopal's mother was invited. She stayed with them for a few days. Kashibai Kanitkar, the Marathi biographer had said that Anandi became pregnant within 2 years after her marriage that means before March 1876. The couple had settled in Alibag at the end of 1874. Hence, between December 1874 and March 1876, that means within 15 months, she went through the experience of menstruation, intercourse and pregnancy, one after the other and could not gain time to adjust herself to the changes within her body and mind.

Menstruation, the first sprout of womanhood shakes the mind of a girl from its very root. Her mind becomes an admixture of unidentified anguish, agitation, disquietude, qualm, ardent longing and excitement, which a novice cannot fully understand. In this period, a girl needs help from a motherly person who would be warm, affectionate, open-minded and would delicately tackle the problems that disturb her. Of course, this kind of help was given by elderly women, but in that period, girls could never get a breathing space between the first turn of menstruation and the beginning of sex life. Immediately after the first turn of menstruation, they had to prepare themselves for intercourse, leaving aside their bashfulness and shame. Then if their bodies responded, they had to pass through the ordeal of pregnancy, childbirth and had to shoulder the responsibility of their premature motherhood. Because sex was forced upon them, it came into their life not as a natural phenomenon but as an unnatural, dirty act. The same thing happened with Anandi.

From Alibag she was brought to Kalyan for her first delivery. Everyone was happy as she gave birth to a boy. But 10 days later, her son died, casting gloom upon the whole house. The little mother was beside herself with grief, as no one could save her child. Later on, she told Caroline Dall, "A child's death does no harm to its father, but its mother does not want it to die."[1] After pondering over why her baby died, she arrived at the conclusion that it died because proper and timely medical help was not available. Then, slowly it dawned on her that thousands of women and children in the country were dying because there were no women doctors, except a few foreign lady doctors, and women could not accept medical help from the hands of male doctors. "How could the situation be changed for the better? What can I do for those suffering women?" Anandi contemplated, "What if I become a doctor? Oh…. can I? Why not? Yes, I can!" Thus, the great dream was born out of her intense suffering. This was a turning point in her life. Coming out of her grief, she had begun to think about a serious social issue. At this juncture, the hoyden of yesteryear grew into a thoughtful, mature woman who dreamt of becoming a doctor. She was longing to tell her secret to her husband who, she was certain, would be thrilled by it. She returned to Alibag in an eager state of mind. Though her arms were empty without her child, her mind was pregnant with a fascinating dream, which she was to pursue here onwards.

When Anandi shared with Gopal her idea of becoming a doctor, he was enchanted by its magnificence. He had little dreamt that his girlish wife would stretch her wings so soon. By now, Anandi had cultivated the habit of reading newspapers to keep herself abreast of the time. She had also spontaneously taken the charge of family correspondence which satisfied her husband very much. Now he thought that it was his responsibility to develop her abilities. So, Gopal started teaching her English. But Alibag was such a backward place that nothing could have been done from there to pursue her dream. Hence once again, Gopal decided to ask for a transfer.

While trying to locate a town with good educational facilities for women, the state of Kolhapur attracted Gopal's attention. This state had the tradition of broad-minded Kings who had the courage to implement progressive schemes, despite public disapproval. Rev. Royal Gold Wilder who had founded the American Marathi Mission in December 1852, was a person aflame with religious zeal. Being suspicious of his religious activities, people thought of him as a public menace. They feared that he would convert people using all tactics. They were so agitated that they wrote a letter to the Political Agent of the British Government for his banishment from Kolhapur. But knowing that the spread of knowledge alone would change the fate of his uneducated subjects, Babasaheb Maharaj, the King of Kolhapur, firmly supported Rev. Wilder, when he wanted to organise a school. People used to learn various skills of their forefathers to earn a livelihood, but most of them were illiterate. Only 4% of the population could read and write. Wanting to change this picture, Babasaheb Maharaj encouraged Rev. Wilder. Aoubai and Balabai, the sisters of Babasaheb Maharaj also extended co-operation to Wilder's wife, in launching a girls' school and offered a place for it in their palace. In 1867, the first government's English Medium School was established which was soon converted into the Rajaram High School. When in 1870, the foundation of the high school was laid, Rajaram Maharaj, the successor of Babasaheb Maharaj, promised the organisers that they would always get his support. No wonder, Gopal felt that Kolhapur was a perfect place to settle in.

When Anandi-Gopal reached Kolhapur in the middle of 1877, the state was governed by Mahadeo Vasudeo Barve, the Diwan of Kolhapur, on behalf of King Shivaji the fourth, who was a minor. Barve had set many reforms in motion, paying special attention to town planning and health services. The town was divided into 6 wards for the convenience of municipal undertakings. A strong fortification surrounded the town. The area near the wall was densely populated with small, earthen houses of poor people. But the interior part of the town looked splendid with spacious houses and temples. The most beautiful and the oldest one was the temple of goddess 'Ambabai' which was built in black stone. All the houses were properly numbered. The royal roads were well-paved and illuminated at night with bright lanterns. Near the main gate of the town, there was a public dispensary run by Dr. Sinclair. The north-west region of the town was cleaned and a huge Town Hall was erected there with a beautiful garden around it. Due to the clement climate and refreshing West winds, Kolhapur was a nice place to live in.

In 1877, Kolhapur was not connected to other places by railway. Bullock-carts and horse-carriages were the only means of transport. Gopal was provided with a horse carriage by the post office for travelling from Alibaug to Kolhapur. The journey was long and tedious. So, they took a halt at Satara, where they spent a night in the house of their friend. The next morning, they resumed their journey. Once they settled comfortably in Kolhapur, Gopal enquired about the girls' school. He found out that the government's school for girls was of good repute and was run by a renowned English lady Miss Meesi. But the only problem was that it was far away from their house. As no public transport was available, it was difficult to send Anandi to this school. Engaging a horse carriage for her was too expensive for his small purse and it was not advisable for Anandi to go alone on foot in the unknown town. But luckily, the bungalow of the headmistress, Miss Meesi, was very near to Anandi-Gopal's house. Gopal met her and candidly explained Anandi's problem. Meesi who had her own carriage, agreed to take Anandi with her, if she would come to her bungalow in time. At last, to his great satisfaction, Gopal succeeded in putting Anandi into the school.

Thinking that the Missionaries would appreciate Anandi's aspiration to become a doctor and would give them proper guidance, Gopal began to call on them along with Anandi. He befriended Rev. J. M. Gohin of the American Presbyterian Church and his wife. Soon Anandi-Gopal became welcome visitors in Rev. Gohin's house. But it gave rise to suspicion among native people that Gopal might embrace Christianity. Since 1870, there was a continuous flow of Missionaries in Kolhapur who had succeeded in converting some of the low caste persons. Now a high caste Hindu lady like Anandi going to school, in the company of a Christian lady was an eyesore to people. They strongly felt that the unruly behaviour of the Postmaster and his wife was a threat to their prestige, so they should not close their eyes to it. Some people of high rank brought this issue to the notice of Diwan Mahadeo Vasudeo Barve, who himself was a Brahman like Anandi-Gopal. When rumourmongers generated a whispering campaign about the possible conversion of the Brahman couple, it created havoc. In effect, Miss Meese was ordered to dissociate herself urgently from Anandi-Gopal.

After all, Meese was a government servant. She could neither afford to quarrel with her means of livelihood nor could she have animosity with the authorities of the State, for the enlightenment of the wife of a Postmaster. But she lacked the courage to reveal honestly her helplessness to Anandi-Gopal. The path of least resistance that she chose was to discourage Anandi by insulting her. She expressed her unwillingness to help Anandi in many ways. When Anandi went to her house, Meese didn't offer her a seat, but deliberately kept her waiting. Sometimes she would hurriedly go away, without waiting for Anandi to come. In her carriage, she arrogantly ordered Anandi to sit at a distance. This kind of treatment spoke for itself. So Gopal thought it wiser not to send Anandi with Meese. It was possible to enrol Anandi's name at the Ester Paton Girls' School, which was established by some Missionaries in 1872, but that school was also far away from the town. Yet Gopal didn't stop hunting for someone who would take interest in teaching Anandi and came across Miss Mc Zaneis, a Missionary lady, who taught in the Mission School. She was ready to teach Anandi whenever she could get time. But the problem was that she did not understand Marathi and Anandi's knowledge of English was hardly enough to understand any subject in English. So, it was difficult for Mc Zaneis to explain anything at length. Having no other choice, Gopal started teaching Anandi at home. She had already perfected Marathi grammar, could turn Marathi matter from her textbook into English, loved to locate various places on a map and could perfectly understand the decimal system. All the time, she was so anxious to learn something new that Gopal faced a real challenge of watering her fertile mind with the constant supply of knowledge.

Though the experience in Kolhapur was disappointing, their stay was not futile because they could get at least a peep of their cloudland. Gopal was convinced that nowhere in India, Anandi would be allowed to learn peacefully and the same obstacles as in Kolhapur would block her way. Then how would she learn Medicine and become a doctor? While discussing this problem with sympathetic Rev. Gohin, Gopal and Anandi came to know about the Feminist movement of women's liberation and particularly the struggle of women doctors in America, for their right to Medical education. They were astonished that women could fight for their right to suffrage and self-expression, the right to protest against slavery and the right to live as human beings. Their hearts throbbed with joyous wonder: "Could women be so courageous, as to fight with the society for their human rights? Could they be so fired with ideas as to demand their rights, fearing nothing, fearing nobody? Who must have kindled the spirit of freedom within their hearts?" They pondered on and on. They were also told that in America, there were separate women's Medical colleges and women from all over the globe flocked there. "Could I be one of them? Could I go to the college of those dauntless women?" Anandi brooded over the possibility. "This is the country on earth, for my wife to live in." Gopal reflected. The hearts of Anandi-Gopal which were now in unison, echoed the same hope of sailing to America where Anandi's dream could be realised.

People remained at a distance from the Christian Missionaries due to the fear of conversion. But being self-respecting persons who strongly believed in their own Hindu religion, Anandi Gopal freely mixed with them without any fear. Gopal had no doubt that the Missionaries would try to convert him and his intelligent wife and it would be a major victory if they could succeed. But instead of running away from them, he decided to use their hidden motive for his advantage. He thought that only by showing an interest in Christianity, he would be able to get good advice and help for Anandi's project. More than that, he looked up to his Christian friends as representatives of the land of freedom.

One day Gopal went to Rev. Gohin and expressed his wish to go to America for Anandi's Medical education. It was so unexpected and sudden that Rev. Gohin was flabbergasted. Crossing the sea was thought to be a horrible sin in the Hindu religion and hence, a woman daring to take this step and going against her religion was unimaginable. He requested Gopal to think it over, but Gopal firmly told him that he was ready to face any calamity. Rev. Gohin decided to seek the advice of Rev. Royal Gold Wilder, the founder of the American Marathi Mission in Kolhapur, who had returned to America in 1875, due to his ill health. He asked Gopal to write a letter to Rev. Wilder explaining his idea. With zeal, Gopal committed to paper. Objectively explaining the problem of women's education in India, Gopal informed Rev. Wilder about his scheme to send his wife to America for her Medical education. Through his simple but earnest words he poured out his mind, "Ever since I began to think independently for myself, female education has been my favourite subject. I keenly felt the growing want of it, to raise the nation to eminence among civilised countries. It is the source of happiness in a family. As every reform must begin at home, I considered it my duty to give my wife a thorough education, that she might be able to impart it to her sisters, but customs and manners and caste prejudices have been a strong barrier to my views. Besides, our attempts have been regarded with suspicion by foreigners. On the other hand, female education is much looked down upon among all Brahmins, the highest class of people in India. My attempts have been frustrated; my object universally condemned by my own people. I have difficulties to encounter and no hopes to entertain in India, and yet I cannot give up the point. I will try to the last, there being nothing so important as female education for our elevation morally and spiritually.

"I should, therefore, if it pleases God, like to take my wife to America for being thoroughly educated. I am not in a position to undertake the journey and to defray my expenses of settling down in America without assistance. I should, therefore like to know, if I can get a footing in any department in America, so that I can go and stay there for some years. I don't want to live on charity, but I am very much in need of assistance in securing a place suitable to me.

I beg of you to help me by inquiring and ascertaining if I can get a chance of fulfilling my object."[2] Along with Gopal's appeal, Rev. Gohin attached his own letter in which he requested Rev. Wilder to help Gopal and his wife. Rev. Gohin also disclosed his secret hope of Gopal's conversion. "I have a great hope that he will first of all give his heart to God and then his own as well as his wife's influence would be a great blessing to his fellowmen.... I never told him this... I have never known of anyone going from this country to America on such a mission."[3]

Both Rev. Gohin and Gopal were proceeding with great prudence and tact. Like contemplative chess players, their actions were neatly planned and calculated. Propagation of Christianity was the mission of Rev. Gohin's life whereas the fruition of Anandi's aim was Gopal's passion. By fanning Anandi-Gopal's ambition Rev. Gohin wanted to achieve his own goal. Similarly, just by showing interest in Christianity, Gopal aimed at gaining help and guidance from him. Each one was trying to use the other party's ambition for his own purpose. Caroline Dall had sharply reacted against the attitude of Gopal, "It is probable that he had come into contact with the Missionaries in every town in which he had lived. He kept a steady eye to the advantages to be gained by Anandabai's thorough education and perhaps he was not perfectly frank when he wished to gain their co-operation."[4] Caroline suspected the lack of sincerity on Gopal's part but then one cannot blame Gopal alone. Even Rev. Gohin had veiled his real purpose behind his friendly help. Actually, in doing so, none of them meant any harm to the other. Both were devoted to their respective goals and concealing the real purpose was a part of their prudence.

Surprisingly Rev. Wilder whose wife had founded the first girl's school in Kolhapur did not find it proper to encourage Anandi-Gopal. In his letter to Gopal, he insisted that Gopal should embrace Christianity and remain where he was. He threw cold water on Gopal's enthusiasm by saying, "Now my dear friend, if you were worth a lakh rupee and would go and live in any part of the world you pleased, I would say don't go. Stay right where you are. Avow your honest convictions and confess Christ as your saviour and only hope of heaven, right there among your friends and countrymen."[5] This means without giving it a serious thought, Rev. Wilder tried to nip the plan in the bud. Neither the earnest letter of Gopal nor the humble request of Rev. Gohin could evoke fellow feelings and interest in his mind. He just gave cold shoulder to Gopal and asked him to work out his own salvation.

Here lies the difference between Rev. Wilder and Rev. Gohin. Both wished to convert the couple but at the same time, Gohin was a real well-wisher of Anandi-Gopal, who honestly wanted to see their goal accomplished. He was sure that if Anandi got an opportunity, she would become a doctor. He himself would have accompanied them if he were to visit America at that point in time. His words show how he cared for them, "If I were going home and had the means to educate them, I don't think I would hesitate to take them with me. But to send them alone and without any assurance of their being kindly received and cared for, I don't think would be wise." [6] On the other hand, the square refusal of Rev. Wilder was certainly not in accordance with his profound longing for Hindustan, the country which was dearer to him than his homeland. He visited America many times but always eagerly returned to Hindustan, except in 1875 when he was seriously ill and a long voyage was not advisable. But he simply could not forget Hindustan, Kolhapur and his work there. Hence for years, he cherished the hope of returning to Hindustan. In 1887, he grew so restless that he urged his doctors and relatives to send him back, "I will get well only if I return to Kolhapur; if not, I would at least die in peace among my people and my work. If I die in the voyage, throw my dead body into sea, so that sea would carry the particles of my body to the shore of Hindustan and my wish will be fulfilled."

To respect his last wish, his relatives decided to send him back to Hindustan, but just 2 days before he was to start his journey, which was on 10th October 1887, he died. No doubt, this is a touching account of his overflowing love for Hindustan. But then it surprises more that such an intense devotee of Hindustan could coldly turn down the benevolent proposal of a Hindustani woman who wanted to become a doctor to save her countrywomen. Though Rev. Wilder's letter disappointed Anandi-Gopal, neither did they lose heart nor did they relinquish their idea. They were prepared to bide their time. Being disillusioned about

Kolhapur, Gopal decided to ask for a transfer. This time, he turned his attention towards the big city of Bombay.

References:

1. *The Life of Dr. Anandabai Joshee* – Caroline Healey Dall. 1888. Page 32

2. Source: *The Nancy Cobb Stone Collection of Letters*.

3. Ibid

4. *The Life of Dr. Anandabai Joshee* – Caroline Healey Dall. 1888. Page 33

5, 6. Source: *The Nancy Cobb Stone Collection of Letters*.

7

Unexpected Developments

Once the decision was taken, Gopal directly approached Colonel Snayder, the Political Agent of Kolhapur, for his transfer to Bombay and explained that he wished to go there for the schooling of his wife, which had become impossible in Kolhapur. All his life, Gopal was known for his outspokenness and fearlessness. He dared to approach any authority or a person of high rank without hesitation. His striking personality and an uncommon passion for women's education aroused respect and curiosity in the minds of the Missionaries, reformers, and the British. So, going out of the way, they helped him and did whatever they could; Colonel Snayder being no exception. In his personal capacity, he wrote a letter to the Chief Postmaster of Bombay for Gopal's transfer. When a Political Agent himself was in favour of Gopal, no one would have refused the request. Not stopping there, Colonel Snayder spontaneously wrote a letter to Miss Prescott, who had organised a girls' school in the Fort area, requesting her to give admission to Mrs. Anandibai Joshi. The very fact that a man of importance like Colonel Snayder was taking so much interest in the personal matters of a mere Postmaster indicates how impressive Gopal might have been.

From the small, peaceful town of Kolhapur, Anandi-Gopal migrated to the big city of Bombay, at the beginning of 1879. He was transferred to the Girgaum Post Office, which was at the centre of the city. Even in the 19th century, Bombay was the economic capital of India, full of bustle and business, with its offices, banks, factories, mills, huge markets, railways and trams. People from small villages and towns rushed to Bombay to earn their bread or to try their luck. Enormous opportunities were available for industrious people who were ready to adjust themselves to the city life and keep pace with its speed. Different quarters of the city were connected by public transports like horse-driven trams and railways. Palanquins and horse carriages were available for those who could afford or wished to travel alone comfortably, avoiding the crowd.

The suburbs of the city like Parel, Mahalaxmi, Mahim, Bandra and Kurla were rather free from industrialisation and looked like villages with their green fields, winding by-paths, brick-red houses and cottages. In the residential area of Girgaum, big chawls were erected to accommodate the increasing population. Yet, handsome bungalows with small gardens and fountains were not a rare sight. Broad, paved streets of Bombay were washed twice a day, by the staff of the Municipality. The city was illuminated with gaslights and small by-lanes had their kerosene lamps.

The life of Anandi-Gopal became livelier in Bombay. The Society for the Propagation of Gospel or the S.P.G. Mission had founded a girls' school which was at a smelling distance from Anandi-Gopal's house. It was run by a Missionary lady called Miss Robson. Gopal enrolled Anandi's name in this school instead of Miss Prescott's school which was far away. As Gopal was very busy in the city Post office, he could hardly get time to look after Anandi's studies. But now she was in able hands, so he did not have to worry about her education. The grandmother was still with them and by now, she had adjusted herself to their lifestyle. To the satisfaction of Gopal, she managed housekeeping and cooking and kept Anandi free for her studies. Anandi was engrossed in her studies and was very happy to go to school. The only obstacle was the frequent visitors from Kalyan who always urged Gopal to send Anandi to Kalyan, inventing all sorts of reasons, to which Gopal reacted curtly. He would allow this once in a blue moon, but the constant insistence irritated him. Surprisingly, even in the modern city of Bombay, women's position in society was not much different from elsewhere, as people mentally belonged to the past era. Even here, the wife of a Postmaster who went to a Christian school, learnt English, recited poems, read books and put on fine shoes and stockings, was an eyesore for relatives, neighbours and even the unknown passers-by or shopkeepers who in fact, had nothing to do with her personal life.

The freedom that Gopal had given to Anandi, enraged even his father Vinayakrao Joshi. He did not mind her learning at home, but could not understand why she had to go to a Christian school, neglecting her connubial duties. He came all the way from Sangamner to Bombay, just to convince Gopal that he was wrong in sending his wife to a Christian school. Her most important responsibilities were to look after their house and to cook food for the family members. But Gopal stood by Anandi and earnestly expressed his views about women's education. He tried his best to convince his father that his fears, doubts and arguments were baseless but the father was not in a mood to listen to anything. Hence Gopal put his foot down and told his father that for no reason Anandi would stop going to school. The heated arguments finally turned into a serious quarrel and the dispute remained unresolved. Vinayakrao was hurt to see that his arrogant son was disregarding his views and overlooking his sound advice just for the sake of his wife. Unable to change Gopal's mind, he left their house in anger, vowing that never in his life he would see Gopal again. The meeting really proved to be the last one, as very soon the old man died. Like his father, most of the relatives disapproved of Gopal's modern outlook and reformative ideas. But Anandi-Gopal had their own circle of well-wishers, who shared their views and appreciated their courage to swim against the current, a well-known activist Mama Parmanand being one of them. Mama himself had taught his wife to read and write and had written many articles in support of women's education. Now he was delighted to meet a woman like Anandi who cherished a great ambition.

It was not possible for an agile person like Gopal to get stuck into the rut for long. Now that Anandi was well-settled in her school, Gopal decided to take a tour of North India. He requested the school authorities to allow Anandi to stay in the school, when he would be out of town and sent back Anandi's Grandmother to Kalyan. Now the only question was to make arrangements for Anandi's meals. But being afraid of public anger, most of the relatives were not ready to take this responsibility. At last, one of them who lived in the Angre's chawl which was near Anandi's school, mustered the courage and agreed to provide morning and evening meals to Anandi. Feeling satisfied with these arrangements, Gopal went away to the North. For the first time in her life, Anandi was living totally alone. In a way, this was like a grand rehearsal of her future stay in America. Gopal wished his wife to be an independent and confident person who would be able to leap any fence. Being ahead of his time, he was trying to carve the figure of the 20th century woman in the 19th century. He knew that unless a staff was taken away from her, Anandi would never be aware of her own capacity and strength.

Early morning Anandi came to her relative's house to take a bath. She had her food around 10 and then she went to school. In the evening, she returned for dinner, after which she went back and retired to her room in the school. Thus, she had to walk on the same road four times a day. Noticing that Anandi was living alone, people openly started pestering her whenever they saw her walking alone. They amused themselves by making fun of her or by throwing pebbles at her. Anandi herself had described those days in a public meeting held at Shrirampur, Bengal, where she delivered a lecture before sailing to America. "Passers-by whenever saw me going, gathered round me. Some of them made fun and were convulsed with laughter. Others sitting respectably in their verandas made ridiculous remarks and did not feel ashamed to throw pebbles at me. The shopkeepers and vendors spat at the sight of me and made gestures too indecent to describe. I leave it to your imagination what was my condition at such a time and how I could gladly have burst through the crowd to make my home nearer."[1] Those ruffians didn't feel ashamed to scare a young girl of 15, for her choice to learn and they vehemently exhibited their collective strength. The presence of a woman on a street itself was an eyeful event in those days and here was a married girl who courageously went to school right under their noses. Interpreting this as a serious challenge to their convictions, they thought it their duty to break her spirit by scaring her. In spite of such calamities, Anandi was happy in Bombay because she got an opportunity to go to school and the freedom to learn. The freedom demanded independence, self-reliance and a sense of responsibility. She rose to the occasion by accepting the challenge of living alone in Bombay.

It would be interesting to see how she learnt to make her own decisions and how she matured under the able guidance of Gopal. Since Anandi competed for the top rank in her class, she attracted Miss Robson's attention. One day Miss Robson ordered her to read the Bible, thinking that if a clever girl like her was acquainted with Christianity, she would influence other students. But Anandi refused it as she didn't like this compulsion. For her disobedience, Anandi was threatened to be expelled from the school by Miss Robson. Those harsh words stung Anandi to the quick and the righteous anger was aroused. She felt that it was unjust on the part of her teacher to compel her to read the religious book. To Miss Robson's surprise, Anandi accepted her challenge and went home. In the evening, she narrated the whole incident to Gopal and declared that never again she would go to Miss Robson's school.

Though Gopal sympathised with her, he looked at the incident from a different angle. He discussed the issue with Anandi and convinced her that there was no harm in reading other people's holy books. On the contrary, it was an opportunity to study a different religion, which she should not lose. Having understood the mistake, Anandi corrected it by going to school and following the order of Miss Robson. In the future, she developed a keen interest not only in the Christian religion but also in various religions of the world. Yet she could never forgive the teacher who thus compelled her students to read the Bible. In a letter, written after some months to her American friend Theodosia Carpenter, she wrote, "I love these Mission ladies for their enthusiasm and energy, but I dislike blindness to the feelings of others."[2]

Anandi could enjoy the life of a schoolgirl only for a short while. Suddenly Gopal was transferred to Bhuj and Anandi had to leave Miss Robson's school. Soon after Anandi went to Bhuj, all 90 girls left the school, because Miss Robson compelled them to read the Bible. As a result, the obstinate headmistress had to close down her school. From the city of Bombay, Anandi-Gopal were thrown into a small town of Bhuj where, once again, her home became her school. Gopal was her only teacher and intellectual communication was the strongest tie between the teacher and the disciple.

Anandi-Gopal reached Bhuj on 25th February 1880. Previously they were to sail by the ship named 'Vengurla,' but their programme changed at the eleventh hour and the tickets were cancelled. This change in plan proved to be very fortunate because 'Vengurla' turned turtle and sank mid-voyage. Not a single passenger could be saved. Thus, by sheer chance, they escaped the deathly calamity. Bhuj was the capital of Kutch, a province in Kathiawad, which was 400 miles north-west of Bombay. On the 3 sides, Kutch was surrounded by the Indian Ocean and the 4th side was a salty marshland. During the monsoon, the marshland got filled with water, turning Kutch into an island. Bhuj was a fortified town that stood on the slope of a hill. With its low roofed houses, clusters of date trees, white mosques and the pinnacles of temples shining against the blue dome of the sky, Bhuj looked picturesque. The King of this State belonged to the Jadeja tribe. Anarchy prevailed in most of the states of Kathiawad, like Jamnagar, Batawa, Limdi, Gondal, Rajkot and Kutch.

On one hand, rulers had to face internal strife and power politics and on the other, they had to be cautious of the Political Agents who closely watched their activities. Most of the rulers were almost powerless and nominal. They were so busy stabilising their tottery thrones that they had little time to look after the welfare of their subjects. The insolent administrators of those weak Kings had invented several ways of looting people. Those who opposed, were tyrannised.

Having no education, no hope and no idea of a value-oriented, meaningful life, the subjects had become languid and lethargic. They were addicted to alcoholism and were victims of vicious habits. Female infanticide was so rampant that it had caused a great disequilibrium in the male and the female population. Hence, the people of Kutch had to procure their wives from other tribes. To live in such a bleak atmosphere was a punishment to Anandi-Gopal. No wonder, girls' school was not even in the imagination of people. Except for a few friends, there was nobody with whom they could have a dialogue. Without her school, without good neighbours and also without her dear grandmother, who had returned to Kalyan, days seemed long and gloomy to Anandi. Her only companion was Appa, the youngest brother of Gopal, whom Gopal had invited to stay with them, after their father's death.

Mama Parmanand, a friend of Gopal and the former Deputy Minister of Kutch came to their help in the time of calamity. Years back when Mama was the editor of a daily *Native Opinion*, he had given voice to the outcry of people in Jamnagar, though it was a dangerous undertaking. Impressed by this, Raja Pragmalji, the King of Kutch, had invited him in 1868 to adorn the position of the Deputy Minister of Kutch, which called for a man of absolute integrity and a sense of justice. Mama accepted the invitation and soon won the reputation as a benevolent administrator. But a thoroughly honest man like him could not stand the political pollution for more than 6 months. So, resigning from his post, he returned to Bombay. But Mama still had some good contacts in Bhuj, Vinayak Narayan Bhagwat, a bosom friend of Mama, who was now the Deputy Minister of Kutch, being one of them. When Gopal was transferred to Bhuj, Mama wrote Bhagwat a letter and requested to take care of the Joshis. Very soon, a warm friendship developed between the two families. Many times, Bhagwat's wife fondly invited Anandi to stay with them for a few days and treated her like their own daughter. The

Joshis also befriended Colonel Batty and his wife. Anandi could improve her English with the help of the lady, as well as learn needlework, sewing and knitting. Friendship with these two families was a real solace to Anandi-Gopal in their solitary confinement.

Here, for the first time, in the absence of her grandmother, Anandi shouldered all the responsibilities of a housewife and whole day remained busy with cooking, cleaning, washing, etc. The heavy workload tired her, yet she managed to keep aside some time for her studies. Since Gopal was not burdened with his office work, he could devote time to teach Sanskrit and English to Anandi. In Bhuj, Gopal invented a game that was amusing as well as thought-provoking. Gopal used to give an interesting topic on which Anandi and Appa had to make preparations for a speech, to be delivered before Gopal in the evening. He used to warn them that if he did not find their performance up to the mark or if he suspected laziness on their part, they would not get their dinner that evening. The purpose behind this game was to generate confidence and to motivate them to think independently. Both the children took the job seriously and took pains to make a good presentation. The game kindled a friendly competition between them which they enjoyed. Both Appa and Anandi who belonged to the same age group, were well disposed towards each other. They loved to exchange their emotions, thoughts and opinions on various subjects, the favourite among them being the freedom of Hindustan. Appa used to declare that when he grew up, he would fight with the British for the freedom of their Motherland. Mere thoughts excited them. All her life Anandi cherished memories of those pleasant afternoons spent in the company of her brother-in-law.

Anandi, Gopal and Appa had created their own beautiful world in the darkness of Bhuj. Yet Anandi needed something more, a female companion in the house, with whom she could share some feminine topics and problems. Particularly she felt lonely in her illness and wanted someone as affectionate and helpful as her dear old grandmother. Sensing her restlessness, Gopal decided to send her away from the undesired surroundings where she was not at home. There was no other place as dear to her as Kalyan. The change of climate, rest and the company of her near and dear ones would have improved her health and spirits. So, Anandi was sent to Kalyan with Appa. Though the days of Bhuj were clouded with gloom and unrest, a ray of hope penetrated through the darkness, in the form of an unexpected letter from an American woman. No mail that Gopal had received in his post office till then, was as delightful and exciting to the Postmaster as that unique letter from Mrs. Theodosia Carpenter.

Neither Anandi nor Gopal could have imagined that the letter that was coldly received by a person like Rev. Wilder, would inspire a stranger to offer them a helping hand and ultimately it would pave the path to America for Anandi. Rev. Wilder had printed the correspondence in the *Missionary Review* of January 1879 which attracted the attention of an American lady, by sheer chance. Mrs. Theodosia Carpenter of Roselle, New Jersey had an appointment with her dentist, in a nearby town of Elizabeth on Saturday, 6th March 1880.When she reached there, the dentist was busy with another patient. Just to pass the time, she picked up an issue of the *Missionary Review* lying on the table among other issues. This issue was the same that contained the correspondence between Rev. Wilder, Rev. Gohin and Gopal Joshi, which she read with interest. She found Gopal's letter very appealing. Even Rev. Gohin's letter was friendly, but the way Rev. Wilder had repulsed Gopal's cry for help, was simply disgusting. 'Wilder's letter must have shattered the dream of that couple. How sad,' the sympathetic Mrs. Carpenter thought. She imagined herself in Anandi's place and perfectly understood her disappointment. She felt so drawn to the Indian couple that she copied down their address and decided to do something for them. A few days before that, Theodosia had by chance met a Missionary who had returned from India. While conversing with her, she had pondered, "Can I get some work to do in the Orient, without leaving my home?" Now the opportunity had presented itself before her and she decided to write a letter to Mrs. Joshi. But on her way home, she realised that she did not know anything about the British India. Nor did she have any idea as to how to get information. So, the idea faded away. Next morning, her little daughter Eighmie, who was 9 years old, awakened her saying, "Mama, I dreamed, you were writing a letter to someone in Hindustan." Theodosia had not told anybody about the previous day's incident. Naturally, she was surprised by Eighmie's dream. She thought that her duty had been marvellously shown to her through her innocent daughter. One possibility was that Eighmie might have heard the conversation of Theodosia and the Missionary lady and 'Hindustan' being a queer word for her, might have lingered in her memory. But the coincidence motivated Theodosia to do something urgently. She immediately gathered her family members, talked with them about her plan and getting the consent from them, sent a letter to Anandi, bearing words of sympathy and encouragement.

Theodosia had encouraged Anandi by saying that her aspiration was praiseworthy and that she would pray to God for its realisation. She also offered the shelter of her home, if Anandi would decide to come to America. She suggested that to understand each other better, they should regularly correspond. This letter was posted to the Kolhapur address which she got from Gopal's letter in the *Missionary Review*. But the issue of *Missionary Review*-January 1879 that Theodosia saw, was a back number and in the meantime, Gopal was transferred to Bombay and then to Bhuj. Hence the letter found its way through the changed addresses to Bhuj, and took a few months to reach there. Gopal was wonderstruck to receive in his routine mail, a letter to his wife, from an American lady. He took it home and put it in her hands. Trembling with excitement, she opened the letter and her eyes eagerly followed the matter written by an unknown hand. It was not a daydream, neither was it a vision but reality. She was so excited to get such a wonderful letter from an unknown American lady that she sang and danced all day long and read it over and over again.

Turning her back to the undesired surroundings of Bhuj, she set about answering the letter, with overwhelming joy. Thus began the delightful pen-friendship between Anandi and Theodosia. Various questions were asked out of curiosity and for a better understanding and they were answered promptly by both of them with the same spirit. Their letters revealed their family lives, habits, likings, festivals, rituals, customs, social problems and special features of their respective cultures. Theodosia says, "Then began for me, … a regular course of education in Hindi manners, customs, religious rites and everything of interest which her ready pen and remarkable mastery of English could set forth, while I in return answered all her queries. Newspapers, magazines, pictures, flowers and seeds were exchanged. The exchange of photograph was most interesting to me because of the peculiar style of dress. How strange seemed the bare arms, the bare feet with their anklets and toe-rings and a mark on the forehead. That I should be corresponding with a young woman dressed like this who could write elegant English seemed past belief."[3]

Being puzzled by a small blemish on Anandi's upper lip, Theodosia asked about it. Actually, it was not a blemish but the nose ring. In her next letter, Anandi beautifully described how a nose ring looked like. "It consists of one gold wire, upon which are fastened pearls, some pendent and others fixed and star-shaped. We are fond of many ornaments. Our hands, feet, necks and waists are all adorned 'to the teeth.' Even our noses and ears are bored in many places to hold them. Holes are bored through the lower part of the left nostril for the nose-ring and all around the edge of the ear for jewels. This may appear barbarous to the foreign eye, to us it is a beauty!"[4] Once they exchanged locks of hair. While sending her lock Anandi explained that in India, except widows, women did not cut their hair. But, in spite of this custom, she did not mind sending her lock, as it was a friendly sharing. Anandi also presented to Theodosia an ornamented silver pot and to Eighmie a silver needle and a thimble, to show the superb Indian workmanship.

The dialogue between Theodosia and Anandi continued even when she went to Kalyan to rest. From Kalyan, Anandi went to Nashik, from where she sent a nose ring, about which Theodosia was so curious. Anandi's new-found friend was so sensitive and thoughtful that the pen-friendship afforded great satisfaction to Anandi. It served as an outlet for her inner thoughts. In these letters, she could ponder over the subjugation of Indian women, the pitiable condition of child-wives and the unhappy lot of widows. Once she wrote, "When I think over the sufferings of women in all ages, I am impatient to see the Western light dawn as the harbinger of emancipation."[5] She herself was also struggling hard to be emancipated but she knew that because she was married to a person like Gopal, she was in a better position. Added to this, now she had a friend in America, who could understand her thoroughly.

Reference:

1. *The Life of Dr. Anandabai Joshee*- Caroline Healey Dall. 1888. Page 86
2. Ibid Page 51
3. Ibid Pages, 36, 37
4. Ibid Page 37
5. Ibid Page 38

8

In the Land of Reformers

The letters of Theodosia Carpenter had brought the distant land of America in the field of Anandi's vision, but it was difficult to advance towards it from a place like Bhuj. Calcutta, then the Capital of India, which was situated in the province of Bengal, attracted Gopal's attention for various reasons. Bengal was a land of great reformers like Raja Ram Mohan Roy, Ishwar Chandra Vidyasagar and Keshav Chandra Sen. Secondly, the Joshis were aware that just a few years back, that is in 1878, reformers and learned people in Calcutta had warmly welcomed their kinswoman Pandita Ramabai Dongare and had highly appreciated her merits. Ramabai was an exceptionally brilliant Maharashtrian lady who had mastered an old language like Sanskrit so thoroughly that she could give a lecture in Sanskrit with fluency and ease. In Calcutta, she surprised the assembly of Sanskrit pandits by spontaneously composing a beautiful poem in Sanskrit before the audience. They bestowed upon her the titles 'Pandita' and 'Saraswati' (The Goddess of Arts and Knowledge). Keshav Chandra Sen was so impressed by Ramabai's scholarship that he urged her to study Vedas, though women were then prohibited to do so. The reformers in Maharashtra were jubilant over her grand success. Knowing this success story, Gopal felt that people in Calcutta would appreciate Anandi's aspiration as well. Thirdly, a resolution was passed in the province of Bengal to employ women in the Postal department. Gopal was tempted by the idea of Anandi and himself working in the same office. Gopal decided to approach directly H. E. M. James, the Director General of Post Offices in India with whom he was slightly acquainted. He wrote a letter to him expressing his wish to work in the Calcutta office. He received a positive response from the Director General and soon he was transferred to Calcutta.

Before migrating to the faraway place, Anandi-Gopal visited their relatives in Kalyan and Nashik and then proceeded to Calcutta by railway.

Though the journey was long and tiring, they were delighted to go away from the salty marshland of Bhuj. Bengal was a beautiful land of lakes, full of lotus flowers, and it was a welcome change. The travellers did not fail to notice the thick groves of banana, coconut, the verdant rice fields stretching up to the horizon and the humming canals that enhanced the beauty of the colourful landscape. Against the backdrop of lush green countryside, Calcutta stood out as a city of palatial buildings. Anandi-Gopal reached Calcutta on 4th April, 1881 and on the 6th, Gopal took charge of his work. The Joshis had found accommodation in the house of a German milliner.

When they arrived, this German lady was peeping through her window and she noticed that their appearance was quite different from the Bengalis. She found their costume so funny that she laughed in their face. Not stopping at that, she insulted them before the servants in the building, who had gathered to have a look at them. Somehow, the lady had taken a strong dislike to them from the first day. Thereafter, she kept a watchful eye on whatever they did. Anandi-Gopal had cultivated a habit of reading to each other in the evening for relaxation, when the day's work was done. But the lady frowned at it and asked them to stop the 'noise' which troubled her sleeping children. She gossiped that the couple quarrelled the whole night, disturbing others. Anandi was deeply hurt when a rumour went around that she was not Gopal's wife. As their costumes, manners, habits and customs were different from those of Bengalis, they were constantly watched and scrutinised by their neighbours also. No wonder, they felt awkward and self-conscious.

When they reached Calcutta, they found that some of their large parcels containing furniture, essential household commodities and cooking utensils had not arrived. While loading parcels in the luggage compartment, their parcels were left behind by somebody's mistake. Since they could get their things only after two weeks, they faced the real problem of running the house without the essential commodities. Having no pots to cook in, they had to fill their stomachs with whatever snacks they had brought with them. Those were the days when there were no hotels and no ready-to-eat food available in the markets. In a letter to Theodosia Carpenter, whom she had begun to call 'dear aunt,' Anandi described her difficulties and gave vent to her feelings. She wrote, "We have our food cooked by ourselves. We do not get these things ready in the Bazaar. As we had no pots in which to cook, we could not do otherwise than go without, till we had our own furniture brought home. We never employ low caste people to attend to household affairs, and as we were but two, in a place where servants and other things available were of no use to us, we could but remain fasting."[1] Caste consciousness was so deep rooted that food cooked by a low-caste was not even touched by a high-caste person. People preferred to go without food than breaking the custom, Anandi-Gopal being no exceptions.

The first summer in Calcutta was simply unbearable to them. Due to the luggage problem, they had nothing but mats to spread on the damp ground on which they had to sleep at night, resisting the shivering. Sleepless nights, wet beds, pangs of hunger, hot and humid climate told upon Anandi's health. She suffered from headaches, fever, boils and indigestion. Being depressed and lonely, she had a feeling that she might not live long. But all those adverse conditions ultimately became instrumental in bringing Anandi-Gopal mentally closer. While living alone in an unknown city, their sense of togetherness increased and they felt attached to each other like never before.

At last they found some solace when they were introduced to two Maharashtrian families. The Maharashtrian community in Calcutta was a close-knit group, as they were very few. One day Krishna Patwardhan, a gentleman settled in Calcutta for a few years, came to know about the new Maharashtrian Postmaster who had recently arrived in Calcutta. He immediately called on Gopal in his office and inquired after him and his wife. Gopal told him about their difficulties and Anandi's illness. Then Patwardhan went to his neighbour Raosaheb Dandekar whom the community held in high respect and told him about the problems of the new Maharashtrian Postmaster and his wife. To give the necessary help to the newcomers, Dandekar went to Gopal's house along with his wife, on the same evening. Seeing Anandi's condition, they invited her to stay with them and with Gopal's permission she was removed to their house at Bara Bazar immediately. Had Gopal been hesitant to send his wife at night, Dandekar's wife was prepared to stay there. But sensing their earnestness, Gopal agreed to their plan. The carriage that was waiting outside took Anandi to Dandekar's house and the kind-hearted couple urged her to stay with them till she was fit to resume her work. Very soon, the two families came closer and the Dandekars, who had a seven-year-old son but no daughter, felt that God had sent them a daughter in the form of Anandi.

As the days passed, Anandi-Gopal became acquainted with the new city and forgot their troubles in the company of their friends. Both of them were full of travel lust and there was much to see in the magnificent capital of India. The Anglican Church of St. Paul's Cathedral which was a beautiful specimen of Indo-Gothic style, was constructed in 1847. St. John's Church was another historic edifice where Job Charnock, the founder of Calcutta was buried. Then there was the famous temple of Kalimata built by a religious-minded landlord Santosh Roy Choudhary. The beautiful temple of Dakshineshwar, built by a wealthy widow Rani Rasmani was the most revered place because a great sagely philosopher Ramkrishna Paramhans lived and worshipped there. The huge Muslim shrine erected in 1842 by Prince Ghulam Muhammad, the son of Tipu Sultan graced the Dharmatala Street. The other attraction in Calcutta was the well-known Botanical Garden that had been developed since 1786. The Asiatic Society of Bengal founded by Sir William Jones for the study of languages, literature and antiquities of Asia was the pride of Calcutta.

Though Anandi-Gopal enjoyed visiting places, they began to sense that the people living in this modern, cosmopolitan capital of the British India, were the same as elsewhere. For example, when they went out for evening strolls, astonished faces and rude glances greeted them. In a letter to Aunt Theo, Anandi narrated this experience and made some significant observations regarding the women's condition in Bengal. "Calcutta is trying to the utmost. Physically, we are reduced in health and strength.... We go out for a walk and the Europeans talk and laugh when they see us. The natives stand still and order their carriages to stop, while they stare at us. They can never be persuaded that we are married. There is so much of the [F1]Zenana system here that a woman can scarcely stand in the presence of her relatives, much less before her husband. Her face is always veiled. She is not allowed to speak to any man, much less to laugh with him. Even the [F2]Baboos who have spent years in England, will not drive here with their wives, in open carriages. If it is so with the educated people, how much more prejudiced must be the illiterate! One sepoy insulted us when we were walking on the Esplanade. He asked my husband who the woman was, that he had with him. My husband was angry and asked his name

F1 Zenana – Purdah System. There were two types of purdah systems. 1. Women used to cover their faces with purdah or veil which used to be a portion of sari. 2.Curtained area in the house specially reserved for women.

F2 Baboo – a gentleman.

to report him to the commissioner. This brought him to his senses and he went away courteously."[2] It was obvious that even in Calcutta people stubbornly stuck to the old, antiquated ideas regarding women. The veil or purdah system was followed by women of all castes. Under the pretext of righteousness, women were deprived of many joys, including that of learning. The success of Pandita Ramabai was an exception and reformers were facing a real challenge to change the mentality of people.

No wonder that as the behaviour of Anandi-Gopal didn't fit in with their conventional ideas, people ridiculed the couple. But Anandi-Gopal had no idea that this was nothing compared to the unimaginable calamity which was in store for them. A very important dispatch from the Viceroy to the Governor of Bengal arrived on 14th August 1881, which was received by Gopal on passing the receipt. Immediately, Gopal and his assistant set out to deliver the urgent letter personally to the Governor. They were rushing through the crowd to get a carriage for going to the railway station. To the shock of Gopal, his assistant who was carrying the letter, dropped it somewhere in a hurry. Both of them desperately searched for it everywhere on the street without any success. The letter had just vanished mysteriously and both stood aghast at their mistake. The police were sent everywhere, people on the roads were examined, Gopal and his assistant were interrogated, but the letter was not found. The disappearance of the letter created havoc in the city. From Gopal to the high officers, everybody was in trouble. A meeting was held on the highest level to solve the problem. It was essential to take some action urgently, therefore gathering evidence against Gopal and his assistant, the authorities put both of them behind the bars and Gopal was suspended from his service for some time.

That was the blackest day in the life of Anandi-Gopal. Humiliation and shame had begotten frustration. No one knew if Gopal would be forgiven or punished severely for his gross mistake. The event had brought so much disgrace on Gopal that it was not possible to share his agony with anybody but Anandi. Gopal was guilty in the eyes of the law, but he had aroused nothing but sympathy and love in the heart of his wife. Here was an agonising moment that demanded profound understanding and trust, which the seven years of their married life had earned. So, the grief brought them closer, deepening their love for each other, as never before. Her reliance on his goodness pacified his troubled breast. Her letter to Aunt Theo is a witness to the fact that both bore the affliction with great fortitude. "We gave up all hopes of service and were prepared to start for any place. We first determined to go to Rangoon, in Birmah and stay there for a time. It was my intention to make an address before the English-speaking people there and thus obtain pecuniary assistance to leave for another place. From there we were thinking of going to Hong-Kong and thence to Japan and from Japan to America. This project may appear very wild to an outsider, but it was necessary. We could not retrace our steps to Bombay, nor was it easy to travel to Bengal or Punjab, where the Zenana is rampant."[3] Since she valued Gopal's prestige the most, she did not choose the safest way of returning to Sangamner or Kalyan. More than that, even in this troubled time, she did not give up her dream to go to America. Her words are loaded with love and respect for Gopal and contempt for Calcutta. "My husband never lost anything before but in Calcutta, he had never seen police court before but in Calcutta...We had never seen double-tongued men before but in Calcutta. I do not know how much misery is still in store for us. I have been telling him to sever his connection with Government to avoid any further calamities; but he is wavering. He thinks it is very difficult to earn a livelihood, but I think otherwise... I do not know why we should have a thought for the morrow. Man wants but little and for that little he bears a world of care; which I cannot understand. Let me be here or in any part of the globe, I will get my bread.... Had there been no difficulties and no thorns in the way, the man would have been in primitive state and no progress made in civilisation and mental culture."[4]

Anandi did not want Gopal to remain in the place where his reputation was stained. She did not mind that their life would have become financially unsecure, had he really resigned. "If I had been called to share the storms with my husband, I would have done nothing but my duty which I owe him as his deserving wife. There would have been nothing commendable or heroic in it. Let there be any amount of difficulties or distress and I think I shall be more than equal to face them."[5] These thoughtful words reflect her ardent courage and self-confidence. Anandi was so much affected by Gopal's suspension that when a job was offered to her after some time, in the Postal department by H. E. M. James, the Director General of Post Offices in India, she politely refused it. In the 19th century, a government job with a handsome salary of Rs. 30 per month could have been a temptation. But once for all, she had decided not to serve at the cost of her valuable freedom which she could well preserve in her own house.

Gopal was taken into the service again but promotion was denied to him and he was transferred to a small village of Barrackpore which was 12 miles north of Calcutta. It had been the country seat of the Governor Generals for more than 40 years. Barrackpore looked majestic with spacious bungalows built after the fashion of the British houses, beautiful parks and a large military cantonment. The first spark against the British rule in 1857 was ignited here which soon developed into the first war of independence. The Joshis went to Barrackpore in November 1881. Anandi took a liking for the calm and quiet town.

It is interesting to note that while expressing herself in a foreign language like English, she was wielding her pen with perfect grace and ease. Aunt Theo did not fail to appreciate the elegance of expression and the wisdom behind her words. In all her difficulties, her continuous dialogue with Aunt Theo gave her real comfort and the moral support which she badly needed. For the Carpenters, now Hindustan was not an unfamiliar distant country on the world map, but a living entity whose heartbeats they could hear through Anandi's letters. Though they had not met Anandi yet, they had already adopted her into their family and were yearning to see her. Anandi's letters pictured various interesting aspects of Indian life. In one of her letters, Anandi pencilled the daily routine of an Indian woman which was quite hectic. "We get up at five o' clock… We sweep the ground and wash all the copper and brass pots used for drinking purposes and worship. Then we oil and comb and dress our hair with several kinds of ornaments. Then if there be children in the house, rice is prepared for them about half past seven. Children eat it with salt and ghee. Ghee is boiled butter…. We begin to give rice to children when they are one year old …. As soon as vegetables are brought from the market, we wash them and cut them into small pieces. So are rice, pulse and wheat flour cleaned and kept ready for cooking…. Our stove is earthen, by the side of which we sit to cook after bathing and changing our night clothes and putting on sacred garments which have been washed and dried in a room where no one could go to touch them."

"First we put an iron pan or a brass pot on the stove and put a little oil in that. When it is hot, rye seeds and cumin are thrown into it. When they are properly fried and broken, we put the vegetables in and cook them without water. We take our meals twice a day. The first meal about noon, the second from seven to eight in the evening. As a rule, men take their meals before the women who serve them. A married woman does not eat until she has served her husband. After dinner, the men go to bed, and women are engaged in removing and washing the dishes and cow-dunging the earthen floors, after which we change our clothes.... We cut and sew our clothes till half-past five. We then go to the temple and return home after six o' clock, when we are again employed in preparing articles for supper. This occupies us until nine, when we prepare our beds and sleep. This is what women in India generally do. They have no letters to write, or books to read. They do not receive or make calls, except among their own female relatives. They do not speak with men, even with their own husbands, in presence of somebody."[6]

These accounts were sometimes illustrated with some articles used in the Indian cookery such as, the samples of millet, peas and beans. Herbs, roots and seeds used in medicines were put into tiny glass bottles whereas cooking utensils of brass and pottery, chafing-dishes of earthenware, idols and their shrines were packed carefully and sent from time to time and each one was neatly described, giving the feel of the Maharashtrian lifestyle. Here is a letter depicting the thread-ceremony and the meaning behind it. "There are sixteen such ceremonies among us from birth to death. 'Thread ceremony' is the eighth in order. It is initiating a Brahmin boy of eight years in spiritual knowledge. After this, the boy must live at his preceptor's house and study... till he is twenty years of age... In this ceremony... a triple thread, prepared at home, is taken in hand and made holy by repeating Vedic Verses. This is afterwards worn by the boy round his neck and under his right hand as a garland.... Then the boy becomes a holy Brahmin.... This ceremony is performed by three castes, the Brahmin, the Kshatriya and the Vaishya.... After the ceremony the boy must perform certain religious austerities twice a day. This ceremony corresponds to baptism among Christians. It was good in principle, but now-a-days it is a mere ceremony. Parents ... spend ... to gratify their vanity and do no good to the boy, who is fed at home, instead of being allowed to stay with his preceptor."[7]

Being a natural linguist, Anandi had learnt many languages. She was well-versed in Marathi, English and Sanskrit; knew some of the Indian languages like Hindi, Gujarati and Kannada. In Calcutta, she picked up Bengali. Thinking that before going to America, she should know something about Indian medicine, she started studying the subject. Religion was another subject close to her heart. She enjoyed reading and pondering over various religious scripts. In Calcutta, she could manage to study 10 hours a day and even in her sleep her thoughts were centred on it. "I always labour under inward impressions. I solve many difficult things while sleeping. I was not able to cut different kinds of native dresses for men and women, but I have learnt how, in dreams. While sleeping I dreamed that I had cut such and such shapes and sewed them. Next morning, I … did the same according to memory and found everything fit and complete. Whenever I have to learn anything by heart, I do it when asleep. In the day, I read the passage to be committed to memory but once and in sleep I read it over and over and repeat it next morning, without a mistake…. I do not know who teaches me, but I learn this way." [8] It was no one else but her own overactive brain that worked when she slept.

In January 1882, Aunt Theo sent a New Year's greeting card with a nice little picture of the city of New York which Anandi pasted on a wall. This time, the Carpenters celebrated the New Year in a different way. Their 11 years old daughter Eighmie, prepared a special New Year's dinner for the family and they had great fun. In appreciation of Eighmie's sweetness, Anandi wrote, "Please tell her, nothing pleases me so much as her readiness to cook for Papa and Mama who are our gods on earth. It is the fundamental principle of Hindu religion that children have no other duty but to serve their parents with all their hearts and souls." [9] In the same letter she narrated the mythical story of a young boy Shravan who was highly devoted to his parents and served them at the cost of his life. Anandi sent the sesame comfit prepared for the festival of Sankrant and requested Aunt Theo to distribute it among her friends, according to the Hindu custom, with words "Accept these Tila seeds and be friendly with me throughout the year." Aunt Theo liked the comfit so much that she asked Anandi for its recipe which was readily sent. "Take one pound of sugar and as much water and boil it till it becomes a little thick, so that if dropped on the ground, it will look like a pearl and will run if you blow it, yet will be hardened or dried into a pill. This sugar juice should be kept in a pot. Then the seeds should be wet, their skins removed and again dried. Put a brass pan over a light fire and shake the seeds in it, till they are swollen. Then move them to and fro with your fingers and put five drops of the sugar on them at a time shaking them till all are coated. Then you will have Tilas like mine." [10]

On 20th March 1882, 'Varsha Pratipada' or New Year's Day of the Hindus was celebrated and Anandi described it for her American friends, "We invite friends and relatives for dinner and give them many dishes. A long bamboo…is erected in the compound, on the top of which is placed a beautiful garment and a wreath of sugar over which is fastened a silver or brass cup. This is in other words a new year's flag…This day is particularly noticed by foreigners from having at each door a flag hoisted up in the air. The city appears a picturesque scenery. Our neighbours here are Christians. This morning when they saw this flag, they were not slow to throw stones at it. Fortunately, one of our inmates escaped being hurt."[11] The insult of their religious symbol and the ill-treatment which she received in her own country, by the people of other religions was disgusting.

After coming to Bengal, Anandi was in correspondence with Pandita Ramabai Saraswati who had by then settled in the province of Assam. After her brother's death, Rama had married in 1880, Bipin Biharidas Medhavi, a low-caste but scholarly Bengali youth with whom she had fallen in love. This inter-caste, inter-provincial love marriage of a well-known lady like Ramabai discomposed the people of Maharashtra as well as Bengal. The couple was expelled from the Medhavi family as all the family members were against the marriage. But despite the opposition from all sides, Ramabai and Bipin had begun their new life in Assam. Soon she was delighted to give birth to a daughter Manorama. But on 4th February 1882 Bipin suddenly died of Cholera. Ramabai's short married life came to an end due to the untimely demise of her husband. Ramabai had lost her parents and even her brother a few years ago and now she was totally alone in the world, with the responsibility of her little daughter Manorama to be shouldered. Since her husband's family had severed all connections with her, she had nowhere to go. When the Joshis came to know about it, a letter of condolence was immediately sent to express their deepest sympathies. Anandi who had high regard for Ramabai, was so moved by the unfortunate circumstances that she invited her to stay with them. Ramabai could not accept the kind invitation, but at the same time, she was profoundly grateful for the 'only invitation' that she received from a woman whom she had never met. In a letter to Caroline

Dall, Ramabai had narrated this event with emotion. "My husband being of low caste, my marrying him was altogether against the country's custom and we were despised and shunned by our most intimate friends and relative.... I therefore resolved to... take care of my baby and myself independently.... I made this promise to my husband before he left me. Therefore, I did not accept Mrs. Joshee's kind invitation, to go to her in my distress. I was very grateful to her all the same, for she was the only person in the whole country who cared for me."[12]

After a short duration of four months in Barrackpore, Gopal was transferred to Shrirampur. These two villages were stretched on the opposite banks of Hooghly, a branch of the river Ganges. Crossing the river, Anandi-Gopal reached Shrirampur on 1st April 1882. Though most of the habitants of Shrirampur were Hindus, the place had gained importance in the history of Christian Missions in India. Previously, it was the headquarters of the Protestant Mission. The first Missionary College in India was founded here. Harriet Newell, the first American woman Missionary had landed here in 1812. From the same place, the first Indian woman, Anandibai Joshi went to America to learn Medicine. The small village of Shrirampur, was ceded by Denmark to Great Britain in 1845. The palatial houses of Bengali Zamindars and the magnificent bungalows of the Europeans enhanced the beauty of this tiny village and gave it a royal touch.

Once Anandi invited to her house, some Bengali women living in her neighbourhood. Such invitations were so rare that the women jumped at it. They were bubbling with excitement, to have a look at a Maharashtrian lady's house. As per their custom, they bowed down and touched Anandi's feet to pay respect which surprised her because in Maharashtra, a friend was greeted like an equal. People prostrated themselves either at God's feet or at their elders' feet. The ladies curiously examined Anandi's dress and ornaments which were different from theirs. They liked the Maharashtrian dress because they felt that it properly covered a woman's body whereas the Bengali dress exposed it. Her friends did not know Marathi, but having learnt Bengali, Anandi could converse with them in their mother tongue. Anandi disliked one particular custom in Bengal which was followed by both men and women. "Some of the Bengali women who have been educated follow very barbarous custom. It is customary among us to eat 'vida' compounded of thirteen ingredients, namely betel leaves, betel nut, chunam, almond, camphor, saffron, cloves, cardamom and so on. This 'vida' stains the teeth, tongue and mouth in red colour. Some of these Bengalis stain the outside of their lips and so expose themselves to contempt." [13] Thus, Anandi took great pleasure in sharing her experiences, observations and thoughts with Aunt Theo. In spite of the physical and cultural distances, a sweet bond of friendship had developed between them. On the other hand, a vast chasm separated her from her close blood relations like her mother or sisters for whom Anandi's passion for knowledge was a mystery.

The thought of migrating to America for learning Medicine haunted Anandi day and night. The Joshis were planning to sail to America in May 1882 and Gopal had applied for a furlough for a year, thinking that both would go to America and once she had settled in her college, he would return. So Anandi had requested Aunt Theo to send information about the voyage. But the furlough was not granted to him and he was not sure if it would be granted even after 6 months. Hence, Anandi informed Aunt Theo in June 1882 that she would not be able to come to America at least for six months. The yearning so grew over her that the waiting period and the waste of time became unbearable. But Gopal started thinking about a solution. One day while pondering over it, an idea flashed in his mind. He felt that instead of waiting for him, what if Anandi would sail alone to America? The mere thought excited him.

When other women remained behind the thresholds of their houses, his brave wife would travel alone to a distant land. He was ready to pursue the idea if Anandi agreed. Therefore, he decided to discuss the plan with her. One day, when they were sitting in a small room near the post office, Gopal opened the subject, "I have not heard of any Hindustani woman who has sailed alone, to a far-away country, for learning Medicine. Would you do that? Would you travel alone my dear and set an example, if I can't accompany you? Would you show our people, what a woman can do?" Thus, he talked for a long time. In the beginning, Anandi was taken aback, but she listened attentively to his arguments and began to realise that what he said was right. That was the only way out. Though it seemed difficult, it was not impossible. She felt proud of her husband who could think of such an unusual idea and who had faith in her mental strength. When his countrymen preferred to keep their wives under veils, he yearned to give her freedom for pursuing her dream. Enchanted by his greatness, she thought that she should always try to be his deserving wife. Since then, Anandi was fired with new enthusiasm and Eagle's wings began to grow on her shoulders. She was satisfied that at last they had succeeded in finding out a viable solution.

On 1st July 1882, the Joshis received a letter from Aunt Theo that contained all the necessary information about the voyage to America. The letter unfolded before Anandi the way to her dreamland. But Aunt Theo was worried about Gopal's plan to send Anandi alone. It would be interesting to see how Anandi tried to convince Aunt Theo that there was no harm in it. "You can imagine how difficult it is for a small purse to pay for two passengers from India to America… I am therefore prepared to go alone to America…. You have reasons to think that very distant voyage will be hazardous for a girl of eighteen because the world is full of frauds and dangers, but dear aunt, wherever I cast my glance, I see nothing but a straight and smooth way. I fear no miseries. I shrink not at the recollection of dangers… If this life is so transitory like a rose in bloom, why should one depend upon another? …. Thousands are too violently attached to the contrary opinions…My design meets the approbation of a few… Though I cannot teach courage, I must not learn cowardice, nor at least leave undone what I so long since determined to to…. Their opposition strengthens me more. I promise myself that if my efforts will be successful, I will return to my native country, otherwise I will not see Indian again…. Our ancient Indian ladies were very wise, brave, courageous and benevolent and endurance was their badge. Let it be my badge also." [14] The letter is a graphic picture of her courage and will power. Once decided she never looked back.

Now Gopal was trying to find out a reliable family going to America with whom Anandi could be entrusted. In October 1882, he came to know about an American doctor, Dr. Thorburn and his wife Dr. Anna who lived at 46, Dharamtala Street. Dr. Thorburn was a widower and he had married Anna Jones who was much younger than him. Anna had graduated from the 'Woman's Medical College of Pennsylvania.' They both had sailed to India in 1880 and now they were well-established in Calcutta as doctors. They wanted to do some social work. Thinking that Thorburn could help them, Gopal wrote a detailed letter to him, explaining his plan to send his wife to America. The Thorburns were taken by surprise, as they had not expected to meet such an ambitious couple in a backward country like India. By no stretch of the imagination, Dr. Anna could think of an Indian girl, wrapped in a traditional Indian sari of nine yards, and decked with all sorts of ornaments, sitting in a classroom of an American Medical college. 'This girl would create a sensation', thought Anna. Therefore, she strongly felt that her Medical college should get the credit of educating the first Indian woman candidate.

Soon afterwards, the Joshis called on the Thorburns, to discuss the matter personally. Dr. Anna talked a lot about Woman's Medical College of Pennsylvania and Anandi was all ears. Anna asked her if she was ready to put on American dresses, sari being unsuitable for the American climate and was satisfied to hear that Anandi was ready to do whatever was necessary. Anna bought a dress material; sewed a dress for Anandi after the fashion of the American women and tried it on her. Anandi might have looked at her reflection in Anna's mirror, in delightful amazement and wondered, "Who is the stranger in the mirror? Is that my reflection? Is this how I would go to my college in America?" In an excited mood, Anna wrote a letter to Dr. Rachel Bodley*, Dean of the Woman's Medical College of Pennsylvania on 27th November 1882 and informed her about the Indian woman, wishing to learn Medicine. Dr. Thorburn published an advertisement in a newspaper to find out a family going to America, who might accept Anandi's responsibility in the voyage. But instead of getting a family, the advertisement became instrumental in spreading the news of Anandi's possible migration to America and it produced shock waves in Calcutta. Particularly Raosaheb Dandekar, who loved Anandi as his own daughter, was unable to believe that she could give consent to such an outrageous scheme. He felt for certain that it was the working of her domineering husband. The Dandekars were livid with rage, when they realised that Anandi's overmastering desire to learn Medicine had motivated the whole thing and, in this matter, she would not listen to anybody, not even to them. As the last hope, Raosaheb wrote letters to her relatives in Maharashtra, who might succeed, he thought, in changing her mind. Since Anandi understood that he did all these things out of profuse love for her,

---

*see Appendix No. 1

she harboured no ill feelings towards Raosaheb or his wife who was also on her husband's side. "Their opposition is due to tender hearts, fearful minds and foolish superstitions. They are doing all they can to prevent my going to America, but I cannot blame them. I have been like a child to them, dutiful and I wish to continue so." [15] Come what may, Anandi's sense of duty never left her. She accepted their hatred as the other side of the coin of love. On 12th January 1883 Anandi went to the Dandekars' house to greet them with sesame comfit on the occasion of the festival of Sankrant. But as soon as Raosaheb saw her, his suppressed anger exploded. The Dandekars talked with her so harshly that she could not stay there for long. It was impossible to make them understand her viewpoint. That was the last meeting with them. Realising that the beautiful relation was shattered forever, she left the place in a gloomy mood and never saw them again.

On the same day, she called on the Thorburns before returning to Shrirampur and that meeting was equally unpleasant. Dr. Anna had assured her that two English ladies of her acquaintance were ready to shoulder Anandi's responsibility in the voyage to America. So, in November 1882 she had informed Aunt Theo that most probably she would start in February 1883 with the escort suggested by Dr. Anna. Moreover, Anna had also promised to give letters to her American friends who might be of help to Anandi. But on 1st January 1883, Anandi could notice that Anna's previous enthusiasm was at a low ebb. It was a great shock to her when Anna suddenly advised her to join Dr. Thorburn's Medical school which he was to open soon, instead of going abroad. Anandi firmly told Anna that she could not change her plan. Gopal was also discouraged by Dr. Thorburn when he met him. He was coldly informed that they knew of no escort. On 12th January, when Anandi met Anna once again, she received the same cold reply. Both the Dandekars and the Thorburns had extremely disappointed her. So, she returned to Shrirampur with a heavy heart.

What could be the reasons behind the changed attitude of the Thorburns? Anandi thought of two possibilities:- the Thorburns might have received a bitter letter from her relatives. Or they might have found her unfit for encouragement. There could be one more reason about which Anandi said nothing. Anandi's ambition might have motivated the Thorburns to open a Medical school for women and nothing was more desirable than a brilliant pupil like Anandi. It would have been yet another feather in their cap, if they had trained the first Indian Medical woman. That means they were curbing Anandi's ambition for their own. It is not possible that Anandi did not realise this, but she had kept silent on it. She always preferred not to blame those who were once kind to her. Forgetting the Thorburns, Anandi-Gopal set about preparing an independent plan. Gopal decided to accompany Anandi up to Madras or Eden, after which he was to entrust Anandi to the care of his reliable friend Govind Sathe who was ready to escort Anandi. They were to set sail on 17th February 1883, by a steamer named 'Quetta.' Her letter clearly shows that nothing could shake their confidence. "Dear aunt, every day I learn something new. What I thought to be true yesterday, I find it to be false today and something else tomorrow.... Be that it may, I will see America, the dream of my life and I will stand or fall as I deserve."[16]

Realising that despite their non-cooperation, the Joshis were going ahead with a new plan, the Thorburns rushed to them, showing great concern about their welfare. They informed that in April 1883, some Missionary ladies were to go to America by the steamer named 'City of Calcutta' and Anandi could go with them. Gopal thanked them but politely refused the offer since they had already decided to sail by 'Quetta.' Then Dr. Thorburn warned that the passengers on the steamers of B.J.S.N. Line were rather rough and it was not advisable to send a young woman like Anandi, amidst them. Moreover, an ex-student of the Woman's Medical College of Pennsylvania would be, he told, a co-traveller of Anandi in the 'City of Calcutta.' Gopal told him that they were not in a position to pay the first-class fare of the costly steamer. But now Dr. Thorburn had an answer to every problem. He assured that since Anandi was to travel with a party of Missionary women, she would get a concession in the fare. Still Gopal had his own doubts, which later proved to be true. So, the next day he wrote a letter to Dr. Thorburn. "If this lady takes my wife as a companion to please herself, we shall be very much obliged. But if it is only to please you and there is any grudge, we would rather depend upon Him who has created us all."[17] Even after this, Dr. Thorburn assured that it was safer to travel with the Missionary ladies. So, once again the voyage was postponed. All that waste of time fatigued Anandi but the offered help could not be rejected, considering Anandi's safety. She wrote to Aunt Theo quite helplessly, "I am ashamed to speak of starting. If God pleases, I will start by the 'City of Calcutta' about the first of April. I am not sure of anything. I am not a performer of anything. I am only His instrument. The whole day and night I dream only of seeing you."[18] There was no other way but to wait patiently.

Having gained wider publicity by this time, her decision to migrate to America for Medical education had fomented public anger. They could not believe that though a woman, Anandi was ready to commit the 'sins' like crossing the sea and staying in a foreign land among the people of another religion. According to them, she had become so bold that she didn't care for tradition, religion or public opinion. Now the opposition did not remain limited to her friends and relatives. People rose against her as one person, feeling that Hindustan's prestige was at stake. Filled with the righteous wrath, they thought it their moral duty to prevent her from going abroad. Believing that migration was the first step towards the conversion to Christianity, the Hindus threatened the Joshis with excommunication. The Christians insisted that she should not go to America without embracing Christianity, as she would be taking the help of the Christian community. As the Indian society could not understand the grandeur of Anandi's ambition, she had to face brickbats in place of bouquets.

At any hour of the day, people gathered around the Post Office building where the Joshis lived and angrily shouted provocative slogans. Since this was disturbing the normal routine of the Post Office, it brought discredit on the Postmaster who could not manage his personal matters and allowed them to come into the way of his office work. Therefore, Anandi-Gopal decided to answer once and for all, the various inquiries of people, in a public meeting. Gopal was planning to deliver a speech explaining their position. But Anandi did not want anyone else, not even her husband, to talk on behalf of her. She confidently told Gopal that she would talk in the public meeting because no one but she herself should make her position clear. Gopal was astonished that she wanted to make her own statement, but he yielded to her wish, for the first time in his life.

His little student had grown into a self-reliant woman, ready to shoulder her own responsibilities. The caterpillar had turned into a butterfly. She was not only his better half; but something more than that — an individual having her own mind, wishes and aspirations. On the path to self-development, a stage comes when the individual throws away the supporting stalk, tests his strength by facing problems and seeks the support from within. Every individual is alone on this path and this loneliness is essential for developing one's capacities. Now Anandi had reached that stage and it was Gopal's turn to respect her independence. This event was a forerunner to the future events. Hereafter, she was to take her own decisions using her own discrimination. One would never know whether the traditional male, hidden behind the progressive Gopal was flabbergasted by her self-determination, appreciated her confidence or took it as a challenge to his power over her, but at least at that moment, he stepped back and allowed Anandi to make her own public statement.

References:

1. *The Life of Dr. Anandabai Joshee* – Caroline Healey Dall. 1888 Page 48
2. Ibid, Page 40
3. Ibid, Page 42
4. Ibid, Pages 42, 43
5. Ibid, Page 52
6. Ibid, Pages 56, 57, 58
7. Ibid, Pages 62, 63, 64
8. Ibid, Pages 48, 49
9. Source: The Nancy Cobb Stone Collection of Letters.
10. *The Life of Dr. Anandabai Joshee* – Caroline Healey Dall. 1888 Pages 55, 56
11. Source:- *The Nancy Cobb Stone Collection of Letters.*
12. *The Life of Dr. Anandabai Joshee* – Caroline Healey Dall. 1888 Pages, Preface, vi vii
13. Ibid, Page 54
14. Ibid, Pages 70, 71, 72
15. Ibid, Page 74
16. Ibid, Pages 75, 76
17. Ibid, Page 77
18. Ibid, Pages 77, 78

9

The Public Meeting

On 24th February1883, the public meeting was organised in the Baptist College of Shrirampur where Anandibai Joshi was to speak on the topic, 'Why I go to America'. Rev. Summers, the chief of the Baptist College, was to preside over the meeting. In the mansions of landlords, on tea tables of the Europeans, in temples and bazaars, on roads and in humble houses of the common people, this sensational news was heatedly discussed. 'Could a woman be a way-maker in this tradition-bound country? Would she be able to swim against the current?', wondered the Europeans whereas natives could not believe that the young woman had acquired so much proficiency in a foreign tongue like English, as to deliver a lecture in it. Orthodox people were shocked to observe that Anandibai, wife of the Postmaster, was behaving like a man and they thought that it reflected badly upon her character. Hence, they wanted to excommunicate her.

It was a Saturday afternoon. Out of curiosity, people flocked to the Baptist College at an appointed hour to see the unusual woman. Something strange was happening in a small village like Shrirampur and nobody wanted to miss the opportunity of witnessing it. Even schoolboys didn't lag behind. They crowded the space near the stage so that they could properly see everything. In the large crowd of natives, a few foreigners men and women were conspicuous. Prominent among them was the figure of Colonel Hans Mattison, the American Consul General who had recently developed a keen interest in the activities of Anandibai Joshi. A small corner was occupied by the reporters of Bengali and English newspapers. But the centre of attraction was the young woman on the stage in her Maharashtrian costume who was immersed in her own thoughts and was calmly sitting in her chair.

She stood up when her name was announced and faced the large crowd looking curiously at her. She did not carry any notes in her hands but spoke spontaneously like a seasoned speaker, though it was her first speech.* A wave of excitement trembled through the hall when she fluently began to speak in English. First, she politely thanked the audience for taking the trouble to attend the meeting and made it clear that she was aware of her limitations. "I stand here to fail, as I am not likely to succeed…I have studied but a little while and the language which I intend to speak in, is not only foreign but thoroughly out of command, and entirely unused. I am therefore liable to make thousands of blunders even in grammar…. I wish I had better knowledge of the language." She also thanked the college authorities and particularly Rev. Summers for the cooperation extended to her. After this brief introduction, she took up six important questions which were repeatedly asked to her.

"1. Why I to go to America?

2. Are there no means to study in India?

3. Why do I go alone?

4. Shall I not be excommunicated on my return?

5. What would I do if misfortune befall me?

6. Why should I do what is not done by any of my sex."

Anandi dealt with these questions one by one, neatly constructing her arguments based on facts, observations and her experiences. The atmosphere around her was explosive. People had united to combat like crusaders against the woman who according to them, was sinning against the respected tradition and was violating rules laid down by the Hindu religion. But Anandi handled the delicate situation with utmost care. She wisely began her speech by appealing to the ladies present in the audience. "I now address the ladies present here, who will be the better judges of the importance of female medical assistance….

---

* For Anandi's speech see: Appendix No. 2

The want of female physicians in India is keenly felt in every quarter. Ladies both European and Native are naturally averse to expose themselves…to treatment by doctors of the other sex." It was difficult but essential to convince people that her decision to go to America for Medical education, was public spirited and by doing so, she would be able to help her countrywomen in the time of their distress. Her speech was an amalgamation of emotions and thoughts, delicacy and strength, calmness and courage, dream and reality.

For years, Anandi was pestered by people in different towns. She shared her experiences with the audience, in order to give them some idea of the obstacles in the path of women who wanted to study in India. She said, "No! I do not mean to say there are *no* means, but the difficulties are many and great…. I am neither a Christian nor a Brahmo. To continue to live as a Hindu and to go to school in any part of India is very difficult…. Example is better than precept. Some few years ago, when I was in Bombay, I used to go to school… Once it happened that I was obliged to stay in school for some time and go twice a day for my meals, to the house of a relation. Passers-by whenever they saw me going, gathered round me. Some of them made fun…. The shopkeepers and venders spat at the sight of me and made gestures too indecent to describe. I leave it to your imagination what was my condition at such a time and how I could gladly have burst through the crowd to make my home nearer." Profound truthfulness was the soul of her speech. She neither exaggerated her difficulties nor gave a false colouring to it. Her expressions didn't smell of hatred or sarcasm. Her words were sharp yet truthful, simple but touching and powerful. So, she could touch the right chord with her audience. Like a skilful surgeon, Anandi dissected their wrong concepts and at the same time, appealed to their sense of justice, humanity, truthfulness and goodness.

She also made some general but critical remarks about the Indians who could not understand their own needs. "There is probably no country so barbarous as India, that would not disclose all her wants and try to stand on her own feet. The want of female physicians in India is keenly felt in every quarter. There is a growing need for a

Hindu lady doctor in India and I volunteer to qualify myself for one." Nobody would have imagined that the woman who humbly began, "I stand here to fail, as I am not likely to succeed." would talk so frankly, leaving aside the feminine shyness.

In this speech, she discussed why Indian women particularly needed native lady doctors. She felt sure that a native lady doctor alone would perfectly understand the problems and the needs of Indian women and there would not be a communication gap between the patients and doctors. Importing foreign lady doctors, was not, according to her, a desirable solution. But while emphasising this point, Anandi had passed some incorrect remarks about European lady doctors, "There are some female doctors in India from Europe and America, who being foreigners and different in manners, ... have not been of such use to our women as they might....we Indian women absolutely derive no benefit from those foreign ladies. They indeed have appearance of supplying our need but the appearance is delusive." These statements are not only incorrect but unjust. There were many foreign lady doctors who had provided superb medical help to native women and had helped them, going out of the way. They had also established an excellent rapport with the populace. (Their contribution is discussed thoroughly in chapter no. 2.) It seems that Anandi had not taken into account the hurdles in the path of foreign lady doctors, such as the multi-lingual environment, unhygienic conditions, the unfriendly climate, the undeveloped means of communication and last but not the least, the blind faiths that kept Indian men and women away, even from the available medical help. Despite such problems, those foreign lady doctors worked among Indian women who were absolutely helpless. Barring this misinterpretation, Anandi's other observations were thoughtful.

To those who argued that her plan was dangerous and she was bound to suffer misfortune, she replied, "Some persons fall into the error of exaggerated declamation, by producing in their talk examples of national calamities and scenes of extensive misery which are found in books, rather than in the world and which as they are horrid are ordained to be rare. A man or woman who wishes to act does not look at that dark side which others easily foresee.... When they happen, they must be endured, but...they are oftener dreaded than experienced....Death and misery come alike to good and bad, virtuous and vicious, rich and poor, travellers and housekeepers...Misery and death are always near and should be expected....When the result of any hazardous work is good, we praise the enterprise which undertook it; when it is evil, we blame the imprudence. The world is always ready to call enterprise imprudence, when fortune changes." This is a graphic picture of her mental strength and wisdom. She had prepared herself to face any calamity.

Another important point that she made clear was that her stay in America would be temporary. She would return to India once the purpose was served, because she wanted to work in her own country and among her own people. She knew that the root cause of the opposition was the fear of her possible conversion to Christianity and undesirable changes in her lifestyle, food or dress in America. Though she herself knew that there was nothing wrong with changing the food and dress habits according to the climatic conditions, she thought that she would compromise on this issue. To set people's minds at rest, she gave a promise to them in that meeting. "I have determined to live there exactly as I do here. I propose to myself to make no change in my customs and manners, food or dress. I will go as a Hindu, and come back here to live as a Hindu. I will not increase my wants, but be as plain and simple as my forefathers, and as I am now." She thought it essential to convince them about her steadfast devotion to her country, religion and people.

It is praiseworthy that she succeeded in winning their minds in spite of her challenging statements like, "If my countrymen wish to excommunicate me, why do they not do it now?" It is interesting to note how sweetly she appealed to their conscience. For example, in the midst of her attacks, she asked, "Dear audience, does it become my native and Christian brethren to be so uncharitable? Certainly not. I place these unpleasant things before you, [so] that those whom they concern most may rectify them and those who have never thought of the difficulties, may see that I am not going to America through any whim or caprice." In short, combining her fearlessness, the strength of convictions, profound thoughtfulness and maturity, she won the summit. The debut that she made was her first victory.

10

Tide was on Turn

Anandi's public meeting was successful beyond expectations. It received a prominent place in newspapers and brought Anandi into the limelight. The letters of congratulations were showered on her from different quarters of society. Colonel Henry Alcott, the president of the Theosophical Society, suggested to Gopal to prepare a write-up and send it to American newspapers. Mr. H. E. M. James, the Director General of Post Offices of India, sent a cheque for Rs. 100 along with his letter of congratulations, in support of her undertaking. The Joshis were profusely grateful for this timely help from him, as they were really in need of money and having no other source had sold some of her ornaments. Even in the past, Mr. James had always stood by Gopal. When Gopal had lost the letter to Viceroy, he was temporarily suspended but not thrown out of the job. This could not have become possible without the protection of the topmost authority like Mr. James.

After Anandi's departure to America, Mr. James went out of the way and tried to raise a substantial fund for Anandi's Medical education. He published an appeal in newspapers, requesting people to donate generously, "A young Brahmin lady has recently gone to America to study Medicine and qualify herself as a Medical attendant for native ladies. In doing this, she and her husband have made great pecuniary sacrifices, and her income barely suffices for necessaries. Going alone among strangers, though treated kindly, she has to encounter many obstacles which she has bravely faced. In recognition of her courage and public spirit, it is desired to raise a sum which will pay her tuition fees, and relieve her from pecuniary anxiety… Mr. James, No. 2, Cameo street, Calcutta will be happy to receive subscriptions." [1]

British officers of high ranks, including the Viceroy of India, responded to Mr. James' appeal and sent their contribution for the fund.

Subscriptions

His Excellency the Viceroy and Governor-General	Rs. 200
His Honour the Lieutenant Governor	Rs. 100
The Honourable Chief-Justice Garth	Rs. 50
The Honourable J. Gibbs, C. S. I. C. I. E.	Rs. 100
The Honourable C. I. Albert, C. I. E	Rs. 50
The Honourable Mr. Justice Pigott	Rs. 50
Mr. James	Rs. 200
Total	**Rs. 750**

This was quite a large sum in the 19th century when the purchasing capacity of a Rupee was many times more than it is today. The above list indicates how Anandi's career had aroused interest and sympathy in minds of the British who appreciated her efforts by generously donating to the James' Fund; whereas not a single native was motivated to do so. The relationship between the British and the Indians was multifaceted. Though the British were conquerors, it was not possible for the Indians to treat them only as their enemies. The Indians held the British in contempt as they had enslaved India, but on the other hand, they felt reverence for their rulers who had established law and order, developed the ways and means of communication and transportation, and opened the doors to knowledge for their subjects. English, the language of the rulers, was a window to the world. Anandi's aspiration was also better understood by the British than most of the natives. On the national level, the British were enemies but on the personal level, many of them were true friends. The relationship between the British and the Indians was an admixture of love and hate, attraction and repulsion, regard and disregard, loyalty and disloyalty.

A month after the public meeting, Anandi was to sail to America by the ship 'City of Calcutta.' But her patience was almost spent when suddenly the voyage was postponed by the navigating company till 9th April. In the month of March, Anandi was busy with her preparations. She had sewed warm dresses of coarse woollen cloth, had purchased saris and blouse pieces, bangles and red kumkum powder. As she wanted to show her American friends some typically Indian things, she took with her the idols of Lord Rama, Lord Shiva, his wife Goddess Parvati and some silverware like [F1]Gulabdani and [F2]Attardani which were used in Maharashtra, to welcome guests. Particularly women used these things in their religious gatherings and get-togethers. On 3rd April, Anandi-Gopal met Col. Hans Mattison; the Consul-General of America, who gave her two letters of introduction. To draw public attention to Anandi, Col. Mattison also wrote an article on her, and published it in *Frank Leslie's Illustrated Newspaper* about the time when she reached America. After the visit to Col. Mattison, Anandi wrote to Aunt Theo her last letter from India. "Overjoyed with the approach of the happy time to which I have looked forward so long, I sit down to write what may be my last letter. Everything is settled. I feel better since I know that there is nothing to do but embark… The time draws near in which we shall be in one country and one place. Every moment shortens the time."[2] The countdown had begun. Every setting sun was decreasing the distance between Anandi and her dreamland. At the same time, it was bringing nearer the separation from her husband and motherland. Her mind was swinging like a pendulum between joy and grief.

After the public meeting, the rising tide of public discontent had receded, but Anandi's mother and other relatives were still hoping against the hope to prevent her journey. Knowing that Anandi was very fond of her younger brother Vinayak, her elder sister Varanasi wrote an emotional letter to Anandi announcing that Vinayak was very ill and urged Anandi to start immediately. Not understanding the trick at the outset, Anandi grieved over her brother's illness and felt like going to Kalyan and meet him. But Gopal made her understand that it was nothing but a trap and if she went to Kalyan, she would fall right into it. Her relatives would move heaven and earth to stop her from going to America. Hence, Anandi decided not to go. On 3rd April, the Joshis came to Calcutta and stayed with their friend Krishna Patwardhan. To give

---

F1 Gulabdani - A tall silverware with a rounded bottom and a tiny perforated flower-like head for sprinkling rosewater.

F2 Attardani - A lotus-shaped silverware having a tiny casket with a lid at the centre, around which is chained a thin flat spoon. In this casket, a small cotton ball soaked in perfume or attar is kept. With the help of this spoon, attar is applied to the hands of the guests.

her send-off, Anandi was invited by their family friends to tea or dinner parties. After a long time, Anandi-Gopal who were in a relaxed mood, enjoyed these friendly gestures. But at the eleventh hour, the scheduled date of the ship was changed by the navigation company from 9th April to 7th April. Hence, they had to decline some of the invitations. The night of 6th April 1883 was her last night in Hindustan. The next day she had to start early morning.

On 6th April, Gopal was busy the whole day doing some last-minute errands. He was eager to do anything that would add comfort to her long journey. At night, he suddenly realised that a horse carriage was not engaged for the next morning and he had to buy some fruit and sweetmeats. Though tired, he rushed back to the bazaar. When he returned, Anandi was fast asleep. His tender glance lingered upon her tranquil face for a long time. He was disturbed by the questions to which he had no answers: 'Tomorrow morning, she will go away. I am sending her alone. Will she be safe? Am I doing a mistake? For the last 9 years she was with me like a shadow. How am I going to live without her? When shall I see her again? What would be the outcome of this leap in the darkness?' Choked with conflicting emotions, he quietly shed tears. In those silent hours, the mask of a stern man fell off and the lovelorn husband gave vent to his feelings. But this melancholy face was not to be seen by his wife at the time of parting, as he did not wish her to be unhappy. Gopal could not sleep the whole night.

When the distant clock struck 3, Gopal woke his friend Govind Sathe and sent him to bring the horse carriage. At last, the day of parting had dawned. He woke Anandi. She could not utter a word; instead, her eyes and her trembling lips spoke. The pangs of separation were so unbearable that their grief knew no consolation. With a heavy heart, she made preparations. Govind Sathe, Tatya Baldeo and Rambhau, the three friends of Gopal were to accompany them. They loaded the luggage and got into the carriage. The horse's hooves made a rhythmic sound on the deserted paths of the city which was in deep sleep. Those last moments were so precious that they were spent silently looking at each other and the glances were rich with an unuttered valediction.

At last, they arrived at the port. It was full of bustle and business as usual, but the noisy crowd increased the uneasiness of a novice traveller.

Finding their way through the large heaps of luggage, the Joshis reached the spot where Mr. and Mrs. Johnson were waiting. Mrs. Johnson who was to be in charge of Anandi on the voyage, was chatting with other Missionary ladies. Gopal waited for Mrs. Johnson to take their notice and introduce Anandi to her co-travellers. But without taking any cognizance, they continued their chit-chat and treated the Joshis very coldly. In fact, Gopal wished to request Mrs Johnson to treat Anandi like her own daughter, but he was so bewildered by her frosty smile that he could not utter a word. Not able to understand the unexpected coldness, he turned to her husband as the last hope. But to Gopal's surprise, the husband inquired only about how much money did Anandi carry with her and showed unwillingness to talk about anything else. Since 43.5 Pounds were already deposited with Dr. Thorburn to cover Anandi's expenses in the voyage, Gopal was unable to understand this question. He urged Mr. Johnson to wait till Dr. Thorburn came.

Struggling hard against his nervousness, Gopal tried to start a dialogue with Mr. Johnson and explained to him how difficult it was for them to raise even that much amount. Since it was not possible for Anandi to spend easily in the voyage, he made a humble request to Mr. Jonson, "Would you please request your wife to see that Anandi's expenses are as less as possible?" To this Johnson replied sharply, "If your wife wishes to travel with my wife, she must spend." This was the last straw. Shocked by Mr. Johnson's arrogance and pomp, Gopal did not know what would happen to Anandi on the voyage. He shuddered to see that the Johnsons were openly showing their unwillingness to shoulder Anandi's responsibility. But why did they accept it if they did not wish, since the Joshis had not asked them to do so? On the contrary, it was Dr. Thorburn himself who had advised and urged Gopal to send Anandi with Mrs. Johnson and her friends.

There was a stunning resemblance between the behaviour of the Thorburns and the Johnsons who gave false promises and insulting treatment to the Joshis. Their misconduct was pre-planned and deliberate. Anandi's decision to go to America instead of enrolling her name in Dr. Thorburn's Medical school had angered them and they wanted to teach a lesson to Anandi for disappointing them. So, they instigated Johnsons to ill-treat her and thus indirectly had their revenge.

Gopal who was hit hard by this double game, realised that they were caught in a trap and there was no way out. He could not tell Anandi not to go because it would have shattered her mind. Plus, the money they had invested would have been wasted and they were in no position to spend again. Surprisingly, even in such circumstances, Anandi looked quite composed. Hence, Gopal did not find it proper to discourage her by sharing his anxieties. He only said, "There is nothing but water below and sky above! Take care of yourself. Do not depend much on these ladies." He could not look at her anymore, for the fear that he would break down. Turning his back, he went away and did not look back at Anandi. Gopal and his friends stepped into a small boat that carried them away from the ship. Gopal could see the resolute figure of Anandi standing alone on the deck and looking at him with tearful eyes. Her lone image haunted him for days. Every wave increased the distance between Anandi-Gopal which they knew, would go on expanding over the period of time.

The next day, he wrote a letter to Benjamin Carpenter, informing him that Anandi had sailed from Calcutta. The end part of the letter throws light on his state of mind. "My dear sir, I took good care of her until her departure and now I hand over this precious charge to you and your worthy wife."[3] Though these words appear simple and formal, there is much to read between the lines.

Reference:

1. *The Life of Dr. Anandabai Joshee* - Caroline Healey Dall. 1888 Page 113

2. Ibid Page 93

3. Ibid Page 94

11

A Transparent Moment

Gopal was infamous for his impulsive behaviour, eccentricity, peevish nature and the habit of sailing under false colours. All his life, he had offended many of his benefactors and friends with his sharp tongue and arrogance. His favourite pastime was to perplex people with his self-contradictory behaviour. Only he could deliver lectures in America against women's education while his wife was learning Medicine there. But even in the life of such a whimsical person, a truthful moment dawned when he was separated from his wife, for the duration of some years. [F1]Gopal's letter to Anandi, which was written eight days after her departure to America, has preserved the transparent moment in his life. He had candidly expressed in this letter his profound love and respect for her. Being enchanted by her greatness, it was written in a spellbound state of mind. All masks that he enjoyed wearing, fell off and he gave way to his innermost thoughts and emotions. This unique moment was so pure that it compelled him to look at himself with open eyes. Acceptance of his mistakes and faults; heartfelt repentance and self-abasement are some footprints of his truthfulness. Out of an urgent psychological need, he pronounced in this letter the judgements against himself.

Anandi's fast intellectual growth had raised Gopal's expectations about her. In the beginning, he wished to give her some sort of education so that she would not remain illiterate like other girls and would know the joy of learning. But when Anandi thought of becoming a doctor, her unusual dream delighted him. When it was clear that she would not get Medical education in India, they thought of migrating to America. Since it was financially impossible for them to go together, she agreed to go alone. Not once did she waver in her resolution and accepted all the challenges. And now leaping every fence, his beloved wife and brilliant disciple had left her motherland, in pursuit of her goal. For

---

F1 The original letter was written in Marathi which is translated here.

years, he had pined to carve an untraditional and confident woman out of Anandi. But now being in the doldrums, he could not enjoy the fruition of his hopes. The things had developed so fast that Gopal who liked to puzzle others, was himself puzzled. In this letter, he saluted her for her dauntlessness and mental strength. "I really wonder at your courage and determination…we all are proud of you… you are a unique woman." Till then, he had looked upon the events in his personal life, as the means to social reforms and his own joys and sorrows had little value. But the farewell to Anandi gave rise to grief that was intensely personal and its social relevance was beneath the notice. He had lost his wife to her high aim and now there was no escape. He had to teach himself to live without her for a long time. The deep chasm gaped between them and he was afraid to think about it.

A few days before Anandi went to America, he had gone to Dr. Thorburn's house one afternoon. He was alone in the hall for some time, when suddenly he was overwhelmed with the forthcoming grief of separation. Unable to suppress, he allowed his tears to trickle down. But in the presence of Anandi, he never permitted this luxury to himself. On the contrary, he wore the painful mask of an iron man. But in this love letter, he expressed his heart's deep languor. He says, "I have no words to express my anguish. Only my sense of duty helped me to control myself, up to the last moment of parting. Alas! I think, I was too strict with you and never tried to comfort you. I am the cruellest person God has ever created on earth. But I am sure you would forgive me." The very fact that Gopal asked for forgiveness indicates that, overcoming his limitations, he had achieved a noble state of mind. In the same mood, he compared himself with Anandi and earnestly confessed that she was a better person. "When I think about your mental strength, I feel that mine is nothing. Do not think about us, Indians. You better forget us, I pray, because we are too bad to deserve your attention. Your letter from the Diamond Harbour was simply beautiful. It made me happy because even I might not have written a thought-provoking letter like that." As Gopal's mind was beyond jealousy at that moment, he could experience the pure and simple joy in her achievement. Though she was going away from him, the sense of togetherness had reached its peak, as if they were divided in body but united in mind. Therefore, he promised her with all earnestness, "I will seek pleasure in your success."

After he saw her off, Gopal returned to Shrirampur. The neat and tidy home looked so empty without Anandi that the silence was unbearable. He felt very lonely without Anandi whose scent of existence was still lingering in the house. Everything in the house reminded him of Anandi. The loneliness and gloom became so unbearable that he could not live there. He took 3 months' leave from his job and decided to travel all over India, in order to divert attention from his unbearable longing for Anandi. But soon he realised that he was trying in vain to get rid of his feelings. For the first time in his life, he perceived that he was really in love with his wife. Without hiding his uneasiness, he wrote, "I cannot stay in the same place for more than one or two days. My state of mind is like a restless bird." From Calcutta, he went to Jabalpur, Harda, Nashik, Sangamner and Pune. Though the lovebird wandered from place to place; mingled among friends and relatives, nothing could set him at rest. He felt alienated from everything and everybody around him.

From Pune, he turned to Madras, disguising himself as an [F2]Agnihotri but no city, no friend and no disguise could console his troubled heart. From Madras, he went to Rameshwar, Baroda, Ajmer, Jaipur, and Kashi, but nothing could make him forget Anandi. The elegy of memories followed him wherever he went. "I know I was very unkind to you, but it is not that I do not love you. Every moment seems to me like a century. Please let me know, if you wish me to be with you. I would immediately follow you and would be happy to serve you." For his own peace of mind, he urgently wanted to make sure that Anandi was convinced about the intensity of his love. It is amusing that like a typical love-sick person, he showed a sign of possessiveness in this letter. He inquired after a certain person on the ship, who he felt, had shown an excessive interest in Anandi. He asked if that man tried to befriend her. Before finishing the letter, he once again blessed her with all his heart. "May you be blessed by my heart of flint."

This simple moment was so different from Gopal's normal way of living, that people around him either misunderstood it or were suspicious about it. They could only see that the stone-hearted man had coldly sent his wife away to a foreign land. The friends of Gopal who were eyewitnesses to the farewell, pitied Anandi and hated Gopal. Tatya

F2 Agnihotri – A priest who worships the sacred fire.

Baldeo exclaimed, "I feel like killing you, for you have compelled her to face alone the perils of the long voyage." After Anandi's departure, they had gone back to the house of Patwardhan. The friends who had gathered there, asked Gopal many questions about Anandi. In the course of discussion, two friends remarked that Gopal's sudden decision to send her away aroused suspicion about Anandi's character. These outrageous remarks pierced Gopal's heart. It was more in sorrow than in anger that he poured abuses on them. Another friend commented that Gopal should not have sent Anandi away because a wife is of great use to a man. Gopal could see that the significance of Anandi's migration to America was just beyond their grasp. "This world is very selfish," he reproached, "I do not grieve for my own sake, as I do not care for my creature comforts. My wants are little and I do not like to trouble anybody for them. I am worried about you, but people cannot understand that." This attitude makes Gopal different from others. Another outstanding quality of him was his enormous capacity to dream even in the time of distress. After sending Anandi to America, he wished to educate her younger sister Sundari. "If I could get hold of Sundari, I would take her to Bengal. I would teach her and send her to you," he wrote.

Though the purity of the 'transparent moment' was beyond doubt, it was difficult for a person like Gopal to remain on the zenith for a long time. Very soon, he became his normal self. The whimsical and naughty person hidden within him once again took hold of him and he began to play tricks. In July 1883, Anandi's brother Vinayak wrote a letter to her and narrated an incident. "People had heard that some Mr. Gopal Joshee had send his wife to U.S.A. They asked him if he was the same person. To this he replied that he was not and did not hesitate to vow by the feet of Dadasaheb Mate, assuring that his wife was at Nashik." This clearly indicates that Gopal had recovered from the 'fit' of truthfulness and thus the transparent moment melted into nothingness.

12

The Lone Traveller

On the morning of 7th April 1883, the 'City of Calcutta' set sail, at high tide. In the beginning, the ship moved cautiously at a slow speed, taking 24 hours to cross the river Hugli or Ganges. The river was full of sand bars and they shifted their positions in the current. The most dangerous ones were near the Bajbaj and the Diamond harbours. On the waterway between the port of Calcutta and Gangamukh — the outfall of the Ganges, all outgoing and incoming ships were provided with an experienced local boatman for the safety purpose. His was the last word — even above that of the Captain, as they had a thorough knowledge of the river Hugli and the dangerous spots in it.

Before entering the Bay of Bengal, the ship halted at the Diamond harbour which was starred with thick groves of coconut, mango, jackfruit, lychee and date and looked like an emerald in the water. Anandi enjoyed watching the peaceful lush green landscape. From here, Anandi posted her first letter to Gopal, describing the beautiful landscape spread before her. At Gangamukh, the ship entered the Bay of Bengal. Anandi took a last look at the shore of her Motherland. Swami Vivekanand, the great Indian philosopher, who travelled on the same route a few years after Anandi, had picturesquely described this spot. "See, here the waters of Ganges disappear and here the Ocean begins. Its hair is blue, the body is blue and even its clothes are blue." It was an enchanting experience to witness the union of the great Indian river and the sea. A similar deep-blue ocean of conflicting emotions was roaring in Anandi's heart. It was difficult to balance on it the little boat of her troubled mind. "I must launch my fortune like a ship, on the ocean of life. To what shore shall it go, to a fertile bank or a barren beach? Or will it go to pieces?"[1] Thus, she had once asked herself. Though she did not know the answer, she had prepared herself to breast calamities. She knew for certain that she was totally alone in her voyage, though Mrs. Jonson was supposed to take care of her.

An incident had occurred two weeks before the time of her departure that had made it clear to Anandi that Mrs. Johnson was going to create trouble for her. So, she had to work out her own salvation. One day Mrs. Johnson had called on her at Shrirampur, with a specific intention of turning Anandi's mind towards Christianity. She had read a certain letter of Theodosia Carpenter, with reference to which she started the conversation.

Johnson: To which branch of Christianity does Mrs. Carpenter belong?

Anandi: I think she belongs to no branch. (Anandi was shrewd enough to sense Mrs. Johnson's real intention of finding faults with Aunt Theo, which was veiled behind the innocent question.)

Johnson: Oh, then I would not allow you to stay with such a profane woman. You may go to a tiger's cave instead. Beware, the heartless woman would lock you in her house. What would you do then? Listen to me child, go to Mrs. Parker at Boston. Mrs. Carpenter has no right to compel you to stay with her. She won't be able to do anything against your wish.

Just to frighten Anandi, Johnson had told her various tales of barbarous tribes, cruelties of tyrants and the hateful activities of notorious pimps; expecting Anandi to lose heart and cling to her for support and advice. But to her great surprise, she found that Anandi was not frightened by her hidden threats. On the contrary, she calmly replied,

Anandi: No one would harm me since God is with me. I am afraid neither of Missionaries nor of tigers. I would be safe wherever I go. Please don't say anything against my aunt.

Johnson: Your aunt? How could she be your aunt? Listen child, you are inexperienced. If you would not obey me, you would not be saved from sin and punishment.

Anandi: I don't need any human being for my salvation. The Almighty would save me. But if you yearn so much for salvation, why don't you save your own people first? Save Mrs. Carpenter instead of hating her.

With this logical argument, Anandi silenced Mrs. Johnson who took it as an insult and went back in anger. Predicting that Mrs. Johnson would have her revenge in the voyage, Anandi had mentally prepared herself to deal with unpleasant situations. She did not tell anything about this to Gopal as he was already under tremendous pressure.

The first night on the ship was very difficult for Anandi. She stretched herself on her berth and tried to sleep, but was so uneasy that she could not. The grief of being away from home disturbed her sleep and the volley of questions bulking large at night flurried her: 'To where would this intrepidity of mine lead me? Will I reach safely to America? Would my letter reach Aunt Theo in time? Would she be able to come to the port in time? What if something goes wrong?' In that century, many women rushed to America from different parts of the world to try their luck. But many a time, an utterly miserable lot awaited women and they were found in the most wretched conditions. Anandi was aware of this dark side, so it was but natural that she was worried.

The ship was like a small crowded town where everybody's rights and responsibilities were well defined. The Captain was like a King whose orders were to be obeyed without any excuses. Officers and engineers were the Europeans and servants, seamen, cooks and coalmen were the Indians. Butlers, stewards and pursers looked after the food, kitchen and dining hall. Every Sunday, there used to be a roll-call of servants on the quarter deck and they were supposed to present themselves in clean and tidy clothes. After the roll-call, prayers were offered, for which passengers also gathered. If a priest was not available, Captain took his place and conducted the ritual. As Anandi was with the Missionary ladies, a first-class cabin was allotted to her, at a concessional rate. The cabins used to be of wood in which 4 to 6 berths were hung near the walls like swings. Each berth was separated by a curtain so that people could have some privacy. A cabin contained a washing table, a mirror, some water jugs, glasses and vomiting pots. The water closets were after the fashion of the European ones and the bathrooms had a tub and a shower of hot and cold water. Cabins were located on the upper and lower decks and there were many inconveniences to which passengers were subjected. Some cabins were so congested and without proper ventilation that passengers suffocated. Cabins near the dining room or the kitchen were filled with nauseating smells of rotten food, whereas in the cabins near the engine, the burning sensation and noise of huge engine irritated people.

Days began early on the ship, with the knock of a servant who came in to clean the cabin. Towels of the passengers were changed and beds were tidied. Pots and glasses were washed daily whereas bedsheets and bedcovers were changed once a week. Morning tea was served in cabins, but for breakfast, lunch and dinner, people had to gather in the dining hall when the bell rang to announce the mealtime. Plates, spoons, forks and glasses were neatly arranged on a large dining table and hot bowls of food were kept ready. In the evening, Anandi used to have a stroll on the quarter deck where some open space was reserved for the first-class passengers. At night, this floating town looked enchanting in the dreamy moonlight, when people danced and sang gaily in a lit ballroom. But the soft music created a strange longing in Anandi's heart. As it was her first voyage, Anandi was totally unfamiliar with the cosmopolitan crowd and the Western atmosphere on the ship. Naturally, the lonely young girl of eighteen was haunted by memories of her sweet home and her dear ones.

In the beginning, she was fascinated by the great expanse of water, but as the days passed, the fascination vanished and the want of land was felt intensely. In the vast ocean, stretching beyond the horizon, the ship looked like a little crescent-shaped structure, on which she was supposed to stay for weeks. The railing of a ship marked the boundary of this artificial land, beyond which there was nothing but fathomless water. Passengers took time to adjust themselves to the unfriendly weather, strong winds, salty smell of the sea and the constant motion of the ship. Simple actions like sitting, standing, sleeping or eating became most difficult on a ship. Particularly, a novice like Anandi who had not yet found her sea legs, suffered from sea-sickness. Vomiting, giddiness and fever reduced her strength. She needed good nutritious food to get back her energy, but being a vegetarian, it became difficult for her to get proper nourishment.

Most of the travellers were non-vegetarians, hence that kind of food was in abundance but it was of no use to her. Due to the scarcity of vegetables, the dishes were always very few and even those were prepared carelessly, since there were few patrons to them. Sometimes even stale vegetables were used without bothering for those who would eat them. Therefore, Anandi had to fill her stomach with boiled potatoes, some rice, cakes and bread. The daily consumption of these articles being unsuitable to her constitution, it invited health problems like constipation and stomach ache. At the same time, her tooth of wisdom also started giving her trouble. Her gums were so swollen that she could not talk or laugh.

As days passed, she learnt to fight her battle single-handed. Under the leadership of Mrs. Johnson, her so-called companions took pleasure in making fun of her dress, food habits, religion and even her high aim. The lone suffering girl could not evoke love or sympathy in their minds. On the contrary, they tried to create troubles for her. One day Anandi was lying on a couch when Mrs. Johnson rushed into the cabin and got into a huff for no reason. She ordered Anandi to quit the cabin and go somewhere else. Anandi left the room without a word and walked towards the nearby deck. But she was stopped by a stewardess who asked her not to go out in that cold weather and warned that if Anandi did not take proper care of herself, she would play havoc with her health. Anandi held her tongue and went back. It would not have served any purpose to tell the truth to the stewardess. Pretending to be innocent, Mrs. Johnson would have used the occasion to prove Anandi's ungratefulness. The strong disdain was so conspicuous in the treatment she received from Mrs. Johnson and her friends that many a time, Anandi's heart sank and she felt very sad. Once she felt like urgently sharing her troubles with Gopal and wrote a letter to him. But on second thoughts, she tore it up because it would have increased his agonies. Anandi decided to write to Gopal only after reaching America safely. Until then, she locked her affliction in the blue-black chamber of her mind.

One of the engineers on the ship spotted Anandi suffering alone. Realising that she had no real protector, he began to give special attention to her. He was always lavish of praise and never missed an opportunity to bestow compliments on her. Anandi tried her best to avoid him but keeping a close eye on her, he followed her everywhere. Many a time, he urged Anandi to go with him in the interior part of the ship, to have a look at the working of the huge machines. But she firmly refused to go alone with him and insisted that he should invite all the ladies. On one such occasion, Mrs. Johnson was present there, but instead of protecting Anandi, she encouraged the lustful man. She told Anandi that she might go alone with him if he wished so. This irresponsible behaviour manifests the extent of Mrs. Johnson's hatred for Anandi. When the engineer realised that Anandi would not yield to his desire, he thought of tempting her with gifts. Once he presented his gold watch to her and said, "Have this! You would need it when you go to your college. You won't meet a person without a watch in America." To this Anandi retorted, "I know my needs better. If I need a watch, I would buy it for myself. I don't want yours." Ultimately Anandi found a way to get away from those unfriendly people. The small library on the ship attracted her attention where she began to spend her time. Forgetting everything else, she started reading voraciously and could finish seven large books before the ship reached London.

The ship sailed smoothly on the calm sea and there were no signs of a cyclone. On 12th April, voyagers could see the land of Lanka, which looked like a colourful painting with its dark hillocks and mountains against the blue sky and the golden green groves of coconut trees gleaming in bright sunshine. Being tired of water, travellers were enthralled to look at the beautiful land. But the ship didn't halt there. Then after eight days, which is on 20th April, the ship entered the port of Eden in the evening. Eden was the first stop after the Diamond Harbour, as the ship had skipped the ports of Madras and Colombo. Some of the travellers took small boats and rushed towards the land. Here for the first time, Anandi saw the Africans with their thick lips, stubby noses and frizzy hair. Eden was not a beautiful place like Lanka. It was situated in the desert and the hills were barren due to the scarcity of water. Since it was difficult to grow even small shrubs, plucking leaves was a crime. The Camps of British soldiers were scattered on the ground whereas the fort stood on a hill. Since 1839, Eden was under the British regime and was governed by the Bombay Government. Being an important coaling station and a trade centre on the sea-way, the importance of Eden was growing fast.

Pandita Ramabai had sailed from Bombay to London two weeks after Anandi and had taken the same route, but they both were unaware of each other's plans. Ramabai journeyed by the ship 'Bukhara' which reached Eden just six days after the 'City of Calcutta', which is on 26th April. The memoir of Ramabai, written in Marathi, provides interesting information. Ramabai, her little daughter Manorama and Ramabai's friend Anandi Bhagat disembarked on the port to have a feel of the place. While wandering, she noticed in a valley the tree of Mimosa or Shirish in full blossom, which was a pleasant surprise in that desert. "Even in the desert of Eden, Shirish blooms. Similarly, happiness flowers in the midst of grief," she reflected.

The 'City of Calcutta' departed from Eden on the same day – 20th April and crossing the Red Sea, reached the port of Suez after 5 days. There were dangerous sand bars and sieve-like corals which absorbed water instead of resisting it and their presence therefore was not easily felt. To avoid disasters, all the ships were put under the charge of knowledgeable local guides between Eden and Suez. When the 'City of Calcutta' entered the Red Sea, people caught a rare sight of land on both sides of the sea. Then gradually the sea expanded and the land disappeared. Egypt was on one shore of the Red Sea and the desert of Arabia on the other. There were flying fishes in the sea and birds caught them swiftly, as they flew out of the water. No one could escape the terrific heat waves on the Red Sea. Particularly the condition of coalmen was very pitiable. All day long, they had to work near the engine, adding fuel to the fire. The heat was so unbearable that sometimes they used to jump into the sea, to get rid of the burning sensation.

On the evening of 25th April, Anandi reached Suez. Here she saw the Egyptian and Arabian vendors. The Egyptians were fair and shapely, whereas the Arabians had longish faces, broad brows and large beautiful eyes. They were selling fanciful articles like shells, silks, brocades and decorative pots. Since some voyagers preferred to remain on ships instead of disembarking at the port, vendors went on board to sell their goods. From the descriptions of Pandita Ramabai and Swami Vivekanand, one can have some idea of the port of Suez in that period. Ramabai wrote, "The town of Suez is two miles away from the seashore. Here people ride on donkeys and we too made it a point to enjoy the funny ride. The inhabitants of Suez are the Egyptians. Women are seen on roads but except their eyes they are veiled."[2] The gigantic crocodiles in the waters near Suez produced wild sensations in the minds of voyagers. Swami Vivekanand had described them in a humorous way "Eh, see there!' we heard an outcry. I saw a huge thing graciously sailing towards our ship. The grand person was as if walking in a procession on the carpet of water, surrounded by several fishes. Some were playing on its back while others were fondly embracing its neck. The person was His Majesty the Crocodile."

A ship took 16 to 17 hours to cross the Suez Canal, on the other end of which was the Port Saied. As the ship left the port, first the old town of Suez was visible and then the new one. In the deserts, there were coconut trees and small houses, and pure white camels stood out on the sandy background. The canal was 105 miles long and a maximum of 200 feet wide at certain places. From time to time, layers of sand slipped into the water, making the canal shallow. But they were removed with the help of machines to clear the waterway. Great care was taken to avoid the collision of ships sailing in the opposite directions. Both Suez and the Port Saied were well-informed by telegrams about the schedules, the exact locations of various ships in the Suez Canal and the details of their arrivals and departures. All the details were carefully entered on a map and instructions were delivered accordingly. The Suez Canal was ceremoniously inaugurated on 17th November 1869. Cutting through the isthmus joining Asia and Africa, the Suez Canal was created which benefitted the whole world. By sailing through the Canal, instead of circumnavigating Africa, via Cape of Good Hope, ships saved considerable mileage, fuel and time. Swami Vivekanand had described the Port Saied as the 'meeting place of two civilisations of the world.' Crossing the Mediterranean Sea, Strait of Gibraltar and the Atlantic Ocean, the 'City of Calcutta' reached London after 13 days. No information is available about this part of the voyage in the letters of Anandi or elsewhere. Only a small reference was found in the account of Pandita Ramabai whose ship was just six days behind the 'City of Calcutta.' "After entering into the Mediterranean Sea, the huge waves forced us to close windows of all the cabins and even then, water rushed in, to give us a good bath. They were tossing our ship more than in the Red Sea. Because it was very cold, we had to put away our cotton garments for the thick woollen ones."[3]

Anandi reached London on the evening of 9th May 1883. She was delighted to be on the land, after a full month on water. 'City of Calcutta' entered the 'Victoria Dock' which was a well-equipped modern dock of that time and was built in 1854. Anandi and her companions took a train from a nearby station and got down at another one, four miles away. From there, they engaged a horse carriage and reached the 'London Lodging House' on Gemini Street. The Missionary ladies had some work to finish in London, so they stayed there for a week. When they reached the hotel, Anandi was so exhausted that she rested in her room for the whole day. Even the next day, she felt awkward coming out on the roads of London, thinking that people would laugh at her dress and appearance. This newly developed self-consciousness was the result of the treatment she received on the ship. In London, the Missionary ladies wanted to present Anandi at a social gathering wearing a gorgeous sari and fanciful ornaments, as it would have produced a sensation. But Anandi declined the request. She felt for certain that many of the Londoners might not have seen an Indian woman, so she was bound to arouse curiosity even in a simple dress. She had no wish to attract people's attention. Though she took sufficient care not to become conspicuous, people could not help noticing her among the Europeans. One day, when she was hurrying towards a station to catch a train along with 10 to 12 people, some Irishmen spotted her. They stopped Anandi's group and inquired who the strange woman was. At the outset, it was a mere curiosity but within no time, Anandi was surrounded by many people who began to jeer at her and their curiosity turned into a nuisance. They followed Anandi up to the station, laughing and shouting something in their language.

To win Anandi's mind with love, Mrs. Johnson changed her strategy in London and behaved in a friendly manner. She bought an umbrella, a brooch and a money-purse for her, as those things were costly in America. On 16th May 1883, Anandi and the party reached Liverpool. On 17th May, they embarked on the ship 'City of Berlin' where most of the voyagers were either European or American. There were doctors, engineers, Missionaries, Irish labourers and families with their small children, whose noise and cheerful laughter resounded on the deck. The Captain of the 'City of Berlin' or the 'Master' as he was called, had a list of passengers wherein many details about them like the name, age, sex, country, location on the ship and number of baggage each passenger carried, were entered. There were 222 travellers in all and a particular number was allotted to each passenger. They were numbered from 1190 to 1412, Anandi's number being 1368. She had three trunks and shared a first-class cabin with her companions. Now the second half of the voyage had begun. The ship made headway in the Atlantic Ocean and at the end of it stood Anandi's cloudland. Her eager mind that travelled faster than the ship had already reached the American shore. With fresh enthusiasm, Mrs. Johnson once again tried to challenge Anandi. "You are a married woman. Mrs. Carpenter has no right on you. Your husband has entrusted you with me, hence I may force you to stay with me." But as before, she met with little success.

The long voyage had almost come to an end. The thin line of the American land looked nebulous in the bluish mist. The shore looked much different than today. The famous Statue of Liberty was not there at that time; it was erected in 1886. Neither was the immigration centre on the Ellis Island as it was developed from 1892 onwards. In 1883, ships used to go up to the Southwest Battery or the Castle-Garden. The round red, stony building surrounded by a garden was called 'Castle-Garden' and it was an immigration centre. The same place is known today as Battery Park and the building is called 'Castle Clinton' which is a national monument. Originally, there were 5 batteries built in the Atlantic Ocean, to protect the American coast from the British. The Southwest battery was one of them which was converted into an amusement centre in 1824. From 1855 onwards, this place was developed as an immigration centre. Its need was acutely felt due to the excessive criminal activities in the port area. Immigrants were deceived, misguided or even robbed of their possessions by rogues who kept an eye on them. The centre proved to be very useful, as it provided the essential help and proper guidance to newcomers and hence misdeeds were controlled. Taking into account their needs and problems, valuable information about the city of New York, the means of transport, jobs and business possibilities was made available. Medical help was offered and currencies were exchanged at reasonable rates. It was a busy place, always swarming with people of different origins.

The spring of 1883 was turning into summer and the weather was pleasant while the City of Berlin was travelling towards New York. Being a terrestrial animal, man is more comfortable on Earth than in water. Hence sea voyage creates a yearning for the land which guarantees safety to man. Here he can stand confidently and breathe freely without the fear of drowning. Moreover, America was regarded as a wonderful land of opportunities by those who travelled from various parts of the globe, in the hope of a new life. Here was a free country where they could pursue their goals and be happy. The panoramic view of New York from the Atlantic Ocean always created a joyous sensation in the minds of voyagers. Sailors shouted excitedly when New York was in sight and people generously bestowed gifts upon them, for breaking the happy news. Marie Zakrzewska, a Polish-German woman had come from Berlin to America for learning Medicine in 1853, which is 3 decades before Anandi. She had noted down her first impressions of New York. With the help of this, one can imagine how New York looked like, in that era, "That is New York,' said he [Captain] pointing to a dark mass of buildings with here and there a spire towering in the air.... A bell sounded. We were opposite Trinity Church whose bell had just tolled eight. On our right were masses of brick houses and tall chimneys surrounded by a forest of masts. On our left were the romantic shores of New Jersey...ferryboats-like monstrous white swans glided to and fro the shores; rowboats piled everywhere; the white and red shirts of the oarsmen giving a bright touch of colour to the ever-changing panorama."[4]

Forgetting their tiredness, wonderstruck travellers held in their eyes the misty 'bellevue' of this new land of freedom. When the 'City of Berlin' entered the port of New York on 4th June 1883, Anandi was equally thrilled. With great excitement, she stepped on the shore of America, where her future was to take shape. Theodosia and Benjamin Carpenter were eagerly waiting in the Castle-Garden to receive her. The little woman with a dark complexion, strange dress and a bright red mark on her forehead was conspicuous in the international crowd. Since the Carpenters had seen her photographs, they could easily recognise her. When they saw Anandi, the image in their mind turned into a real face. First their eyes met, then their faces lit up with joyous smiles, which instantly turned into big grins and the Carpenters rushed forward to welcome their Anandabai. The quivering lips, wet eyes and warm handshakes washed away the remaining distance and the next moment Anandi was in the fond arms of Aunt Theo.

Reference:

1. *The Life of Dr. Anandabai Joshee* – Caroline Healey Dall. 1888 Pages 72, 73
2. *Pandita Ramabai* – (Editor) Maharashtra Rajya Sahitya Sanskruti Mandal. Second Edition, 1988. Pages 20, 21. (This Book is written in Marathi)
3. Ibid-21
4. *A Woman's quest: The Life of Marie E. Zakrzewska* – Edited by Agnes C. Victor. 1972 Arno Press New York Times Company New York. Page 75, 76.

PART - II
In America

13

Angry Young Women of the 19th Century

"I long to hear from you that you have declared an independency and by the way, in the new code of laws, . . . I desire you would remember the ladies and be more generous and favourable to them than were your ancestors. Do not put… unlimited power into the hands of husbands. Remember all men would be tyrants if they could. If particular care and attention are not paid to the ladies, we are determined to foment a rebellion and will not hold ourselves bound to obey any laws in which we have no voice or representation." [1] These are the words of Abigail Adams, from a letter, written to her husband John Adams, the second President of America. It was written in June 1774, when he was going to attend the first Continental Congress. Inspired by the motto of the American Revolution, 'No taxation without representation', the First Lady of America had warned her husband not to neglect women.

Though the feminist movement took shape a few decades after Abigail's battle cry, in the second half of the 19th century, it was not a sudden outburst or a chance-happening. The silence of centuries was broken and women were ready to fight for their human rights. In his classic *Republic*, Plato advocated that women possess natural capacities equal to men, but most of the people disagreed with him. Roman consul Marcus Porcius Cato once said, "As soon as they begin to be your equals, they will have become your superiors." So, the opposition to women was fear-oriented. During the ancient civilisation of Rome and Greece, women's rights were narrowly circumscribed. By the Mosaic Law, the rights of a wife were quite negligible compared to those of her husband. Under Roman Law, a husband had the right to kill his wife, if she was found guilty of adultery; but a woman had no such right. Man's word was the law and a public trial was not considered necessary for proving a woman guilty. Therefore, men's ill treatment and inhumanity to women made their lives terribly miserable. A daughter could be forced into a marriage by her father while he had no such power over a son.

For centuries, men and women were expected to remain and work in their separate spheres. Men were supposed to earn their livelihood and take the financial responsibility of their families. They socialised with like-minded people in public places like clubs, bars, parties and meetings. Whereas the lives of women were homebound. They were expected to be nothing else but homemakers. Women living within the four walls of their homes were so isolated and swallowed up by their household duties, that they had little opportunity to educate themselves. In fact, the concept of women's education was not even thought of. The right to education is a birthright of an individual, regardless of sex, caste, creed, religion or nationality. This right is the foundation of self-development. Yet it was denied to women all over the world. For centuries, it was decided by men that women's place was in their homes and intellectual activities were beyond their grasp. In the different stages of civilisation, there were always some women of unmatched wisdom and courage who realised this fact and tried their wings, in spite of the adverse social conditions. But the majority of women were not aware of their due rights and women as a class were shut out of public life. No one thought of their right to learn and earn and be independent; their right to live according to their own ideas and concepts and the right to take their own decisions. It was so pathetic that women did not even know what was denied to them. Bound by the social and religious customs, they meekly submitted to the rules laid down by men, without sensing the injustice behind them. It was so hard for women to realise that the intellectual field was not the monopoly of men and in spite of the physical differences, they were human beings, having the capacity to think, ponder, analyse, decide and act accordingly. It was impressed upon them that to cross the boundaries of their homes, in pursuit of their own achievements, was a hateful, unwomanly act. This was nothing but a clever way of keeping them confined to their houses.

There was little difference between a slave and a woman because basic human rights were denied to both. Even in a free country like America, individual freedom was valued but women were in bondage. Abolition of slavery was fought for but women had to struggle for their political, economic, educational and cultural rights. They had no right to suffrage, no right either to property or higher education. Even the right to participate in social gatherings and express their views was denied to them. During the second half of the 18th century, it was accepted in America that girls might get elementary education, so that they won't remain illiterate. Hence, girls' schools had become a part of American life. Women availed themselves of this opportunity and then the passion to gain more knowledge and to develop their careers was awakened. But most of the men being unable to appreciate ambitious women, reacted sharply and opposed them. No wonder, higher education of women became a controversial issue. It was argued that schooling was more than sufficient since women did not have well-developed brains to grasp higher education. It had become fashionable to ridicule women's yearning to attain some goals in life. It would be evident from some of the titles suggested by men to confer upon women.

"M.P.M. = Mistress of Pudding Making.

M.S.B. = Mistress of the Scrubbing Brush.

R.W. = Respectable Wife

M.W.R.F. = Mother of a Well-regulated Family."[2].

These titles bear witness to the popular belief that a home could be the only field of women's activities. Their well-defined role was that of an ideal house-keeper, a loving mother or an obedient wife. Though men were staunch supporters of this theory, this was not going to be continued forever. Ultimately, education opened women's minds to sense the injustice done to them for centuries. It had dawned upon them that they were not treated like human beings, and were the victims of gender prejudice. Women took a stand that men could not claim the right to speak and decide on behalf of them. As they were capable of taking their own decisions, they might have their own choice. In the 19th century, the 'angry young women' united to fight against male dominance. Some men who were sympathetic to the cause, made them aware of their due rights and also played an important role in the upliftment of women.

The awakened women thought on the same lines as Abigail Adams. In 1792, Mary Wollstonecraft of London published her thought-provoking book, *Vindication of the Rights of Women*. She argued that the educational system of her time deliberately trained women to be frivolous and incapable. In 1826, a brilliant young Scotchwoman, Frances Wright came to America cherishing a high hope about the land of freedom, but was surprised to learn that women there had no right to vote; no place in politics. For several years, she wrote articles and lectured about the enfranchisement of women and tried her best to form public opinion. She was the first person to bring this issue to the forefront so forcefully. In 1836, a Polish woman Ernestine Rose, the daughter of a rabbi, migrated to America and pursued the same issue. She was banished from Poland for her progressive views and ideas. Considering it her mission to create a place for women in politics, she rigorously began to lecture on the role of women in politics and in the government and very soon attracted big crowds. She also demanded the repeal of unjust laws under which women were suffering. In the winter of 1836-37, she circulated a petition in Albany, New York for the law to enable a married woman to hold property. She could convince only five women to sign the petition. Yet she carried it to the legislature. In 1848, that is more than a decade after, the amendment was accepted and it was a significant triumph of the movement. By 1840, Ernestine Rose was associated with the famous feminist leader Lucretia Mott. Another courageous woman, Margaret Fuller of Boston advocated through her writings and lectures political rights for women. She also published a book *The Great Lawsuit: Man vs Woman*. In 1847, Lucy Stone, a graduate of Oberlin College began fighting for women's rights with tremendous zeal.

From the very beginning, women had taken an active interest in the 'Anti-Slavery Movement'. In 1837, the first 'Women's Anti-Slavery Convention' was organised by feminist leaders in New York. Women like Lucretia Mott, Lydia Maria Child, Maria Weston Chapman who were dashingly expressing their views on the banishment of slavery, had become prominent figures in public meetings and debates. And yet, society was divided on the basic question of women's right to self-expression, the right to participate in social meetings. In June 1840, the 'World's Anti-Slavery Convention' was held in London. Eight women delegates from America, including Lucretia Mott and Wendell Phillips went there. They wanted to establish women's right to participate publicly in such movements; but the organisers refused to recognise the women delegates and they were banished from the Convention. Thus, the rights of women were systematically suppressed even by those who talked about the human rights of slaves. Lucretia Mott remained in London for several months, propounding the issue of women's rights before like-minded people. She befriended men and women among the Quakers, who had always recognised the equality between men and women. In England, the thought of starting a movement for giving voice to women's problems took roots in Lucretia Mott's mind.

Yet it was not easy to unite women for giving a fight for their rights. In fact, many women who believed in their conventional role of a homemaker, disagreed with these 'Manly Women.' It took another eight years for Lucretia Mott to commence the feminist movement. In 1848, Lucretia Mott, Elizabeth Caddy Stanton, Mary Ann McClintock and Martha Wright came forward to issue a call for the first 'Women's Rights Convention.' James Mott, the husband of Lucretia Mott presided over the Convention. His stand sent a clear message in society that there were some men who regarded women as human beings and actively supported their freedom fight. The convention was held at Seneca Falls on 19th and 20th July, 1848 in the 'Wesleyan Methodist Church' which created a great deal of sensation. Newspapers gave wide publicity to this unique convention. It drew such a large crowd that there was not a single empty seat in the hall. Elizabeth Caddy Stanton carefully drafted the 'Declaration of Sentiments, Grievances and Resolutions' modelled after the Declaration of Independence. They boldly proclaimed in their now-famous declaration, "We hold these truths to be self-evident: that all men and women are created equal." The document laid out the injustices done to women like their inability to own property, their subjugation to men and their lack of political access. The declaration and the resolutions were discussed and adopted. This vocal agitation motivated wise persons to re-examine the relationship between men and women and the role of women in society.

This convention was an important landmark in the history of the Feminist movement. But the reactions of the general public to the first organised attempt of women to demand their due rights were acrid and bitter. They were denounced for their so-called rude behaviour and frivolity. Elizabeth Caddy Stanton and Susan B. Anthony, a Massachusetts teacher met in 1850 and thereafter worked hand in hand as feminist activists. They raised their voice against the denial of economic freedom to women and encouraged women to take up jobs and work outside their homes. In 1869, they founded the National Women Suffrage Association with the express goal of acquiring the right to vote.

The feminist movement had two-fold significance. On the one hand, women challenged the supremacy of men and demanded equality with them. On the other hand, the movement signified that women's search for identity had begun. They had realised that they had boundless powers within, unused so far. Eager to cast aside her unrealistic, man-made images such as a goddess or an angel, the woman longed to find out who she was. She wished to discover her unidentified capacities and wished to live like a free human being. Over the period of time, various groups of women became so active that they organised protests, rallies and meetings, aiming to bring the cause of women's rights to public notice. In April 1848, women were legally allowed to hold property, for which Ernestine Rose had fought. After that, women demanded equal guardianship over their children, removal of the unjust divorce laws and women suffrage. Their strategy was to accept whatever rights they could gain and demand those which they did not possess. In 1850, the constitution of Indiana was revised and under the leadership of Robert Dale Owen, the laws for women were liberalised beyond any, existing then. Thus, women's efforts were crowned with success.

In the history of women's liberation, Medical education of women met with the most stubborn resistance and the mere idea of a woman doctor drove people to frenzy although there was a dire need for women doctors. Women were prohibited from entering Medical institutions and the mutinous women were despised as if they were enemies of the people. Since it was thought that a woman alone should shoulder the responsibility of a happy home, the majority of people were worried about the effect of women's higher education on family life; they didn't care for the injustice done to women due to this attitude. People opposed women doctors for various reasons. Firstly, religious leaders thought that the movement was anti-religion and anti-church. Taking support of the Biblical sayings, women were commanded to remain in the limited sphere that was supposed to be fixed for them by the divine decree.

Religion had such an impact on the masses that people got carried away by the views of religious leaders. All types of conservatives were against women doctors because a change in any walk of life was undesirable to them. Hence, they tried to crush women into submission. Old beliefs were so deep-seated even in the minds of women that it was hard for them to grasp the wider significance of the feminist movement and the meaning of the newfound concepts and values. The supporters of women doctors had to therefore protest by voice, pen and petition.

The biggest obstacle in the path of Medical women were the male doctors who looked at women's entry into the Medical field as an encroachment. Men did not mind women becoming nurses, since the subordinate position of a nurse was in accordance with the traditional man-woman relationship. But accepting women as doctors was to regard them as intellectual and professional equals. It further implied competition and competition meant an intellectual challenge. They were not prepared to accept a challenge from women. It might have proved at least some women to be superior to male doctors and this was just unacceptable to them. No wonder, women's entry into the Medical field was treated as a misdemeanour. Naturally, women had to organise their own institutes to exercise their right to Medical education. The 'Woman's Medical College of Pennsylvania' founded in 1850 was the first of its kind in history. It was the luscious fruit of the new thought, new consciousness born in the minds of women.

Though women of the 19th century used the word 'women's rights', what they really demanded were the individual rights, the birth rights possessed by each human being. A right is a valuable moral principle that defines and sanctions a person's freedom of action in a social context. Individual rights are corollaries to a person's right to his own life which is the fundamental right. Just because women were deprived of them they were labelled as 'women's rights.' Otherwise, there are no special rights either to men or to women. Individual rights are possessed by a person regardless of his gender. Secondly, though the dominant trend was anti-women, all men did not oppose women. The battle was fought not against 'all men' but against the particular dominant attitude of men and the injustice caused by it. There were many active supporters of the feminist movement among men. Some of them were also instrumental in making women aware of their birthrights. The most significant point underlined by the women's struggle is that men and women should treat each other as human beings and should respect the individual rights of each other because both of them are the molecules of the human race.

References:

1. *The Encyclopaedia Americana* – volume 29 / 1985 / p.p. 449-450.
2. Ibid – volume 9 / 1985 / p.p. 694.

14

Doctors' Dilemma

In the 19th century, 'woman doctor' was a controversial concept all over the world. Struggling hard against social prejudices, mistrust, self-doubt and sex barriers, women doctors created a place for themselves in the mainstream Medical profession. In the first half of that century, a woman doctor was an unthinkable idea, but by the end of the century, thousands of women were serving as physicians all over the world. Though women were forbidden in Medical Colleges, they persistently knocked at the doors to get entry. America and England had become the biggest battlefields where organised groups of like-minded men and women fought against the injustice. It was not at all an easy battle and it went on for years. These pioneers made a deep impression upon the civilisation and their struggle went down in the social history of the world.

Over the period of time, some universities opened their doors to women candidates who wished to study Medicine. In 1854, the University of Zurich showed a willingness to confer Medical degrees upon women. The same curriculum, opportunity and degree was offered to students regardless of sex. Russian women took advantage of this golden opportunity, since they were barred from learning Medicine in Russia. Very soon, the continuous flow of Russian women became noticeable in the University of Zurich and in effect, Russia lost her valuable life-savers. In 1868, the Scientific Society of Russia petitioned the Czar to allow women to study Medicine. Four years later, the request was granted and the Medical Faculty for women was founded at St. Pittsburgh. In the next 10 years, 600 women doctors graduated from the institute, but it was suddenly closed down in August 1882. It could reopen only after 15 years, in 1897. In short, the policy of the Russian Government regarding Medical women depended upon the whims and fancies of the authorities. In 1868, France began to admit women into Medical Colleges whereas England did the same in

1877 and Belgium in 1883, the German universities being slowest in removing the sex barriers.

It would be interesting to note some of the arguments advanced by the opponents to prove that women were totally unfit for the profession.

1. The basic requirement of a doctor was to be a man, since the Medical profession called for a physically strong person. This was not a territory of the weaker sex who had to undergo menstruation, pregnancy and childbirth.

2. By nature, women were dull, coward and unintelligent.

3. Women were bashful, gentle, hyper-sensitive and tender creatures. It would not be possible for them to pass through the ordeal of surgery. They would not stand the discussion and dissection of naked human bodies and the sight of blood would frighten them.

4. The whole purpose of women's existence was to bring forth children for keeping the continuity of the human race. It was argued that the hard study might destroy their reproductive energy. In 1870, a British doctor wrote in *The Lancet*, a well-known Medical journal. "As a body they are sexuality; constitutionally and mentally unfitted for the hard work and incessant toil and for the heavy responsibilities of general and surgical practice."[1]

All these notions were based on a series of wrong assumptions, deeply rooted in the male ego and some of the feminine qualities were used against women like weapons. But the spirited iconoclastic women attacked and destroyed the false, man-made notions about them and proved their ability through their original work in the Medical field.

When there were hardly any women's Medical institutes and the doors of the existing colleges were closed on them, it was extremely difficult to get access to Medical knowledge. In such times, women candidates appealed to the authorities by promising that they would not crave for the degree if they were offered a chance to learn, since they were more interested in gaining knowledge than getting a degree. Mary Putnam graduated from the Woman's Medical College of Pennsylvania in March 1864. Dr. Ann Preston was extremely impressed by Mary's prior knowledge of Medicine. So, she allowed her to appear for the final examination at the end of the first year itself. In September 1866, Mary Putnam sailed to France with the determination to somehow get an entry into the well-known University of Paris. In the beginning, she requested two doctors to allow her to join a group of students who followed them on their hospital rounds. With her tremendous convincing power, she could even gain admission to some lectures in the 'Ecole de Pratique' and the library. But her application for the enrollment as a student was rejected. Not being a person to take defeat, she intensified her efforts, feeling sure that if the main entrance was locked, backdoor entry could be possible. She requested the authorities of the college to permit her to take just one course, without any credit. At last, the permission was granted. After attending the first lecture in the Medical school, the triumphant young girl wrote a touching letter to her mother, on 25th January 1868, "Day before yesterday, for the first time since its foundation, several centuries ago, a petticoat might be seen in the august amphitheatre of the Ecole de Medicine. That petticoat enrobed the form of your most obedient servant and dutiful daughter."[2]

Very soon she won the hearts of her teachers by her sincerity, studiousness and unflinching devotion. The Dean and a few other professors supported her request to take the examination and so it was granted. Fully equipped with her study, she appeared for the examination and passed with flying colours. She wrote her thesis on the biochemical theme, 'On Neutral Fats and Acids' and won the 'Paris Faculty Medal.' She returned to America and began her work with zest. Being a researcher at heart, she never stopped studying various Medical problems of women. In 1876, she wrote an essay on 'The Question of Rest for Women during Menstruation' and challenged the conservative view. Menstruation was looked upon as a mysterious happening within a woman's body that drained her energies. Her essay was based on original research, scientific knowledge, case studies and sophisticated statistical analysis. It won the esteemed 'Boylston Prize' of the Harvard Medical School. The achievements of intelligent women doctors were thus conspicuous despite the obstacles. In 1872, Dr. Mary Putnam Jacobi founded an association for the advancement of the Medical education of women which served as a connecting link among women doctors throughout America.

Harriot Hunt is called the 'Mother of American women doctors' because their struggle began with her. Harriot was a school teacher. Out of curiosity, she used to read Medical books and discuss various Medical issues with friendly doctors. Due to this, she started regarding the human body with reverence. "My mind was greedy of knowledge. The more I investigated; the more was I delighted."[3] Soon her hobby turned into a passion. She had become sufficiently knowledgeable to cure the cases of Dyspepsia, constipation, liver complaints and a few other diseases. While working among the women around, she observed that instead of seeking proper Medical advice, most of the time women abused their bodies through ignorance, negligence, or laziness. She felt that if she could get proper Medical training, she would be able to change this attitude and help them in the time of their illness. In 1838, Dr. George Combe arranged in Boston a course of lectures on 'Medicine for women.' At once Harriot grabbed this chance to gain scientific knowledge. Even this small opportunity to explore made Harriot extremely happy. "To me they were revelation – bread for a hungry spirit and water for a thirsty soul. He gave us the golden clue of connection between cause and effect and end."[4]

Fired with the idea of becoming a doctor, now she thought of entering into a Medical College for systematic study. In 1847, she wrote a letter to Harvard University, requesting them to give her admission to the Medical course, but it was outright rejected. Without getting discouraged, she urged the authorities again and again to accept her as a Medical student, but could not succeed. In 1850, when she was 45, once again she tried to convince them with good grace, pouring her purely scientific mind into her words. "In opening your doors to a woman, it is mind that will enter the lecture room, it is intelligence that will ask for food; sex will never be felt where science leads, for the atmosphere of thought will be around every lecture."[5] This simple but thoughtful letter was a superb answer to the blatant sexism. It mirrors Harriot's healthy attitude towards the process of learning, her optimism and mental strength. In spite of the repeated rejection of her application, she never felt like abandoning her hope. When the so-called intellectual vanguards of science in Harvard University were haughtily rejecting Harriot just because she was a woman, a middle-aged woman like her, who had never been to a college, was trying to make them understand the futility of gender discrimination in the field of knowledge.

After this letter, with some reluctance still lurking in their words, the authorities informed Harriot that they would accept her as a student with no guarantee of a Medical degree. Harriot was ready to compromise; but even this decision immediately fomented revolt in the students' campus. They looked upon the event as a flagrant breach of rules. Passing a resolution against the decision, the students' organisation threatened the authorities that they would all shift to the Yale University if a woman was accepted as a student. "We object to having the company of any female forced upon us, who is disposed to unsex herself and to sacrifice her modesty by appearing with men in the Medical lecture room." [6] Their language reflected their hatred for women whom they looked down upon as inferior beings. In contrast, Harriot's matured personality and scientific mind shine through her letters. Obviously, the students' display of wrath made the University retract its step which had been taken diffidently, without any conviction.

Elizabeth Blackwell, the 19th century pioneer woman doctor in the world, was strikingly fortunate in getting admission to a Medical College. As a young girl, she dreaded the sight of a diseased person and the gloomy atmosphere around that person. Generally, she avoided paying visits to unwell friends, but a certain visit changed her attitude completely. Once Mary Donaldson, a close family friend, was dying of cancer and the visit was unavoidable. Hence, Elizabeth went to her house. She had no idea that it was going to be a turning point in her life. In the midst of their friendly chit-chat, Mary, the girl in the shadows of death, disclosed her innermost thought to Elizabeth which had been troubling her for a long time. She said that to die a gradual death was a terrible thing, but more than that, it was shameful to get examined by a man. The physical pain was bearable compared to the unbearable burden of shame. She would have suffered less, if there was a woman doctor at her side. Mary felt for certain that many women might be feeling like her. Mary's sad eyes rested on her youthful friend and an idea crossed her mind. Anxiously pressing Elizabeth's strong hands, she urged, "Liza, women need doctors of their own sex. You are young and clever. Why don't you venture to become a doctor?" Struck dumb by the shocking idea, Elizabeth did not know how to react, but Mary insisted again, "Please Liza, promise me that you would at least give a thought to it." The pathetic look of her dying friend made her whisper a faint promise.

Yet she could not get over the shock for days and many a time, the incident returned to her mind. In all earnestness, she desired a fascinating goal but she could not digest the idea of becoming a doctor. She pondered over the issue, asking herself again and again how would she keep her promise when women did not take to that profession. One day she approached her mother and indirectly sought her advice by asking who did the mother prefer when she was in labour, a male doctor or a midwife? Her mother truthfully confessed that it was very embarrassing to have a man around at the time of delivery and that any woman would prefer a woman's help. So no further proof was necessary. She was convinced about the crying need for women doctors. The issue was discussed with the family members, who wisely decided to back up Elizabeth's unique ambition.

In 1846, her medical study commenced in the large house of Dr. Samuel Dickson, a prominent physician of the town of Charleston. His encouragement sharply contrasted with the hostility of many other doctors whom Elizabeth had approached before. His large library was a real boon for Elizabeth. The history of Medicine revealed to her the enchanting stories of women doctors of ancient times. Anodise, an Athenian midwife, attended lectures on Gynaecology disguising herself as a man. She was brought to trial for breaking the law, but her grateful patients, the Athenian women, successfully defended the benefactor. Aspasia was such an authority on Obstetrics and Gynaecology that she was quoted in Greek and Latin Medical works. Even in the 18th century, some women were attracted to the Medical profession. But to Elizabeth's great surprise, she came across her own name, in the history of Medicine – 'Elizabeth Blackwell.' She could not believe this coincidence and was filled with wonder. The other Elizabeth had lived just a century ago. The good omen assured her that she was going to be a doctor.

In May 1846, she went to Philadelphia, which was then a major centre of Medical education. Here she was guided by Dr. Warrington and Dr. Elder. According to their advice, she wrote letters to different well-known Medical Colleges but ultimately it was an anonymous Medical college in Geneva, N.Y that made history by accepting her as a student, without any condition or denial of the degree. The college was notorious for the uncivilized behaviour of students, most of whom had entered the college because they had nothing else to do.

When Dr. Lee, the Dean of the college, received the letter from his friend Dr. Warrington regarding Elizabeth, he did not know how to react to it. But he decided to put the letter to the vote of students and let them decide. Immediately he went into the classroom where Dr. Webster was lecturing in the midst of a commotion. Raising his voice the Dean compelled the attention of the students and informed about the strange letter that he had received that day. "Dr. Warrington requested the faculty to admit as a student; a lady who was studying Medicine in his office. She had been refused admission by several colleges, but as the Geneva School was in the country he thought it more likely to be free from the prevailing prejudices against a women student….He heartily recommended the applicant as a good student, eminently respectable, and honestly sincere in her desire to become a doctor"[7]. He further informed them that the faculty had decided to leave the matter in the hands of students. If a single student was against her admission, they would refuse the permission to the young girl.

For the first few minutes, there was dead silence in the classroom, since the students could not understand the situation. But the moment they recovered, the room was filled with noise, laughter and whistles. They just could not believe that the future of a woman candidate rested in their hands. On the same evening, the student-leaders called a meeting. After eloquent speeches and heated arguments, ultimately, they all decided in favour of Elizabeth, with the guarantee of their good conduct. On 20th October 1847, a statement was prepared and sent to the faculty. "Resolved that one of the radical principles of a Republican government is the universal education to both sexes, that to every branch of scientific education, the door should be open equally to all; that the application of Elizabeth Blackwell to become a member of our class meets our entire approbation; and in extending our unanimous invitation we pledge ourselves that no conduct of ours shall cause her to regret her attendance at this institution."[8] Thus, the solemn promise became instrumental in throwing doors of the Geneva Medical College open to the first woman candidate of the 19th century.

When Elizabeth went to her college from the nearby Waller's boarding house, men and women crowded the doors and windows of their houses to have a peep at the 'outrageous woman'. Even small children dared to poke fun at her. Though it was a nuisance to her, she learned to overlook it. Fascinated by the valuable Surgical, Pathological, Anatomical and Obstetrical collections in the institute, she preferred to work there even after college hours. Lost in her work, she hardly realized that she was alone in the deserted college, and the evening had turned into midnight.

Only once a certain incident annoyed her. Dr. Webster, who had then commenced a session on the reproductive organs, grew conscious of her presence. He found it a trying experience to explain the subject with illustrations and a detailed description in the presence of a woman. So he wrote a small note to Elizabeth, requesting her to remain absent during the next few sessions. Feeling sad by this stand of her professor, she wrote a letter to him, stating that regardless of her sex, she was a Medical student and expected to be treated as nobody else but a student. She further remarked that the study of Anatomy was a serious matter and that human birth was so sacred that it could evoke nothing but reverence in her mind. Dr. Webster was deeply impressed by this profound stand and the fervent appeal. He submitted the matter to the students' consideration, as was asked by Elizabeth and the students once again decided in favour of her. After this, no such problem was ever faced by her.

On 23rd January 1849, the degree of M.D. was ceremoniously conferred upon Elizabeth. In remembrance of this great historical event, the New York State raised a pillar at the sight of the Geneva Medical College in 1932 upon which the following words were carved, "Site of the Geneva Medical College. Elizabeth Blackwell received here in 1849 the first degree of M.D. ever conferred upon a woman." Elizabeth's pleasant experience was of course an exception. The same college later denied admission to Elizabeth's sister Emily. Compelled to depend upon the whims of the students, professors and deans, women were thus advancing with stops and starts, not knowing how long it would continue. After all, it was not the question of admitting one woman or the other, the basic issue being, whether or not society respected everyone's right to education, regardless of sex.

A thought began to take shape that if women were not allowed in Medical Colleges, why should they not have their own institutes? The first Woman's Medical College in the world was started in Philadelphia by resolute reformists who showed the courage to swim against the current. Dr. Joseph Longshore, Dr. C. W. Gleason, Dr. Nathaniel Moseley were the founders of the 'Woman's Medical College of Pennsylvania.' They organised preparatory classes for students two years prior to the actual opening, that is in 1848. Ann Preston who became the pillar of the institute in future, was a student of this first batch. A certain building on Arch Street was selected for the college and William Mullane, an affluent merchant came forward to shoulder the responsibility of paying the rent of the building. The college opened on 12th October 1850 and the glorious day marked the major victory of the women's movement. Vowing to provide the best Medical education to all, the founders had removed a huge obstacle from the path of women's advancement. The first and foremost responsibility of the college was to train women who could teach at the institute.

Forty zealous women enrolled their names in the first year of college. Out of them, 32 were potential candidates or listening matriculates whereas eight were expecting the degree. Ann Preston, Elis Susan, Hannah Longshore, Anjanette Hunt, Michel Francis, Anna Longshore, Martha Swain, Fobby Way – were the first graduates of the college. On 30th December 1851, the degree of M.D. was conferred upon those eight women in the Musical Fund Hall, in the presence of well-wishers and supporters of the movement as well as the parents and friends of the students. By sending their daughters to college despite public opposition, thoughtful parents had greatly helped the cause. Lucretia Mott, the eminent leader of the feminist movement graced the occasion with her presence and was deeply satisfied by the signal success of the pioneer women doctors. The event had raised her hope and expectations about the bright future of women. Explaining the historical importance of the event, Dr. Joseph Longshore made the Medical graduates aware of their responsibility and insisted that women will have to sustain themselves in spite of their opponents. He also advised them not to regard themselves as inferior because they were women. In his address, he said, "This day forms an eventful epoch in the history of the race. This day society assigns to women an exalted position"[9]. A few days before the graduation, agitated Medical students had threatened disruption in the ceremony. To avoid this, the police force was called upon to help and 50 policemen stood guard around the building at the time of the women's graduation. With the determination to frown down women's inadmissible adventure, the Pennsylvania State Medical Society passed in 1859 the following resolution: "Members of the regular profession cannot consistently, with sound medical ethics, consult or hold professional intercourse with the professors or the graduates of the female Medical College." [10]. This ban was imposed in the name of Medical ethics and was not lifted for the full 18 years. On the one hand, the policy of non-cooperation was adopted and women Medical students were banished from hospitals, libraries and laboratories. On the other hand, they were accused of having insufficient knowledge and experience. This reflected their double standards veiled under the name of Medical ethics. Thus, closing all roads, the opponents felt for certain that now the women's institute was doomed to fail. But accepting the challenge, the organisers expanded their area of activity by founding the Woman's Hospital which provided the students with the Medical experience as well as extended Medical help towards the diseased women. Ann Preston who had joined the college in 1855 as the Professor of Physiology, got so involved in the problems of the institute that its advancement became the mission of her life. She was a brave champion of the cause, ready to weather any crisis. In 1861, she obtained the Charter, necessary to open a hospital and in September of the same year, a spacious building on the North College Avenue was selected for the purpose.

In fact, those were the most difficult days as the whole nation was passing through the turmoil of the Civil War. Issues like the abolishment of slavery, industrialisation, economic growth were closer to people's hearts than women's rights. Mentally as well as physically, people were so involved in the war that affected their lives from the very roots that they could not centre their attention on anything else. Almost every house had become a camp of warriors and each house had its share of tears and tensions. Naturally, they were least bothered about the growth of the 'Woman's Medical College.' Due to the lack of funds and students, the institute was passing through a serious economic crisis. The expenses of running the college became unaffordable when in 1860-61, there remained a single student. Hence in 1861-62, the college was closed down for one year and was reopened in the winter of 1862. At the time of the national calamity, women doctors and nurses spontaneously came forward to undertake the responsibility of their posts. They treated the wounded soldiers with unflinching devotion and courage in the midst of misery and death. The opportunity of proving their ability had presented itself and they used it fully to let people know how women doctors could be of great help to the nation. Since their kind help was gratefully noted by people, the war proved to be a boon in disguise.

Even in this agitated period, Ann Preston continued with her work of raising funds for the college. In 1864, she found an enthusiastic and efficient assistant in the form of Rachel Bodley who soon became her right hand. In 1866, Ann Preston was promoted to the prestigious post of the Dean of the 'Woman's Medical College.' Not only did Ann teach Medical subjects to her students but she also nurtured their young minds with vigorous thoughts, for making them mentally strong. She also succeeded in giving her students a new outlook on life and their precious womanhood. "Yours is not the fancy of a moment, but a great sacred work...Women must subdue opposition by showing the world that it is unjust. No champion can vindicate their claim if they do not establish them for themselves."[11] In 1866, after becoming the Dean of her college, she wrote a letter to the Medical Society to lift the ban on Medical women which was not even replied to. But in 1867, she wrote another letter which was rebuked harshly giving her a sermon on the limitations of women and their duty to their families. Ann Preston then crossed swords with the authorities of the Medical Society saying, "As a responsible being... for eternity we have decided for ourselves that study and practice of Medicine are proper, womanly and adopted to our mental, moral and physical constitution."[12]

At last in 1869, Ann's firmness and earnest efforts were crowned with success. She had pursued the matter so efficiently that the Pennsylvania Hospital of Philadelphia opened its doors to the students of Woman's Medical College with many other institutes following its example. Due to the superb performance of the Medical women in the Civil War, the opposition to woman doctors gradually weakened. There was a marked change in the attitude of people because women doctors had proved their worth.

On 2nd January 1869, Medical women were invited to the Blockley Hospital to attend a lecture. Ann Preston went there with her little band of 30 students, feeling excited and happy. But when they reached the hospital, they were welcomed at the door by a large crowd of male students who were jeering, whistling and stamping their feet to exhibit their anger. When women left the premises after the lecture, they were actually stoned by the crowd with great gusto. The *Evening Bulletin* thus reported the event: "Ranging themselves in line, these gallant gentlemen assailed the young ladies...with insolent and offensive language and then followed them into the street, where the whole gang. . . joined in insulting them . . . missiles of paper, tinfoil, tobacco quid etc. were thrown upon the ladies while some of these men defiled the dresses of the ladies near them with tobacco-juice."[13] The victory of women was thus 'celebrated' by men. It becomes clear from this, how the moral support of someone like Ann Preston was essential and how difficult it was for women to study Medicine, keeping their heads cool.

Although England was governed by Queen Victoria, herself a woman, the question of women doctors was under a cloud and for years women had to wrestle with the establishment. The exceptional "Dr. James Barry" could receive the degree from the 'University of Edinburgh' in 1812, just because the woman disguised herself as a man. She spent her whole life as a man and always shielded her real identity with the name of Dr. James Barry; her own name was a guarded mystery. She was said to be an illegitimate daughter of Prince Regent and a well-known Scottish lady and was always provided with masculine advantages from her early childhood. Dr. James Barry could manage to enter the British Army and worked as a doctor in many quarters of the globe. She was a skilful surgeon and a dauntless officer whose bravery at the battle of Waterloo was particularly recorded. Her secret remained guarded for years, as she had some close friends in the British Army.

According to the Reform Act of 1858, no one else but the graduates of certain recognised institutes were allowed to practise Medicine in England and women were strictly prohibited from entering those institutes. The doctors holding the degrees of foreign universities were considered unauthorised practitioners, who could not get a permit to work. Thus, every care was taken to close the profession to Medical women.

There were only two exceptionally fortunate women who could obtain a licence to Medical practice. One of them was Elizabeth Blackwell, who went to England after her graduation since England was her motherland and she wished to establish herself there as a doctor. As she had started practising before the Reform Act, she could procure a licence. The other lucky woman was Elizabeth Garret who had taken inspiration from Dr. Blackwell. She privately learnt Medicine and moved heaven and earth to appear for the examination of the Society of Apothecaries. Only these two women were included in the Medical register.

Though with the help of the law, an opportunity to learn and practise Medicine was denied to women, the law had no power over their minds where the quenchless desire lurked in a subdued form. The history of women doctors' struggle tells us how, despite the adverse rules and regulations women explored every avenue for getting Medical knowledge. In 1865, Sophia Jex-Blake of England paid a visit to her American friend Dr. Lucy Sewall of Boston. The American women's movement for their rights and the good work of women doctors did not fail to influence Sophia. The visit to America expanded the limit of her vision and she returned to England inspired to fight for women's right to Medical education. The history of British women's struggle to enter the Medical field began with the same woman, Sophia Jex-Blake!

In May 1869, she wrote a letter to the 'University of Edinburgh' requesting the authorities to accept her as a Medical student. She personally met some of the professors and tried to convince them about the need for women doctors. But Robert Christenson, physician of Queen Victoria, threatened the authorities that if they allowed a woman to take the Medical course, the support of Her Highness to their institute would be taken away. Despite such a threat from an influential person, Sophia fearlessly continued to fight with the establishment. Her courage was appreciated by thousands of British women who spontaneously backed her by writing warm letters and showed that she was not alone. Josephine Butler wrote, "O England, what a wicked amount of conservatism of selfish customs have you to answer for . . . I dare say, to yourself your life must appear sometimes to be wasted, but it is not so! In every good cause there must be martyrs and pioneers who have had the hard task of opening the way for others to work."[14]

At this juncture, four congenial companions Edith Peachey, Isabel Thorne, Matilda Chaplin and Helen Evans joined forces with Sophia, and together they knocked at the doors of the University. They were ready to spend their jolly youthful days campaigning for the cause under the leadership of Sophia. From 1869 to 1877, the long struggle continued for full eight years, but ultimately, they succeeded in veering the public opinion and compelling the conservatives to change their attitude. In the beginning, those fearless five asked the University at least to arrange separate classes for women. Due to the pressure of the public opinion and the support of newspapers, the University yielded and allowed the women to appear for the matriculation examination which was a sort of entrance exam of the University. All five women achieved remarkable success and their names appeared in the list of top-ten, which was a flying start. The first victory added zest to the adventure and Sophia noted in her diary, "The deed of life was done! This morning 11.30 a.m. I, S.J. B. first of all women matriculated . . . Tonight for the first time five women are undergraduates! HURRAH."[15]

Gradually people in the University got divided on the issue of women's Medical education. Some of the doctors granted permission to women to attend their lectures. Encouraged by this, the women asked permission to work in the Royal Infirmary. When this news flared up on the campus, students who were instigated by the anti-women professors, rose in revolt. They were determined to wipe out this rising force of women, by fair means or foul. Some of the students showed their wrath at the five women by chasing them at the late hours, in order to scare them. But the women who were absolutely determined to proceed on their right path, did not bow to the threats. The following words of Edith Peachey could be quoted as the proof of their mental strength: "Each fresh insult is an additional incentive to finish the work begun. I began the study of Medicine merely from personal motives; now I am also impelled by the desire to remove women from the care of such young ruffians."[16]

The misbehaviour of students produced strong reactions from various strata. In April 1871, under the leadership of Lord Provost, the thoughtful citizens of Edinburgh formed the 'Committee for securing complete Medical education to women in Edinburgh.' Money flowed into their coffer from the generous well-wishers of the movement like Charles Darwin, Thomas Henry Huxley and Harriet Martineau. Nine thousand women in England presented a petition to the University against the ill-treatment given to the women candidates and demanded that the women should be allowed to study in peace. Sophia was invited to give a lecture in a public meeting of the Suffrage movement where she could win the minds of the large audience with her effective speech. But despite this public support in Edinburgh, she had a difficult path ahead.

Though the fearless five completed the Medical course successfully, they were not granted permission to appear for the final examination. When Sophia threatened legal action, their path was reluctantly cleared but then the degree was denied, which was the most cunning move since without a degree, no doctor could have recognition or a licence to practise. In this circumstance, the toil and moil of so many years might have become meaningless. Therefore, as the last hope, the Medical women candidates sought the help of law. On 27th July 1872, the verdict was pronounced which went in favour of the women and the court put its finger on the unworthy male jealousy. "It was their demand for degrees, and their announced intention to practise Medicine, that had aroused unworthy jealousy and occasional strife." [17] But in spite of the verdict, the authorities in the University who had made it a prestige issue of the matter, denied to confer the degree of M.D. upon women, seeking some loopholes in the law. The situation was graver than expected. Ultimately, the long struggle culminated in the foundation of a separate women's Medical institute. In the winter of 1874, the London School of Medicine for Women was started, which had its staunch supporters who collected a large fund for the institute.

When Sophia Jex-Blake had been to America, she could not agree upon the idea of separate institutes for women because she believed that women had to get the same privileges as men. But now after years of fierce combat, she had realised the need for such an institute. Yet women had to resolve one more important question: If women were prohibited in the recognised institutes in England, why should recognition not be given to foreign universities? Women now focussed their attention on fighting for this particular issue and as a result, at last the University of Geneva and Burn were recognised. In the winter of 1876, Sophia Jex-Blake and

Edith Peachy received their degrees from the University of Burn and in 1877 their names were included in the Medical register. Ultimately the question of Medical women was given voice in the Parliament. After heated arguments and stormy discussions, the debate was won in the House of Commons on the point that in the Medical Reform Act of 1858, the word 'PERSON' was used which included women too. In the 19th century, the principle of equal opportunity in curriculum and degree was candidly accepted only in this Medical Act of 1886. However, a wedge was driven between, by giving universities the choice of rejection of women candidates. In essence, the conservative British found it difficult to make way for women.

For years, British and American women doctors presented a bold front and removed the various obstacles from the path to their progress. Though the acute need for women doctors was seriously felt by people, their acceptance of the concept was slow and gradual. The placards in America like 'Doctors wanted: No woman need apply' spoke for themselves. Even Elizabeth Blackwell could not attract patients. In New York, she opened a dispensary in the winter of 1851. She took good rooms for her dispensary, but people had no faith in women doctors. So, they took their own time. Those few who visited her place behaved as if they were obliging her by accepting her Medical advice. Without a Medical companion or a fellow worker, she felt very lonely. The male doctors stood aloof and society was distrustful of women doctors. Her financial position was also a source of constant anxiety to her. In addition, ill-natured gossip was spread and insolent letters were sent to her. Even after two years, the situation was as grave as before. In 1853, in a letter to her sister she confessed that, with no support but a high purpose, it was hard to continue. Dr. Hannah Longshore, one of the first graduates of the Woman's Medical College of Pennsylvania, had a strange experience of the non-cooperation of druggists when she opened a dispensary in the heart of Philadelphia. A young lady doctor driving her horse carriage to carry out her mission was not at all a pleasing sight to people. Even the druggists thought it their moral duty to advise the 'rash woman'. When Hannah asked them to fill her prescriptions, they used to refuse her. A certain druggist once advised her to go back to her home and darn her husband's stockings instead of running around as a doctor.

Many times, these lone women doctors came together to extend friendly support to each other. For example, Maria Zak and Blackwell sisters (Elizabeth and Emily) united their forces for founding the 'New York Infirmary for Women and Children' which was opened on 1st May 1857, on 64, Bleeker Street. They had to walk a tight rope, shouldering most of the responsibilities. Once when a woman in the hospital died in childbirth, people swarmed around the hospital, threatening them with pickaxes and shovels, shouting that these doctors were killing women. But the neighbouring police came to their rescue and saved the situation.

The story of the first Ambulance doctor, Emily Dunning Barringer reveals how the pioneers had to face the suspicion of the public on one side and the jealousy of professionals on the other. In the spring of 1902, Seth Low, Mayor of New York, declared that women could appear for the competitive examination of 'Gouverneur Hospital,' on condition that no special concession would be given to them just because they were women. The same terms offered to men applied to women which meant two years' internship. One year in General Medicine, one year in Surgery and a year and a half of it on ambulance duty. This was a challenge to those who demanded equal opportunity for women. Emily Dunning decided to accept it and joined the hospital in January 1903. Unwilling to accept her, four interns there decided to teach a lesson to the woman who was trying to play a man. They planned the work schedule in such a way that it would have broken her neck. To frighten her they constantly talked about the danger involved in the ambulance duty, with the emphasis on the sinful dens and saloons of outrageous criminals where a doctor had to go. Just to drive her out, they assigned her some tasks which patients regarded immodest for a woman to do. But she was ready to accept any challenge.

On 30th January 1903, Dr. Emily Dunning's first ambulance call was announced. In that period, an ambulance was horse-driven and was divided into three major parts. At the back of a carriage, there used to be a small, ledge-like seat on which a doctor had to perch himself. The middle portion consisted of a closed wooden box-like structure for a patient and the front seat was for a driver. Emily thoughtfully prepared herself for the ambulance call. First of all, she sewed a special dress with multiple pockets wherein she kept ready all the necessary medicines and the first-aid things so that she might not forget anything in her hurry to leave. Dick Bateman, the ambulance driver, had taught her an easy way of mounting on the tiny back seat. Though the interns were unfriendly, the ambulance drivers proved to be her true friends and were always ready to give her a helping hand. They also drove her safely back and forth from the hospital, at any hour of the day. Her duty demanded visits to poor districts, slums and red-light zones in New York. Filled with amazement at the sight of a woman doctor in the ambulance, the inhabitants shouted their surprise and crudely disapproved the sight. But since she had taken it for granted, she was unaffected. Tom White was another good-hearted driver whose long experience had turned him into a diagnostician. Hence, his timely advice proved to be very valuable for the novice doctor. He was able to judge by the condition of a person whether he was a patient or a drunkard. All day long, he would whisper, 'Take him in, Doc' or 'He is all right, take him to the police station.'

Surprisingly the four interns were unaffected by Emily's sincerity, zeal or devotion to her work. They burdened her mercilessly with day and night ambulance calls, work in the accident ward and surgery duty. Even when Emily was sufficiently senior not to be on the first ambulance call, they kept her at it. But the devoted doctor never complained. On the contrary, she looked at it as a boon, as an opportunity to learn a lot in the school of experience. In January 1905, the period of her internship was over. The woman who worked silently and tirelessly for two years had won the hearts of patients, nurses, ambulance drivers, police, citizens and also the hospital authorities.

The evening after her departure from the Gouverneur Hospital, the delegation of people presented her with the testimonial, expressive of their gratitude and profound respect: "Dr. Dunning, for two years served the hospital and the people of New York in a manner that has won the admiration and esteem of her fellow-workers and all those with whom she has been brought in contact. Her wonderful skill, conscientious and untiring efforts, charm of manner, devotion to her patients, extreme kindness and consideration for all who laboured with her, have endeared her to all. **AS THE ONLY WOMAN AMBULANCE SURGEON IN THE WORLD,** she has won distinction that is world-wide and brought honour, not only upon herself but upon her sex, her profession, Gouverneur Hospital and the city of New York."[18]

This was the successful culmination of the long struggle given by the 19th century women doctors. This was how people of the 20th century saluted women's work. The women's movement had proved that like any other discrimination, such as caste, religion, race or nation, sex discrimination was meaningless in the field of knowledge and humanity. A person has to be judged by his qualities and values, with no other criteria being just and fair. It was very wise of Sophia Jex-Blake who wrote, "I never care to argue at all about the relative capabilities of men and women. I mean to try to do my own work up to the very best of my power and that is all that really concerns me."[19]

References:

1. *Woman Gains a Place in Medicine* – Edythe Lutzker/1969/ preface p.1
2. *Women in White – The Role as Doctor through the Ages* – Geoffrey Marks and William K. Beatty/1972/p.124
3. *Glances and Glimpses* – Harriot K. Hunt/1856/p.
4. Ibid p.142
5. *Doctors Wanted: No Women Need Apply – Sexual Barriers in the Medical Profession* (1835-1975) - Mary Roth Walsh/1977/p.31
6. *Women Doctors of the World* – Esther Pohl Lovejoy/1957/p.78
7. *Lone Woman – The story of Elizabeth Blackwell: The First Woman Doctor* – Dorothy Clarke Wilson. Hodder and Stoughton, London. 1970. p. 5,6
8. Ibid p.10
9. *Women Doctors of the World* - Esther Pohl Lovejoy/1957/p.24
10. Ibid, p.33
11. Ibid p.33
12. Ibid p.36

13. *The Evening Bulletin*- January 2 1869

14. *Women Gain a Place in Medicine* – Edythe Lutzker/1969/p.p.51,52

15. Ibid p.57

16. Ibid p.91

17. Ibid p.107

18. *Women in White – Their Rule as Doctors through the Ages* – Geoffrey Marks and William K. Betty/1972. 139

19. *Women Gain a Place in Medicine* – Edythe Lutzker/1969/p.144

15

In Aunt Theo's House

The ship 'City of Berlin', reached New York, on 4th June 1883. Now remained a short journey from New York to Roselle. Along with Benjamin and Theodosia Carpenter, Anandi went to a nearby railway station to take a train going to Roselle. Roselle was a small town and the Carpenters' house was not far away from the station. The house looked cosy with papered walls, large windows, carpeted floors, a frontal garden and a backyard. The rooms were soberly decorated with pretty little paintings, showpieces and vases; but the much-adored things were books. The house of a middle-class businessman like Benjamin Carpenter was like any other well-regulated American house. But on 4th June, it became the centre of attraction, since it was to receive an outlandish guest from India. Some relatives of the Carpenters had gathered to welcome Anandi and they were waiting in ecstasy for the arrival of the young Indian girl in a bizarre dress and strange ornaments, whose photographs they had seen.

Soon she arrived and stood right before their curious eyes. The little woman with a somewhat dark complexion and jet black, curly hair looked tired but happy. She was not wearing a divided saree as in the photographs which produced the effects of the Turkish trousers. But she had wrapped herself in a long, flowing, shawl-like material with some folds arranged neatly on her body. She talked with them in English as fluently as she wrote, as if English was her mother tongue. Now she was to stay with them for a few years to learn Medicine. Even in America, girls seldom learnt Medicine, but she had come from a faraway country with that signal purpose. After the hearty welcome, Aunt Theo took Anandi to her room so that she could relax. Now onwards, she was to live in this room. But instead of relaxing, Anandi started writing a quick letter to her husband who she knew, was restlessly waiting for the news of her safe arrival in Roselle.

While she was hurrying through the job, Eighmie, Helena and three other children came to her room one by one and greeted her with flowers.

Very soon, Anandi settled comfortably in Aunt Theo's house and found that like Aunt Theo, the other family members were also warm and friendly. Uncle Benjamin owned a small factory of ironworks and ceramics and though not affluent, he was well-off. Aunt Theo had given birth to seven children but five out of them had died early. Only Eighmie, the third daughter and Helena the youngest one had survived. Eighmie who was six years younger than Anandi, was then in high school while little Helena had just begun to attend her school. Their days were full of study, games, friends and merriment whereas evenings were spent with the parents. On Sundays, they went to the Church and visited friends in their Sunday best.

Little Helena could not have an idea then, that the memories of this Indian girl were to remain with her throughout her life and they were to influence the mind of her granddaughter Nancy as well. When Helena grew old, she would fondly take little Nancy in her lap and share those beautiful memories with her. Thus, memories of Anandi flowed in the next generation and they remained green in Nancy's mind. It was my privilege to meet the same granddaughter of Helena, Mrs. Nancy Cobb-Stone who shared those memories with me. I sensed that her mind was still imbued with a tender longing for Anandi, whom she had never seen but whose influence she had never escaped. While talking about Anandi and her grandmother Helena, she told me, "In June 1883, Helena's life changed forever. A young woman named Anandibai Joshi became a member of her family. This amazing girl changed the lives of all who knew her during her brief stay in U.S.A. and she changed my life too. Anandibai lived in my grandmother's heart all her life."

Eighmie and Helena were delighted to have an elder sister like Anandi. She was so unique, so different than anybody else whom they had met, that they were proud to have her with them. By the sweetness of her manners and loving nature, Anandi had endeared herself to everybody around her. When she moved around in her bright, colourful saris, Eighmie and Helena watched her curiously. The girls were

Anandi's ancestral house at Kalyan, in ruins

Photographs of Anandi with her signature in Marathi and English

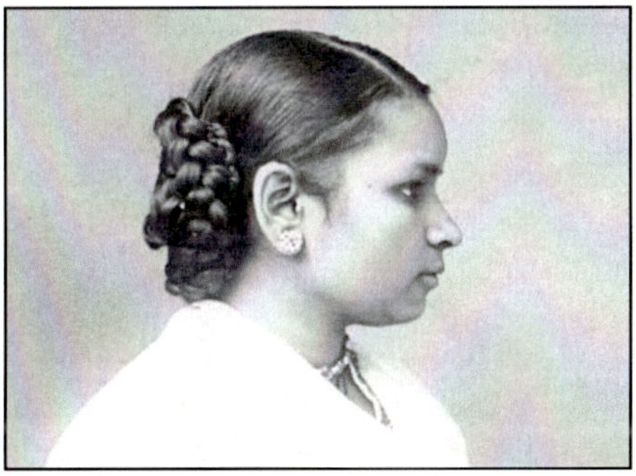

Anandibai Joshi

Maate wada- The house in Pune where Anandi was born and where she died.

Ganpat Joshi, Anandi's father

Rev. Royal Gold Wilder of the American Mission, Kolhapur, India

Theodosia and Benjamin Carpenter

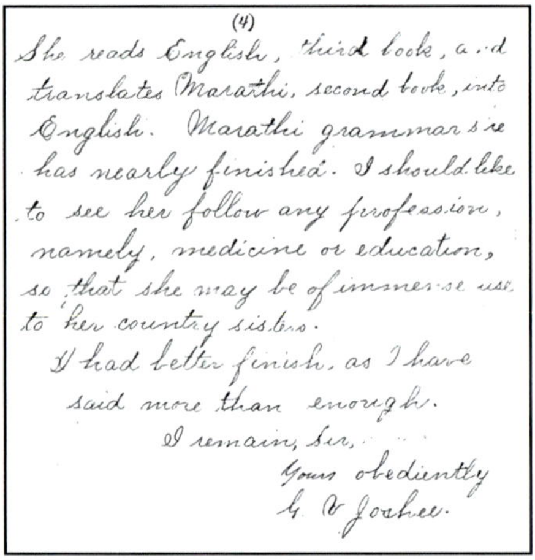

(4)

She reads English, third book, and translates Marathi, second book, into English. Marathi grammar she has nearly finished. I should like to see her follow any profession, namely, medicine or education, so that she may be of immense use to her country sisters.

I had better finish, as I have said more than enough.

I remain, Sir,

Yours obediently

G. V. Joshee.

Handwriting of Gopal Joshi

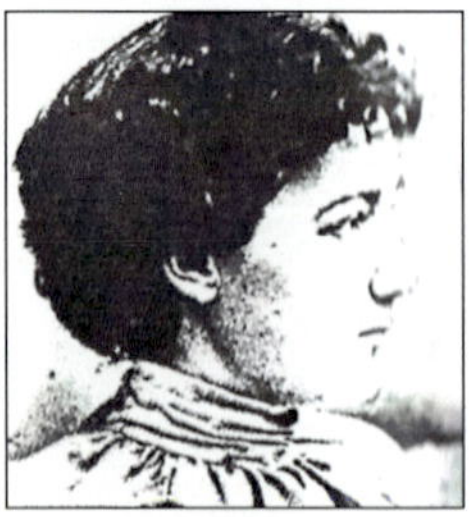

Eighmie Carpenter

Woman's Medical College of Pennsylvania was founded in this building

Dr. Ann Preston

Dean Rachel Bodley

Dr. Clara Marshal

Dr. Frances Emily White

Dr. Hannah Croasdale

Dr. Anna Broomal

Dr. James B. Walker

Dr. Marie Zakrzewska

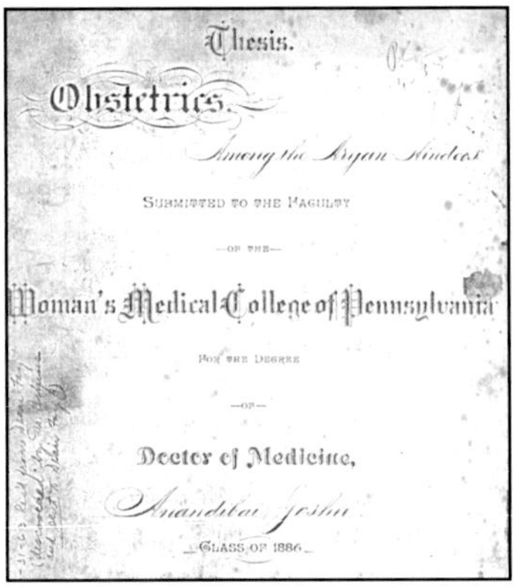

Thesis.

Obstetrics.

Among the Aryan Hindoos

SUBMITTED TO THE FACULTY

—OF THE—

Woman's Medical College of Pennsylvania

FOR THE DEGREE

—OF—

Doctor of Medicine,

Anandibai Joshee

CLASS OF 1886.

Front page of Anandi's thesis

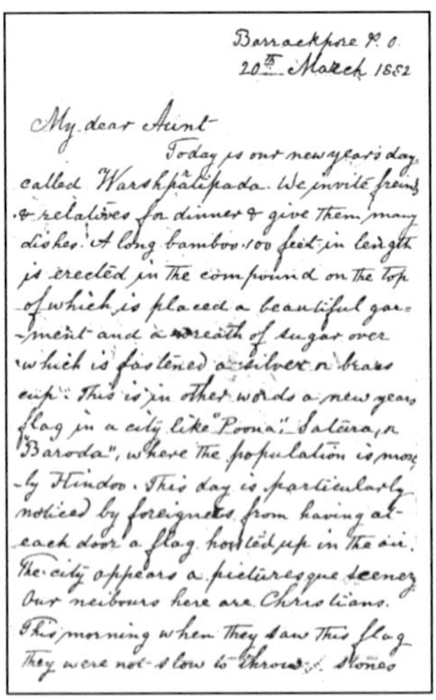

Barrackpore P. O.
20th March 1882

My dear Aunt

Today is our new year's day called Warshpatipada. We invite friends & relatives for dinner & give them many dishes. A long bamboo 100 feet in length is erected in the compound on the top of which is placed a beautiful garment and a wreath of sugar over which is fastened a silver or brass cup. This is in other words a new year flag in a city like "Poona", Satara, or Baroda", where the population is mostly Hindoo. This day is particularly noticed by foreigners from having at each door a flag hoisted up in the air. The city appears a picturesque scene. Our neibours here are Christians. This morning when they saw this flag they were not slow to throw stones

Handwriting of Anandibai Joshi

Dr. Anandibai Joshi at the time of her graduation

Dr. Maria Formed -
Anandi's Russian classmate

Pandita Ramabai

Dr. Anandibai Joshi

Anandi, Keiko Okami
and Sadat Islambooli

Jennet Millar, Head of the
Archieves of Medical College of
Pennsylvania (1991)

Anjali Kirtane in the archieves of Medical College of Pennsylvania

Nancy Cobb Stone and Anjali Kirtane

Anjali Kirtane, Nancy Cobb Stone and Nancy's husband Jimmy

Theodosia Carpenter's things preserved by Nancy Cobb Stone

Albert Edward Hospital, Kolhapur, where Anandi was to start her career

Gopal Joshi holding Anandi's dead body

Anandi's grave in the Rural Cemetery of Poughkeepsie. This is the original grave stone. Now the Indian community has replaced it by the new one.

charmed by the flutter of her dress, the crisp sound of her toe-rings and the tinkle of her green glass bangles. They could not understand why there was a sea-green tattooed mark on her forehead, between her eyes which looked like a tiny anchor? Anandi told them that it was inserted there soon after her birth, as per a custom in the Hindu religion. The mark could not be erased either by water or by oil. Eighmie and Helena who seemed to miss nothing, let out a volley of questions and Anandi enjoyed quenching their innocent curiosity. They wanted to know why Anandi never removed a particular necklace of black beads and a golden wire with a golden pendant at the centre. Every morning after bath, Anandi used to put on her forehead a fresh spot of the reddish paste called kumkum and she was never seen without it. The girls had noted that while putting on kumkum, her lips quivered, as if she was muttering something. What was the meaning of all those things? Anandi explained that it was a special string put on a woman's neck by her husband at the time of her marriage and a married woman was supposed to wear it all the time. The black necklace or the Mangalsutra, the green bangles and kumkum, all these things were signs of the married state of a woman and it was a custom to repeat the marriage vows silently while applying kumkum.

Anandi also loved talking about her country and her people. She described how Indian houses looked magnificent with large rooms, a separate idol-room, women's chambers, a common kitchen of the joint family and the swings, gardens and house-yards. Anandi sang for them melodious songs that Indian women used to sing while performing hard tasks like grinding, pounding or other rough household occupations. Even various games were accompanied by songs. She didn't hesitate to tell them about the dark side of woman's lives, their problems and struggles. Sometimes she would narrate Indian stories connected with Gods, festivals or various customs. Thus, she unfolded before her American friends the magical carpet of Oriental life.

Anandi's dressing was never complete without putting flowers in her hairdo. In America, she badly missed the scented Indian flowers like Jasmine, Champak and Rose. But she satisfied herself with whatever colourful flowers she could get. It was a normal thing for

Anandi to entangle and comb the confused mass of her long curly hair and wear it in beautiful braids, a shapely knot, circlet or a graceful crown. But Eighmie and Helena watched with wide eyes the skilful, swift movements of her hands. Knowing that her hairstyles had caught the fancy of her sisters, Anandi gladly arranged their hair in styles and decked them with flowers which made them stand out in their friend circles. Anandi had given Indian names to the girls. Thus, Helena was 'Tara' and Eighmie was 'Pramila.' But to Aunt Theo's surprise, Anandi never addressed her by her name. Once she asked Anandi the reason behind this and Anandi explained that in India, not to address elders by their names was a mark of respect. Aunt Theo appreciated this silent way of showing respect. In the company of Anandi, the Carpenters had acquired the habit of greeting each other with 'Namaskar' instead of Good Morning. Even her dolls, said Helena, preferred sarees to their American dresses. Sometimes Anandi would prepare Indian delicacies for her American family. In appreciation of all these things, Aunt Theo would say, "Instead of Anandi cultivating the American habits, we are becoming Hindus, day by day."

In Aunt Theo's house, Anandi relived in a better way, her lost childhood. Her real childhood was spent enduring the punishments of her hot-tempered mother, whims of her husband, premature sexual experience, pangs of early pregnancy and the death of her child. She never really had a chance to behave like a carefree child. Therefore, many of her childish wishes had remained unexpressed or unfulfilled. At the age of 18, she was blessed with the unalloyed joy of being a child. That first American summer was like a long holiday stretched between her strict life in India and her future years of hectic study. Hence, Anandi felt that it was the happiest summer of her life. In her American family, she was no more a grave, married woman. Like a young child she romped with her sisters and their friends; ran behind a ball, enjoyed jumping ropes and laughed merrily if she fell. Once the friends of the Carpenter girls had gathered to play jackstones. They taught this game to Anandi in all seriousness. Though she listened quietly, a smile of amusement lurked on her face because she was familiar with that game since her childhood. When it was her turn to play, the girls were amazed to see that she could play it with perfect ease. She could rhythmically swing her palms inside and outside and could catch all the jackstones at a time.

Anandi was not considered beautiful either in her own country or in America, but the beauty of her mind could be felt like a flash of light. Caroline Dall says, "Very few people thought Anandabai beautiful at first sight. Almost everyone found her complexion darker than had been expected and her form less graceful, but to everyone, sometimes during the years that followed, there came a sudden revelation, a day when the soul seemed to flash through the flesh, to burn in the dark eyes, to inform the every fingertip and sway every fold of her wonderful dress."[1]. One Sunday morning, Aunt Theo asked Anandi if she would go to the Church with them. Anandi went to her room to get ready. When she returned, Aunt Theo saw her descending the stairs and she could not believe her eyes. The pleasant young girl, lost in her thoughts simply charmed her. The beauty of Anandi was a revelation to Aunt Theo. She blamed her own eyes for not showing her this beauty before. But thereafter her watchful eyes noted many graceful things about Anandi. Particularly her shapely little hands attracted her attention. It seemed as if the hands had a separate personality of their own. They were brisk while eating her food without a spoon, quick while helping Aunt Theo, steady while writing and tender while playing with small children. They possessed both the humbleness of a traditional woman and the confidence of a modern woman. Anandi evoked profuse love in Aunt Theo's mind, when she saw Anandi swiftly moving in her house humming a song in an unknown language. The Carpenters called her 'well-spring of delight'.

Being a newcomer, Anandi was trying to understand the American way of life and her family was of great help to her. Some of the discussions with Uncle Ben made her aware of the new heroes of this enterprising land like industrialists, traders and businessmen. Uncle Ben toyed with the idea of calling Gopal to America as a businessman and asked her what kind of business he would like to do. A trivial incident helped her in answering the question. Somebody gave her a pack of Indian tea. It was so tasty that whoever drank it took to it. Some of them went to the bazaar and asked for that particular brand but could not get it. Anandi thought that in the beginning, Gopal could trade in tea and then studying the needs and demands, could decide upon other goods. The idea excited her that her husband could be an Indian export-import agent and through his efforts, business relations could be established between the two countries. She eagerly put pen to paper and communicated with Gopal.

Anandi not only observed the rosy side of the American society, but also the blue one. She was bewildered by the accounts of conjugal quarrels and the applications for divorces with which American newspapers were flooded. Her Indian mind could not understand how people could destroy their own family life and make their own children miserable. But of course, the family who had given her the shelter was a happy family, so Anandi was quite comfortable in their house. She received a fair share of love even from their relatives and friends. On 13th July 1883, they went for a picnic along with some friends to a huge park. The whole day, Anandi was wandering and playing there with the girls. A small tent was raised where they rested and ate their food. Anandi wished to have a photograph of the group in memory of the day. There were many professional photographers around, one of whom was called by Aunt Theo and the jolly band posed itself for a snap. Once Anandi visited a factory of jewels where she observed a few Eastern novelties in a small museum attached to the factory. Sensing her interest, the guide showed with zest some choicest things and requested her to visit the museum again.

Anandi had aroused so much curiosity in Roselle, that many visited the Carpenters' house just to have a look at the would-be Indian woman doctor. They were amazed to see that the strangely dressed young woman was adorned with curious ornaments and her hairdo was decorated with colourful flowers. They would always ask her questions about her dress, food manners and the Indian lifestyle. If the questions were posed earnestly, she would answer them elaborately. If not, answering them shortly she would pursue her own study of Sanskrit. In any case, her fluent English never failed to astonish them. If she was requested to sing a song, she would sing without being timid. Caroline Dall says, "Her perfect dignity was never sacrificed to the indulgence in curious questions or rude stares which were so freely bestowed upon herself, yet she seemed to miss nothing.

She was always gracefully courteous, but the words of approbation or admiration with which her efforts were greeted never seemed to touch her. Quick to note every fact presented to her, grateful for every bit of information, flattering words never seemed to be understood?"[2]. Thus, Anandi had left behind beautiful impressions of her matured personality.

The curiosity and the wonder about her were not limited only to Roselle. Even before she had put her feet on the American land, some of the press reporters had written letters to Rachel Bodley, the Dean of the 'Woman's Medical College of Pennsylvania' enquiring about Anandi's possible admission to their college. For example, the editor of *Evening Telegram* wrote, "The editor of *Evening Telegram* would feel much obliged for information, as to the probable date of arrival at the college, of Mrs, Anandibai Joshee who it is understood, will enter the Female Medical College of Philadelphia, on her arrival in this country."[3] In the letter of 19th June 1883, written to Alfred Jones, the chief of examination committee, Dean Bodley informed about the profuse interest of reporters regarding the advent of Anandi's arrival in America. "The doyen reporters of the city press, representing as many city papers, have been calling upon me and writing to me in regards to her, during the last month, so remarkable do they regard her coming to be."[4]. Anandi had received standing invitations from colleges in New York, Boston and Philadelphia. Aunt Theo had corresponded with many institutes and before taking any decision, wanted to make sure which one would offer the best educational facility at minimum expenses.

Since the 'Woman's Medical College of Pennsylvania' at Philadelphia had shown great interest in Anandi, Aunt Theo had written a letter to Dean Bodley and asked, "Believing that you and other eminent Philadelphians had already taken interest in her, before her arrival, I feel willing and glad to respect that interest by asking your advice at the outset and what preparations if any have been made for her and what her advantages will be in going to Philadelphia rather than New York?"[5]. Aunt Theo had indirectly asked about a scholarship and the same thought had arrested Dean Rachel Bodley's mind, who was eager to get this student. There was a strong reason behind this extravagant eagerness — the competition between colleges. In that period, many European women had migrated to America for Medical education, but an Asian woman was a rare species. A statement of Pearce Louise in her article 'A Century of Medical Education for Women' seems significant in this respect. "It was the acceptance of this high-caste Brahmin woman by the Woman's Medical College of Pennsylvania . . . served as the first step in gaining world attention for the institute and its efforts to provide Medical education for women."[6]. No wonder, in a letter to Alfred Jones, Dean Bodley insisted upon offering a scholarship to Anandi. She felt that by doing so, they would be able to put an end to the competition. "This will at once, distance all the competing institutions and make her sojourn with us."[7].

A scholarship was offered to the candidate whose age was between 20 and 30 years, but Anandi was only 18 years old. That means she had sought admission in the Medical College even before reaching the age that was considered as the minimum by the American standard. The makers of the college like Ann Preston, Robert Dodd, Hannah W. Richardson, Isaiah V, Williamson had offered donations for the scholarships and they were open to all, regardless of caste, religion or race. In all, there were 4 scholarships and each one was of $600 for the full course. Out of that, $240 were offered for the First and the Second Year each, and $120 for the last one. For getting a scholarship, a student had to first apply to the committee headed by Alfred Jones and the applications were subjected to careful scrutiny. In her application, Anandi stated the purpose behind the venture. "The voice of humanity is with me and I must not fail. My soul is moved to help the many who cannot help themselves ... I ask nothing for myself individually, but all that is necessary for my work."[8]. Dean Bodley had already recommended her name and her thoughtful words might have impressed the committee, since the scholarship was granted to her.

A small event would cast light on the genuine interest that Dean Bodley had felt in Anandi from the very beginning. In the town of Elizabeth lived Dr. Muaileg, a relative of Dean Bodley, who was acquainted with Theodosia Carpenter. It seems that with the help of this lady, Dean Bodley tried to attract Anandi's attention towards her institution. This becomes clear from the letter of Dr. Muaileg to Dean Bodley. "I am doing all in my power to prevent her going to New York to study although some keep holding out...tempting ideas...I feel there is such a grand field for useful work for your college in her country and which a number of your graduates have already toiled in, that you will be personally interested in this lady."[9]. The same Dr. Muaileg advised Anandi, "Be, rather than appear to be a true, earnest, well-educated, intelligent physician and surgeon and the future of the women of your country depends upon your course here."[10].

Anandi had started preparing for the matriculation exam which was mandatory for students as per the rule, for getting admission in the Medical College. Therefore, she devoted many hours of the day to her studies. The remaining time was spent reading newspapers, playing with the Carpenter girls and helping Aunt Theo in her work. Aunt Theo had a sewing machine and she had taught Anandi to sew and darn old dresses. Anandi had brought with her a sufficient stock of cut-pieces. Moreover, Gopal had sent some beautiful cut-pieces from Madras. Never before Anandi had worked on such a machine and was fascinated by its speed and efficiency. With great enthusiasm she sewed her garments, a fanciful quilt, six aprons and a few night dresses.

Before going to Philadelphia, Anandi treated her friends to a splendid Indian feast and it was the most memorable event of that summer. Innovatively using the available stuff, she cooked the food after the Brahminical Maharashtrian style. To give them the feel of an Indian party, she changed the American dining room into an Indian banquet hall. All furniture was removed out of the room including chairs and the dining table, so that she might get sufficient space to arrange the things in her way. In all, there were 18 people including Anandi, therefore 18 smooth planks took place of chairs, on which people were to sit, folding their legs like the Indians. Everything was done according to Anandi's instructions. Eighteen squares were drawn with ochre and the flat wooden seats were placed within them, near the walls. Anandi had brought with her 'Rangoli', a sort of smooth white powder used for drawing patterns and a perforated brass cylinder with a handle to emboss the patterns on ochre. She filled the cylinder with Rangoli and briskly rolling it on the crimson ribbon of ochre, produced a lace-like delicate design. Then she ornated each square, swiftly drawing thin-lined recess and some flower-like patterns with her hand and enhanced them by spreading kumkum in the empty spaces. This skill was then inherited by almost all Indian girls, who acquired proficiency by observing elderly ladies and it was a part of their daily routine to draw Rangoli in front of their houses.

The verdant green leaves of Buttonwood were stitched together to make plates. In India a long, silky Banana leaf is used for the same purpose, which was not available in Roselle. Using the Buttonwood leaves, she also improvised small bowls. The dinner consisted of rice, dal, ghee, pickle, curry, Indian jam, cereal, salad, cucumber, chapatti, sweetmeat balls, sweet rice, sweet and spicy varieties of stuffed food, a sweet dish of banana and milk, etc. The house was filled with unfamiliar but tempting aromas. When Anandi served the food, the green leaf-plates looked simply tempting. The Oriental charm of the banquet would have vanished if ladies had appeared in their American dresses. Therefore, Anandi emptied her wardrobe and distributed her sarees among her friends. She helped them in wearing the Indian dress and also decked their hands and necks with whatever ornaments she could procure. The ladies looked truly Hindu when kumkum was applied to their foreheads. Though eager to devour the food, the buoyant little group waited excitedly for Anandi to begin. They didn't dare to touch the colourful plate since spoons, forks or knives were not supplied. Anandi was to demonstrate how to eat like a true Indian without cutlery. So, they waited for her to take her seat. At last, finishing all the duties of a hostess, Anandi took her seat. A Sanskrit prayer was recited before they ate. Then she demonstrated how to eat using one's right hand fingers instead of a spoon. "Anandabai would pick up a morsel, bring it a few inches from her plate and then with a dexterous twist of her fingers toss it into her mouth. It seemed to fly magically to the right spot. 'To miss,' she said, 'would be vulgar."[11] She also told them that to miss a morsel was improper. The novice friends were as if on trial, who tried their best to follow Anandi's instructions and had great fun.

Dinner was over in a playful spirit and coffee was served at the end. After the dinner, they were invited in another room where a large mat was spread. Leaning against thick white cushions ladies sat on the mat while gentlemen stood in the room or squatted on the mat. The spectacular display of the colourful sarees looked like a rainbow. Beaming with joy, Anandi distributed tiny bouquets of flowers among her guests, then pressed a trace of rose perfume from an Attardani or phial on everybody's wrist and sprinkled rose water from a long-necked silver vessel called 'Gulabdani.' Feeling satisfied that everything was done perfectly and the demonstration was complete, she sat down among her friends. Some of the guests knew that it was customary to recite songs at the end of an Indian feast. Therefore, they urged Anandi to sing and with her melodious recitation, the feast drew to a close. The guests returned to their homes cherishing the imprints of beauty, artistic sense, deliciousness and decorum.

Before going to Philadelphia, Aunt Theo asked Anandi to fill up a sort of question-album, then popular in America; in which questions regarding personal likings, hobbies, views, etc. were asked. The title of the album was, 'What is your favourite?' On 3rd September 1883, Anandi filled the album as requested by her aunt. This is in a way Anandi's self-portrait or a mental graph.

What is your favourite?

1) Colour – White.

2) Flower – The Rose.

3) Tree – The Mango.

4) Object in nature – Mountains.

5) Hour – Sunrise and Sunset.

6) Season – Spring.

7) Perfume – Jasmine.

8) Gem – Diamond.

9) Style of beauty – Perfection of form and manner.

10) Names – Male and Female – Rama, Tara, Annie, Gopal, Vishnu, Krishna.

11) Painters – I love all.

12) Musician – Those who play on the violin and lyre.

13) Piece of architecture – The Taj Mahal.

14) Poet - Pope, Manu and Kalidas.

15) Poetess – [F1]Muktabai and Janabai.

16) Prose Author – Goldsmith, Macaulay, Addison, [F2]Shastri Chiploonkar.

17) Character in History – Richard Coeur de Lion.

18) Book to take up for an hour – The Bhagvad Gita.

19) What book, not a Bible, would you part with last? – *The History of the World.*

20) What epoch would you prefer to live in – The Present.

21) Where would you prefer to live? – In Roselle now, hereafter in Heaven.

22) What is your favourite amusement? – Reading.

23) What is your favourite occupation? – Whatever is necessary to the common comfort.

24) What is your favourite trait of character? – Sincerity.

25) What trait do you most detest? – Dishonesty and infidelity.

26) If not yourself, whom would you like to be? – No one.

27) What is your idea of happiness? – Faith in God.

28) What is your idea of misery? – To follow one's own will.

29) What is your bête noir? – Slavery and dependence.

30) What is your idea of pleasure? – To be rewarded for what I do.

F1 Muktabai and Janabai – Two Marathi saint poetesses.

F2 Shastri Chiploonkar – A well-known Marathi writer.

31) What is your distinguishing character – I have not yet found.

32) That of your husband? – Benevolence.

33) What is the sublime passion? – Love.

34) What are the sweetest words? – Love, Charity, Truth and Hope.

35) What are the saddest? – Lost, Forsaken.

36) What is your aim? – To be useful.

37) What is your motto? – The Lord will provide.[12]

This is a rising graph of her value-oriented, optimistic and idealistic mind. Her choice of the most preferred book (*The History of the World*) reflects her respect for great heroes. The object in Nature that she liked was a mountain which could be called a symbol of the person who is firmly rooted in the earth but whose greatness lies in his high ambition. The values that she respected the most were sincerity, honesty, truthfulness, love and independence which were her own qualities. It seems that she was not particularly interested in Music and Painting, therefore her answers to the questions regarding those arts were vague and general. Reading was her favourite hobby, as she belonged to the book culture. The vast span of her choice expanded from Eastern authors like Manu and Kalidas to Western authors like Pope and Goldsmith. Anandi was thus a beautiful conflux of East and West. She was so intensely fallen in love with her American family that after Roselle she preferred to live nowhere else but in heaven. Roselle was her heaven on Earth where she experienced love, joy, satisfaction and peace of mind. Nothing could stand in comparison with it.

Leaving this heaven behind, very soon she was to migrate to Philadelphia. So, she began packing her things. She took with her some books from Aunt Theo's collection and a few paintings to decorate the walls of her lonely house in Philadelphia. Uncle Ben's useful gift of an alarm clock pleased her very much, since never before she had seen a clock like that. Hereafter her life was going to be tied up with the clock. The joyous holiday was over and the days of hard work were ahead. Hard yet long-wished for!

References:

1. *The life of Dr. Anandabai Joshee* – Caroline Healey Dall 1888.p.101
2. Ibid page.96
3. Source: Archives of the Medical College of Pennsylvania, Philadelphia, U.S.A
4. Ibid
5. Ibid
6. *Independent Woman* 29: 4 April 1950/ 104-105
7. Source – Archives of the Medical College of Pennsylvania, Philadelphia, U.S.A
8. Ibid.
9. Ibid.
10. Ibid.
11. *The life of Dr. Anandabai Joshee – Caroline Healey Dall 1888. p.99*
12. Ibid, p. xi, xii

16

In Philadelphia

On 28th September 1883, Anandi and Aunt Theo reached Philadelphia by train, at 5 in the evening. Taking a cab, they went to Dean Rachel Bodley's house on North College Street. Now onwards, Anandi was to live in this city of 'Brotherly love' founded by an English Quaker, William Penn. The father of this city had dreamt of creating a refuge for people of all sects and religions, where they could live in harmony and work together without any fear or tension. The city had a lion's share in making history of the nation. The Liberty Bell in the city was a beautiful symbol of freedom and the message carved on it was 'Proclaim liberty throughout all the land unto the inhabitants there of.' In this city George Washington was appointed as the General of Continental Army and Thomas Jefferson had written here the Declaration of Independence. The first American flag was also made here, in the Betsy Ross House, on Arch Street. All these historical memories were green in the minds of citizens. From the pinnacle of the City Hall, the statue of William Penn looked fondly at the growing city of his vision, which had developed into a leading centre of Science, Commerce and Education. It was no more an old city that sank into darkness after the sunset. Now the roads were illuminated with gaslights and the electric lights were on their way. In December 1882, the first electrical bulb was fixed up on a street in Philadelphia, by the Brush Company. On 7th April 1883, the first electrical cable streetcar or the tram was run from Fairmount Park to the Twenty-third Road. It was the same day when Anandi had sailed from Calcutta. With the advent of locomotives, the industrial city acquired speed.

The cab halted in front of the house numbered 1400, and Dean Bodley came out to welcome Anandi and Theodosia Carpenter. She looked at the tender girl in the first flush of youth, standing at her door in a plain blue cotton sari. "Is she the same mutinous woman?" she wondered. Dean Bodley who never forgot this first meeting, wrote after a few years,

"Since that hour, when speechless for very wonder, I bestowed a kiss of welcome, upon the stranger's cheek, in lieu of words, I have loved the women of India."[1].

The next day, that is on 29th September, Dean Bodley gave a grand reception to Anandi, for which she had invited professors, students, college authorities, doctors and eminent Philadelphians. Decked in a crimson gold silk sari and a few ornaments, Anandi was the centre of attraction. She stood between Dean Bodley and Aunt Theo to receive the guests. Aunt Theo who was looking fondly at her felt proud that among the fashionable, ornate ladies, Anandi was conspicuous by her simplicity and her unassuming personality. The other woman who watched Anandi with scrutinising eyes was a feminist writer Caroline Dall, who was specially invited by the Dean. She was not much impressed by Anandi's appearance or looks. Caroline was well-informed about life in India as her husband Rev. Dall had settled there a few years back. When she conversed with Anandi and let her know the interest that she felt in India, Anandi's face brightened and she began to talk with great enthusiasm. This brought over the change in Caroline's first impression and gradually her disappointment vanished. At the end of the reception, they became friends and Caroline felt warmly towards Anandi. They parted with a promise to meet again.

Caroline had beautifully pencilled in her diary the graph of her mental oscillations. This is an eyewitness account of a splendid evening in Anandi's life. "I had promised to pass the evening at Dr. Bodley's, that I might meet the young Mahratta woman, who has come here to study Medicine. As I had a high opinion of the intelligence of her tribe, I was surprised to find that a 'nose-ring' formed part of her costume, although she wisely refrains from wearing it . . . She insists on wearing her native dress and although she wore three necklaces, three pairs of earrings, her nose-ring as a brooch, six pairs of bangles and a saree of crimson and gold, at the reception held for her by Dr. Bodley, she was so plainly dressed to-night, that she would have attracted no attention in the street, provided she had worn a bonnet. She was however so ill that I ought not to judge her. She looks like a stout dumpy mulatto girl, not especially interesting, until her yellow face lights up and light up it did as soon as she gathered from a helping word of mine, that I was familiar with the customs of her people. I cannot describe the effect. It was magical. She speaks seven languages, of which English, Sanskrit and Mahratta are three. Her English is exquisite. There is hardly a flaw in pronunciation or construction. If I had not known, I should have thought her born in this country... She has none of the delicate features which distinguish the Bengalis.

"Her feeling of caste is still uppermost. She receives her guests with impassive dignity like a true Oriental, . . . she has shown curiosity but once, however much she may have felt it. Among those invited to meet her was a mulatto lady, who took a Medical degree two or three years ago and is highly esteemed in Philadelphia. Anandabai looked her all over and evidently did not make her out. There was nothing to show her that the mulatto was not a Hindu, except the European dress.

"I was much interested in my conversation with this woman however disappointed I felt as to her personal attractions. She had a blue tattooed mark between her eyes, a little like an anchor. She told me that this was inserted soon after birth, that she might be recognised as a Hindu, not mistaken for a Mohammedan...

"When we parted, she put out her hand. 'I feel as if I have found a friend.' She said. 'It is the first time anybody has known about me,' and then I saw beauty in the lambent eyes."[2] Caroline was 43 years older than Anandi, but despite the disparity between their ages, they were friends. After the reception, Anandi and Aunt Theo went to Bodley's house. From the next day, Anandi was to reside at Hallman's house where the Dean had rented a room for her. There were a few rooms on the fourth floor of the college, but since all of them were vacant, the Dean thought that Anandi would have felt lonely there whereas Mrs. Hallman was a nice lady. Plus, the house was so close to the college that even in snow, Anandi could have walked down with little difficulty. On the morning of 30th September, Anandi and Aunt Theo moved her things in the Hallmans' house. Aunt Theo stayed with her for a day and then returned to Roselle the next evening. Before that, she helped Anandi in putting her house in order. After arranging the cooking utensils, packages of food articles, and a bed, the room looked homely and comfortable. But Aunt Theo was worried to find that the stove in the room was defective. It smoked badly, choking the room, because the anthracite was not responsive. It was a trying job to make fire and cook food. Aunt Theo tried her best to mend the stove, but with little success. She did not know how Anandi would cope with her first American winter without a good stove in the house to keep her warm.

The next day after lunch, they went to the market and purchased some necessary household things. Except for a looking-glass, they could get everything. After shopping, both went to the railway station as Aunt Theo was to return to Roselle. When they reached there, the train was about to start. So, Aunt Theo hurriedly caught it at the last moment and two gentlemen helped her to get in. Everything was so sudden that Anandi could not even say goodbye to her. The train left the station and Anandi stood alone in the unknown city crowd, with tears rolling down her cheeks. For the first time since she had come to America, she felt so lonely. The station and the roads of Philadelphia were full of bustle and business, but without her dear aunt, they seemed gloomy and empty.

With a heavy heart, she slowly returned to her home and the ticking of Uncle Ben's clock underlined the deep silence. To get the heavy burden of loneliness off her chest, she showered letters on Aunt Theo, from 2nd to 5th October, forgetting her usual cool and composed disposition. On the evening of 2nd October, she wrote, "I write this to you to testify my uneasiness in not hearing from you. I know you have no time to write a long letter, but I hope you will get time to write a postal card to let me know how Eighmie is . . . I am not very well. I feel lonesome."[3] To forget her loneliness, she tried to keep herself busy with some household tasks. One day she spent her time unpacking and arranging her books and paintings but again, they reminded her of the happy summer at Roselle. While looking fondly at the paintings, she thought that she should not have brought so many things from her aunt's house. Feeling that the beautiful paintings looked out-of-place in her small den, she decided to take them back whenever she would visit Roselle next. Some time was spent in reading, writing and paying a couple of visits to Dean Bodley and her good-hearted neighbour Mrs. Hallman. Just to keep herself engaged in something, she experimented with American cookery. One day she baked her bread and the other day she succeeded in baking a cream cake. When the uneasiness was unbearable, in spite of all these activities, she slept off her boredom.

"I slept very well last two three nights and did not fail to take any chance during the day times. When I am asleep, I do not know anything in this world. So, whenever I was quite uneasy, I laid down and rested a while."[4] Writing letters to her relatives in India also eased her anxiety to some extent. Though her husband was far away from her, his mind moved around her in orbit. He longed to know in detail what was happening in her life. The means of communication were limited, slow and undeveloped and a letter was the only bridge between them. Therefore, a delayed letter would always upset him. Before leaving Roselle, Anandi was not able to write to him. When he did not receive her letter around the expected day, he angrily blamed her for being lazy. She replied to this letter, on 2nd October and let him know how down-hearted she was feeling.

Anandi was matriculated on 3rd October and the Winter Session of 1883 was inaugurated on 4th October. No details of this examination could be available anywhere. Anandi came to Philadelphia on 28th September. The next day, a grand reception was organised to welcome her and immediately on 3rd October, she was Matriculated. There was no time gap in between. No account of the nature of this exam is given, even in the letters. So, the examination might be something like a nominal entrance exam. On that day, she rose early in the morning, took a bath, had her breakfast and sat down to write a letter to Aunt Theo. "I am 'all right.' The college opens at 4 p.m. Students buy their tickets from 9 to 4. My name, I hear, is the first one. The Dean has told not to give the… ticket to anyone else. So, I am obliged to go at 8.45 and buy ticket."[5]. Anandi had come far away from her motherland in quest of knowledge and her efforts were gratified by accepting her as a student. It was a red-letter day in her life. At last, the golden opportunity to study Medicine was within her reach. Now nobody was going to throw pebbles at her or abuse her. She was fondly received in this country and her dream was understood. The clouds of gloom vanished and she waited eagerly for the moment to go to college. The mere thought excited her that the persons who made or witnessed the history of women doctors' struggle were to be her guides and teachers. Her mind was filled with joy, gratitude and a sense of responsibility when she entered through the gates of her college.

Just in the front of her college, stood a temple-like magnificent building of 'Girard College'. It was an institute for white orphans, founded by Mr. Girard, an affluent businessman. The organisation supported helpless children, ranging from 6 to 18 years. They were provided with food and shelter and were taught various useful skills that would have helped them in leading a respectable life. The institute reminded Anandi of the orphans in her own country for whom there was no such shelter. She had always wanted to do something for orphans. The noble work of Girard College breathed inspiration into her mind. Even after a century, Girard College stands erect. Today it is not the house for 'only white orphans' but 'any' orphan. Considering the growing need for larger premises, 'Woman's Medical College' was shifted from its original building on Arch Street to North College Avenue. The new building was exactly at the corner where the North College Avenue and the Twenty-second Road met.

Young women in their colourful dresses swarmed through the gates of the college to attend the inauguration. Anandi had aroused a great deal of curiosity because she was the first Asian woman to enter this institute and secondly, she was the first student who had come from a foreign land, wearing her native dress. In the college, Anandi befriended many students and a close friendship was also formed with a few, Abbi Charlotte, a British girl from Birmingham being one of them. William Alexander Hamilton, the great grandfather of Abbi had sailed to India, long ago, with the East India Company. There he had married an Indian princess, so Abbi was partially Indian and she was proud of it. Since Anandi belonged to the native place of her great grandmother, Abbi felt attached to her. When Anandi saw Abbi for the first time, she watched Abbi's silky black hair in silent wonder. But when she came to know about her Indian heritage, she was not surprised. The mutual attraction between Anandi and Abbi soon turned into a strong bond of friendship. Abbi had decided that after her graduation, she would sail to India with Anandi and serve the native women of her great grandmother's country. Abbi's heartfelt sympathy for Indian women did not fail to touch Anandi's mind.

Anandi was introduced to Jessica Carlton, a daughter of an American Missionary settled in India. The American Mission of Ambala in the

Punjab province had sent Jessica to the Medical College. Even she was to work in India after her graduation. There was a comely and ebullient Russian youth, Maria Formed in Anandi's class. Maria's brother Henry Formed was a demonstrator of Pathology in the same college. Dr. Henry Formed had settled in America a decade ago and he was known as an expert pathologist. In 1882, the Medical College of women in St. Pittsburgh, Russia was closed down by the command of the Czar and there was no way for women to learn Medicine. Since her ambition was to become a doctor, Dr. Henry invited Maria to America. Along with Maria, her mother and younger brother Robert also migrated to America.

The majority of students in Anandi's class were American women and many of them like Harriet Brook, Jennie Eagleson, Lucretia King, Emma Richardson and Elizabeth Kending were Pennsylvanians. Jessi Thompson came from Ohio. The open-minded, friendly Jessi belonged to the well-educated, cultured family of Dr. Thompson who was also an eminent writer, social worker and an advocate of the temperance movement. Jessi's mother was an artist, skilled at portrait painting. Jessi was the eldest daughter of this couple. Before coming to this Medical College, Jessi had taken the 'Bachelor of Arts' degree from the Otterbein College, of which Dr. Thompson was the president. Jessi was free to learn whatever she wished.

The women in Anandi's class belonged to various age groups. Elizabeth Kending was 29 years old. She was a student of the State Normal School of Millersville. Jane Lord Hersam from Maine Province was a middle-aged woman of 43. Jane had married Dr. Hersam of Portland but his sudden death ended her happy married life. Jane was so inspired by the good work of her husband that after his death, she decided to be a doctor, to follow in his footsteps. Jane was the first woman from Maine to enter the Medical College.

Anandi who had not been able to finish even her elementary schooling in India, was facing the challenge to create her own place among such well-bred girls. It was noteworthy that she did not suffer from an inferiority complex in that sophisticated atmosphere. On the contrary, she was among those students who were competing for the highest rank. In December 1883, she told Gopal that she had concentrated her full attention on her studies as she wished to stand first in her class. This was neither boasting nor wishful thinking. Dr. Bodley's significant remark proves this fact. "Her faculties developed rapidly under Western opportunities, . . . scientific acquirements placed her high in rank among her peers in the college class."[6]

References:

1. A reprint of the '*High-caste Hindu women* – Pandita Ramabai Saraswati / Introduction by Dean R. L. Bodley / February 1981 / p.(i)
2. *The life of Dr. Anandabai Joshee* - Caroline Healey Dall.1888. p.p. 114,115,116.
3. Source – *The Nancy Cobb Stone Collection of letters*.
4. Ibid
5. Ibid
6. A Reprint of *The High-Caste Hindu Woman* – Pandita Ramabai Saraswati.

   Introduction by Dean R.L. Bodley. February 1981 page iii

17

The First Winter Term

The academic year of the 'Woman's Medical College' was divided into two terms: the winter term and the spring term. The winter term extended from October to March and the spring term from March to June. From June to September, the students had a long summer vacation. Anandi's college life began with the winter term of 1883. During this first term, Anandi attended lectures on Chemistry, Anatomy, Physiology, Histology, Materia Medica, General Therapeutics and Surgery. The dissection of one or two divisions of the cadaver was also taught. Students were expected to work daily in the clinics of the Woman's Hospital. Examinations in Chemistry, Anatomy and Physiology were held regularly. So, the students had to keep abreast of these subjects.

The college building was built in 1875, especially for women doctors' training and the Women's Hospital was in the same premises. This college was a memorial honouring women doctors' victory. More than 4,000 patients were treated there annually. The college was well-equipped with various laboratories, which were under the supervision of senior professors. In Chemical laboratories, students were trained to analyse toxins and urine. The Histological laboratory was well equipped with microscopes of high quality. In the Physiological laboratory, a pendulum, a myograph, a revolving kymograph, a high resistance galvanometer, a manometer and other necessary apparatus were available for students to study various interesting and important concepts in Physiology. The Pharmaceutical laboratory was under the charge of a skilled pharmacist. Excellent facilities were provided to students for becoming familiar with standard Medicinal preparations. The Pathological laboratory was under the direction of Dr. Henry Formed. In the beginning, demonstrations of bandaging, fracture-dressing and operative surgery were performed on manikin and cadaver.

Chemistry was taught by the Dean herself. Dr. Clara Marshal was the professor of Materia Medica and General Therapeutics; Dr. Frances Emily White was the professor of Physiology and Hygiene. Dr. Anna Broomal taught Obstetrics whereas Gynaecology and Paediatrics were taught by Hannah Croasdale. Some male doctors also taught in the women's college. Dr. William H. Parish was the professor of Anatomy, Dr. William W. Keen was the professor of Surgery whereas Dr. James B. Walker was the professor of Principles and Practice of Medicine. For the benefit of the students, guest lecturers were specially invited and their lectures were arranged in the amphitheatre. After the long struggle, now women had access to a number of hospitals like Will's Hospital for Diseases of the Eye, the Eye and Ear Department of the Philadelphia Dispensary, the German Hospital, the Orthopaedic Hospital and Infirmary for Nervous Diseases. Here they could attend clinics, lectures and obtain private tuitions as well.

The reading room of the college was up-to-date with valuable reference books and journals. It was open to students at all hours and they could take advantage of it by paying 50 cents at the beginning of the academic year. The library of Pennsylvania Hospital was open to all those who had registered their names as clinical attendants in that institute, on the temporary deposit of $10 with the librarian and the payment of $3 annually. Students could take advantage of the library of the College of Physicians which was the largest in the country, excluding the library of the Surgeon General's Office of the U.S. Army.

The Association of Alumnae was founded in 1875 with a view to promoting the interests of their college. Some of the ex-students were now professors in the college and they had taken a keen interest in forming the Alumnae Association. In the third annual meeting of this organisation, it was decided to donate yearly, one half of the surplus fund to the library. The other half was to be used for the establishment of an educational fund for students. When Anandi was a student, an amount of $50 was contributed by the association for improving the tables in the Physiological laboratory. The Board of Managers of the Woman's Hospital had a fund of $1,000, the interest of which was offered in small sums as premiums to the graduates and the students, for inventions or improvements of surgical instruments or Medical appliances. Such an institute with abundant educational facilities was a real boon for a studious person like Anandi.

In her letter to Aunt Theo, which she wrote immediately after the college opened, she depicted her first day at college. "I sit down to write a few lines to you (hungry and tired as I am) while my rice is on the stove. I just came from college. I went to the college at 10 A.M., bought my matriculation ticket, went to the lecture on Children's diseases, went to the Hospital and saw two surgical cases. One of the new students fainted. Then I came back to the college and signed on B Board. Any of the students wishing to dissect sign on the board. At about one o'clock I came home with a friend who came to see my room . . . After she was gone, I ate my dinner and went back to the college. I went to the lecture on Obstetrics."[1]. In spite of her hectic schedule and strenuous work, she was ever ready to learn as much as possible. Therefore, she attended the lecture on Obstetrics, though she was not supposed to study that subject in the winter term.

On 3rd November 1883, in a letter to a certain Indian lady, which was written in Marathi, she said, "You have asked me, how many hours of a day do I study. To this I can say that whenever I find time, I do nothing else but study." But cooking food on the defective stove consumed a deal of her time. Sometimes in the evening, she went to Hallman's house to cook on her stove. But in the morning, she had to rush without eating anything if the stove gave trouble. If the fire went out at night, she had a sleepless night, due to the unbearable cold and the irritating smoke. Feeling very sorry for the lone foreigner, one day Hallman tried to repair the stove when Anandi went to her college, but it was of no use. As Anandi had no mirror, she had to apply the spot of kumkum at the centre of her forehead just by guess. Since Anandi could not find time to go to the market, Mrs. Hallman herself bought a mirror for her. Hallman was a good-hearted woman, who wished to help Anandi in every possible way. Dean Bodley was quick to notice that with that troublesome stove, it was very difficult for Anandi to cope with the first American winter. Moreover, her loneliness might have turned into homesickness. Therefore, Dean Bodley invited Anandi to stay with her and Anandi heartily welcomed the idea. She knew that in Dean's house, she would be able to devote more time to her studies which was wasted here in kindling fire. On 22nd October, she informed her aunt, "I am thinking of boarding. While keeping house, I cannot possibly get time to get regular meals. Housework and making fire keep me busy and I can hardly get time to study. I do not find study very hard, nor do I take much time to learn my lesson, but I want 'some' time at least to read them once or more."[2] Soon after the college opened, Dean Bodley arranged a gathering of the First-Year students. While they chatted gaily, Anandi became interested in certain 'Mrs. Luther' who offered her notes and friendly help in her studies. Due to the warmth of friendship and the affection of Dean Bodley, Anandi felt at home in Philadelphia.

Dean Rachel Bodley was a scientist of national repute and a sympathetic teacher who understood her students very well. She had a history of her own. When she was a child, her mother had organised a girls' school in their house. Rachel was graduated at the age of 18, from the 'Wesleyan Female Seminary.' In 1860, she came to Philadelphia and studied Physics and Chemistry at the Polytechnical College. In 1865, she was appointed as the professor of Chemistry and Toxicology at the 'Woman's Medical College of Pennsylvania.' Though women taught Chemistry in that period, no woman was appointed before as a Professor of Chemistry. In 1874, when Dr. Emmeline Cleveland resigned her deanship and left the college, the prestigious post was offered to Rachel Bodley. In the same year, the college was shifted from the hired building on Arch Street to the new building on North College Avenue. With tremendous zeal, Dean Rachel Bodley began to work for the advancement of women doctors. To acknowledge her good work, the honorary degree of Doctor of Medicine was conferred upon her by President T. Morris Perot on 13th March 1879 in the 27th Annual Commencement. The period of her Deanship was the golden era of the institute when many women doctors were trained and sent out in Asia. It could be said in all fairness that it was Dean Rachel Bodley who made Philadelphians interested in Anandi.

Students found Chemistry, the subject that Dean Bodley taught, very interesting but the most difficult one. Dr. Kate Campbell Hurd Mead who entered the college two years after Anandi, had given the reason behind this. "Experiments were few and Organic Chemistry in its infancy...We came betwixt and between the old and new Chemistry and we had to memorize both for examination."[3] The soft-spoken and lively Dean was a favourite of her students. Kate had described her as a 'tactful, subtle and friendly' teacher who knew how to get the best work out of her students. Her girls who drew inspiration from their noble professor, felt proud to tell that they were students of Dean Bodley. Professors like Dr. Francis Emily White, Dr. Anna Broomall, Dr. Clara Marshal, were Dean Bodley's students a few years back.

In the 19th century, the importance of Pathology was yet to be fully grasped in the Medical field and the subject was in its infancy. An amusing story that Dr. Formed, the demonstrator of Pathology, used to tell his students every year, ran like this: Once Dr. Formed was called for a post-mortem by a family, living on the outskirts of a certain town. Dr. Formed found that the brain of the dead man was in a very good condition which would have proved valuable for brain study. He requested the family to give him the brain for his study. But the mere idea of removing brain threw them into a violent rage and they thought of Dr. Formed as a heartless demon. But, not ready to give up, he quickly worked out a plan to trick them. On the face of it, he made peace with them, agreeing not to remove the brain out of its skull. Then he asked them to provide him with some flour, as he needed, he said, to make dough, while sewing the dissected body. It was given to him, without any suspicion. The doctor carefully placed the soft dough into the skull, bagged the brain and took leave of the family in a great hurry.

Among the male professors, an agile and jolly Dr. William W. Keen, the Professor of Surgery, was most liked by his students. He taught them how to operate on brain tumours; how to cut, sew and mend a human body. He had his own style of communicating with his students. The enthusiastic Dr. Keen began his lecture even before entering the classroom with "As I was saying last time," and at the end, he often declared, "After any operation a patient needs rest, Rest, REST in BED." To support his statement, he banged his fist on the table with such force that the specimens fairly danced as if revitalised. Then pulling on his overcoat, he dashed down the stairs, hurriedly jumped into his carriage and went away, as fast as his horse could carry him. "The quiet and dignified manners of Dr. James B. Walker presented an amusing contrast to the swift and vehement movements of Dr. Keen....Nothing but a cinematographer could picture Dr. Keen's rapid and vehement motions, but a time exposure would do justice to Dr. Walker's quiet and dignified pose while he lectured to his class,"[4] says Kate Campbell Hurd Mead, a student of these professors. Kate had skilfully pictured the difference between Pro. Keen and Pro. Walker. Dr. Walker taught his pupils how to see and hear subtle symptoms of various diseases. He was against the excessive use of medicines and recommended sunshine and fresh air for his patients. The shrewd teacher would always know if a student was just guessing and was not sure of herself. Playfully exposing her ignorance, he would give one more chance to answer correctly. This joyous and open atmosphere helped students to understand their mistakes, without being afraid of their teacher.

Thus, Anandi's college life began in an atmosphere aflame with intellectual zeal. There used to be 30 to 40 students in the classes of the First Year, the Second Year and the Third Year. All the students came together for a special lecture or an important surgery or a visit to a hospital. Hence, Anandi came in contact with Frances Coleman Smith, a married woman older than Anandi by 11 years, who was a student of the Second Year Class and Anandi was glad to meet a matured woman like Francis. Very soon, a bond of trust and affection developed between them. Originally Frances belonged to Cincinnati but after marrying Dr. Willis Violet Smith in 1879, she settled in Warrensburg, Missouri and was encouraged by her husband to join the Medical College.

From the very beginning, Anandi proved that her disposition was suitable for the Medical profession. In the first winter term, students had to dissect human bodies, the mere thought of which was frightful or even repulsive to some of the new students. On top of it, when an infant's dead body was brought on the dissection table, they were filled with nausea and pity. As the dissection proceeded, the demonstrator supplemented it with necessary information and the verbal description was an added horror. Unable to withstand it, one by one, all the girls left the room except Anandi, who remained there throughout the demonstration. Instantly she was in the news, surprising students and teachers as well. Not that Anandi was a cold-blooded person. The infant's dissection was painful to her also, but she tried her best to endure the agony. Just before a few years, she had suffered the death of her own suckling and the dissection might have been a sad reminder of the past tragedy. Yet bottling up her tears and emotions, she rose to the occasion and proved that she was a truly dutiful Medical student. When the sensational news reached Caroline Dall, she inquired about it, to which Anandi simply replied, "It would have been better if it had not been a baby."[5]

On 7th December 1883, Anandi had a strange dream wherein she was accused of stealing 3 pearls. Some men and women filed a lawsuit against her. The judge asked her, "Is there any evidence of your innocence? Who is your advocate?" To this, Anandi replied, "The justice and the truth are on my side." Under suspicion, Anandi was sentenced to six months of solitary confinement. Troubled to think that due to this punishment she would not be able to continue her studies, she requested the Judge, "Would you please be kind enough to inform my aunt and tell her to send all my books? I cannot stop reading, since I have decided to study, up to the end of my life." Then she was confined to a clean, small hut in a forest, but books made her forget the loneliness.

The dream symbolised the conflict between her intense urge to learn and the strong social opposition to it which she had faced in India. People in the dream who accused her of theft, represented her natives who wished to block her path to knowledge by fair means or foul. Three stolen pearls could be indicative of 3Rs (Reading, Writing and Arithmetic) and ultimately knowledge to which women had no right. Even in the dream, Anandi was confident that justice and truth were on her side. So, she needed no lawyer to defend her case. Despite her innocence she was punished, yet she used the situation to her benefit and studied in her solitary confinement with unflinching devotion. Her humble house in Philadelphia where she lived in the beginning, took the shape of a hut in her dream. In short, her overmastering desire to learn manifested in her dream.

Before the Christmas of 1883, Dr. Muaileg, a relative of Dean Bodley at Elizabeth, whom Anandi held in high respect, suddenly died. Shattered by the news, Anandi pondered, "Is she taken away from those who love her dearly and need her so badly? What a mystery this world is! Happy today, miserable tomorrow! How true that our deepest sorrows flow from our deepest affections. What an instrument of torture one's own heart is."[6]. Not being ready to accept the reality of her death, Anandi kept Dr. Muaileg alive in her world of fantasy. Hence, she saw her walking on a street or entering a house. It seems that behind the hard shield, Anandi was a tender-hearted woman.

In spite of the hard work and the hectic schedule, she experienced a deep satisfaction in learning to her heart's content. But when she started receiving rude letters from her countrymen full of harsh comments and unwanted preaching, a portion of her joy was taken away. Though they were far away from her, they were keeping a close watch on her activities. Their invisible eyes as if followed her everywhere. Pandita Ramabai who was then in England, embraced Christianity in 1883. This event was instrumental in heightening people's suspicion about Anandi. Letters were showered on her, advising her not to follow Pandita's step. Anandi was tired of stating repeatedly that she respected and loved her own religion and that her only passion was to become a doctor. In such times, she expected loving words of encouragement from her husband Gopal which would have healed all wounds and made her stronger. But sadly, a note of discord had begun to creep into their relationship as well.

From a certain photograph, Gopal came to know that instead of the divided type of sari, Anandi had adopted the undivided, Gujarati sari. Feeling annoyed that she made this change without informing him, he looked askance at the photograph and in a fit of anger, imagined that the folds of her sari, covering bosom, were not arranged decently. His letter full of quips and angry words arrived, which was a bolt from the blue to Anandi. She could not believe that the same person who had urged her to change food and dress habits if she found it necessary, was now agitated by a trifle change. It was just not possible to wear the divided sari which exposed her body to severe cold. But without understanding her difficulty, or perhaps in spite of understanding it, he accused her of levity. As a wife and an honest person, she was pained by his crude remarks.

Against this background, one can imagine how Anandi found solace in the company of the Carpenters who understood her well and never failed to offer her the fund of love. Roselle was to her what 'Tara' was to 'Scarlet' of the novel *Gone with the wind* – a power station that generated mental strength. With the approaching Christmas, she prepared herself to go to Roselle. "Perhaps you would not know dear aunt," she wrote, "how delightful it is to get ready to go home."[7] After the separation of some months from her American family, she was longing to meet them and enjoy her first Christmas with all her heart.

She had her first experience of snow at Roselle when she arrived there for Christmas. She was surprised to see that snow had totally changed the appearance of the town. The calm beauty of snow simply charmed her. The snow-capped roofs, snow-clad trees, dazzling white roads, heavy with snowdrifts cast a spell on her. Leaves of all trees, except Evergreen, had vanished. The snow-coated, leafless and shining vines looked like thin glass tubules. This presented a striking contrast to the flood of colourful leaves in the fall season. The white silence of snowfields, consoled her troubled breast. It made her so tranquil that for some time, she felt removed from her worries. She loved watching snowflakes falling noiselessly from the sky as if like a dream. Eighmie and Helena took her to play in the snow and she joined them in snowballing. In front of every house, children were making snowmen. Anandi too heaped up snow and carved a huge belly out of it, on top of which she kept another small snowball for the face of a snowman. Eyes of black seeds, a red scarf, a tiny cap and a cigar in its mouth, made it a perfect snowman. Anandi was so engrossed in this game that she did not feel Uncle Ben's presence until he clapped and admired her snowman and a shy smile lingered on her face. When Aunt Theo was free from her household jobs, she took Anandi for a sleigh ride which she enjoyed the most and they took many rounds till she felt satisfied. New Year's Eve was celebrated with delicious food, guests, gifts, greetings and decorations after which she returned to Philadelphia, feeling fresh and happy.

She was unaware of what was in store for her. A certain letter from someone in India, whom Caroline Dall calls 'bitter enemy' and Kashibai Kanitkar describes as a 'brut' was lying on her table. It is not known who was the person or what was the content, but the letter completely shattered Anandi's peace of mind and she took days to recover from the shock. She wrote to Aunt Theo, "My face was clouded by my indignation. My friends said my colour changed from red to blue and thought I was sick."[8] In her disturbed state of mind, once again Anandi took the support of fantasy. "All at once a beautiful young lady with a sweet voice came and sat down by me and pressing my hand with her own, said, 'Dear child, do not despond. Providence is just and merciful and means you no harm. Have courage to endure many more such things. Do you not remember how I was persecuted in the presence of my husband, the king? Be true and faithful.' Then she seemed to disappear. I felt her presence though I could no longer see her and was comforted."[9] Being very personal, she did not disclose her grief to anyone but Aunt Theo. To soothe her wounded mind that was suffering alone, she fancied that she had met a queenly woman who in the time of agony stood by her. In her day-to-day life, she had come across good women like Dean Bodley, Aunt Theo, Dr. Anna Broomall and Frances Smith, who had given her true love and moral support and had guarded her as their own. Adding divine colours to that image, she created a figure of the queen in her fantasy, who understood her and was convinced about her innocence.

That year it snowed heavily. The snowfall recorded in Philadelphia on 9th January 1884 was 30 inches. For days, the sun disappeared behind the thick white curtains of snow and the sunless days as well as chilly nights were equally depressing. On 8th January, Anandi was so feverish that she was advised to take rest for a few days. On 30th January, the snow cleared up and the sun reappeared, shining softly in the wintery sky. Wearing her thick shoes, when one day Anandi was carefully walking through snow towards her college, the rays reflecting from snowdrifts dazzled her eyes. As Gopal was not there to share this unusual experience, she felt like bottling the shining snow and sending it to him. On the same evening, she sat down to write a letter to him in which she sketched a word picture of her experience of the snow. But being pressed for time during that week, she could only finish the long letter, bit by bit. It was completed at last on 4th February. Thursday was the most tiresome day when students had to perform various tasks from 9 a.m. to 9 p.m. having very little free time, which was just sufficient for lunch. In the above-mentioned letter, she requested Gopal to send her a Sanskrit dictionary and a couple of textbooks useful for a beginner, because Dean Bodley had shown interest in learning Sanskrit. The letter ended with a complaint about her health.

While she was dining one evening, she started suffering from a headache and also had a throat pain. When she was warming up her cold feet, she looked so tired that Dean Bodley advised her to go to bed. At night, she had a severe attack of Diphtheria. So Dr. Anna Broomall and Dr. Schultze were called immediately and an experienced nurse was stationed at her side for 24 hours. A letter was sent to Theodosia Carpenter to inform her about Anandi's illness. The news so upset Aunt Theo that she fainted out of nervousness. With great affection, she wrote to Anandi and urged her to tell what she should do for her. For two weeks, Anandi was asked to take complete bed rest. For the first week she was put on a milk diet. Dr. Broomall visited Anandi twice or thrice a day despite her busy schedule. Her friends too came every day to cheer her up with flowers, fruits and small plants, and their delightful company acted as a tonic. Yet the burden of unproductive days was too heavy to bear, as her feeble health did not allow her to study. She trembled to think that all her efforts might go to waste if her health did not improve fast.

On 16th February, she was a little better. Having sought permission to get up, she moved about in her room. On 17th February, she mustered up the strength and went to the college library, but till 21st February, she could not attend lectures regularly. To catch up with the class, she began to study at home. Since childhood, she was habituated to turn her home into school if difficulties cropped up, so there was nothing new in it. Now also, remaining at home, she began to prepare herself for the examination for which she had to appear at the end of the winter term.

References:

1. Source: *The Nancy-Cobb Stone collection of letters*.
2. Ibid.
3. 15th Anniversary Volume of Woman's Medical College of Pennsylvania – Name of the article – *40 Years of Medical Progress: Reminiscences and Comparison* – by Kate Campbell Hurd Mead / p.p. 171-174.
4. Ibid.
5. *The life of Dr. Anandabai Joshee* - Caroline Healey Dall 1888. p 190
6. Ibid, p 107
7. Ibid, p 107
8. Ibid, p 108
9. Ibid, p 108

18

The First Spring Term

As winter turned into spring, the snow melted and there was pleasant warmth in the air. Tender leaves had started appearing on trees. At the end of the winter term, students were examined in Inorganic Chemistry, Anatomy and Physiology. Their entry into the Physiological and Chemical laboratories depended upon the result of these examinations. Anandi's illness did not allow her to study hard, but in spite of it, she scored well. She was keenly interested in Obstetrics, as this subject was directly connected with her future work in India. It was taught by her favourite professor Dr. Anna Broomall, who was very intelligent and was adept at teaching. Dr. Anna was an ex-student of the 'Woman's Medical College of Pennsylvania.' Though she was born in a family of lawyers, she had no interest in law. One fine morning, she declared that she wished to become a doctor. Though her father wanted her to become a lawyer, he respected her decision. He fondly advised her, "If you wish so, then at least try to be a good doctor." In 1871, the degree of 'Doctor of Medicine' was conferred on Anna, but the next year, she again took the same course for a deeper understanding of the subjects. This suggests how seriously she had taken her father's advice. After becoming a professor in her own college, she took a great interest in the training of nurses. Very soon, Broomall nurses gained a good reputation and were constantly in demand. There was no substitute for a Broomall nurse if a difficult surgery was to be performed.

In 1883, Anna opened her own dispensary on 1411, Walnut Street. In 1880 she became the first woman doctor performing abdominal surgery. At the outset, the management of the 'Woman's Hospital' had laid down a condition that when Anna would operate, the presence of a male doctor was a must. But Dr. Anna Broomall was so efficient a surgeon that the male doctor had nothing else to do but to cool his heels. Hence, the previous decision was soon overruled. The slender lady in her simple black cloth was regarded as a gentle but disciplinarian teacher. Her eyes which looked as if partially closed, were in fact sharp enough to observe indiscipline, carelessness, lethargy or inattention. Dr. Kate Campbell Hurd Made had underlined Dr. Anna Broomall's special qualities in her article. "To her nothing was so precious as a living baby and a perfectly healthy mother. Nor did she tolerate any nonsense about the beneficent role of nature in repairing a tear, nor the use of force instead of skill with low forceps, nor would she allow saving the operator's time by the too early application of high forceps. She taught us to do prenatal work long years before it was attempted elsewhere. Her quizzes paralysed the students who could not think and act quickly, for as emergencies are the rule in maternity cases, she felt that a doctor should be eternally vigilant and always prepared for every kind of abnormality."[1]. As Anandi had a natural interest in this subject, she tried to learn the Broomall methods thoroughly.

In this spring term, Anandi started learning French, German and Botany as a pastime and needed no other entertainment or relaxation. But once her friend Miss Bee persistently urged her to come to the famous Barnum's Circus, which was advertised as the 'Greatest Show on the Earth.' In that period, it was a novel entertainment, popularised by Phineas Taylor Barnum, since 1830. Even after 50 years, the Circus was known by his name. A huge tent, which could accommodate 1,000 people was raised and the owner claimed to have the biggest animal collection. So, Miss Bee wanted to take Anandi to see the circus. Anandi went to the circus with Miss Bee and her father, but somehow, she could not enjoy it. She was more interested in intellectual activities like reading, letter-writing, discussions, debates and giving or listening lectures. As she had become famous in Philadelphia, she was invited by different organisations to deliver lectures, which she thoroughly enjoyed. In America, Anandi was closely questioned about her country, people, the Hindu religion, the practice of child marriage and the female infanticide. Anandi was pained to observe that the Americans looked down upon India as a tribal country and were ignorant about its merits. So, whenever she got a chance to speak in public meetings, she defended her country and the Hindu religion. One such opportunity presented itself in April 1884, when the organisers of the Ladies Missionary Society invited her to deliver a lecture in their annual meeting. The large audience was eager to understand the views of a young Indian Medical woman like her on the subject of child marriage which she herself had chosen for the lecture. Women felt sure that on the Medical ground, Anandi would disapprove of the disgusting practice of child marriage.

Anandi could not get time to prepare her speech but she knew what she wished to say. Because of her exquisite English and elegant performance, she won the prize of $10. Yet she shocked her audience by strongly defending the national custom. Could it be possible that Anandi was unaware of the frightful effects of child marriage on the mental and physical development of little girls? Didn't she know that just because of child marriage, undesired sex, early pregnancy and premature motherhood were imposed on underage girls? Was she really unaware that the biggest obstacle in women's path was nothing but this custom of child marriage? Even Caroline Dall and Dean Bodley were disappointed by Anandi's speech. Yet they tried to seek answers to such questions in their own ways and tried their best to understand Anandi. Caroline Dall wrote, "If she favoured early marriages, was it strange? She had been married at nine years. All the happiness of her life had been flowed from the instruction of her husband and from that liberal sympathy which she supposed to move him in assisting her to come to this country."[2] Whereas Dean Bodley explained the situation in a different way. "She chose her subject 'Child Marriage' and surprised her great audience by defending the national custom. If there are any who still cherish the feelings of disappointment and regret engendered that April afternoon, let them turn to Ramabai's chapter on Married Life in this [F1]book and learn how absolutely impossible it was for a High caste Hindu wife to speak otherwise."[3]. According to Caroline, Anandi approved of child marriage because it had brought happiness to her, whereas Dean Bodley thought that the limitations of Anandi were that of a Hindu

---

F1 The High Caste Hindu Women – by Pandita Ramabai, introduction by Dean R. Bodley.

wife. No doubt, both of them were sincerely trying to read Anandi's mind but their explanations are incorrect and scanty. They had not sufficiently taken into account the personality of Anandi, who was thoughtful enough to consider any question objectively. Knowing that her life was an exception, Anandi would not have defended the custom of child marriage, just because it had made her life meaningful. It is also not true that she defended child marriage under the pressure of the tradition. Without caring for public opinion, she had fearlessly analysed the drawbacks of her countrymen, in the public meeting at Shrirampur.

In the process of understanding Anandi, both Caroline Dall and Dean Bodley had wrongly imposed on her the limitations which were not hers and overlooked those which were real and significant. Child marriage was not the 'only thing' that she defended. Though it was a proven fact that the cruel practice of female infanticide existed in certain parts of India, she furiously denied it when questioned by an American lady doctor. In America, Anandi was constantly exposed to climatic changes like extreme cold, frost-bite and contagious diseases. Doctors had suggested that she might at least take broth, as she needed good nourishment. But despite their wise advice, she maintained that it was not necessary. Later on, at a meeting in Boston, she emphatically told that she did not feel the need for any other food than what she ate in India. Therefore, the real question that needs to be probed in is, why did she defend in America whatever was Indian? Why was it difficult for her to be objective about the Indian way of life?

The reasons behind her defensive policy were hidden in her peculiar position in the American society, where the Americans regarded her as the representative of India. Feeling sure that the rebellious woman like her would not mind discussing frankly any issue at hand, they closely questioned her about India and were outspoken in their remarks. Similarly, they questioned Pandita Ramabai also, when she visited America a few years later. Ramabai did not hesitate to discuss frankly any issue but somehow Anandi could not. In America, Anandi was annoyed to observe that a non-Christian was generally looked down upon as a heathen and Hindustan was thought to be a land of uncivilised people. Therefore, she thought it her responsibility to let them understand the magnificence of the Indian heritage. Shielding herself with a self-defensive pride about the Indian culture, customs and people, the vanguard crossed swords with those who had so-called wrong notions about her country. There was nothing wrong to stand by values, but when she went on defending even vices, self-esteem turned into false pride and ultimately it imposed obvious limitation on her personality.

When Anandi was in India, she had openly attacked her people. She was very frank with Aunt Theo when she wrote that due to child-marriages, many of the women in India became weak. It should be remembered that when she made such a statement, she was only 15 years old, not a Medical student and yet analytical. And now, when she was sure to know the scientific reasons as to why child marriage was injurious to mental and physical growth of a budding girl, she was defending it, just because it was an Indian custom. Dr. Ida Scudder, who had worked in India for years, had thrown light on the sorry state of the Indian child-wives. She wrote, "Educating the populace through our medical graduates and nurses will help to do away with the custom of child marriage and child-wives. Probably there is not a practitioner here who has not stood by one of the little wives in labour and felt that it was time something desperately should be done to save the little girls of India from the sufferings forced upon them. Only a few weeks ago a little girl of 13 was brought in labour. She hardly realised what was happening and everyone present in that operating room rebelled against this custom of child marriage."[4]. Dr. Scudder wrote this in the early 20th century. If this was the condition in the 20th century, one can imagine what it would have been in the 19th century. Anandi herself had experienced the ordeal of child-bearing at the early age of 12. She had also witnessed the deaths of child mothers. It was quite disturbing that in spite of this, she was defending the custom.

But there is another side to this issue. Anandi was fighting on two fronts at a time. On the one side, she had to answer the inquisitive questions about her country and people, raised by the Americans. On the other side, some of her countrymen were suspiciously observing every move of her because she was living in a foreign land with people of different religion. Many of her countrymen strongly believed that one day, Anandi was bound to embrace Christianity. No doubt, Anandi was highly impressed by the teachings of Jesus Christ and loved to discuss religion with Christian priests. In Philadelphia, she often visited a certain church on Spring Garden Street to hear the sermons of Rev. Amis. He did not fail to notice the silent and attentive young Indian girl. Soon they became good friends and sharing her thoughts with Rev. Amis, afforded profound satisfaction to Anandi. In spite of this deep interest in Christianity, she did not feel like abandoning her own religion. It was just not possible that Anandi would have adopted another religion, however attracted she might have been towards it. While talking with Caroline Dall, once she explicitly made her position clear "I came to America, simply to study Medicine ... I devoted myself to my Sanskrit to the exclusion of everything else. I wanted to read the Shastras to women of America, to prove to them that I have no need to become a Christian. God gave the truth to my people in the beginning and although I love to read of Jesus and take pleasure in Bible, I have an older script of my own."[5]

Another significant reason for not feeling like embracing Christianity was that, the conversion would have at once distanced her from her people and they might have looked at the act as a breach of loyalty. This she did not want to happen, since her ultimate aim was to work among her own people. In the public meeting at Shrirampur, she had given her precious word that she would go to America as a Hindu and would come back as a Hindu, which she earnestly wished to keep. It would have been very difficult for her to enter public life in India, if she had fallen in the eyes of her people. Though she was against her conversion, deep down in her mind, she always cherished love for Jesus Christ. Many times, she would fall into deep consideration, asking herself, 'Why Christ is loved so much, even after eighteen centuries?' Her mind would reply, 'Christ was the last Sage, the last Prophet, the last and the best.' Being conscious of the religious turmoil within herself, sometimes she was even afraid that she might become Christian, in spite of her decision of not doing so. Once she wrote to Gopal that she was alone in a Christian land, so her mind might change, but she would pray to God to help her. This remark indicates the fact that she was in conflict with her own self. She was afraid that she might embrace Christianity. But ultimately her sense of duty, love for her own people and deep attachment to her own religion helped her to come out of this situation.

In May 1884, Anandi and her class twice visited the 'Morris Town Insane Asylum.' Due to her Indian dress, she stood out in the Western crowd. When she was passing through different wards, insane women frenziedly rushed towards her to have a look at her. Lots of crazy faces pressed closer, making her position awkward. One of them came forward and shook hands with Anandi while the other held her in a tight embrace and was not ready to leave her alone. With sweet words, Anandi slowly diverted her attention and freed herself. She had perfectly understood that, those mad women meant no harm to her but welcomed her in their own fashion. A woman asked Anandi, "From where have you come? And what for?" To this Anandi replied, "I've come from Hindustan to meet you." The woman who was obviously pleased by this reply urged, "Then do come again." But a woman in the next ward, who somehow did not like Anandi, aimed a pillow at her. When the Medical students were thinking of changing their ward, a small group of mad men approached them, who took Anandi to be a Chinese woman. One of them exclaimed, "Eh Chinese, only you seem to be a woman," and others joined him in hilarious laughter.

After a few days, students visited the same asylum for a post-mortem. A student from the upper class dissected a body in the presence of their professor who provided the necessary information. After it was over, all the students went out except Anandi who was making some observations. Standing on the attached balcony, her friend Francis Smith was adjusting her bonnet. In the twinkling of an eye, an incurably mad, robust woman stormed in the room, who had escaped from the hands of her attendant. She was wildly curious about the operation theatre and the surgical instruments.

She herself wanted to do something, but when she saw that the body was already opened and Anandi was standing near the dissected body, she flew into a violent rage. Rolling her eyes, she asked Anandi in a frightful tone, "What are you doing here?" The heart which was removed from the body, was placed in a tray. Thinking that Anandi had killed that person, she shouted, "What have you done? Come on, now I am going to operate you." Anandi did not utter a word, because it would have added fuel to the mad woman's anger. Anandi stood at her post, without making a single movement. Francis Smith, who saw everything from the balcony signalled Anandi to run away, but that was not possible as the angry woman stood between Anandi and the door. Had Anandi tried to run away, the woman would have easily caught her. So Anandi was thinking of cautiously moving towards the door without her knowledge. But luckily, her attendant came running to take charge of her and Anandi was saved.

When the spring term was over, the college closed down for the summer vacation and Anandi went to Roselle. There she used her spare time in perfecting her Botany. She collected different types of wild flowers and leaves, dried them and pasted them in her notebook, with their proper classification. She also sewed summer and winter clothes well in advance. The relatives of the Carpenters also treated Anandi as their own. This summer, Aunt Theo's sister, Barto, who lived in Saratoga, invited Anandi to stay with her and took her around, to visit different places of interest. One of them was the 'Medicinal Springs' at Saratoga, situated at the foot of the southernmost spur of the Adirondack Mountains. The Saratoga Lake was 4 miles east of Saratoga Springs and it was a famous place for regattas. It was believed that the spring water was good for health. Since 1826, the waters were bottled and sent to various parts of the world. In Saratoga, Anandi visited houses of Red Indians and befriended a young girl who quenched Anandi's curiosity about their way of life. At the time of departure, the girl bestowed some attractive Red Indian objects on Anandi and in return Anandi gave her some Indian curiosities. She bought a few things from Red Indian women and out of that, presented a nice wooden box to Aunt Theo in which she kept

Anandi's letters. Though Anandi enjoyed the holidays, her health did not improve much. She constantly suffered from headaches, but she wrote to Aunt Theo in a sportive mood, "Ever since I left Roselle, I have not spent a day without my new companion, the headache. Every movement gives me pain; but you need not worry about it, for I do not let it interfered with anybody's happiness, nor even with my own." [6] She had accepted her headache as a troublesome but unavoidable companion.

She enjoyed the blissful quietude of the country places. This summer, Anandi also visited Troy which had begun to grow as an industrial centre. In addition to the rapid advancement in Commerce, Troy had acquired fame even as an educational city. At Troy, she saw some cucumbers which were unnaturally green. Anandi suspected copper in them, but no one could assure it. So, she took a needle and ran it into one of the cucumbers. Within a few minutes, the needle turned bright red and she felt satisfied that her guess was correct. Happy days of the summer vacation were almost over and soon she was to join the college.

She had spent almost one and half years away from her husband. The lovelorn wife was thankful to the man who had invented the idea of letter-writing. Anandi-Gopal were at the opposite ends of the globe and only letters could cross the vast expanse of ocean that separated them. It was possible to fill this 'paperboat' with one's memories and dreams, tears and smiles, weal and woe and send it at the beloved's door. Her anguished heart so longed to meet her husband that one corner of her life always remained empty without him. As the days passed, the desire to meet him turned into an irresistible yearning. Gopal's love for Anandi was not less in intensity, however whimsical he might have been. Out of profuse admiration, he once asked her if he could call her by the name Saraswati, the Goddess of Learning. Touched by this, she replied shyly that she did not deserve that title but he could call her Saraswati, if he wished so. The other time Gopal suggested that, they should collect the material about her which was printed in America and India and make a book out of it. She understood that his excessive love made him think of such an inadmissible idea. So, she told him very tenderly not to do so, as it would not do any good. She was calm enough not to lose her balance of mind while Gopal was excited by her success. Gopal was a complicated man whose troubled disposition sharply contrasted with Anandi's self-control. His praise and admiration were as extravagant as his harshness and cutting remarks. The initial outburst of the joy of Anandi's success gradually receded and the pang of separation took its place. At a certain point, the grief of separation was so unbearable to him that he hated Anandi for being so ambitious. He was tired of her high aim which was once fondly nurtured by him only. Since he was unable to turn the clock back, he started inflicting his wrath upon her. He would deliberately misunderstand her, whenever he wished to start a quarrel. The simple grumbles soon turned into serious accusations which indicated his agitation. He could not bear that Anandi was enjoying her pursuit of knowledge in spite of their separation.

The undercurrents of gloom, loneliness, fear, anxiety, helplessness and worry flowing in his mind slowly turned him into a sadist. He started writing disdainful letters for poisoning Anandi's happiness. He felt that she had no right to be happy without him. To give vent to his impotent anger, he tortured her with dirty accusations like disloyalty, greediness and frivolity. The far-sighted man of yesteryears completely lost the balance of his mind and soon began to take perverse pleasure in her pain. Knowing that the torrent of angry words was deliberate, Anandi trained herself to remain cool. She searched in his letter for small particles of love scattered among the bitter ones and sought satisfaction if there were any. With all her heart, she wished that the physical distance should not turn into a mental distance. Therefore, she tried to evoke the old love that was hidden behind the misunderstanding. She urged him to remember that he knew his wife better than her own pen knew her. So, he should not lose faith in their meaningful relationship. Since she had given her life to a cause, it was her prime duty to work hard for it but that did not mean that she had forgotten her husband. Her letters were full of such requests and explanations. But it depressed her if Gopal did not respond to her honest efforts. It was hard for her to believe that her own husband did not realise the depth of her heart. Letters took a deal of time to reach and in the meanwhile Gopal's mood, causes of discontent, complaints or a particular situation used to change so much that the arrived replies could not make a desired impact on him and hence it gave rise to another quarrel.

In spite of this, Anandi never forgot that he was the man who had stood by her like a tower of strength when the whole society was eager to nip her ambition in the bud. She let him know that she remembered everything and regarded him as her Guru, her leader and her benefactor. There was nothing in the world that could take his place. After Anandi went to America, the united world of Anandi-Gopal was split into two. Gopal had remained where he was whereas Anandi had entered a new world, altogether different from that of Gopal. It was quite difficult to bridge the gulf between them. Anandi grew rapidly under the changed conditions around her and became more confident, self-reliant and independent. Years back, Gopal had vowed that he would educate at least one woman in his life. He might not have anticipated then that Anandi, his first and the only disciple would reach such a height that he would feel dwarfed before her. He never realised that he was successful in his mission beyond limits and it was *his* victory that his creation had surpassed him. As the sculpture grew taller than the sculptor, the sculptor suffered from the inferiority complex. A traditional husband within him found it very hard to accept that his wife was his intellectual superior. Accepting the ups and downs in her emotional life, Anandi had decided to march on her chosen path. She had trained herself to shut the doors leading to worries and tensions when she stepped into the territory of her studies. At the end of September 1884, the summer vacation was over. In the winter of 1884, she entered the Second Year Class.

References:

1. 15th Anniversary Volume of Woman's Medical College of Pennsylvania

   Name of the Article – *40 Years of Medical Progress: Reminiscences and Comparison* – by Kate Campbell Hurd Made.

2. *The Life of Dr. Anandabai Joshee* - Caroline Healey Dall. 1888. P,109

3. A reprint of the *High-Caste Hindu Woman – Pandita Ramabai Saraswati*

Introduction – Dean R.L. Bodley / Feb 1981 / ii, iii

4. *The Southern Medical College College for Women* – by Dr. Ida Scudder / The Journal of the association of Medical women in India / May 1916 / Vol V No 10 / p.5

5. Caroline Dall's letter – "Christian Register", Boston, on June 30, 1887.

Source: Clippings of Ramabai preserved in the Mukti Mission, Kedgaon, Dist. Pune, Maharashtra State. India

6. *The Life of Dr. Anandabai Joshiee* - Caroline Healey Dall. 1888. p 111

19

The Second Year Winter Term

The winter term of 1884 commenced on 2nd October. Now Anandi was a student of the second year class. In this term, the first Australian woman, Constance Stone, took admission to the Medical course. Even in Australia women were not allowed to learn Medicine. Constance Stone received her Medical degree in 1887 and in the same year, the ban on Medical women was lifted by the University of Melbourne. This year, the opening address was delivered by Professor Parish, on the Practical Hygiene and he had a large audience. During this term, the students had to attend lectures on all the subjects except Materia Medica and Surgery. In addition, there were practicals of Anatomy, visits to hospitals and clinical jobs which kept them busy the whole day. The students had to take weekly examinations in Chemistry, Anatomy and Physiology. At the close of the second winter term, the students were eligible for the final examination in these subjects.

Professor Frances Emily White, who was absent for the first few days, gave her first lecture on 8th October. Dr. White was also an ex-student of the college like many other teachers. After receiving her degree in 1872, she joined the college as a demonstrator of Chemistry, Anatomy and Physiology and within a few years became the Professor of Physiology. In 1876, she sailed to England and worked at the 'Cambridge University', under the guidance of reputed doctors. While returning to America, she brought with her some of the modern medical equipment for her college, the Pendulum Myograph being one of them which was exhibited to the visitors, with due pride. Professor White was the first person to introduce Pendulum Myograph in America. She was also one of the founder members of the Alumnae Association.

For Anandi's future work in India, the study of Gynaecology was as important as Obstetrics which was taught by Professor Hannah Croasdale. She was a conspicuous figure in the college, with her fashionable dresses of velvet, silk and laces. The watch with a long golden chain always hung from her neck and her fingers were adorned with diamond rings. Girls curiously observed Professor Croasdale's fashions and found this stylish lady very attractive. But while operating, the diamond rings were removed from the fingers without fail. Wrapped in a simple white apron, she looked like any other doctor. As a lecturer, students found her uninspiring, but she was a marvellous surgeon. In the operation theatre, she would stand patiently among the students who crowded the room and explained skilfully the case at hand.

While attending operations, the students had to wear an apron on their usual dress. But no particular type of apron was recommended, so they were free to choose the fashion of their liking. Maria Formed's apron was very big and on the white background she had patched a brown shape of some kind. Elinor Jones had an attractive apron with ruffles. Anandi had kept aside an old sari and a blouse for wearing at the time of operations or dissections and she had sewed some simple aprons on Aunt Theo's sewing machine. During that period, the use of masks and gloves was unknown. In 1865, Dr. Joseph Lister had proved that Carbolic Acid could be used as an antiseptic. The Lister's Carbolic Acid spray was nick-named by students as the 'Spouting Biddies.' A lamp emitting the spray of acid was fixed on a stand alongside the operation table which enveloped people in a cloud of vapours. The acid spray was irritating to the mucous membrane of the respiratory tract, but there was no solution. Dr. Croasdale had specialised in the operations of tumours and cancers. She always insisted that students should without fail, keep the surgical instruments away from the interior parts of a patient.

The sponges used in those operations were not man-made. Neither were they sponges only in name; they were a kind of porous sea animal. After every operation, blood was washed off from them. Then they were soaked in the permanganate solution followed by the oxalic solution. Finally, the clear sponges were dried and kept in jars, all ready for the next operation. After every abdominal operation, patients were drained with the help of long test tubes of hard black rubber with small holes at the rounded ends. At the open end a hard rubber syringe was fitted to withdraw peritoneal fluid. The duty of performing this task every 2 hours, for 24 to 48 hours was assigned to assistants who were supposed to sit at the bedside of a patient turn by turn. Even after 50 years, Maria Formed had preserved one such drain as the memento of her college days.

At the beginning of this year, Dr. Emily Du Bois, the demonstrator of Anatomy left the college for health reasons. Though her early retirement came as a shock to her students, she herself was aware of her hopeless condition. With a heavy heart, Anandi said goodbye to her dear teacher who was also her good friend. Another friend of Anandi whose company she enjoyed the most, was Francis Smith. On 3rd October, Anandi and Francis visited the electrical exhibition in Philadelphia which was the first of its kind in America. Electricity was quite a new source of energy and it was yet to become a part and parcel of day-to-day life. The exhibition had become a talk of the town because never before people were exposed to new-found energy like electricity, on such a large scale. Along with this, the National Conference of Electricians was also held under the sponsorship of the Franklin Institute. A total of 216 exhibitors participated in the exhibition. The thronging multitude felt aghast by the glaring brightness of electricity which was to illuminate their dark nights in the near future. They watched curiously the attractive display of lamps of various shapes and sizes and the models of locomotives running on electricity. In all 2,82,779 tickets were sold, in addition to which, there were numerous guests and celebrities who were specially invited by the organisers. Anandi and Francis who had met after the long summer vacation, enjoyed the evening together. The college had just begun, so they were yet free to amuse themselves.

This year, Anandi started dissecting the head, the third and the last part of the body in dissection, which she found very interesting. But had she not been tormented by acute backache, she thought, it would have been more enjoyable. Being very busy on all other days except Wednesday and Saturday, she could hardly devote any time to letter-writing. After working for 15 to 16 hours a day, she was simply exhausted. Sometimes an examination was announced suddenly at the eleventh hour, causing panic among students. In December 1884, the examination of Anatomy was thus announced. Burning the midnight oil, the students desperately tried to cram their brains with the details of 400 muscles and bones. But Anandi decided to study only that selective portion which she had digested properly. She informed Aunt Theo about her way of studying. "I only strive for all within my reach, but do not struggle for what I could not digest or what my undeveloped brain or insufficient strength could not retain, for everything must have its time. Prematurely born babies seldom live longish, nor are the prematurely ripened fruits the best."[1] This is how small events provoked big thoughts in her mind.

In November 1884, Anandi was informed by Uncle Ben about the arrival of Gopal's friend Govind Sathe in Roselle and Anandi went to meet him on Thanksgiving Day. Govind distributed Gopal's gifts among the family members of the Carpenters and Anandi was glad to get her share of beautiful sarees. The year 1884 was drawing to a close. Caroline Dall had invited Anandi to her Georgetown house near Washington for Christmas so that they could have spent some time together. Their friendship was sealed on their first encounter which then developed further through the regular correspondence, evoking profound love for each other. From Philadelphia, Anandi took a train going to Washington, which was delayed for some reason. Caroline waited at the station feeling uneasy, because the horse carriage that she had engaged went away. When the train arrived, all passengers hastily rushed to catch the carriages. The demand was much more than the available carriages. So, Caroline could not engage another. They had no other choice but to get in the horse-driven tram. In fact, Caroline wanted to avoid it on account of the attention Anandi would attract. But she observed with admiration that the curious glances of their co-travellers and passers-by were calmly endured by Anandi. She also had a heavy handbag which Anandi herself carried, in spite of Caroline's request to allow her to help.

During her stay, Caroline took her to visit the White House which was then occupied by President Chester Alan Arthur; Congress House and many other public buildings. They also attended a service in the Unitarian Church. Anandi was invited by many of Caroline's friends for lunches and dinners and 29th December was reserved for those friends who were to meet Anandi at Caroline's place. She had recorded in her journal that on that day, they had 52 callers and out of them, 30 remained for supper. Several questions were asked to Anandi about the Indian culture and the Hindu religion which were answered earnestly by her. In her journal, Caroline had written down the detailed account of the memorable evening with Anandi. "To-night, before quite a large company, she talked in an earnest and excited way about the religions of the world, showing a profound intelligence as well as scholarship. Then for a while in a very entertaining way about jewels and costumes. Her best talk was with the Rev. Theodore Wynkoop, after most of our friends had gone.

"To-night she wore a close satin vest embroidered with gold and a white…saree deeply bordered with gold; also, her collars and necklaces of jewels, and for the first time, at my request, her 'nose-ring.' This is a spray of flowers two or three inches long and made of fine old, pearls... The centres of the star-like flowers are of ruby and emerald. A fine wire attaches it to the left nostril close to the cheek. It is very effective, much prettier than ear-rings, and looks as if she were holding a spray of flowers between her lips."[2]

One can easily see through these words, how the quaint little ornament like nose ring appeared to the curious eyes of an American woman like Caroline Dall. At the time of their first meeting she had turned up her nose at the same 'nose ring' saying, "As I had a high opinion of the intelligence of her tribe, I was surprised to find that a 'nose ring' formed part of her costume, although she wisely refrains from wearing it."[3] But now when she saw it on Anandi, she was impressed by its unusual beauty. She was also charmed by Anandi's personality who had disappointed her at the outset and about whom she could never think of as a beautiful woman. "As time went on, I grew familiar with what had at first disappointed me and saw the fascinations of the movements and manners that others felt so deeply. It was the Oriental charm, but I do not think that in her own country she would ever have been called handsome. Her motions were sinuous, not serpentine like those of the Bengalis. Her beautiful hands and feet, her elastic muscles belonged to her race, rather than herself. In one respect from the first to last, she was herself alone, in the sweetest truthfulness, the most entire candour that ever belonged to a mortal."[4]

One day after visiting the White House, Caroline interviewed Anandi about her life in India and took short notes of the conversation. Caroline who wished for several such intimate meetings, could not have suspected that it was her first and the last chance. After Anandi's untimely death, she grieved over not taking longer notes. Caroline's house differed from the other American houses in one respect. It had the touch of Indian culture which pleased Anandi very much. Caroline had displayed several interesting articles sent by Rev. Dall from India. Moving quietly in the house, Anandi touched those articles with deep affection and delight. Feeling rejuvenated by her visit to Caroline's house, Anandi returned to Philadelphia in the first week of January 1885 and buried herself in studies, because the final examinations of some subjects were approaching. One Sunday she decided to study hard from early morning to 10 at night and almost succeeded, except that at 9.30 p.m. fatigue so took over that her eyes shut automatically. Within a moment, she was fast asleep and the gaslight burnt on the whole night. When she woke up in the morning, sunlight was seeping through the curtains. Previously she had a few sleepless nights and the sudden attack of sleep was restful for her tired body and mind. Away from Philadelphia, Aunt Theo was in a tizzy and waited for Anandi's letter to know about her health. Knowing this, Anandi comforted her, "Let not your dear heart be burdened with any anxiety. I am very judicious in regards to my work and food."[5] Yet the ups and downs in her health troubled Aunt Theo's motherly heart. Anandi tried her best to take whatever care she could, in her busy schedule. Whenever the weather was clement, she went out for a long walk, as it was a good exercise. In spite of her aversion to non-vegetarian food, she had started consuming an egg every day, for extra-nourishment. Yet the climatic changes, heavy workload and mental tensions told upon her health.

Next to Aunt Theo, Frances Smith was Anandi's mentor. Frances was a funny woman whose cheerful company offered infectious joy to Anandi and the girlish teasing that went between them helped Anandi to restore her sense of amusement. Once Anandi described an amusing incident to Aunt Theo: "I think that it was for the first time that Mrs. Smith came to ask me for needle and thread, as she wanted to sew buttons on her shoes and when she got through, she found she had one button extra at the top, very near the edge, for whose acceptance, she could not find a hole. A needle very seldom has the pleasure of being handled by Mrs. Smith, so I was very much amused at it."[6] For some reason the intimacy between Anandi and Frances, who also lodged at Dean's house, was disagreeable to Dean Bodley. As Frances was to return to her home after her graduation in March 1885, the remaining few weeks of togetherness were precious to both of them. Except at the breakfast table, they could hardly get time to chat. Noticing for a few days that both sat there for a long time, one day Dean gave a sharp scolding to them and a certain word stung Anandi to the quick. As she was in a habit of reporting everything to Aunt Theo, she wrote, "I do not care for any style, nor for vanity, but that one word touched my pride, for I am always very prompt and regard it as my pleasure as well as duty to be so. Besides it was Sunday and I did not hear the bells." [7]

The relationship between Anandi and Dean Bodley needs to be probed into for finding out if there were any tensions or misunderstandings between them. Kashibai Kanitkar, the Marathi biographer of Anandi, had brought some serious accusations against Dean Bodley.

(1) Employing various methods, Dean Bodley tried to force Christianity on Anandi.

(2) Annoyed by Anandi's square refusal, she neglected her meals and starved her. Being unable to consume meat, Anandi needed a sufficient quantity of milk, butter and other vegetarian food, but those things were not properly supplied to her by Dean Bodley.

(3) After her graduation, Anandi was invited by the State of Kolhapur to take charge of the female ward, but Dean Bodley created obstructions in Anandi's career.

All the 3 accusations are extremely grave. If they are true, it would prove Dean Bodley to be a mean-minded fanatic who played a double-game with her own student. If they are baseless, untrue and therefore harmful to Dean Bodley's reputation, the injustice has to be wiped out by finding the truth. Though Kanitkar had made these charges, she herself was not sure if they were true or false; because the source of information was Gopal. Knowing Gopal's habit of vacillating his opinions and loyalties according to his whim and caprice; his disregard for the truth and his relish for exaggeration, Kanitkar wrote this chapter of Anandi's life in a confused state of mind. On the one hand, she looked askance at Gopal's statements but on the other hand, she could not be sure of Dean Bodley's innocence. She knew only Aunt Theo with whom she had corresponded for some time. But for her, Dean Bodley was an unknown woman whose guaranty she could not give. She had no proof either of her innocence or her guilt. It is true that she herself made bitter comments about Dean Bodley and put forth the information without analysis. But while brooding over this issue she had also expressed her surprise that in spite of the Dean's good treatment to Anandi, how come Gopal called her names and how bad the Dean might have felt.

Mrs. Nancy Cobb Stone, the great-granddaughter of Theodosia Carpenter, generously entrusted the treasure of Anandi's letters to me, where I could locate a letter written by Anandi to Aunt Theo, which would throw light on this issue. The matter in the letter, dated 12th February 1885 runs like this: "Professor Bodley had commenced a few weeks since, to talk to me on that 'most serious and sacred' old subject 'The Religion.' She said she never talked on the subject before as one dear Mrs. Smith was here and had the 'bad influence' over everybody that came in. I asked her if she has observed any change in me and if so where about. She replied in the negative. I never fully understood the pain and sorrow she had to suffer for me. She said she never spent a Sunday without shedding tears for me and Mrs. Smith. She said, 'you are taught to regard sacred things as very sacred. I will understand it better than Mrs. Smith. I said, 'Certainly and [I] was first taught to receive the thorough rationale of anything before I accept it. If you will give me a reason to accept your theory, I will be only too thankful to you.' After long talk (no arguing) she asked, begged me to promise her to keep Sundays as long as I live. Of course [I] could not do it. I am not prepared to misuse my word even for one day far less 'life.' I generally keep silent unless there be an attempt made to force answer out of me. I had several talks with the Prof. and from [F1]Mrs. B too numerous to mention. I hope it won't go far enough to create any unpleasantness between us (I mean Professor and myself.)"[8] It becomes clear from this letter that both Dean Bodley and her old mother tried to put emotional pressure on Anandi for embracing Christianity. Another proof regarding this matter is a bit oblique. The Archives of Medical College of Pennsylvania had prepared the 'Brief Biographical Sketches of Three Foreign Students.' The short note on Anandi alludes to the above fact, "It is interesting to notice that Doctor Bodley expressed some qualms of conscience

F1 Mrs. B = Anandi refers to Dean Bodley's mother who stayed with her.

regarding her hospitality towards a so called 'heathen,' since she was in every respect a Christian missionary-minded woman."[9]

It also becomes clear from Anandi's letter that her friendship with Frances was disagreeable to Dean Bodley because Frances strongly supported Anandi's stand regarding religion. Anandi who was armed with resolute convictions, was not afraid either of Dean Bodley or her mother. Anandi loved to discuss religion with a truly religious person, but she despised this mentality of disrespecting others' religions. In essence, there was a germ of truth in one of the three accusations. But the crux of the issue is, whether Dean Bodley tortured Anandi for not agreeing to get converted. Dean's deep interest in Anandi was quite noticeable from the very beginning. Not only did she invite her to her college but also strongly recommended her name for the scholarship. Though it was not a Dean's duty to solve the housing problems of students, out of sheer regard for Anandi, she hunted a suitable house for her and when it was found to be unsuitable, she offered the shelter of her own house. Could a woman like Dean Bodley who had fought for the cause of Medical women, degrade herself by starving her own student just because she refused to become Christian? Was she more a Missionary than a wise professor? Was the religious fervour so overmastering as to drown love and sympathy? Dean Bodley was well aware of the health problems of Indian women. When she was shaping the first Indian woman doctor, could she destroy her own creation by sapping the energies of the feeble girl? Had the tension between them really swelled up to that limit, Anandi was sure to give vent to her feelings in her letters to Aunt Theo. But her letters indicate that in spite of all these things, Anandi held Dean Bodley in respect and referred to her as a dear loving woman. "She is a dear loving woman, nor will I ever think of her with anything else, but gratitude and love."[10] Anandi's letters to Gopal carried the same mark of admiration and she was truthful enough not to praise the imaginary qualities. Neither was she superficial as to exhibit the unfelt emotions.

Gopal had informed Kanitkar that Dean Bodley would never allow latecomers to dine, so whenever Anandi was late due to some work, she had to fast. Hence, Kanitkar painted Dean Bodley like a stubborn innkeeper, who pinched her boarder's belly to save her food. When Gopal met Anandi, he could perceive that his sick wife was a mere shadow of her previous self. This blow desolated him. Therefore, it is highly possible that in his desperation, he put the whole blame on Dean Bodley with whom Anandi stayed. But the fact is that in the 19th century, it was not easy to provide nutritious vegetarian food all along the year. Particularly in winter, it posed a big problem for Dean Bodley to feed Anandi, without including meat in her diet which constituted a large portion of the American meals. But without considering these difficulties, Gopal nurtured the misunderstanding and did not fail to tell the tale to Kanitkar.

Moreover, there was a vast difference between Indian and American meals. In India, Anandi had ample rice, chapatis, fried and cooked vegetables, dals, salads, pickles, Indian jams, curd, and buttermilk in her daily diet. But in America, she had to feed herself mainly on potato, beet, tomato, lettuce, radish or cucumber which were consumed either raw or in a boiled form. But vegetables were neither fried nor flavoured with different spices as in India. A pepper-pot, a salt-cellar and a phial of vinegar were the only taste-makers. So, it was but natural for Anandi to find the food tasteless, after continuously consuming it for two years. Compared to the main meal, desserts like cakes and fruits, were interesting. Pandita Ramabai, who had to face the same problem in England and America in the same period, had observed that those who had no liking for meat, had to fill their bellies mostly with milk, bread, salads and fruits.

Hence, it was a common problem of all the vegetarians and not specifically of Anandi. Not only at Bodley's place; but in any house, Anandi might have faced the same problem. If Anandi was not fed properly, it was not because of Dean Bodley; but in spite of Dean Bodley, who on the contrary faced a challenge to hunt vegetarian food for Anandi. One cannot forget that, when Gopal and his countrymen were suspicious about Anandi's dress and food manners, it was Dean Bodley who came to her help and assured that Anandi was keeping her word. In a letter to Gopal she stated, "During her residence in Philadelphia she has spent her time entirely in study. She is modest, dignified and prudent and she has won the hearts of all those associated with her steadfast devotion to duty. She dresses as a Hindu lady and abstains wholly from animal food."[11] This is a sort of character certificate issued by Dean Bodley which speaks a deal about what she felt about Anandi.

Anandi's wish to invite Pandita Ramabai for her graduation, who lived in England was rather expensive. Yet Dean Bodley took initiative and promptly corresponded with her. Ramabai had reservations about this invitation, for two reasons. Firstly, her well-wishers in England had advised her not to go to America leaving her own work unfinished. Plus, the sea-voyage was very unsafe in February-March and Ramabai was hesitating as her daughter Manorama was a mere child. Yet Dean Bodley succeeded in convincing her why her presence was essential in the graduation ceremony of Anandi, who was to become the first Indian woman doctor.

Dean Bodley's letter to Ramabai sheds light on her convincing power, capacity to understand problems of other people, her profound love for Anandi and the vigilance about women's welfare. "I regret that unconsciously I have been the means of unhappiness and unrest for you. . . . The impression I have received from your relatives concerning you is that your mission in India is that of an inspirer rather than that of a teacher. In years past, you have led on and sought to break down barriers and to lift up standards; your countrywomen looking out from their secluded lives have been encouraged to follow on. . . . My thought in inviting you to come to America early in1886 has been that if the tidings might be sent to India that you braved a wintery ocean to witness Anandibai receive her degree as a Doctor of Medicine, you in a certain sense gave your sanction to her act and enfolded her and her work in your own future leadership. . . . Mrs. Joshee has proved herself a faithful and successful student; if her life and health are spared, a grand professional future awaits her in her native land . . . Should you decide not to come to Anandibai's graduation, there is no other event of sufficient importance to bring you...dear Ramabai...I release [you] wholly from my obligation which your acceptance of my invitation may have implied. I understand the whole situation...Do not think of us in America as you decide."[12]

She would not have written this, if she wanted to ruin Anandi's future work. Considering this evidence, one can say that Dean Bodley surely tried to persuade Anandi to embrace Christianity, but she was not a mentally sick person as to starve Anandi or put a spoke in the wheel of her student. On the contrary, Dean Bodley who wished nothing but success to Anandi, prepared the ground and gave the necessary support for her career. In the introduction to *High Caste Hindu Woman*, a book written by Pandita Ramabai, Dean Bodley had emphatically said, "I had been familiar with the statements concerning the condition of the native women of India. My sympathies had always been with them."[13] Some natives had expressed their suspicion that Anandi was not a doctor. She might have completed only a nursing course. Dean Bodley, who was pained to know this, had immediately sent a letter in support of Anandi. On 20th March 1887, using this letter, the news was published in a well-known newspaper 'Maratha' which was founded by the great leader Lokmanya Bal Gangadhar Tilak. The editor had appreciated Dean Bodley's sense of justice and had thanked her. He didn't fail to criticise the people who had tried to dwarf Anandi. The news runs like this —

"The Late Dr. Anandibai Joshi"

Dr. Rachel L. Bodley, M. D. Dean of Faculty of Woman's Medical College of Pennsylvania, where the late lamented Dr. Anandibai Joshee studied Medicine thus wrote to us.

"Dear Sir, I am informed that it has been stated in India that Dr. Anandibai Joshee is not a Doctor of Medicine but has only acquired the position and knowledge of a mid-wife while in United States.

I beg to state as Dean of Woman's Medical College of Pennsylvania that Dr. Joshee has followed full course of Medical studies prescribed by our Faculty (a copy of which I enclose herewith) and that she had the Degree of Doctor of Medicine conferred upon her at a public commencement held in Philadelphia on March 11th 1886: She is therefore recognised by the laws of the commonwealth of Pennsylvania as a fully educated and qualified practitioner including all its branches.

With great respect, I am

Truly yours,

Rachel L. Bodley M.D.

Dean of Faculty.

"We are sorry that the honoured and loved lady who was the cause of this letter has 'shuffled off this mortal coil.' How very grateful would she have felt towards her late preceptress for her kindness in hearing testimony to her worth and qualifications. This is the difference between India and America! Here the only return that we make to Dr. Anandibai for her noble act of self-sacrifice and heroic devotion to a noble object, is to sneer at her and suggest the most uncharitable and wicked doubts about her qualifications. We have a faint recollection of having read in some worthless but venomous print a doubt expressed as to whether the late Dr. Joshi was not merely a Doctor of Midwifery. This paper may not think fit to correct its mistake.... But we thought it our duty to publish the letter...to do justice to the memory of the diseased lady and to show to our friends the worthiness of the American character. We cannot but thank Dr. R. L. Bodley for her kindness to Dr. Anandibai individually and through her the weaker sex of India generally."

This is the strongest evidence of the benevolent character of Dean Bodley. At the same time, it is very shocking that in spite of Dr. Bodley's timely help, Gopal gave wrong information about her to Kashibai Kanitkar, when she was writing Anandi's biography.

References:

1. Source: The Nancy Cobb Stone Collection of letters
2. *The Life of Dr. Anandabai Joshee* – Caroline Healey Dall. 1888. p. 119
3. Ibid, p.p. 114, 115
4. Ibid, p.p. 116, 117
5. Source: The Nancy Cobb Stone Collection of letters.
6. Ibid.
7. Ibid.
8. Ibid.
9. Brief Biographical sketches of Three foreign students – prepared by the Archives of the Medical College of Pennsylvania.

10. Source: The Nancy Cobb Stone Collection of letters.

11. From the letter, which is preserved in the Government's Archives in Kolhapur, Maharashtra State, India.

12. *The letters and correspondence of Pandita Ramabai* – compiled by Sister Geraldine. Edited by A.B. Shah, / 1977 / First Edition p.p. 164, 165,166.

13. A Reprint of *The High Caste Hindu women* – Pandita Ramabai Saraswati.

    Introduction Dean R.L. Bodley. February 1981 p. i

20

The Second Spring Term

At the end of the winter term of 1885, Anandi and Frances Smith were busy with their own studies. After completing the thesis on 'Physical Phases of Epilepsy' which she had to submit for her degree, Frances began to prepare herself for the final examinations. Whereas Anandi concentrated on Anatomy, Physiology and Chemistry, the subjects in which she was to take her final examinations. She passed the examination with good marks and the delightful news was delivered to Gopal by Dean Bodley. "She passed the examinations creditably taking higher rank in her class, which consisted of forty-two ladies."[1]

Frances Smith graduated on 11th March and received the degree of Doctor of Medicine. She had invited Aunt Theo for her graduation, but some domestic problems held her back. This year, the degree of Doctor of Medicine was conferred upon 22 students by President T. Morris Perot and the valedictory address was delivered by Dr. William Keen, the Professor of Surgery. In the evening, a grand reception was given in the honour of new graduates. Saying goodbye to her college and colleagues, Frances returned to Warrensburg on 16th March. Thereafter Anandi was all alone on the upper floor of Dean Bodley's house and missed Frances very much. The spring term commenced on 15th March, during which Anandi and her class worked in the Pharmaceutical and Pathological laboratories and took a course in bandaging and fracture-dressing. Several special lectures of guest lecturers were arranged in this term. A course on Dental Physiology and Pathology was conducted by Prof. C. Newline Peirce of the 'Pennsylvania College of Dental Surgery.' The most frequent surgical diseases of the gums and teeth were illustrated by examining clinical patients from the Woman's Hospital. A course on Toxicology was conducted by Dr. Jno J. Reese, the professor of Medical

Jurisprudence and Toxicology at the 'University of Pennsylvania.' In addition to those special lectures, private tuitions on various subjects were also available. Anandi took a private course in Gynaecology from Dr. Hanna Croasdale. Those who had failed in March could reappear at the end of the second spring term.

So much time was consumed by lectures and practicals that Anandi could hardly get time for self-study. Hospitals were scattered all over the city and students had to run from one end to another which consumed their time, energy and money. To make both ends meet, Abby Charlotte worked in the summer vacation as a correspondent and an agent to a certain journal, where she was to get a good percentage on profit. Therefore, Anandi tried to get subscribers to Abby's journal through Aunt Theo. Even Anandi had to manage her financial affairs very carefully. Yet, the financial tensions were nothing compared to the emotional tensions given by her near relatives and countrymen. Finding out her address in America, unknown people also showered letters on her and tormented her by demanding explanations about her food habits, clothes, way of living and observance of religious duties, though they had no right to do so. But she never affirmed that the change in food and dress habits was essential for her survival in a cold country like America. Some of her countrymen thought it their moral duty to keep a watch on Anandi, while others took pleasure in spreading various rumours such as — Anandi had forgotten her Nation, her near ones and dear ones; Gopal had lost his wife forever and soon she was to embrace Christianity. Anandi was hurt to see that her countrymen were treating her like a criminal though she had done nothing wrong.

It is really amazing that despite this torture, Anandi tried her best not to lose her patience. She knew that ultimately, she was going to work among the same people. Though their harsh words and baseless criticism saddened her, she understood that their ignorance, thoughtlessness, fear and anxiety made them suspicious about her. They had not still recovered from the shock of her migration to a foreign land. She hoped that one day, her good work would speak for itself and they would realise their mistakes. She was hurt to observe that even those who knew her very well were not ready to take her side. She was particularly pained by the attempt of Raobahadur Dandekar to poison Gopal's mind. She sadly remembered that the same person had once loved her like his daughter. Except for the warm, friendly and encouraging letters of Gangadhar Ketkar, with whom she could share her problems, tensions and thoughts, she had no other solace. On the American front, she defended her nation and on the Indian front, she had to defend herself. Hence a large amount of her valuable energy was wasted in giving unnecessary explanations. This struggle was too much for the girl who was just out of her teens.

It was painful for her to accept the fact that even her husband brought accusations against her. He had the heart to take away the moral support which she badly needed and hence she had to fight alone. Gopal, who had joined forces with her opponents, attacked her relentlessly, exercising the rights of a husband, a Guru, a moral guard of the Hindu culture and last but not least, a male. The husband reproached his wife's disinterest in him. The Guru announced that the success had gone to her head. The moral vanguard dogmatically criticised her levity, whereas the possessive male went off the rails when he seriously charged her with disloyalty. These unfair charges jarred on her nerves. Oscillating between gloom and grief, she wrote to him that she possessed neither tears nor sighs to give vent to her feelings. Gopal never realised or rather he did not wish to realise that since their precious qualities were complementary to each other, he and his wife were interdependent. To educate a woman was his greatest dream, which could be realised only because Anandi had the potentials. Similarly, Anandi could pursue her off-beat goal, only because of Gopal's strong support. But it is a rule that while the glory is written in the name of a King, the benevolent satisfaction is the share of a Kingmaker, which must be enjoyed silently. No wonder, Gopal was to remain in the background and Anandi was to be in the foreground of public attention. Though her success was the triumph of his conviction, she was to receive name and fame. But being unable to accept his secondary role, he refused to remain in the background and thus defeated not Anandi, but himself. His baseless charges against her were nothing but an expression of the inferiority complex. He tried to impress upon Anandi's mind that however intelligent she might be, he was her husband and therefore he was superior. By belittling her, he tried to gain confidence and her suffering was for him a sure sign of his power over her. The confidant person of bygone days now needed to torment his wife, to make sure of his own existence.

Anandi was sharp enough to understand that the real purpose of Gopal's accusations and blames was to trouble her and to make her feel guilty. Yet she went on giving explanations and proving her innocence. Her letters show that she was not a woman to accept anything just because her husband ordered her to do so. When Gopal let loose his tongue, she fearlessly exhorted him to remember that she did not look at him as an average husband and he too, in turn, should not be conventional in treating his wife. When it was impossible for her to overlook his biased opinions, she showed him his proper place. She boldly reminded him, what devilish treatment he had given to her when she was a small girl. She remarked that Gopal had felt free to beat her blue, because for centuries no law existed in the country to prevent a husband from tormenting his wife. A wife was left with no choice but to endure her affliction with fortitude, since the law had offered her no right to protect herself or to complain. These events are enough to prove that in no way she was afraid of Gopal. Even though she tried to make peace with the Indian public by accepting their views regarding food and dress, she never compromised on the basic principles. One cannot forget that she had made people accept her migration to America for her Medical education in those days, when women's education as well as migration to a foreign land were treated like sins. She had prepared herself for the excommunication also, when she gave a lecture at Shrirampur, Bengal. In one of her letters, she told Gopal that she would be sorry if people disliked her decision to be a doctor, but she would never give up.

Anandi had no doubt that women could play an important role in the upliftment of society, and she was in the process of preparing herself to play her role as a doctor, as a lifesaver, as a reformer and as a social worker. Yet a thin fabric of traditionality was closely woven by the side of modernity in the complex texture of her mind. All through her life, those two outlooks conflicted with each other and Anandi was unable to overcome this subtle conflict. When the advanced woman was stronger in her personality, she could fight back her husband's attacks, throwing aside the traditional view that a wife should obey her husband. As a letter-writer, Anandi dealt with Gopal on a personal level and that was their private communication. Here she did not mind using strong words to oppose him. She never obeyed him at the cost of her own values and conviction. But in public, Anandi was a different person. Not wishing to hurt his pride and self-respect before others, she behaved like a typical meek, and obedient wife and did not utter a word against him.

Anandi did not answer even a friendly question from Caroline Dall, "Why did Gopal resign his job before coming to America?" Anandi did not prefer to answer this question because the truthful answer would have exposed his carelessness. In fact, Anandi herself had advised him not to give up the job, since it would have created grave financial problems. But she did not admit this fact even before Caroline who was her trusted, mature and elderly friend. Cleverly avoiding the real answer, she said briefly and with a deep sigh that Gopal was tired but did not pursue the subject further. After becoming better acquainted with Gopal's whimsical ways, Caroline was very much worried about Anandi, but no question about Gopal was entertained by Anandi, and her only answer was silence. "No word escaped her lips. Obediently she stooped to lift her heavy burden." [2]

Here some questions could be raised about Anandi's dispositions as well. Why did she protect Gopal all the time? Why a truthful person like her did not admit that Gopal was wrong, when she was absolutely convinced about it? Was she still afraid of her husband in the depth of her mind? Or did she think that her frankness would instigate Gopal to create more problems and he would put her in an awkward position, and both would fall in the eyes of their well-wishers in America? But her silence did not save her. Anandi was reputed to be rebellious woman, but her dumb endurance and meek acceptance of the unacceptable things disappointed her friends in America very much. No doubt, like Gopal, Anandi too defeated herself as a person, despite her signal success in her studies. But one cannot forget that both Gopal and her countrymen who constantly exposed her to mental torture had a lion's share in her defeat.

References:

1. Source: The Government's Archives in Kolhapur, Maharashtra State, India.
2. *The Life of Dr. Anandabai Josh*ee - Caroline Healey Dall. 1888. p. 148

21

Talk of the Devil and...

Even before his arrival in America, Gopal was a known figure among the well-wishers of women doctors. He had earned respect as Anandi's broad-minded husband, mentor and staunch supporter of women's higher education. Wherever Anandi went, she was pleased to hear good words about him. Anandi who was utterly grateful to Gopal, once told Caroline, "I know there are many good husbands in the United States. I see that they make their wives happy. But among them all there is no one so good as my husband."[1] Frances Smith who was eager to meet Anandi's husband, had asked her to bring him to Warrensburg whenever he would come to America. But except Aunt Theo, no one was aware of Anandi's inner conflict. She knew for some time that he was thinking of resigning from his job at the Post office and coming to America. In a letter written to him in January 1884, Anandi had urged him not to do so. "Have patience. There is no point in doing anything hastily. Please don't resign your job." But the letter had no effect on Gopal. Anandi wanted him to come to America as a businessman and do something of worth. But having no dream, no aim of his own, he did not consider her suggestion with seriousness. Anandi was disturbed by his untimely arrival in the spring of 1885, though it was not unexpected to her. She did not know how both were to survive without any source of money.

One day an Anglo-Indian inspector in the Post office gave a scolding to Gopal for a mistake. Gopal was annoyed because he thought that he was not the culprit. Outwardly feeling insulted, but inwardly happy to find an excuse to resign, he gave up his job. He did not care that by doing so, he had lost forever a stable source of income. Packing up his belongings, he left for Nashik to meet Gangadhar Ketkar, in whom he confided that very soon he would be going to America. He kept his belongings at Ketkar's house and went to Bombay. There he purchased a ticket of the cheapest vessel going to Burma, which cost him 5 Rupees. Before reaching America, he wanted to visit various countries.

The ship was crowded with poor labourers going to Burma, to earn their livelihood. Putting on red-ochre clothes, Gopal disguised himself as an ascetic and mingled among people as a respectable sadhu. It was raining heavily and the weather was very rough. After 3 days, the ship reached Rangoon, the capital of Burma. He stayed there for a few days doing some odd jobs to earn money. He had vowed that he would conduct this tour without spending a single penny of his motherland. So, he sent back Rupees 5 to India with which he had purchased the ticket from Bombay. Away from his home, job and country and not tied either to his wife or relatives, he wandered like a free bird doing whatever he wished. Without burdening his mind with a thought for tomorrow, he lived like a tramp, from hand to mouth.

In June 1884, Anandi came to know from his letter that Gopal had left his job and was wandering in strange countries doing all sorts of unthinkable activities. Very scanty details are available about his tour. From Burma, he went to Thailand at the end of September. From Bangkok, he wrote a letter to Anandi on 30th September. In November, he went to China, then to Japan and after 10 months or so, reached New York. What kind of jobs Gopal did for his livelihood? How did he survive for months in those unknown countries without money or friends? How did he communicate with those people whose languages were unknown to him and when English was not commonly understood by the masses? All such questions are unanswered. The only certainty is that in every country, he delivered lectures before the educated class who understood English and received an honorarium for that. A letter to Anandi sent from China, carried this address — 'Post Office, Hongkong, China.' So, it is quite possible that being a former Postmaster of the British Government, he might have taken shelter under the roofs of Postmasters of various regions. In China, he succumbed to a queer disease. He was all alone and there was nobody to help him. To get rid of the tiresome disease, he drank a cup of kerosene with sugar and played havoc with his health. What made him think of such a queer remedy and how he recovered, no one could know. Or it could be another tale woven by him to create awe. Those days in Gopal's life are wrapped in mystery. But one cannot help appreciating the astonishing travel lust, the daring and the relish for adventure. Anandi reached America via England, whereas Gopal took exactly the opposite route, thus combinedly both encircled the globe.

In the last phase of his travel, he didn't communicate even with Anandi. In a letter to Aunt Theo, written on 12th February 1885, that is a few weeks before his arrival in America, she said, "I have had a short letter from my husband. He is well."[2] But on the next day she wrote, "I have not heard from my husband in nearly three weeks. It is the longest time, I ever passed without any word from him. I feel very anxious."[3] The obvious inconsistency was the result of her perplexity and tension. At the beginning of March 1885, Gopal landed in New York. But instead of going straight away to Philadelphia to meet Anandi, he just wrote a letter to her from New York. She expected him to arrive in the spring of 1886 but he had arrived a year before. Gopal's untimely arrival disturbed Anandi and she was unprepared to meet him. So, she was tensed up. She couldn't guess why he arrived so soon and what exactly his plan was. Being aware of his eccentric nature, she anticipated that he was bound to create problems. Not knowing how to react, she took her own time to answer his first letter from New York. She explained later that she was very busy, so she could not find time to reply. Busy she was, but more than that, there were certain things on her mind which she found awkward to discuss with Gopal. She was not sure if Gopal would take them in a proper spirit. Unable to delay any more, at last on 13th March, she replied to his letter and made a clean breast of her thoughts.

Anandi wanted to make him understand that there were two problems that they had to solve together. For a long time, she was habituated to talk, write, read, study and think in English, with a one-track mind. In America, there was not a single soul with whom she could communicate in her mother tongue Marathi and remain in touch with the language. Hence it would have been difficult for her to talk with Gopal in Marathi. She was sure that this was going to make Gopal angry. But she felt that only if Gopal would show some patience and offer her a little help, she would be able to pick up Marathi very quickly. Secondly, she wanted to decide about the mode of their first meeting on the American grounds. Like a long-separated American couple, they could not have embraced and kissed each other in the presence of others, as it was beyond the Indian sense of decency. At the same time, it would not have looked proper just to shake hands because Gopal was not a stranger but her husband. Nor could she have been able to run out of the room, bashfully covering her face with her hands like a typical Indian woman, as she did not feel that way. Now that she was a different person, she thought that it would have been out-and-out hypocrisy. For days, she had put on her thinking cap, yet was unable to decide about their first meeting. It is not known for how long Gopal was in New York and with whom he stayed but on 16th March, Anandi informed Aunt Theo that she had received his letter from San Francisco. It is possible that, offended by Anandi's silence, he might have gone to the other end of America to teach her a lesson. When Anandi wrote him a letter on 13th March, she had no idea about his departure. Only on 16th March she came to know about his move. "I had a letter from my husband today. He is in San Francisco. He intends to stay there until June, as he is afraid, he might interfere with my studies." [4]

Anandi had decided that at the close of the spring term in June, she would go to New York, along with the Carpenters to meet Gopal and then they would go to Roselle. But not waiting for this or not even meeting Anandi in Philadelphia, he went away to San Francisco. Knowing for certain that now Gopal was bound to give lectures and interviews to newspapers without much thought, she mildly warned him to be careful with reporters. She was also worried about his health and felt that rest, homely atmosphere, good food and her love were the things that he needed the most. But he did not let her into his plans. Once he wrote that he would return in June, but the other day he conveyed that he might not come till her graduation. Before the actual meeting, they entered into an argument over her letter about their first meeting. Gopal did not fail to misunderstand it and instead of giving a thought to it, he picked a quarrel with her, saying that she wrote such things out of disloyalty. He quickly used the opportunity for giving an acrimonious sermon to her about her extravagance and lure of money, though there was no reason to say all those things to her. Anandi received the letter on 31st March 1885 which was her 21st birthday. She was upset to receive this bitter birthday gift and felt that Gopal had no feelings for her.

As she had predicted, Gopal began to give lectures in San Francisco, the topic of his first speech being 'The Best Women.' He greatly astonished his audience by attacking the higher education of women and prescribing the cult of domesticity for them. "This," he declared in his high-pitched voice, "unfitted them for the domestic duties of wives and mothers." Shocked by the inconsistency between his deeds and words, someone from the audience cried, "I thought your own wife was studying Medicine in Philadelphia." In answer to this, he just shrugged his shoulders, spread out his hands and exclaimed, "Oh, yes!", as if he could not help it. Being a sensationalist, he did not mind that he spoke contrary to his own conviction. Gopal's image of a benevolent supporter of women's education was shattered by this speech. In fact, Gopal himself acted deliberately as an iconoclast and enjoyed it. The Americans did not know that he had just begun the game and Gopal could cross any limit of rashness if he wished.

He perfectly knew what he was doing. Knowing that 'Anandi's husband' was his only qualification and that people were all ears to listen to his liberal thoughts, it was an easy game to strike wonder by saying the opposite. The newspapers gave wide publicity to his lecture and within a day, he was in the news. The clippings were immediately sent to Philadelphia and it did produce the effect that Gopal desired. The friends and well-wishers of Anandi stood aghast at the outrageous speech delivered by her own husband. A clipping was sent to Caroline Dall also, who was more sad than angry for Anandi's sake as she knew that Anandi was sure to get hurt by his behaviour. It was beyond the understanding of the people in America who had always believed Gopal to be a man of conviction, that he could publicly denounce higher education of women. It was unbelievable that he could behave in such a hypocritical manner. Though they did not know, Anandi knew that Gopal was capable of doing such things just to create a sensation. He would not hesitate to make fun of any serious matter, regardless of its aftermath.

One day suddenly Gopal visited Caroline Dall's house, without giving her any idea about his visit. Caroline was not at home. So, the housekeeper received him. As she also knew about his speech in San Francisco, she questioned him sharply and demanded an explanation. Gopal was so amused by her anger that he answered her very lightly.

"Mr. Joshee . . . went to my house, and there encountered the lady who had charge of it in my absence. More ignorant than the rest of us of various embarrassing complications, this lady, who had been greatly attached to his wife, looked at him sharply and said, 'Was it you then, who made that speech in San Francisco?' 'Yes', replied Gopal. 'And what did you do it for?' she persisted. 'Just for a little fun,' was the answer. 'I thought I would stir them up a little."[5] This answer produced an acrid reaction from Caroline Dall. She wrote, "Mr. Joshee could have had a very inadequate idea of the interest Anandabai had aroused in this country, and he could have understood very little the character of his wife, if he expected her to be pleased by fun of that sort. I have recorded this reply, because I never gratified him by any inquiries concerning the matter, nor am I aware that any of his wife's friends ever did so."[6] Though Anandi's friends never held her responsible for Gopal's behaviour, it made her nervous because her own husband had hurt the feelings of her friends with his irrational pranks. Caroline noticed a subtle change in her when they met. "No one seemed to know whether Anandabai had received the news, but the moment we met in the autumn, I knew that she had seen the paper. A change had passed over her, as subtle as that the hoarfrost breaths over summer grass."[7]

Had Anandi registered her protest, Gopal might have done something more ridiculous to amuse himself. Knowing this, she did not give vent to her real feelings in her letter. On the contrary, she decided to appeal to the goodness hidden within him. She informed him in a lighter vein that her friends were angered by his speech, but those who knew him to be a staunch supporter of women's education, felt that he would never be so harsh upon women. With deliberation, she gave him a benefit of the doubt, when she remarked that it might be a misinterpreted or a biased report, skilfully made by reporters. She pretended not to understand the real meaning of his action but in the depth of her mind, she knew with certainty that Gopal was capable of anything. She further added with caution that some of her friends asked if he was filled with remorse for allowing his wife to study Medicine. The letter is a manifestation of her tremendous self-control, patience and wisdom. She took every care not to hurt him or instigate him while she spoke her mind. She did not want to waste her energy in quarrelling with him. So, in a way she did this for self-protection also. Using the mask of 'somebody', she posed before him her own questions and indirectly gave way to her feelings. She mildly warned him that perhaps he would not have meant what he said, but people were bound to take his statements at the face value, thinking him to be an anti-women person. Hence a joke of that kind was out of place.

Despite her care and deliberation to hide her mind, the mental disturbance was apparent at the end of her letter when she confessed that she was at a loss of words and her hands trembled when she set to write. "Some tasks are such" she told him, "that they can be better done only in dreams, than in real life." Who knows, she might be giving an outlet to her anger in her dreams and controlling it in her wakefulness, not wishing to sap her remaining energy by fighting with Gopal. In short, Gopal's arrival proved to be nothing but a nuisance and an encroachment on her freedom. Till then, she was alone in America and he was at a safe distance in India. But now that he had come, the tiresome responsibility of performing the role of his wife had unavoidably fallen on her shoulder.

The spring term of 1885 ended on 30th May and Anandi went to Roselle for her summer vacation where Eighmie and Helena were eagerly waiting for her arrival. Summer was always full of fun, games, guests, tea parties and picnics. The previous summer, Anandi had gone to Saratoga but this summer all remained in Roselle, in expectation of Gopal whose plan they did not know. Gopal did not inform Anandi when he would come and she could do nothing but wait patiently. The first meeting of Anandi-Gopal which had worried Anandi a lot, took place without much ado. Gopal found out an easy solution of going to Roselle unannounced. But when he arrived Anandi had gone out with Eighmie to a friend's house for a tea party. So, he had to wait for her return. Generally, guests were received in the guests' parlour. But for the Carpenters Gopal was not a guest but a relative. Therefore, Aunt Theo invited him into their family room. Plus, she knew that as usual Anandi would go directly into the family room and would get her pleasant surprise. When Anandi came home, no one told her about Gopal's arrival. As was expected, she went straight into the family room, and was stopped short to see Gopal sitting comfortably on a sofa reading newspaper. The couple being united after a long time, was left alone for some time. As there was no witness to their first meeting, it took its natural course. Gopal could silently watch the play of emotions on her face and she could shed tears of joy without any restrain. They were meeting after 2 years. On the morning of 7th April 1883, Gopal was separated from Anandi. Like a candle in the wind, Anandi was standing alone on the deck of the ship. But Gopal had no strength to look at her and say goodbye. Furiously trying to control himself, he had gone away. Now in the summer of 1885, they were united. At last the period of separation was over and now she was standing before his eyes trembling with joy like a delicate flower.

This summer was unique in the lives of the Carpenters. Their house resonated with cheerful talks, chitchatting, discussions and laughter. Aunt Theo and Uncle Ben were busy arranging picnics and parties for Anandi-Gopal. People in Roselle curiously visited their house to have a look at Anandi's husband, who was much older than her. 'How come Anandi was married to him at the age of 10? She looks like his daughter!' They whispered. The tall man wearing his Indian costume with a red turban, who spoke in his high-pitched nasal voice didn't fit in their concept of Anandi's husband. Yet he commanded respect because he was instrumental in sending Anandi to America for her Medical education. Plus, they were happy for Anandi's sake that at last she was united with him. Gopal was exhausted by his long journey that stretched over a period of 10 months and had fallen prey to Rheumatism. Now he needed homely comforts like good food, medicine and rest. Now his wife was there to look after him. Though they were placed comfortably in the house of the Carpenters, Anandi did not wish to burden them with an additional expense, so she suggested to Gopal that they should pay for their food. Once she had thought of selling her gold chain for raising money, but she realised that she would not be able to procure even 1/10th of the original price. Hence, she dropped the idea. She requested Gopal to make some arrangements and also urged Aunt Theo not to take any unnecessary trouble for them. But the Carpenters regarded Anandi as their own daughter and were glad to put out the welcome mat for Gopal. They tried their best to make him at home.

One Sunday, Anandi-Gopal visited Brooklyn which was an important city in New York State. The East River that separated Brooklyn from Manhattan was spanned in 1883 by the Brooklyn Bridge and it was a pride of the city. Brooklyn was famous for its educational institutes, the Brooklyn Female Academy being one of them. Magnificent churches and other monuments were landmarks in the history of this city and the city hall had a prominent role in public life. But the purpose of the Joshis' visit was different than sightseeing. They had gone there to listen to the lectures of Thomas De Witt Talmage and Beecher Henry Ward. Talmage, the editor of *Frank Leslie's Sunday Magazine*, was a Presbyterian clergyman, who had served as a chaplain in the Union Army during the Civil War. Beecher Ward was also clergy and was well known as a giant among orators of the anti-slavery time, who could easily deliver several lectures in a day. No other champion of the anti-slavery movement was more hated and abused than the 'Abolitionist Beecher.' His series of speeches in England in the fall of 1863 had helped turn the course of the English opinion in favour of North America which was fighting against slavery. The prime reason for his success was his tremendous physical and mental vitality. If people attempted to howl him down, he would make them know his muscular power. He believed in free trade and women's suffrage and vigorously advocated those concepts. He was 72 years old when Anandi-Gopal heard his lecture but he had the same energy and enthusiasm. When Anandi-Gopal attended the meetings of Talmage and Ward, their messenger met Anandi and told that both Talmage and Ward wished to talk with her. As Anandi always liked to discuss religion or any other serious topics, she was more than pleased to talk with these great persons. On the same day, Anandi-Gopal visited Greenwood country, which was a cemetery. It was so beautiful, serene and lush green that Anandi thought it was the best place to rest in peace.

This year Anandi went to Philadelphia a little early. She wanted to attend the wedding of her friend who had urged her to come along with Gopal. Anandi's wish to enjoy snow in the company of Gopal was to be fulfilled this winter. Soon the winter term of 1885 was to begin which was the last term of her Medical course, and at the beginning of the spring term, she was to receive her degree.

References:

1. *The Life of Dr. Anandabai Joshee* - Caroline Healey Dall. 1888. p 177
2. Source: - The Nancy Cobb Stone collection of letters.
3. Ibid
4 Ibid
5. *The Life of Dr. Anandabai Joshee*- Caroline Healey Dall. 1888. p 124
6. Ibid, page 124
7. Ibid, page 124

22

The Winter Term of 1885

The winter term of 1885 commenced on 1st October. The Medical course was divided into 5 terms. After completing it, students had to work for a year as interns in one of the hospitals, where women doctors were welcomed. During the third-year winter term, attendance at lectures and weekly examinations in all branches in which the final examination had not already been passed, was required. A course in Operative Surgery was given prime importance in this term for increasing the practical knowledge of students. The candidates had to apply for the degree six weeks before the close of that session and they had to exhibit evidence of having completed the requirements. They were supposed to pay the graduation fees and complete satisfactorily the thesis of their own composition and penmanship on any Medical subject of their choice. This year, the graduation was fixed on 11th March 1886. The annual examination was arranged in the first week of March. A student's degree depended upon the result of this examination as well as her thesis.

The old friends like Frances and Dr. Schultz had gone away to their respective towns but Anandi had some new friends like Keiko Okami, the first Japanese Medical student, who had aroused much curiosity. The condition of women's education was so bad in Japan that till the Second World War, women were not accepted in Medical institutes. Though the general atmosphere in Japan was anti-women, Keiko's house was governed by her progressive father who was a man of the broad horizon. He had decided to impart higher education to his daughter. He was also possessed by the idea of establishing business relations with foreign countries. So, he had understood the importance of learning English. Though in the 19th century, the Japanese were not interested in educating their women, there were a few girls' schools which were established by Christian Missionaries. Being himself a Christian, Keiko's father had sent her to one of those schools. The family had already drifted away from the Japanese tradition by embracing Christianity and now by sending Keiko to a school, in spite of the disapproval of their people, they further broke themselves away from the commonly accepted ideology. Under such favourable conditions, Keiko developed herself very fast. Since childhood, she took pains to master English. In 1881, she joined Sakurai Girls' School as an English teacher. In 1884, Keiko was married to Sekichiro Okami, a well-bred youth who strongly believed in women's education. Missionary work and upliftment of the poor were the goals that brought them together and soon love developed between them which ultimately culminated in their marriage.

A month after their marriage, Sekichiro joined 'Michigan College of Agriculture' in America and Keiko followed him to join 'Woman's Medical College of Pennsylvania' about which she had heard a lot from the Christian Missionaries. It is true that no woman of any caste, creed or religion was prohibited in the college, neither was it thought necessary for a student to mention her religion. But a special encouragement was given to those who desired to study Medicine with a view to become Missionary physicians. They were admitted annually at half the price of all tickets excluding matriculation, laboratory and graduation fees. They had to furnish only the certificates of the Foreign Missionary Society whose wards they had been. The applicants were supposed to pursue Medical work abroad under the direction of the society issuing the certificate. Dean Bodley herself had taken a profuse interest in this work. Being an Asian Christian who had decided to give her life to Mission work, Keiko could easily obtain the special advantages.

This year, Sadat Islambooli, a Syrian woman from Damascus, also entered the college. Dean Bodley arranged a reception for Keiko and Sadat on 10th October 1885. She snapped their photograph along with Anandi, and all the three women posed for her in their native dresses. To the great satisfaction of the organisers of the college, this year, Pierre La Flesche, the leader of a Red-Indian tribe Omah sent his daughter Suzan to the college. This was an indication that their painstaking efforts of years were bearing good fruits. Of all the new students, Anandi liked Keiko Okami the best and wrote to Aunt Theo about her, "She is very intelligent in her looks and a very sweet little woman. She is married and is with her husband. She is an artist."[1]

The conflict between Anandi's physical strength and willpower reached its climax this winter. A severe headache had become her constant companion. Her resisting power was so reduced that she fell prey to

different diseases. One day in November, her condition was so bad that she was unable to walk properly. Leaning on Abby's arm, she returned home and could not go to college for the next few days. Her letter to Aunt Theo written on 28th November depicts her disappointment with her own self because there seemed no end to her health problems. "I am sorry to say I am not through the course of my sickness. As soon as the originally affected organ began to recover, another one in the neighbourhood took its tern. So, we have to begin the story over. I am not in bed and hope never again shall be until next March, more than 7 hours, but am rather miserable."[2]

Though Gopal was staying with her, he used to go out early morning and return home very late. Once Rev. Amies of the Unitarian Church on the Spring Garden Street gave him a letter of introduction which he was to present to a certain professor in the University of Pennsylvania for a job. What exactly happened is not mentioned anywhere but nothing materialised. In America, Gopal did nothing particular to earn his bread. The only thing that he really enjoyed was to deliver sarcastic lectures and criticise harshly people in America, their religion and of course women's higher education. He didn't feel awkward to accept an honorarium from the organisers for hurting them without any rhyme or reason. This was his only source of income. No wonder he made his wife suffer a lot and increased her tensions. Had he given some satisfaction to Anandi; it would have reflected in her letters to Aunt Theo. But on the contrary, her simple words are the manifestation of her disappointment and gloom. The subdued grief could be sensed hidden between the words like 'He is out as usual', 'He is out again', 'He is talking of going to Washington tomorrow,' etc. It is clear that she wanted him to be with her, in the hours of her trouble but he left her alone and wandered aimlessly wherever he wished.

A strange kind of indifference and coldness had crept in, in their relationship from Gopal's side. One night Anandi was copying the lectures that she had missed during her illness. As she had to write a lot, she requested Gopal to help her a little. But sharply remarking that he would not indulge her with such help, he refused to copy the lectures. She was not asking much and Gopal had nothing else to do but sleep peacefully. She was not keeping well and certainly needed a helping hand. But his refusal made her work till late at night, in spite of her backache. He was less troublesome from a distance, when he was in India. But now that he was staying with her, his nuisance value had increased. The emotional burden

was so unbearable that she reported all such things to Aunt Theo who was her only solace. Her letter of 8th February 1886 would cast light on Gopal's queer ways of harassment. "My husband came to see me at the college this afternoon with attitude…of a severe critic; …The criticism I doubt not was rational, proper…but I must confess it was too harsh for my sensitive nature. He condemned me for my weak style of writing which he knew, I always possessed. I did not wish to utter a word to anyone, but swallow everything as is my practice… I was told I gave you an impression that I shall not see you again until after my hospital duty is over. You know that is not true …What I intended to say in my previous letter was simply that I would not have anything like the vacation we anticipated."[3]

There always dwelt a forlorn child in Anandi's mind who was hungry for true and unmixed love which she didn't receive either from her husband or from her mother. Aunt Theo was the only person who could comfort Anandi's troubled mind with her affection. Therefore, Anandi felt better after pouring out her grief or sharing her joy with Aunt Theo. Even when Gopal tried to create misunderstanding between them, Anandi knew that he would not succeed. "We know each other a great deal better than we are understood by others. I therefore trust, our hearts will speak for themselves and understand each other."[4]

When Gopal came to America, he bitterly noticed that his wife had become a celebrity, who had earned name, fame, friendship, popularity and love. Whereas he was nobody but 'Anandi's husband.' Being a victim of jealousy and hatred, he could hardly admire Anandi's success. His ego was so hurt that he took pleasure in shattering her peace of mind, which she needed the most. Having no other choice, she bore her affliction with great fortitude. Yet she thought it was her 'duty' to love him. "Love and duty are sacred and my own . . . I can always love though I cannot claim to be loved."[5] But if love could be looked at as the response to values, was it really possible for her to love a malevolent person like Gopal, just out of duty? Was she compelling herself to love him? Or was she conventional in loving him, just because she was married to him? It is unthinkable that in her mind there was no conflict between love and duty. She was perhaps attempting to bury her despair deep down, so that she herself might not know the real nature of her feelings. Or perhaps, she was hoping against the hope that if she would continue to love him, regardless of his ill-treatment, one day she might get back her lost love.

This year she had not been able to finish even one-third amount of the work that she had done the year before. She was simply keeping up with the lectures. Being unsure of her physical strength, she could not go to Roselle for Thanksgiving Day. "The long trip may tire me so much that I am afraid, it will cut off a large part of my pleasure…My health is improving but I am far from being well yet. I am trying to save every bit of strength."[6] She could go to Roselle only for Christmas and enjoyed her last Christmas in America with the Carpenters. She returned to Philadelphia on 3rd January, and concentrated her whole attention on completing her thesis on the 'Obstetrics Among the Aryan Hindoos.' Only after submitting it to the college authorities, she felt a bit relaxed. Her thesis which contained 50 pages, was the largest one.

This winter, for the first time in all those years, she had a fall on the snow. She was not much hurt but all the bangles around her right forearm were broken. Being a married Hindu woman, she was not ready to go without them and had refused to take even a drop of water without putting on bangles. So, Gopal bought her a gold bracelet for $5.50. The very fact that she was wearing nothing but glass bangles indicates that in order to meet her expenses in America, she might have sold many of her gold ornaments, including bangles. Being jobless and disinterested in doing something regularly to earn money, Gopal had increased her pecuniary problems. Her educational expenses had already reduced her bank balance to almost nothing, so there was no other go but to sell off her valuables. Hence, this additional expense worried her. "If every fall will bring in as much gold, would you consider it a misfortune? I called it so, because those $5.50 might have brought me an instrument that would have been useful or a book that would have been instructive."[7]

Anandi's letters are mirrors of her profound mind. Though Gopal blamed her for having a weak style of writing, her letters show that she had a real flair for writing, and the images that she used were born out of her experiences. At one place she wrote about her health. "My physical self is like the days of September and my brain and nerves seem 'dissected up' like the warp on the loom, distinct and bare, but sensitive."[8] Anandi perceived the similarity between the constantly changing weather of September and her equally unstable health. She linked the experience of dissecting the brain and nerves with the warp on the loom and drew a vivid picture. In February 1886, she had a second attack of Diphtheria but it was diagnosed at an early stage and so was cured fast.

In the first week of March, when she appeared for the final examination, the struggle between her weak body and strong mind had reached its climax and sheer force of will helped her to go through the examinations. "On the last day of examination, I was more tired than I remember being ever before. In examination when I was on the last question and I think on the last, because I would not think any more, my patience for once gave vent and I could not write another word on my paper. I did not stop even to see if I had finished the sentence. I pinned the papers together and left the room abruptly."[9] About two hours later, she had her oral examination with Dr. Walker.

The Japanese woman Keiko Okami did very well in her examinations, but the Syrian student Sadat Islambuli was so ill that she had to leave the college that year. The result was announced on 7th March, and to her heart's delight, Anandi had passed and was through with her studies at last, completing her mission successfully. But the joy of her success was shadowed with sadness, as she was not in dark about her physical condition. While talking about the illness of Sadat Islambali, she reflected, "Her condition is sadder than death, if death is at all sad."[10] Why did Anandi felt that way? Had she heard the death-bells tolling for her? Was she trying to console herself by saying that death was not sad? Had her Oriental wisdom taught her to accept death as an inevitable fact of life? But just before a month, which is on 8th February, she had written, "Heaven, if it be only for its riches, and banquets and no duty, has no charm for me."[11] Thus, she had expressed her wish to perform her duty on Earth, but as the days passed, she was disappointed and was trying to seek consolation in thought that death was not at all sad. But at the same time, she did not want to lose courage. In a letter to Aunt Theo, she said, "It is always well to look far in future, just far enough to guide our steps and prepare for the immediate obstruction . . . but I think it is foolish if not worse to mourn over the future which is probably to come, when the present claims our care, attention and strength."[12] It seems that through these words she was trying to make herself stronger.

References:

Source: The Nancy Cobb Stone Collection of letters. - 1, 2, 3, 4, 5, 6, 7, 8, 9, 10, 11, 12

23

Anandi's Thesis

Candidates of the 'Woman's Medical College of Pennsylvania' were supposed to write a thesis for their degree of Doctor of Medicine. Though it was called a thesis, it was more or less a research paper of a small size. Hence, Anandi's thesis consisting of 50 pages of a medium-sized notebook was the longest one. The subject of her thesis was 'Obstetrics Among the Aryan Hindoos.' The subjects selected for their thesis by some other students were as follows:

1. The Ophthalmoscope in General Practice – Jessica Carleton.
2. Clinical Medicine – Jennie Eagleson.
3. Some Notes on Criminal Abortion – Mary Formed.
4. Puerperal Mania – Francis Hatchett.
5. Ovarian Tumour – Elizabeth Kendig.
6. Diagnosis of Neurotic Poisoning – Emma Richards.
7. The Urine in Health and Disease – Jessie Thompson.
8. Report of Obstetrical cases- Gertrud W. Van Pelt.
9. Scarletina – Lucretia King.

The subject being vast, Anandi sketched a broad outline of the Aryan Obstetrics and provided at places quotations of the Indian thinkers like Manu and Sushruta. For explaining her approach, she stated, "We must not entirely overlook the history of past ages and consider the superior minds which laboured with marked success, in the same field of investigation under the promptings of the same motives, as far back as 15th century B.C. They may enable us to the better appreciation of the science and pay due respect to the discoveries, thesis and mode of application of remedies of minds of different nations at different times.

I therefore need not apologize for choosing this subject." The nature of Anandi's thesis was general and descriptive whereas the other students had selected particularly Medical issues for writing their thesis.

Anandi dealt with various aspects such as the signs of conception and pregnancy, the development of the foetus, preparation for lying-in, possible emergencies and life-saving methods used by native doctors, the causes of abortion, the care of a newborn, the diseases of an infant and some valuable remedies. According to Anandi, the remarkable characteristics of the Obstetrics among the Aryan Hindus were as follows:

1. The importance attached to hygiene than to medicine.
2. The tendency to avoid interference in nature's work.
3. The conspicuous role of the pulse-rate test.

She wrote, "I have known at least two native physicians positively deciding pregnancy from the pulse alone while in one case of my personal acquaintance there was no other sign." She presented a case where a woman and her child were saved by a Hindu surgeon performing a difficult operation. While narrating how an almost still-born child could be given life, she wrote, "Place the child in warm water, place the placenta as far from it as the cord will allow you to do with safety. A few shreds of cotton should be next placed over the placenta at short distance and set fire to them. As they ignite, the blood will be warmed and remove the difficulty if it be caused by the infant being chilled after birth."

In her thesis, Anandi supplied some cultural details, encircling childbirth. She described, how in India, primipara was fondly indulged and how she enjoyed the utmost attention of her family and relatives. "A primipara is invited to parties, where young women, especially those in the similar condition, are invited. Garden parties, moonlight parties and candlelight parties have no end. Singing, playing, gentle dancing (strictly among women) constitute chief amusements. She is daily asked by friends and relatives as to her desire for certain things, food or drink." Anandi's thesis was full of cultural details and information about customs among the Hindus, which seem unnecessary in the thesis of a Medical student. Had she concentrated her attention on some scientific aspects of the Aryan Obstetrics, it would have been appropriate. At the end of the thesis, she wrote, "I have said too little to do justice to what is taught and practiced among the Brahmans but on account of the rarity of valuable time and space, I am obliged to say no more."

I was curious about Anandi's thesis for many reasons.

1. The only specimen of her Medical study that survived is her thesis.

2. This could have enabled me to understand her approach to traditional Obstetrics, after being trained in the modern Western branches of Medicine.

3. Anandi herself had passed through the ordeal of childbirth and the death of her child at the tender age of 12. The suckling had died because it could not get medical help in time. In fact, she was inspired to become a doctor due to the premature death of her child. Her great interest in Obstetrics being supported by her own experience, her comments on the subject were sure to carry weight.

4. I had already met the sensitive, contemplative woman having the depth of character in her multiple letters. Now here was an opportunity for me to meet an intelligent Medical woman.

I went on reading pages after pages, in search of that person, with little success. Descriptions without discernment or careful scrutiny have occupied a large part of the thesis. Kashibai Kanitkar, the Marathi biographer of Anandi had remarked that Anandi had translated the matter from various books on the Aryan Hindoo Obstetrics. This was sure to impose a limitation on her thesis. Students were not supposed to 'translate' opinions of others but were expected to 'present' their own observations supplementing them with analyses and comments. Though at places Anandi stated that she was quoting from her own experience, she seldom noted her observations and drew conclusions. For example, she wrote that she had known two native physicians who positively decided pregnancy from the pulse alone. But she did not analyse how and why this method was scientific.

The lack of critical attitude and the emphasis on only the plus points of Aryan Hindoo Obstetrics made the thesis one-sided. Neither did she refer to the negative points and limitations nor expressed her own doubts. One cannot find in her thesis, her own stand as a modern Medical woman, about the traditional Indian Obstetrics. It seems that she wanted to show the Americans who thought the Indians to be illiterate and unclean tribal people, that the Indians had their own well-developed Obstetrics. There was nothing wrong with it, but she did not have to depict a one-sided, rosy picture at the cost of her objectivity. She did not have to adulate the Indian science, forgetting that she was soon to become a doctor. One cannot take her side and say that she wrote her thesis in a hurry or that she was ill. From the very beginning, she was aware that she had to submit a thesis in the last term of her course. She was not a person who would have done such an important job in a hurry. Long before writing this thesis, she had asked Gopal to send some books on the Aryan Hindoo Obstetrics. In short, it was pre-planned work, done with a specific purpose.

If the Indian Medical science was so advanced and perfect as she had depicted, why did she feel the need of going to an American Medical College? The lack of practical knowledge in Indian Medicine was no matter of dispute. In India, to dissect a human body was thought to be a sin, therefore a sheep was used instead. Naturally, the native physician could not have a chance to study properly the human body. Therefore, it had prompted an eminent native physician like Bapusaheb Mehendale to learn dissection after the Western method. When Anandi went to America, the 'Madras University' had opened its doors to women. But since women were allowed to take a partial course, Anandi did not want to enter that University. She was overwhelmed by the idea of learning Medicine thoroughly in an advanced country like America. She had boldly stated in her public speech at Shrirampur, "There is probably no country so barbarous as India that would not disclose all her wants and try to stand on her own feet."[1] By publicly making a statement like this, she had frankly pinpointed a drawback of her countrymen. Even from her own experience, she was convinced that the available medical knowledge and help were not at all sufficient for treating women and children. Then had she forgotten these facts while she wrote her thesis? If she was really of the opinion that it was possible to get well equipped with Medical knowledge in India itself, she would have never migrated to America.

It is shocking that a brilliant candidate like Anandi, who was soon to appear for the final examination had stated at three different places in the thesis that the Indian thinkers had asked to pray to God in the time of emergency. If there were symptoms of abortion, along with other treatments "Prayers should be recited." To avoid any disaster "Prayers should often be repeated by the woman." If it was a difficult case and surgery was necessary, "If the foetus is alive, manipulation and prayers should be tried." Whether a person should take support of the concept of God or not is a different issue, but why should it be repeatedly referred to in a Medical research paper?

After describing what kind of presents should be offered to a pregnant woman, she made it a point to say, "All these rules, says Sushruta, 'must be observed in order to avoid any catastrophe and disaster such as making the foetus congenitally deaf, dumb, blind or deformed." Could she really believe that if the rules of giving particular presents were not observed, it badly affected a foetus? Anandi did not hesitate to make unscientific statements like, "If the mother is emotional, selfish or generous so will be the child." In that case, Anandi and all her sisters and a brother should have become hot-tempered and quarrelsome like their mother and then what about the qualities of her father? She wrote about a newborn child as if its personality was a hereditary factor like a disease. If her statement is accepted, there would be no meaning to individuality, willpower, thinking power or mental development. If she was quoting it as someone's opinion, then what was her opinion? Did she agree or disagree with it? But she had not stated her own opinions.

The rosy picture of native doctors and nurses that she painted was pretty misguiding. No one would have believed after reading her thesis that Indian people badly needed Medical help. Anandi wanted to become a doctor in order to provide Medical help to her countrywomen but surprisingly enough, she had not even touched a single burning issue like:

1. The causes of the high death rate among women and children in India.

2. The urgent need to train ignorant midwives.

3. The premature motherhood imposed on young girls by child marriages and their horrifying side effects.

Instead of dealing with these problems from the angle of a Medical woman, she satisfied herself with quotations from the works of old masters.

She had described at length how a nurse was supposed to examine the body of a newborn baby. "After the cord has been tied and divided the new-born should be smeared all over with sesame oil and gently rubbed. While doing this the nurse should examine the child's body and note that there is no imperfection anywhere. She must anoint the little finger and carefully pass it in the anus if she can. This will decide that there is no imperforate anus. Let her next pass her another little finger under the tongue and see that the Phlegm does not extend too far. Then pass the same finger farther on and look out all that may lodge in the throat. Examine other parts of the body at the same time . . . This will take but a moment for an experienced and skilful nurse and require little skill . . ., but will save many an hour of suffering." While describing the skillful method of a native nurse, she had overlooked the fact that many a time, those ignorant nurses did not observe even the simple rules of hygiene like washing hands before touching a baby or keeping their nails short and clean. Hence their uncleanliness and ignorance had become instrumental in causing the deaths of newborn children.

Even in the first half of the 20th century, the need to train native nurses was acutely felt by many of the foreign doctors who worked in India. So, one can imagine how grave the situation might have been in the 19th century. Dr. Ida Scudder wrote, "Here again every one of us present could give instances of the horrible tortures women are constantly subjected to by the ignorant, untrained dais. Our sympathies have been taxed by the poor sufferer who has been brought to the hospital in such a condition that her life cannot be saved and our hearts are often touched by the appeals from such a woman to save her for the sake of the little group of children waiting for her at home."[2] Realising problems of native women, Anandi had consciously decided to become a doctor. She herself had passed through the ordeal of early pregnancy and the death of her child. So, it is just not possible that she had no knowledge of the situation in India. She herself had mentioned in a letter to Gopal that when she saw the 'Girard College' of white orphans, she remembered the motherless children in India who were mostly neglected and some of whom had to live in a miserable condition. With great concern, she had expressed her wish to organise an orphanage and give new hope to children.

It is much surprising that nowhere in her thesis did Anandi expound the need to equip nurses with the rules of hygiene and proper Medical knowledge. Anandi's rosy description of a good doctor also seems out of place in the thesis, "The physician should be of a good family, of a healthy body, young (or old experienced one when a family physician), handsome, pure, vigorous, modest, discrete, patient, firm and intelligent." It seems that without asking herself if it was necessary for a physician to be young, handsome, modest or of a good family, she had accepted the description of an ideal physician as it was written in the old script. Secondly, when it was not customary to get treated by a male doctor, what was the use of such a doctor? There was a yawning chasm between the fictitious and bookish description of the Medical situation in India presented by Anandi and the harsh reality which was overlooked by her. Had she objectively taken into consideration the facts and produced medically valuable details instead of citing quotations, her thesis would have turned into an authentic research paper. Here are some more examples of her unscientific attitude.

1. Regarding the rules laid down by the Aryan legislator, she said, "The following good rules are laid down by Manu, the great Aryan Legislator, Sushruta and other physiologists. They say, 'transgressing them means committing sin." How could a concept of sin have a place in the thesis of a Medical student like Anandi?

2. About the doctor-patient relationship, she wrote, "A patient rejecting a physician will be punished here and hereafter." But she did not define what kind of a doctor? If by chance, a patient would fall into a trap of an ignorant doctor, what would happen to him if he had no right to change his doctor? It is just not understandable what made her write about all such things, wasting her time and energy?

Anandi who had studied various religions nursed no grudge against any. Yet the caste-feeling was deeply rooted in her mind. While describing the characteristics of a wet nurse, she mentioned, "The wet nurse should be of the same caste or class as the child. . .She should present a good family history . . . When it is found to be absolutely necessary to have a wet nurse, these pre-conditions are religiously observed." Was the caste of a wet nurse and her family history more important than her healthy body and a good sense of hygiene?

At the end of her thesis, it becomes clear that she had before her mind, only the Brahman class. She wrote, "I have said too little to do justice to what is taught and practiced among Brahmans." If so, the title of her thesis is not appropriate. Aryan Hindoos did not believe in the caste system. In ancient days, Brahman, Kshatriya, Vaishya and Shudra were not the castes but the professions. People were free to select their professions. A person who was Brahman by birth could become a warrior or a trader if he wished so, because the social system was pretty flexible. But during the course of time, it became customary to stick to the profession of one's forefathers. The social system thus became rigid, turning a profession into a caste. If Anandi had titled her thesis as 'Obstetrics Among the Aryan Hindoos', how could she think only of the Brahmans? In that case, the title should have been 'Obstetrics Among the Brahmans.' It is unfortunate that a Medical woman like Anandi who had cherished a great dream of upliftment of her countrywomen, was thinking in terms of caste.

In the public meeting at Shrirampur, Anandi, who was fired with rebellious ideas, shone like a bright star. There she had frankly affirmed, "In going to foreign countries we may enlarge our comprehension, perfect our knowledge or recover our lost arts."[3] This statement is proof of her impartial and healthy outlook regarding knowledge. Ready to pay any price for her dream, she challenged, "If my countrymen wish to excommunicate me, why do they not do it now?"[4] Where had this spirit vanished while writing the thesis? It is clear that the thesis was the product of the same defensive and extra-protective attitude towards the customs of her country that made her talk in favour of child marriage; that made her deny that female infanticide prevailed in certain regions of India.

Of course, though she avoided being analytical in her thesis, she was not dull or unintelligent. It would be unjust to judge her merits only on the basis of this thesis which was one of the many expressions of her study; her examination papers, journals, notebooks being the others, which are not available today. Moreover, there is no way to know her surgical or diagnostic skills. There is enough evidence to show she was regarded as a promising student. Even when Anandi was not a celebrity and had just begun to learn, her brilliance was admired by those who came in her contact. For example, in a letter to Rev. Wilder, Rev. Gohin wrote, "his wife is bright and quick to take up anything and ...she would be capable of acquiring a first-class education if she had an opportunity to do so."[5] Dean Bodley had also appreciated her intellectual capacity in a letter to Pandita Ramabai and the introduction to *The High Caste Hindu Women* written by Ramabai.

It must be remembered that in spite of her various health problems and mental worries, she always scored good marks and aimed at securing the first rank. Every year, only two or three graduates of the college were selected to appear for the competitive examination of the Blockley Hospital and Anandi was chosen from her class. Before Anandi went to America, Aunt Theo had sent a letter of her writing to a psychiatrist whose analysis and conclusions are worth considering: "This is an intellectual well-balanced mind, cultivated with great care... The writer is a lady of more than ordinary brain power, ... not afraid to investigate any subject . . . Her penetrative mind is constantly reaching for more light....I see her in future as the one who has no superior."[6] Due to her untimely death, she could not get a chance to bring her knowledge into practice and to prove her ability as a doctor. Her greatness lies in the fact that fighting against all odds, she achieved her goal of becoming a doctor.

References:

1. *The Life of Dr. Anandabai Joshee* – Caroline Healey Dall. 1888. p 84
2. *The Southern Medical College or Women* – by Dr. Ida Scudder – *The Journal of Association of Medical women in India* / Vol V May 1916 No. 10/ p 5
3. *The Life of Dr. Anandabai Joshee* - Caroline Healey Dall. 1888. p 89
4. Ibid, p 88
5. Source – The Nancy Cobb Stone collection of letters.
6. *The Life of Dr. Anandabai Joshee* – Caroline Healey Dall. 1888. p p. 120,121 For Anandi's Thesis: see Appendix No.3

24

The Short Span of Togetherness

Anandi and Pandita Ramabai never met in India though for some time they were living in the nearby provinces when Anandi was in Calcutta. But they could meet in America because Ramabai was invited by Dean Bodley to witness Anandi's graduation. In spite of their people's disapproval, both these women had migrated to foreign countries in pursuit of their goals. So, people often compared them. When Ramabai embraced Christianity, people suspected that Anandi might do the same. Both were public-spirited and were thoroughly interested in improving the lives of Indian women. Like Anandi, Ramabai also wanted to become a doctor but because of her incurable deafness in one ear, she had to give up the idea. Though Ramabai was disappointed, she found out another way of leading a useful life. In India, little girls were frequently married to old men, many of whom became widows even before reaching the age of puberty. The poor unwanted creatures had no hope, no education, and no chance to remarry since widow marriage was prohibited. Physical and mental abuse, starvation, heavy workload and sexual harassment used to be the lot of a widow. Ramabai was so touched by their pitiful condition that she had decided to devote her life to their upliftment. After returning to India, she was to open an asylum for widows where she wished to offer them shelter, education and peaceful life. She was determined to turn those helpless beings into self-confident and independent human beings. When Ramabai came from England to America, she gave voice to the miseries of Indian women and appealed to the Americans to donate generously for her widow house. Wishing to help this benevolent woman, 'Pandita Ramabai Clubs' were founded in various cities and the fund-raising activity was conducted with great enthusiasm. Ramabai wrote the book *High Caste Hindu Women* which was published in America and the entire profit was to go to her project. In all these activities, Dean Bodley played a major role and helped Ramabai in every way.

On 17th February 1886, Ramabai and her little daughter Manorama sailed to America by the ship 'British Princess.' Her well-wishers in England had urged her not to take the risk of going to America because that year many ships had wrecked. The month of February was considered to be the most dangerous month for a sea voyage. But listening to her inner voice, Ramabai decided in favour of Dean Bodley's invitation. In a letter written to her friend Dorothy Beal of Cheltenham on 13th January, she said, "the inner voice tells me nothing but to go to America which decidedly is my duty for the present. I must follow this voice at any sacrifice."[1] Ramabai felt that the only way to conquer fear was to jump into the frightful situation instead of avoiding it. On the fourth day of her journey, the 'British Princess' reached a dangerous spot known as the Devil's Pot. The devastating thunder was brewing there so dangerously, that the ship was storm-bound for full 6 days. When the ship reached America, they found that the coast was besieged by thick rolls of snow. The voyagers' patience was almost spent but the difficulties had no end. One evening, they entered the outfall of river Delaware, 60 miles away from Philadelphia where Anandi was eagerly waiting to welcome Ramabai. But the ship was bogged down in the mud and could not be moved an inch, for whole 2 days. At last, on 6th March 1886, Ramabai and Manorama arrived safely.

Ramabai's beauty never failed to evoke admiration even in America and the charming impressions of her personality were cherished by many. Caroline Dall saw Ramabai for the first time, on the occasion of Anandi's graduation and remarked in her journal. "Ramabai is strikingly beautiful. Her face is clearcut oval; her eyes dark and large, glow with feeling. She is a brunette, but her cheeks are full of colour."[2] Francis Willard, a well-known American educationist wrote, "Pundita has dark grey eyes full of light, a straight nose with tiny tattoo between the brows, mobile lips, close blue-black hair and perfect white teeth."[3] The mother of Francis Willard too pencilled in her diary the unique personality of Ramabai. "Marvellous creation! She has a surprisingly comprehensive intellect, as open to perceive truth as a daisy in the Sun; with face uplifted she marches straight into the effulgence, caring for nothing."[4] When Anandi saw her for the first time, she marvelled at the unmatched union of tender body and strong mind. She was also enthralled by little Manorama. "Her child is here, a little darling. She is as bright as Sunshine and as sweet as a fresh rosebud. She must give a great deal of comfort to her mother, who has passed through too many sorrows for one woman. ...She is a woman, tender with feeling, as tender as a flower, timid as can be and impatient of pain, but her courage has outweighed that of the sternest and bravest warrior. She has filled my heart with real joy."[5]

Anandi and Ramabai had corresponded with each other before they met and now, they had a chance to be together for some time. Since both the women were yearning for the emancipation of their native women, their goals were complementary to each other. Anandi wanted to establish a women's hospital and a Medical College for women, whereas Ramabai had decided to found a widow-house. Under Dean Bodley's roof, Anandi and Ramabai might have spent hours, planning with zeal, their future plans. There might have been thought-provoking discussions and heated arguments between them about their religious convictions. Anandi was bound to express her doubts about Ramabai's conversion to Christianity. But after their open discussion, they might have respectfully agreed to differ. Now that they were together, sharing one's thoughts and experiences was easier and pleasant. Their gleaming eyes, smiling lips, tender touches, firm grasps of hands, intense voices and significant silence might have manifested the subtle ripples of meaning.

Their correspondence is not available today because Ramabai had destroyed her private letters a year before her death, but Anandi's letters to Gopal and Ramabai's letters to her British and American friends are available. Anandi's letters to Gopal show how Anandi and Ramabai were held in comparison by their countrymen. Particularly when Ramabai embraced Christianity, people had no doubt that Anandi was to follow in her footsteps. Taking umbrage at such a remark, once Anandi told Gopal that Ramabai was not Anandi and Anandi was not Ramabai. They were two different persons meant for different purposes. Anandi emphasised that Ramabai was 20 times more intelligent than herself and that there was no likeness between them. Though Anandi felt so, the deeper study of their personalities shows that in spite of the differences, there were many similarities between them. Activities like reading, letter-writing, debating, lecturing, and travelling were their favourite pastimes. Both Anandi and Ramabai were question-raisers. Being contemplative by nature, they took immense pleasure in grappling with abstruse questions and left no stone unturned while seeking the answers. They took immense pleasure in the intellectual process it involved. The restlessness which originated from this process was an inseparable part of their personalities. The alert, spontaneous and evergreen state of their intellectual prowess was an important common factor between them.

Their quenchless thirst for knowledge was a motivating force behind their all-important decisions. Ramabai once wrote, "To study, I am wedded for all my life and study is my immortal husband that shall not be robbed from me like the mortal one."[6] Anandi and Ramabai could speak and write English with great fluency and ease. Both were excellent orators and their skills were admired by people in America. The only difference was that being acquainted with English since her childhood, Anandi could understand the foreign language very well when she went to America. Whereas when Ramabai went to England, she was not much familiar with it; she had scant knowledge of English. Many times, she felt sad that she could not express herself properly in English, could not take part in any discussions, and could not give vent to the religious conflicts in her mind. "I knew then almost nothing of the English language . . . I myself remember those times with much sorrow how I struggled with myself, not being able to express my doubts to anyone."[7] Her deafness was another obstacle in learning English. But overcoming these problems, she mastered the language before going to America. Caroline Dall gave due credit to her when she said, "Ramabai spoke . . . as if English were [her] native tongue."[8]

The high sense of duty was another characteristic common between Anandi and Ramabai and the enlightenment of their countrywomen was regarded by them as the most important duty. Many people felt that neither Ramabai nor Anandi would return to India. Even Gopal had once advised Anandi to settle in America but the idea failed to attract her. Similarly, despite her conversion to Christianity, Ramabai was thoroughly Indian at heart. Her love for Sanskrit was so profound that she was insistent about the Sanskrit words on her Cross, instead of the Latin ones. "all the good old things are very dear to me and if I do not find anything in them that is contrary to our blessed Religion, I will not and must not part with them. I do not want to take from others what is not wanted and what is not good for my country."[9]

Their chosen goals had become their all-consuming passions. But those missions were misunderstood by their people as dangerous activities. Every action of theirs was regarded with suspicion and they were threatened with ex-communication. Yet neither Anandi nor Ramabai ceased to care for the welfare of their natives. But there was one basic difference between their attitudes. Ramabai was more open-minded and franker than Anandi. For example, like Anandi, she too was closely questioned about child marriage, child widows and female infanticide but she never defended the horrible customs just because they were practised in India. Any custom, belief, convention or concept whether Hindu or Christian, was regarded by Ramabai with absolute objectivity. *High Caste Hindu Women*, the book of her writing is the best manifestation of her just and thoughtful approach. All those issues which were defended or avoided by Anandi, were discussed clear-headedly by Ramabai. About female infanticide she wrote, "After considering how many girls could safely be allowed to live, a father took good care to defend himself from caste and clan tyranny by killing the extra girls at birth, which was as easily accomplished as destroying a mosquito… Who can save a baby if the parents are determined to slay her."[10] After providing the details of what methods were employed to kill the infants, she wrote with contempt, "Then there are not a few child thieves who generally steal girls, even the wild animals are so intelligent and of such refined taste, that they mock at the British law and almost always steal girls to satisfy their hunger."[11] These quotations are sufficient to show the basic differences between Anandi and Ramabai as intellectuals.

Ramabai was rebellious enough to challenge any authority or any power centre. No one could stop Ramabai, the fearless truth-lover, from challenging a statement that was disagreeable to her. She would never accept a theory or an opinion unless she was fully convinced about it. She was neither afraid of the Christians nor the Hindus; or for that matter of any society, while implementing her decisions or taking the essential steps which were in accordance with her judgement. She could deal with any issue in a detached and impartial manner, without giving an emotional colour to it. While dealing with female infanticide, she took into account the psychological, social, religious and economic factors and analysed the problem with the objectivity of a scientist. It would be interesting to see how she goes to the root of a problem. "A lady friend of mine in Calcutta told me that her husband had warned her not to give birth to a girl, …or he would never see her face again, …there was another woman, …She had been notified by her husband that if she persisted in bearing daughters, she should be superseded by another wife, …and she should be made the drudge of the whole household. Not unfrequently, it is asserted, that bad luck attends a girl's advent, and poor superstitious mothers in order to avert such a catastrophe, attempt to convert the unborn child into a boy, if unhappily it be a girl. Rosaries used by mothers of sons are procured to pray with; herbs and roots celebrated for their virtue are eagerly and regularly swallowed; trees and son-giving gods are devoutly worshipped. . . .After the birth of one or more sons, girls are not unwelcome, …both parents lavish love and tenderness upon her, for natural affection, though modified and blunted by cruel custom, is still stronger in the parent's heart…But alas! the dark side is too conspicuous to be passed over in silence....Female infanticide though not sanctioned by religion, and never looked upon as right by conscientious people, have nevertheless,…been silently passed over unpunished by society in general."[12] Still going deeper, she pinpointed that the root cause of this problem was in the custom of dowry and the extravagance in Indian marriages of which poor parents were always afraid. In the end, she remarked, "Large expenses might be stopped by law, but a belief, deeply rooted in the hearts and religiously observed by the people for centuries, could not be removed by external rules."[13] These detailed quotations would cast light on Pandita Ramabai's deep understanding of her people and culture. Ramabai could dissect any problem, any issue at hand as coldly as an able surgeon and had the courage to strongly criticise wrong deeds; yet her love for her people was no less than Anandi, qualitatively or quantitatively.

Anandi's temperament was different. She was emotionally disturbed and hurt when her people or their customs were criticised by others. She did not compromise on the issues like her Medical education. She dared to cross the sea and live among strangers belonging to a different religion though it was thought to be a sin by her natives. But in many other respects, she accepted the prevalent norms which were actually disagreeable to her. For example, as a Medical student, she knew very well that according to the geographical conditions one has to change food and dress habits. Yet she stuck to her Indian manners even when they had proved to be injurious to her health, just because she didn't want to hurt the feelings of her native brethren. On top of it, all the time she defended her decision. Caroline Dall was right in criticising her when she remarked, "In reference to what she said of diet, she was doubtlessly glad to reinforce her husband's opinion, but I think it certain that if she could have taken animal food or at least broths, her chance of life in this climate would have been greater."[14]

Since her childhood, Ramabai's life went off the beaten track. Her father Anantashastri was a learned man and a Sanskrit scholar. Being a staunch supporter of women's education, he taught his wife and daughter without caring for society's adverse reactions. Therefore, from the very beginning, Ramabai was exposed to books, magazines, newspapers as well as old Sanskrit scripts. Going against the religious rule, her parents had decided not to marry her early. So, the child remained free to learn whatever she wished. After her parents' death, Ramabai and her brother Shrinivas travelled as pilgrims throughout the country, right from Madras to Punjab, Assam and Bengal. Toiling on with the singleness of purpose, they advocated women's education. The long travels revealed to them the degraded conditions in which women were held by cruel superstitions and customs. Thus, her experience of her people was much wider than Anandi. The young pilgrims often suffered from poverty, hunger and other wants while they were travelling all over the country. These unprotected, lonely journeys turned the young girl into a grown-up woman with a remarkable insight into the problems of her country. No wonder Ramabai never defended the cruel customs of her Motherland for any reason. Whereas in America Anandi went on defending in vain, the undefendable customs like child marriage, just because she wanted to break down their prejudices. This attitude imposed a serious limitation on her personality.

Religion was a subject of their common interest. But in quest of the ideal religion, each had chosen a different path. Anandi had arrived at the conclusion that no religion in the world was bad in itself, since all of them preached the same values like truthfulness, righteousness and honesty. Therefore, she felt no need to change her religion. Whereas Ramabai thought in a different way: "Hindoo religion gave me teaching but not an example. The Hindoo religion brings the Supreme Being the

Holy God to the level of a creature like myself, but Christianity lifts man up to God. ...I would not have accepted Christ's religion as mine if I were not convinced of its beauty and superiority."[15] In 1883, the news of Ramabai's conversion to Christianity gave a terrible shock to Anandi. Her immediate reaction was that by embracing Christianity, Ramabai had brought disgrace to women's education, devotion to God and truthfulness. But soon she recovered from the fit of anger and after reconsideration tried to understand Ramabai's mind. Giving benefit of doubt to Ramabai, Anandi wrote to Gopal that if Ramabai was not motivated to change her religion just for seeking help from the Christian community, she would never utter or write a word against her. On the contrary, she would respect Ramabai for acting in accordance with her conviction.

Their views regarding the founder of a religion and his followers concurred with each other. They looked up to the founder as a great man of wisdom, compassion and love, whereas blamed the followers for being the bigoted mis-interpreters of the humanitarian message of their Guru. At the time of her conversion, Ramabai had made it very clear that though she had chosen the Christian religion as her own, she would never surrender her 'right to study' the Bible, the right to formulate her own opinions, regardless of what the 'Church of England' felt about it. Not caring that she was regarded as a proud, haughty woman, she always refused to be a blind and meek follower. Her resoluteness is clearly reflected in her letter written on 12th May 1885 to Sister Geraldine of England. "I have a conscience and a mind and a judgement of my own ... Although priests and bishops may have certain authority over the Church, yet the Church has another Master who is superior even to the bishops. I am, it is true a member of the Church of Christ, but I am not bound to accept every word that falls down from the lips of priests or bishops.... Obedience to the law and to the Word of God is quite different from perfect obedience to priests only. I have with great effort freed myself from the yoke of the Indian priestly tribe, so I am not at present willing to place myself under another similar yoke by accepting everything which comes from the priests as authorised command of the Most high."[16]

A quotation from Anandi's letter would show the remarkable similarity between their fundamental views about the founder-follower relationship. "No religion is bad, but its followers and selfish interpreters.

Our priests are prejudiced and corrupt as are those of other religions. I dislike them as a class. ...If there had been no priesthood, this world would have been advanced ten thousand times better than it has now."[17] There is another profound comment on religion made by Anandi, "Take any religion you like and you will find that its founder was a holy man; go to its followers and you will find holy man the exception."[18]. The Americans looked up to Anandi and Ramabai as the sparkling examples of brilliant women who were born in an undeveloped country like India, but who achieved their great dreams, fighting courageously against all odds.

Both Anandi and Ramabai reciprocated their heartfelt love and respect. When Ramabai's little daughter Manorama fell ill, forgetting her own health problems, Anandi fondly looked after her as if she was her own daughter. Anandi was ready to take Manorama with her to India so that Ramabai could finish her work fast, without any tension. The darling child had aroused tender motherly feelings in Anandi, which had remained dormant so far. In America they visited together ladies' clubs and associations where they participated in discussions or gave lectures. Anandi spent the last few months in America, travelling with Ramabai and it was a real relaxation. Together they experienced the splendour of Niagara Falls and were fascinated by its grandeur. Those serene and beautiful moments were very precious to both of them. Anandi and Ramabai thoroughly enjoyed their short span of togetherness.

But day by day, Ramabai's heart was saddened to see that Anandi was losing the battle against her weak body and the depletion of strength was a serious problem. For a few days, she was admitted to the 'Woman's Hospital' at Philadelphia, but as she was not responding to the treatment, she was sent to Roselle in the care of Ramabai, from where she was to return to India. It had become obvious that Manorama could not go with Anandi, since she herself was a patient. Therefore, Ramabai decided to send her to England with someone else. Yet Ramabai was hoping against hope that Anandi would recover. It was thought that the voyage to India would be all for the best and Anandi might improve as she was accustomed to Indian food and climate. So, cherishing a hope of meeting again, they parted. But the brief span of their togetherness was to end there and the separation was final. Thereafter in the future, bereaved Ramabai was to travel alone on her chosen path, without her dear friend.

References:

1. *The letters and correspondence of Pandita Ramabai* – compiled by Sister Geraldine. Edited by A.B. Shah / 1977 / p.167
2. Source: The collection of Pandita Ramabai's clipping in Mukti Mission, Kedgaon, Dist. Pune, Maharashtra State. India
3. Ibid
4. Ibid
5. Source: Nancy Cobb Stone collection of letters
6. *The letters and correspondence of Pandita* Ramabai – compiled by Sister Geraldine. Edited by A.B. Shah / 1977 / p. 125
7. Ibid – p.141
8. *The Life of Dr. Anandabai Joshee* – Caroline Healey Dall. 1888. p.135
9. *The letters and correspondence of Pandita Ramabai* – compiled by Sister Geraldine. Edited by A.B. Shah / 1977 / p. 28
10. A reprint of the *High Caste Hindu Women* – Pandita Ramabai Saraswati 1989 / p.13
11. Ibid – p.14
12. Ibid – p.
13. Ibid – p.
14. *The Life of Dr. Anandabai Joshee* – Caroline Healey Dall. 1888. p.155
15. *The letters and correspondence of Pandita Ramabai* – compiled by Sister Geraldine. Edited by A.B. Shah / 1977 / p. 151
16. Ibid – p.59
17. *The Life of Dr. Anandabai Josh*ee – Caroline Healey Dall. 1888. p. 50
18. *The Life of Dr. Anandabai Joshee* – Caroline Healey Dall. 1888. p.54

25

The Graduation Ceremony of 1886

On Thursday, 11th March 1886, Anandi and her batchmates were to be graduated in the 34th graduation function of the Woman's Medical College of Pennsylvania and the degree of Doctor of Medicine was to be conferred upon them. Since the first graduation in December 1851, the college had come a long way. It had become well-known as one of the best institutions providing Medical education to women. It was the pioneer institute that had laid the foundation of women's Medical education and now their work in the Medical field was continuously expanding for three and half decades. Only at the time of the Civil War, the organisers had to close the college for 1 year. Barring this exception, every year, women doctors were graduated. Not that the Medical field was completely free from the hatred for women doctors, but now they had gained much more active supporters.

The graduation of 1886 was not a routine ceremony but a golden event in the life of the institute. Anandibai Joshi, the first Asian student of the college was to receive the degree of Doctor of Medicine and it had caused a great deal of sensation in Philadelphia and Roselle, where people personally knew Anandi. Many of Anandi's friends in Roselle had expressed their wish to be present for the occasion, one of them being Dr. Galt who was an ex-student of the college. Anandi had sent a bunch of invitation cards to Aunt Theo to distribute among her friends. Dean Bodley personally saw to it that as many of Anandi's friends as possible could be accommodated. Days before the graduation, an affluent lady in Philadelphia had presented a beautiful gold watch to Anandi, which was both useful and ornamental. Aunt Theo also wanted to give something to her but Anandi did not want Aunt Theo to spend money on a graduation present. Therefore, in January 1886, she wrote a letter to Aunt Theo and requested, "Don't buy me anything for next March. I shall be sorry if you put yourself into any unnecessary expense, for it is unnecessary. Your presence will make me a great deal happier than if you brought me anything for any price." [1]

The Graduation exercise commenced at noon in the Green Room of the Academy of Music which was known for its excellent acoustics. Bubbling with excitement, people had crowded the auditorium to witness this historical event. Many of the seats were reserved for the invitees and there was not a vacant seat when the function began. Yet the unstoppable crowd rushed into the hall and people stood against the walls, sat upon the steps and filled every aisle and doorway. Smiling eyes, eager faces and young girls in their colourful dresses marked the jubilation. The students of the college filled the front seats in the pit, but Anandi had a special place reserved for her on the stage. The Faculty members and their invited guests like Caroline Dall and Pandita Ramabai with her daughter Manorama took their seats on the stage and the function began. Their presence was an added attraction of the function. The immense crowd of 3,000 people consisted of parents and friends of 33 candidates who were soon to be graduated, well-wishers of the feminist movement, ex-students, reporters, doctors, professors and the elite of society, and of course Gopal and the Carpenters, whose joy knew no bounds. Anandi, Ramabai and Manorama were the cynosure of all eyes.

The degree of Doctor of Medicine was conferred upon the 33 students by President T. Morris Perot, among whom was Mary Formed, Jessica Carlton, Elizabeth Kending, Lucretia King, Emma Richardson and Jessy Thompson. The seats in the front row were reserved for the students to be graduated. The valedictory address was delivered by Dr. Clara Marshal who heartily congratulated the Graduates, made them aware of the various responsibilities of their profession and the difficulties in their path. Dr. Marshal also reviewed the situation of the Medical women on the Indian scene and referred to Anandi and Pandita Ramabai with profound respect. "On behalf of the Faculty...I now extend to you the right hand of fellowship and salute you as Doctors of Medicine! ...Teach your students also to regard with respect and gratitude... those women of the profession who acted the role of pioneers, who suffered social obloquy and professional ostracism that we might prosper...We learn of the lady Dufferin movement, ...under the inspiration and command of Royalty, that has been established in India and 'National Association for supplying Medical Aid to the woman of India.' One of the objects of this Association, . . . is the 'Teaching and Training in India of women as doctors, nurses and midwives' but as yet with the exception of one of our graduates of to-day no native women have been trained for this work."[2] Thus, Dr. Marshal emphasised the historical value of Anandi's achievement.

The journal of Caroline Dall, who was specially invited for the occasion, had preserved an eyewitness account of that memorable day in Anandi's life. "Mrs. Joshee wore a pure white saree richly bordered with gold. Although not in the least beautiful, she is the sweetest impersonation of pure womanliness that I have ever seen. All eyes were on her. Ramabai, who wears the plain white 'chudda' of the Mahratta widow, has a really handsome face, a delicate skin flushed with brilliant colour. She and her little girl look like Spaniards. ... An immense quantity of flowers was distributed at the close of Dr. Marshall's address, and Anandabai had many valuable presents, books, instruments and money, to help her carry out her purposes. She could hardly be insensible to the fact that she was the observed of all the observers; she must have heard the frequent and honourable mention of her name, nor could she have been deaf to the applause of that immense audience when she went forward to take her Diploma, but not even the quiver of her lips betrayed her."[3] Anandi's graduation dress was criticised by some of the American reporters. They remarked that Anandi received the degree certificate wearing an artificially brocaded cheap sari. But that was not true. It was in fact her wedding dress. To stop this gossip, an explanation was sent to the press "The friends of Anandabai who are accustomed to associate a simple and childlike sincerity with everything relating to her, were at first amused and then a little pained, when several of the daily papers spoke of her degree, in a robe 'trimmed with tinsel!' There was no more tinsel on her robe than there is in her character. The snowy gold-bordered dress she wore was part of her wedding outfit, made to her father's order. It was made in the old city of Chunder, famous through many centuries for the product of the finest handmade Indian mull. ...This muslin sari is four-yard-long and two and half wide. The gold... borders are not even made of gold thread, but of flat drawn gold so pure that it washes like a gold ring...No one who has seen the sari daintily worn can fail to be charmed by it."[4]

Some questions regarding this incident have remained unanswered. Who had spread this rumour? Instead of concentrating on Anandi's success, what made them discuss her dress? Who was behind this? American reporters had no idea about Indian costumes. What made them think that Anandi wore a cheap dress? How come they confidently made such statements? Who motivated them? They would not have passed such remarks unless backed by some Indian source. Was it a trick played by Gopal, to divert people's attention from Anandi's success? Had his hatred and perversity reached such a limit? Though the shrewd person had left no proof behind, one cannot deny the possibility.

Those who valued Anandi's achievement and realised its importance, gave her the due credit. The detailed account of the graduation was sent to Queen Victoria, by Dean Bodley in order to inform her about the signal success of her subject. It was a fact that even though England was ruled by a woman, women could enter the Medical field only after a long and fierce struggle because Queen Victoria herself was not much in favour of women doctors. Over the period of time, there was a change in her attitude and when she came to know about the distress of her Indian daughters, she had commanded Lady Dufferin to shoulder the responsibility of providing Indian women with Medical aid. Therefore, it was very wise of Dean Bodley to let the Queen know how a young Indian woman rose from nothing to become a doctor and leaping every fence achieved success.

The letter that Dean Bodley wrote to the Queen of England is not available but the reply from the Queen was as follows –

"From

Windsor, July 14th 1886

I am commanded by the Queen to request that you will kindly thank Dr. Bodley for having sent Her Majesty the account of Dr. Joshee's graduation at the Woman's Medical College of Pennsylvania, and to assure you that the Queen has read it with much interest."[5] This letter was written by Sir Henry Ponsonby, the private secretary to the Queen and it was addressed to the British legation in America.

Anandi's graduation did not mean the fruition of her aim alone. It had a different significance for different people. It gave deep satisfaction to Aunt Theo whose solemn undertaking had borne the succulent fruit. It offered immense pleasure to Pandita Ramabai whose own unrealised ambition to become a doctor was in a way realised by her dear friend Anandi. When Ramabai was in Hindustan, she had tried to get admission in 'Madras Medical College', but the authorities denied it. In spite of his jealousy, it had afforded a sense of fulfilment to Gopal, who had vowed to educate at least one woman. Moreover, her success had brought great credit to her college since she was the first Asian student of the institute. On top of it, her victory was a milestone in the history of Indian women's education.

References:

1. Source: The Nancy Cobb Stone collection of letters.
2. Source: The archives of Medical College of Pennsylvania, Philadelphia, U.S.A. – The valedictory speech of Dr. Clara Marshal.
3. *The Life of Dr. Anandabai Joshee* – Caroline Healey Dall. 1888. p.135
4. Ibid,141-142
5. Ibid, page,164

26

The New-found Paths

In 1886, the 'Woman's Medical College of Pennsylvania' added 33 new doctors on the map of American women doctors. Each one of them faced a life ahead, full of challenges to establish herself as a doctor. Graduation was just the beginning, after which they had to bring their knowledge into practice and had to deal with human beings for solving their health problems. More than that, they had to win people's hearts, win their confidence as people were not free from prejudices against women doctors. If a patient died in the hands of a woman doctor, the opportunity was seized to use it as a proof of her inefficiency. Against the names of some doctors from Anandi's class, no achievement other than their graduation was recorded in the archives of the college. Some got married and the youthful sense of achievement was lost or forgotten in the cult of domesticity. Some could not cope with the problems in their personal lives and go ahead with their careers whereas some died early. But there were some women who marched on with the single-mindedness of purpose, Dr. Mary Formed from the class of 1886 being one of them.

Not willing to waste a single day in her life, Dr. Mary Formed set out on the very next day of her graduation to do something purposeful. Out of habit, she walked from West Philadelphia, cutting through Fairmount Park and was driven towards her college by the inner urge to learn more. She entered the Woman's Hospital and turned in the direction of the Gynaecological Clinic where she found Dr. Rebecca Hunt and Dr. Marie Werner at work. The young graduate shyly asked permission to assist them which was granted instantly and Mary started working under their guidance. At that point in time, she could not have imagined that she was to work there for the next 50 years. In 1888, she was formally appointed as the Clinician in Gynaecology Department. Later she assisted Dr. Mary Fullerton until Dr. Fullerton left for India and then Dr. Hannah Croasdale until she resigned. Ultimately in 1903,

Dr. Mary Formed became the Head of the Gynaecology Department. Under the influence of her brother Dr. Henry Formed, Mary had developed a keen interest in Pathology. From 1887 to 1889, she worked as a pathologist in the Woman's Hospital. She was also the first pathologist in the 'West Philadelphia Hospital for Women' and worked there from 1890 to 1893. To develop her own private practice, she opened her clinic on the corner of Fifth Road and Poplar Street. At the time of World War I, she went to France in 1918 with the Women's Overseas Unit and for 14 months offered her service to the wounded soldiers. On completion of the 50 years of her service at the Woman's Hospital, a grand celebration was held on 16th March 1936. The whole life of Dr. Mary Formed was an expression of her loyalty to her profession. No other student in her class achieved the height of success that Mary did, but many of them devoted themselves to the Medical profession and achieved remarkable success.

Returning to her home from Philadelphia after her graduation, Dr. Elizabeth Kending found her sister Barbara severely ill of the nervous prostration. Abandoning all hopes of recovery, the doctors had predicted that she might live only for 6 weeks. But determined to save Barbara from the clutches of death, the novice Elizabeth confidently took the responsibility of her sister on her young shoulders and succeeded in curing her first patient. Very soon, Barbara was on the road to recovery and had a life long enough to survive Elizabeth. In appreciation of her skill and efficiency, the happy father gave her $100 which was the first and the highest fee she ever received. For 12 years, Elizabeth practised in Chicago after which she settled in Lancaster and lived there till her death. Elizabeth lived a long life of 90 years and spent it practising Medicine, until her illness forced her to retire at the age of 88.

Dr. Jane Lord Hersam also made quite a name for herself. She returned to Portland Maine after her graduation. Jane had turned to Medicine to fill the vacuum created by the untimely death of her husband, who was a doctor. Now well-equipped with the Medical knowledge, she wished to carry out his mission. When Dr. Jane started practising, there was not a single woman doctor in the Maine Province. She was the pioneer who worked very efficiently and set a high standard in the Medical field. To appreciate her work, the membership of the 'American Medical Association' was awarded to her. Dr. Jane Lord Hersam lived a long life of 87 years.

Dr. Jessie Thompson was married to Charles L. Bogle of Springfield, Ohio in October 1887. There were many obstacles in her path which made it difficult for her to work as a doctor. But she was so spirited that nothing could deflect Dr. Jessie from her goal. She began her career in Cincinnati and practised there for a few years, after which the Bogles moved to New York. There she started practising and confined herself to the diseases of women and children. After 17 years, Jessie left New York and settled in Yellow Springs, Ohio, on account of the illness of her husband. There she continued her practice for some years but when she suffered a serious back and hip injury, she had to give it up. During this period, she became very lonely because she lost her husband and parents. The family was all gone except her sister Clara Crandall. Therefore in 1931, Jessie and Clara resided in the 'Otterbein Home', where she rendered valuable help to the matron Mrs. Young. Even the attending physicians of the old house found Dr. Jessie Thompson's advice valuable.

Upon her graduation, Dr. Emma Richardson set up practice in Norristown and in a short time gained the reputation as one of the leading physicians. She was an active member of the 'Montgomery County Medical Society' and was one of the Society's delegates to the State Medical Society in 1889. On 10th October 1890, the first Medical staff of the Charity Hospital was elected and Dr. Emma Richardson was one of the physicians. She also served as a member of the board of directors for six years from 1899 to 1904.

Dr. Francis Hatchett was not fortunate enough to have a long life like Dr. Mary Formed or Dr. Elizabeth Kending. Just 14 years after her graduation, she died of Pneumonia on 11th April 1900. But she devoted all those years to the Medical profession. She worked as an intern at the 'Lying-in-Charity Hospital' after her graduation. Like Dr. Mary Formed, she also turned towards her own college for building up her future work. She was appointed as a clinician in the dispensary of the Woman's Hospital of Philadelphia and was also appointed as an assistant in the Gynaecological department. Being a sympathetic and kind-hearted person, she was popular among her patients. It was unfortunate that she died in the prime of her life.

Though American by birth, Jessica Carlton was more attached to India where she was brought up and had decided to work. In due course of time, she returned to the 'Presbyterian Mission' at Ambala where she built up her Medical practice. The people of Ambala had high regard for the public-spirited doctor whose charges were so low that even the poorest among poor could avail himself of her Medical help.

Anandi's road to her career led her to India where a grand professional future awaited her. In India, the huge tidal wave of joy and wonder had swept away the doubts and suspicions about her and newspapers were ahead of everybody in showering praises on Anandi, the pioneer Indian woman doctor. Sometime before her graduation, the State of Kolhapur had entered into correspondence with Dean Bodley in order to enquire if she could supply a woman doctor for the 'Albert Edward Hospital.' They were not aware that Anandi was a student of the same institute and was going to receive her degree in a few months. But on the realisation of this fact, the State of Kolhapur showed interest, particularly in Anandi. In the letter dated 10th March 1886, it was clearly mentioned how they thought of appointing Anandi: "Dear Madam – I beg you will kindly excuse me for not replying to your letter of November 25th before. After I wrote to you, my first letter, the fact that Dr. Anandibai Joshee would appear for her final examination at your college in the current month was brought to my notice by the Hon. Rao Bahadur M. G. Ranade. Thinking that nothing could be more desirable than to have a native of India for our 'Lady Doctor' I placed myself at once in communication with my friend, that he might ascertain from Mrs. Joshee whether she would accept the appointment alluded to. I hear that she is willing."[1]

Before writing to Dean Bodley, the proposal was sent by the Kolhapur State to the Political Agent, Lee Warner, for approval and it was approved on certain conditions. On 4th March 1886, the decision was conveyed to the State. "I cordially approve of your proposals which are conditional on Mrs. Joshee's success in the examination. I think you will do well to place yourself in communication with the Dean. Perhaps the passage money might be repayable if the lady leaves your service in less than a year. The general supervision by the Durbar Surgeon is I think right; but I expect that it will be a contested stipulation. I would add to the words 'private practice,' 'to such an extent as not to interfere with her public duties.' I believe that private practice does occasionally lead to the neglect of the class or the ward."[2] This means just before

Anandi's graduation, the plan of action regarding her appointment was taking shape.

Anandi's graduation fulfilled the first and foremost condition put by the Political Agent. The other terms and conditions were mentioned by the Diwan Meherji Cooverji in the letter written to Dean Bodley. Anandi was appointed in the 'Albert Edward Hospital' as the 'Lady Doctor of Kolhapur.' The engagement was for seven years; but both the parties were free to terminate it, on giving a six months' notice. Anandi was to be in charge of the female ward of the hospital but there was to be general supervision of Dr. Sinclair, the Durbar Surgeon. Private practice was allowed to the extent that it would not interfere with public duties. Secondly, no fees were to be charged for attending on the ladies of the Palace or on the wives of the contributors to the Hospital Funds. She had to instruct and train the class of girls in Medicine. The expenses of a single passage from United States to India were to be borne by the State of Kolhapur. But it would be refunded if Anandi would leave the service in less than one year. Her salary per month was to be Rs. 300 at the beginning and was to be increased to 400 after two years' service and to 500 after five years. A bungalow with ordinary furniture was allotted to her but it did not include service or board. In the letter of agreement, two things were made clear by Meherji Cooverji: 1. The supervision of the Darbar Doctor would be friendly. 2. Anandi was under impression that they wished to train the pupils only as nurses. But the Diwan emphasised, "Our object is much higher – to enable them to be general practitioner."[3]

Dean Bodley placed this letter before Anandi for her perusal and Anandi requested to give her a week's time for consideration and after a week, she cordially accepted the offer. She did not find anything objectionable in those terms except one, that she should not charge the ladies of the palace. To this she reacted, "Our Shastras require us to impart the gifts of healing and of religious truth without pay, and to this practice I shall adhere; but if I ever meant to take a fee from any one, it would assuredly be from those who are rich and powerful, and never from those who are poor and depressed."[4]

To Anandi's delight, the golden opportunity of bringing her knowledge into practice was offered to her and it afforded tremendous satisfaction to Dean Bodley who conveyed her feelings to the Diwan of Kolhapur in these words: "[I] assure you that it has afforded me great pleasure to serve the State of Kolhapur in this noble effort to give to the suffering women in the Albert Edward Hospital a woman as their physician and [I] rejoice that this skilful woman is herself a native of India."[5] After finishing her internship, Anandi was to return to her motherland. She eagerly looked forward to begin her new life.

References:

1. Source: The Government's Archives at Kolhapur, Maharashtra state. India.

2. Ibid

3. *The Life of Dr. Anandabai Joshee - Caroline Healey Dall. 1888. p. 145*

4. Ibid, p. 146.

5. Source: The Government's Archives at Kolhapur, Maharashtra state. India.

27

In Boston

Authorities of the Kolhapur State were expecting Anandi to join the 'Albert Edward Hospital' by 1st June 1886, but Dean Bodley explained to them why that was not possible. As a rule, every graduate had to work for one year in a chosen hospital as an intern. The arrangement was made for Anandi in the 'New England Hospital' at Boston. But considering the severity of the Boston climate and Anandi's poor health, the rule was relaxed in her case. She was allowed to finish her internship within 6 months. Being anxious to welcome her at their institute, the authorities of the hospital had given some concessions to Anandi. Though all the posts of interns were filled, they had accepted her as an extra student. An extra student was required to pay a certain amount towards the instruction, but they invited her as their guest. She was told that in Boston, she could visit other infirmaries and asylums to observe a great variety of work. Before going to Boston, Anandi was glad to spend some weeks in Roselle with the Carpenters, Ramabai, Manorama, Gopal and Govind Sathe.

She reached the New England Hospital on 2nd May at about 7 p.m. Two college friends had come to the railway station to receive her. Boston was the Capital of Massachusetts and a major Atlantic seaport. It was situated on Boston bay, South bay and the rivers Charles, Mystic, Chelsea and Neponset. Therefore, it offered a splendid display of the beauty of both river and the sea. From 1840 onwards, Boston had become a leading literary centre and was called the 'Athens of America.' During that period, there lived noted historian William H. Prescott, George Ticknor and many other literary figures like Emerson, Longfellow and James Freeman Clarke. Anandi wanted to meet her favourite author James Freeman Clarke whose books she had read with interest, but was disappointed as she could not get the opportunity.

The New England Hospital was not in proper Boston but in Roxbury, and was situated on Codman Avenue. But Roxbury had been annexed to

Boston in 1868. The beauty of this town was enhanced by the alternation of hills and hollows and the diversified surfaces. Enthralled by it, Anandi wrote, "I am so impressed with the beauty of Boston! I am prepared to say that it is the prettiest place I have seen in U.S.A."[1] Immediately after reaching the hospital, she went on her duty and helped a woman in labour. Her letter to Aunt Theo dated 3rd May gives a clear idea of her busy workday. "This morning at seven o'clock I visited the wards, Medical and Surgical; again at 8.30 I went with Dr. Pope and other interns. I paid another visit at 12.30 as one of the regular visits. I have to visit again my own ward in the evening. So, you see how busy I am. I have to make three visits besides the one with Dr. P. to all the hospitals, after which the consulting physicians, resident physicians and students meet in the office to discuss. My sleeping room is on the third floor, dining is on bottom floor and patients all over. I have to fill up the papers that belong to my own patients. I am so tired . . . You will be sorry to hear that I have such a cold in my throat that I can hardly talk. I can only whisper."[2] [F1]

Anandi was very much impressed by the well-disciplined administration of this hospital and their business-like attitude which she found lacking in the Woman's Hospital, Philadelphia. She was also happy to notice that this hospital was not crowded with the whimsical nurses, having a nuisance value. There were two Doctor Popes in the hospital who were twins and Anandi had corresponded with one of them before she went there. The sisters looked so alike that people found it difficult to know one from the other which amused the twins very much. Only their friends knew that one of them had a tiny mole on her cheek and that was the only mark of differentiation. Apart from them, Anandi worked with Dr. Hall, Dr. Sterling and Dr. Keller who took Anandi with her to attend some of her most interesting surgical cases. Occasionally, she was invited by Dr. Keller to dine with her, and also by some of the women's organisations for a discussion over tea. Those were the pleasant changes in her hectic schedule which helped her to relax; otherwise the workload was very heavy for her. Caroline Dall strongly felt that the authorities of the hospital failed to notice her delicate condition. Had she been kept free from the tiresome duties of an intern and allowed only to observe the variety of

F1 This quotation is taken from the original letter of Anandi which I found in Nancy Cobb Stone's collection. The same letter in Caroline Dall's book was found not to be authentic, as she had made some unnecessary changes in it.

cases, as was promised, it would not have sapped the little fund of her strength. Caroline remarked, "Her disappointment in connection with the work at the hospital was much greater than she ever acknowledged."[3]

One of her college friends left the Hospital and the other was seen rarely. Exhausted and chilled in the Bostonian climate, Anandi went on performing her duty. She had no time to look after her own problems because as a doctor, she had to take care of her patients belonging to various age groups. She had a seven months old baby in her charge who suffered from Pneumonia. Two patients were so sick and needed constant attention that Anandi had to visit them 4 times a day. There was another patient who had almost every possible trouble with the digestive system. At night, Anandi had to fill up their papers and prepare the records. But day by day, the graph of her own health was falling down. Ultimately it became impossible for her to pull through the hectic schedule. She described her deplorable condition in a letter to Aunt Theo, "My heart bellows . . . at the strain every time. My legs rebel at the injustice done to them. So, there is a civil war in me."[4]

In the Boston Hospital, Anandi was introduced to a very famous Polish-German doctor, Marie Zakrzewska, who was called Dr. Marie Zak in America. She belonged to the first generation of women doctors who gave a solid fight for entering the Medical field. Dr. Marie had her own interesting history. She was a professor of Nursing and the Head of the Nursing Department in the 'Charity Hospital' of Berlin. She had also started learning Medicine privately under the guidance of a benevolent doctor, Dr. Schmidt who supported women's Medical education. In March 1852, he showed Marie a circular that he had received from the 'Woman's Medical College of Pennsylvania' and told her excitedly that in America, women could become doctors like men. This letter became instrumental in turning Marie's attention towards America. She was thrilled to learn that the first batch of women doctors was graduated from this college despite the opposition of male doctors. In her day-to-day life, even Marie had to face male dominance and hatred for women in the Medical field. So, this great news made her think of migrating to America. She was discouraged to do so by her friends and relatives, because America was considered to be a dangerous country where all sorts of notorious activities were carried out. So, the country was not safe for a lone woman. Not getting scared by these frightening accounts, Marie decided to go to America, along with her younger sister. They reached America, on 22nd May 1853. The first few months were extremely difficult. When they reached America, they were almost penniless, but doing whatever odd jobs they could, the sisters survived. One day, Marie came in contact with Dr. Elizabeth Blackwell, the first woman doctor in the world. She was so excited by this meeting that she wrote in her diary, "I saw Dr. Elizabeth Blackwell. From this call of 15th May 1854, I date my new life in America."[5] Now Marie was not alone. She had gained Dr. Blackwell's support. Even Elizabeth was delighted to get in the form of Marie a student having such a passion for learning Medicine. She wrote, "I have at last found a student in whom I can take a great deal of interest. There is a true stuff in her; and I shall do my best to bring it out. She must obtain a Medical degree."[6] No wonder, Dr. Marie Zak was impressed by Anandi, the first Indian woman doctor, who had also migrated to America in spite of the opposition of her countrymen and received the Medical degree. Students of Dr. Zak were scattered all over the world and she had preserved their addresses, Anandi's address being one of them. In this respect, she wrote a few words about Anandi in her autobiography, "Among the interns whose address in India was, unfortunately not for a long, was the charming Dr. Anandibai Joshee, the first Hindoo woman to seek Medical education in America. …Coming to Boston in the summer of 1886, she served only for a short time."[7] It was very disappointing for Anandi as well, that she could not complete even the partial term of her internship.

Following in Anandi's footsteps, Gopal too had shifted to Boston. While Anandi kept her nose to the grindstone, Gopal fomented trouble by his thoughtless speeches. During the last week in May 1886, Gopal attacked Christianity in a meeting of the 'Free Religious Association' where he asserted that Christianity lacked every noble attribute including justice, righteousness and humanity, and charity was absent through the length and breadth of Christianity. Unable to prove his extravagant charges with any coherent arguments, he went on piling up all sorts of absurd statements. Gopal was not at all blind to the fact that his wife was generously aided by her Christian friends and she would not have achieved her goal without their kind and friendly support. He was also well aware that by his irresponsible behaviour he was hurting their feelings and was doing injustice to the Carpenters, Dean Bodley, Caroline Dall, Rev. Amis and many others who had lavished nothing but love upon Anandi. Neither were his speeches an outcome of his ignorance or stupidity. All those harsh statements were the deliberate expressions of his sadist and perverse mentality. By delivering anti-Christian lectures, he was killing two birds with one stone; he was hurting the Christians as well as his wife.

In June, Gopal delivered another lecture in a meeting arranged by his friend, Chamberlain, on the Missionary life in India. Forgetting what he had said before, he emphatically stated that he was not against Christ and his teachings but he found his followers unworthy of the prophet. He said, "The more I look into their characters, the darker is the dye that stains them. Christians have manufactured all the vices and exported them to the countries where simplicity and innocence reigned."[8] Someone from the audience asked if he thought the same about Rev. Dall. He was taken unaware yet recovering within a moment, he said, "I do not know Mr. Dall." His hypocrisy did not stop here. A month later, when he heard the news of Rev. Dall's death, he wrote in his condolence letter to Caroline, that Rev. Dall was much loved by the Indians. No wonder, Caroline was deeply hurt by his outright hypocrisy.

Gopal's double-dealing was highly shocking in another meeting where he profusely praised Christian Missionaries. Both Anandi and Gopal were invited to this meeting where Gopal surprised everybody by giving a pleasant speech full of delightful stories of the good work of the Christians. When asked by a friend how did this account agree with what he had told her the night before, Gopal said, "I must tell them what they want to hear . . . This is what they were expecting."[9] Unable to control her rough-mannered husband, Anandi attended the unavoidable meetings under tremendous tension and suffered silently whereas Gopal cleverly counted on her helpless silence. Knowing that in spite of her disapproval, his obedient wife would neither challenge him nor utter a word against him in public, but would be a dumb onlooker, Gopal felt free to talk whatever he liked. He was also conscious that her submissiveness would definitely create doubts in people's minds regarding her rebellious spirit and intelligence. Thus, this was his easiest way to ruin her reputation.

At this juncture, a question could be asked regarding Anandi's silence also. If her husband was repaying the kindness of her friends with ill-treatment and unjust criticism, was it not her duty to register her protest since she was a dutiful person? Why she did not come forward to say that she did not agree with Gopal, did not approve of his misconduct and was not a party to it. By remaining silent, she, in a way, gave a sanction to his irresponsible behaviour. It was unfortunate that when the situation demanded her to be an impartial, truthful and dutiful person, she behaved like a conventional Indian woman, taught to regard her husband as God. More than that, she missed the opportunity to express her heartfelt gratitude for those who helped her in every way. Instead of opposing her husband, she avoided taking sides. Once again, the traditional woman who defended child marriage took over the rational and thoughtful person. In a meeting at Concord, when Anandi was meekly sitting near Gopal without saying a word, while Gopal was loudly talking as usual, a lady in the audience said, "I wish, she would tell us what *she* thinks."[10] No doubt, this was the most natural reaction of those who expected her to speak her mind, but all her words died in the gloomy silence and she didn't utter a word against her husband.

References:

1. Source - The Nancy Cobb Stone collection of letters.
2. Ibid.
3. *The Life of Dr. Anandabai Joshee* - Caroline Healey Dall. 1888. p. 158
4. Source – The Nancy Cobb Stone collection of letters.
5. *Send Us a Lady Physician: Women Doctors in America* – Edited by Ruth J. Abrum 1985 p. p.82
6. Ibid, p. 83
7. *American Women: Images and Realities. A Woman's Quest: The Life of Marie E. Zakrzewska* – Edited by Agnes C. Victor 1972 Note23 p 497
8. *The Life of Dr. Anandabai Joshee* – Caroline Healey Dall. 1888. P158, 159
9. Ibid, p160, 161.
10. Ibid, p161

28

Declining Health

The hectic workload in the 'New England Hospital of Boston' pulled down Anandi and after a month it became impossible for her to continue. She could no longer drag her weak body behind her strong mind. Having no other option, she decided to give up the hospital work and take complete rest. Her decision was conveyed to Aunt Theo by Gopal. When Caroline Dall went to meet Anandi on 5th June 1886, she was sorry to know that Anandi was very ill and was confined to bed. When Caroline went into her room, she found that Anandi was quietly lying on her bed. But she was very much delighted to see her. Gazing sadly at Anandi, Caroline felt that Anandi was just a pale reflection of her former self. In lieu of words, they clasped hands for a long time, and suddenly Caroline thought that Anandi was right when she had once said, "I have no need of words. I know what my friends think without words."[1] And yet there were many questions which Caroline wished to ask her. But perceiving that Anandi had no strength to talk much, she did not ask her anything. From whatever little Anandi said, Caroline gathered that she was not much worried about her health, but was thinking about her future work with Ramabai. Though she was not in the dark about her condition, a thin hope flickered in her mind that she might improve after returning to India. But if at all, her life was not spared, she was prepared for the inevitable. While talking to Caroline, a few lines from Longfellow's '*Golden Legend*' were repeated which were fresh in her memory.

Not so much even as the lifting of a latch,

Only a step into the open air,

Out of a tent already luminous

With light that shone through its transparent walls.

These lines cast light on Anandi's inner mind. Caroline realised that the thought of death did not horrify Anandi. Her Oriental mind looked at the unavoidable end as 'Mukti' or the ultimate freedom.

Till 9th June, Anandi was in the hospital after which she was removed to Dr. Keller's house for taking rest. In the early part of her stay at the hospital, she had received a call from Mrs. Underwood who wanted to invite Anandi to the 'Free Religious Association' for their annual function. She had requested Anandi to deliver a speech on the needs of Indian women. But being very busy with her hospital work, Anandi had not accepted the invitation. Now that she was free from those duties, she decided to attend the meeting. Underwood's account of Anandi's meeting is valuable to a rare degree, because it conveys the first impressions of a person who was not much acquainted with Anandi. It manifests some interesting shades of Anandi's personality and appearance. "She wore no bonnet, but instead a fawn-coloured wrap enveloped her finely shaped head and gracefully draped her shoulders; this was removed on entering. Her robe of some fine dark woollen material was edged to the depth of several inches with gold-coloured embroidery and in spite of its flowing drapery at one arm, fitted nicely her plump petite form. Gold bracelets adorned her wrists. The dark face was round, with full lips. She had a handsomely shaped brow, broad and intellectual looking. Between the eyebrows was a small tattooed mark, in shape somewhat like a cross. The eyes were beautiful and expressive, large, black, softly shining, as capable of smiles as of tears, with a strangely pathetic look in them. The prevailing expression of Dr. Joshee's face was grave, dignified, almost sad, but the rare smile which marked her appreciation of the ludicrous was charmingly bright and girlish. The talk drifted during the evening into channels which in spite of her modest diffidence drew her out.

"The car of Juggennauth was discussed, and in speaking of the mothers who distraught with poverty sometimes throw their babies into the Ganges, Dr. Joshee said that during her Medical experience in Philadelphia, a large number of newborn infants, either murdered or deserted, found their way into the dissecting room, and she might as well on her return to India relate this fact, making it a custom of

American mothers to kill or desert their children, and adducing it as a result of Christian belief, as to charge the Hindu faith with the drowning so often reported.

"In discussing the right of men to kill and eat animals, Dr. Joshee said that she had lived in America for three years without feeling the need of any other food than that she ate in India. Her acquaintance with the American and English scientists and persons of note was something phenomenal. As she glanced over a large collection of portrait photographs, a word or two would show that she was familiar with the story of each man and his work."[2] Curious Mrs. Underwood had minutely observed and nicely described Anandi's costume, manners and facial expressions. It gives a clear picture of how Anandi looked like. Barring Caroline Dall, no one else had depicted her so well. Mrs. Underwood was wise enough to see that there was a hidden sadness on Anandi's face and her bright, girlish smile was rare.

Saying goodbye to Boston and her student's life, Anandi started for Roselle and reached there on 1st July 1886. Now she wished nothing but to be among her near and dear ones and if possible, she wanted to take a small sightseeing tour before returning to India. On 10th July, Anandi and Eighmie went to Delaware country where there were several relatives of the Carpenters as well as the Eighmies. Eighmie was the surname of Aunt Theo's father but she had given the same name to her elder daughter. Several marriages had taken place between these two families, hence the relationships between them were rather complicated. For example, Grandma Eighmie was both step-mother of Aunt Theo and her sister-in-law and Grandma Carpenter was the mother-in-law of Aunt Theo and the mother of Grandma Eighmie. When Anandi went to Delaware, both these ladies were staying there.

The girls reached Delaware at 4.30 p.m. and a buggy was sent for them to the station. Someone to whom Anandi referred as J.C. had come to receive them. They rode home together and Anandi enjoyed the ride very much. At last, she was free from all duties to have fun and her happy mood reflected in her letter. "The road was very smooth and the ride very pleasant. The mountain scenery is most charming and so are the woods. We were afraid it would be raining when we arrived here. We were most pleased to find it otherwise. It was shining and warm."[3] Aunt Theo had sent some presents with the girls for the ladies in the house, which consisted of Calico, Turkish towels and candies. After distributing them Anandi wrote mischievously to Aunt Theo, "Grandma took the blue one [Turkish towel] and aims at the yellow one."[4] The girls stayed with Aunt Jennie for some days. One day, after breakfast, she took Anandi and Eighmie for a walk in the nearby woods. They were under the impression that they would encounter wild animals or at least a rattle-snake; but Aunt Jennie told them that no wild animal or snake inhabited that wood. While roaming around, sometimes Anandi and Eighmie came across nice little patches of strawberry and ate them heartily. The peaceful, slow-paced country life, serene atmosphere, sweet silence of the woods and the joyous wandering with Aunt Jennie and Eighmie gave deep satisfaction to Anandi.

When it rained heavily and the girls could not go out, Anandi took out her unfinished [F1]silk quilt and started stitching it. She had collected colourful silk pieces of different shapes and sizes from her friends. Stitching them together, Anandi was going to make a crazy quilt out of them. Her friends had embroidered their names and designs on those pieces. On three blocks Anandi had embroidered Gopal's name, her own name and also the year of her graduation, that is 1886. This quilt was in a way, a symbolic representation of her days in America; a memento of all her friends, so it had an emotional value for her. While selecting the pieces that were to go together, Anandi saw that their colours or designs would match. It was a time-consuming and tedious job but she liked it. Sometimes Aunt Theo and Eighmie also helped her in making it. Anandi wanted to prepare some fancy article for J. C. so, she requested Aunt Theo to bring with her the little bottle of gold paint, pink satin, a ribbon and a coloured paper which she had kept in the closet. Anandi had an interest in handicraft but could rarely spare time for it. In Boston, she had planned to learn wood carving and her friend from Roselle was to send her a particular

F1 The quilt is preserved in The Raja Kelkar Museum, at Pune, Maharashtra, India knife. But realising that she would not get time, she had told her not to send it.

From Delaware, Anandi wrote a letter to her mother-in-law to let her know the future plan and to convince her that she would be the most obedient daughter-in-law. Anandi had carefully worked out a plan so that she could justly divide her time between her house and the hospital at Kolhapur. During her stay at Delaware, Anandi helped a relative of Aunt Theo who was in labour. In a letter to Aunt Theo, she gave an account of how the case was handled. "Franky is very low. I spent ten hours with her, …The doctor came in and I had a consultation with him. We decided what was to be done… According to the discussion, the labour was brought on by rupturing the membranes, as that was the only chance of saving her life. There was she suffering intense agony…so unnatural interference was necessary. She was not expected to be able to stand the child birth, but she did better than was expected of her. She brought forth a child that weighs ₤b 1½, like Helena's small doll-baby. It was born at 6 p.m. yesterday and is living yet. It is so feeble that we doubt if it will live longer. ... pulse has not been felt for over three hours and they think she will die soon."[5]

Though Anandi felt satisfied performing the duty of a doctor, the overexertion ultimately told upon her health. Moreover, the sudden change from the lowlands of Roselle, to the elevation of about 1,500 feet above sea level in the Delaware country proved harmful to her delicate health. She had chills three times a day and a fever after each one. Her whole body ached. Anandi was nervous and was longing to meet Aunt Theo. So, on 20th July, she wrote a letter to her, urging her to come to Delaware urgently, "How I wish you were here. I won't stay here very much longer for I have been ill ever since I came here…If you do not come here within a reasonable time, I shall leave this place and go to you."[6] On 23rd July, she piteously repeated her complaints. "I am now having two chills daily, and fever after each one. My throat is so inflamed that it keeps me coughing all the time. Last night, I did not have five minutes' rest."[7] Not wanting to keep her waiting, the Carpenters and Gopal immediately arrived in Delaware. But when they came, Anandi's health had picked up. Except for coughing, there was no other complaint and to Aunt Theo's great relief, Anandi was happily working on her quilt.

According to Anandi's wish, her friends had planned a sightseeing tour and Dean Bodley and Ramabai were to accompany her. On 9th August, Anandi went to Rochester from where they were to go to Niagara Falls, Cincinnati, Chicago and St. Louis. Gopal had gone to Rochester before Anandi and he was to come to the station to receive her. Anandi had a pleasant and comfortable journey. She had informed Gopal that the train would reach Rochester at 9.55 p.m. but somehow that night it arrived before time, at 9.05 p.m. Naturally, Gopal was not there at the station. Instead of waiting there for an hour, Anandi decided to search for the house. She inquired at the station and took the nearby tram. The conductor told her where to change the cars and how to reach the particular street. When she reached there, it was so dark that she could not understand where she was. She saw a few people sitting on a piazza, whom she asked what number their house bore. As it was the house numbered 70th, she turned and went back and found the desired house. Gopal who had gone to meet her on station came back 40 minutes after she found the house.

Anandi had faith in the goodness of people which was strengthened by the pleasant experience of a streetcar driver, while she was travelling alone that night in Rochester. "I had a terrible coughing spell in the street car. I found a white piece which I thought was five cents, and dropped it in. The good driver looked in the box and asked me if I had put in some money. I said, Yes, when he showed me that I had put in 25 cents. He was very sorry, and so was I, but I did not say anything. The honest driver could not open the box, but he managed so nicely that I got twenty cents back. A gentleman who stepped in was told by the driver of my mistake and paid me his fare; nor did the driver let anybody put in another fare till I had my twenty cents back. I could not help feeling extremely grateful to the stranger for his kindness.... This is the way I have always found people."[8]

Anandi had decided to leave Rochester with Gopal for Niagara Falls on 20th August. Thereafter Gopal was to put her on the train going to Chicago. Anandi's friend in Chicago had promised her to show various places of interest. From Chicago, Anandi had planned a trip to Warrensburg as she intensely wished to meet her close friend Dr. Frances Smith before returning to India. From Warrensburg, she was to go to Cincinnati where Dean Bodley and Ramabai were to join her. For this long journey, Anandi took with her only plain dresses instead of brocades, but Frances wished to present Anandi in her pretty saris. Hence Anandi requested Aunt Theo to send her red silk sari and either her graduation dress or a shawl by post, at Warrensburg. Aunt Theo was like a mother to Anandi, hence neither Anandi felt awkward to ask such favours nor did Aunt Theo feel that Anandi was troubling her.

But unfortunately, Anandi had to abandon her nicely worked-out plan. Keeping all the important matters aside Dean Bodley and Ramabai arrived at Rochester itself, instead of joining her later at Cincinnati, so that Anandi might not have to travel alone. But the moment they met her, Dean Bodley realised that Anandi was in no position to take such a long journey and it would be nothing but a waste of her remaining strength which she badly needed for her voyage to India. Therefore, it was decided that they would visit only Niagara Falls and return. The town of Carlisle was on the way to Philadelphia and Anandi wanted to visit the school for Red Indian children at Carlisle, organised by Captain Pratt. Dean Bodley took her to the school and then they all returned to Philadelphia. Immediately Anandi was admitted to the Woman's Hospital and from 31st August to 9th September, she stayed there.

For all these years, Anandi's health went on declining continuously. At many places, various complaints are recorded but it becomes difficult to understand what exactly the nature of her illness was. Her poor health could be traced back to the days at Bhuj. Before that she had enjoyed the best of her health. She had undergone the ordeal of pregnancy at the age of 12. It is not known if something went wrong in that period. In America, she suffered from severe headaches, backache, common cold, throat pain, chill, fever, Malaria and Diphtheria. Anandi herself was a Medical student; her friends and teachers were doctors. It was not possible that her problems were not diagnosed. Yet nowhere it is recorded if she underwent a full medical check-up. On the contrary, Caroline Dall alluded to it in a negative way, "Her friends … saw that something needed to be done, but a thorough medical examination does not seem to have been thought of."[9] The way Anandi herself had described her physical condition from time to time, it is obvious that her illness could not have gone unnoticed by those who came in her close contact. It is not possible to believe they could be in the dark about her health. There are 2 references that clearly indicate that neither Dean Bodley nor Anandi herself was unaware of her serious condition.

1. In a letter to Ramabai, written on 28th December 1885, Dean Bodley had said, "*if her life and health are spared* a grand professional future awaits her."[10] The statement is conditional. The word 'IF' indicates that Dean had found out 'something' which was injurious to her health. What was that?

2. A statement by Caroline Dall is sufficient to show that it was a disease of the lungs. "She thought the sari very inconvenient for a working woman …but she never experienced the slightest inconvenience from wearing it as a student, until her *lungs began to fail*."[11] That means her lungs had begun to fail right from her college days; and Anandi was well aware of the problem which was discovered certainly before December 1885, since Dean had mentioned it in her letter of 28th December 1885.

Yet it is not known precisely when was Anandi affected by tuberculosis or when was it diagnosed or had she undergone any tests and what did the report of her medical check-up say. So, these questions remain unanswered. The only thing one can say for sure is that people close to her knew very well that Anandi suffered from tuberculosis. In that period, tuberculosis was an incurable and common disease even in America. Its symptoms were known to people very well. A house without a patient of tuberculosis was thought to be a fortunate house. A few years after Anandi's death, which is in 1899, Eighmie Carpenter also died of tuberculosis.

For 10 days, Anandi was treated in the Woman's Hospital in Philadelphia, where she had worked for the last two and half years as a Medical student. The place was like her home where she was happy to be with her friends and professors in the hours of her illness. She had a chance to meet everybody before returning to India. Greetings were exchanged and promises were made to remain in touch while Anandi took her adieus. Though she did not allow her pains to interfere with those sweet moments, the suffering found its way in a letter to her close friend Caroline Dall, "Even the least breeze seems to abuse me. No one in the house realizes the trouble as my Doctor and I do, and no one need."[12] After spending 10 days in the Woman's Hospital at Philadelphia, on 10th September 1886 Anandi went with Ramabai to Roselle, which was her last destination in America.

During her college days, she had travelled umpteen times between Philadelphia and Roselle, but on the 10th September, it was her last journey and she was never to come back to Philadelphia. This city, where the happiest days of her life were spent, had a special place in her heart. Her quest for knowledge had brought her here from a faraway country and the tiny seed of her hope was nurtured here with care. She owed the satisfaction and delight that she obtained in her life to this city of 'brotherly love.' Hereafter, she was never to see those roads and lanes familiar to her like the lines on her palms; those buildings, gardens, churches and her college. The memories of the days spent here were to linger in her mind forever. So, with a heavy heart, she said goodbye to Philadelphia.

At the time of parting, Dean Bodley might have remembered the day when she had met for the first time, the plump and happy girl in her blue cotton sari at her doorstep, who contrasted with the thin and weary patient before her and the parting might have become more painful. Though Dean Bodley could not shut her eyes to the reality, she hoped against the hope that Anandi's health might improve after returning to India. Leaving the Philadelphia station, the train speeded up. It was early September and the signs of approaching fall were seen in the form of a few reddish leaves among the green clusters. Very soon, the trees were to turn into colourful masses of golden, brown, yellow, red or orange leaves. But by that time Anandi would have gone away, without witnessing their amazing beauty. The fall season had begun within her body and there was no guarantee of her long life. If the end was near, she was prepared for it but her only wish was to rest among the Carpenters after her death. She was sure that if she would die in India, her husband would show courage to send her ashes to America despite people's opposition and doubtlessly the Carpenters would respect her last wish.

Anandi reached Roselle. The hearty welcome dragged gloom out of her mind and she was delighted to be among her beloveds. The house of the Carpenters became livelier with the Indian guests like Ramabai, Manorama, Gopal and Govind Sathe. Anandi's friends rushed to meet her and their loving company cheered her to a great degree. Taking into consideration all her needs, a room was kept ready for Anandi where she lived for 4 weeks. She had grown so weak that most of the time she preferred to remain in bed or sometimes she would sit for a while in her easy chair. But she would always join the family at lunch and dinner, enthusiastically taking part in jolly social conversation. Though everyone was worried about Anandi's health, they took good care to hide their gloom and tears from her. They deliberately maintained cheerfulness and the bright atmosphere made her almost forget her illness, the only unavoidable sign of it being the medicines that she had to consume periodically. The precious memories of those last few weeks which the Carpenters spent with Anandi were to remain green forever. Anandi was worried about the final packing of her luggage, as she had no strength to do such a job. When she had arrived in America, she had only 3 trunks with her. But now she possessed various books, notebooks, surgical instruments, botanical specimens which she had collected; her degree certificate, letters, clothes, the crazy quilt, multiple gifts and photographs. All those things were not mere inanimate objects. They represented beautiful memories of her life in America. Anandi was anxious about packing her coffer neatly but was satisfied to see that her friends packed everything very carefully according to her instructions. In all, 11 trunks were packed, including those of Gopal.

With so many guests residing in the house, Aunt Theo had no time to raise her head from the household affairs, but the thought of her Indian daughter never left her mind. The unstoppable questions regarding Anandi's future troubled her very much: 'Would Anandi be able to endure strains of the long voyage to India? Would Gopal treat her with honest love and tenderness? Would he take proper care of her or would he be quarrelsome as usual? What would happen to her in India? Would her people welcome her or would they excommunicate her? Would she be rewarded or punished for her rare merits and success? Would her health improve in India or not?' Aunt Theo prayed to God for her well-being, good health and safe journey. Recalling those days, she once wrote to Caroline, "It was too hard to believe that all the efforts of her physicians would be in vain and we tried to shut our eyes to the heart-rending truth."[13]

Anandi's nature and manners were so pleasant and lovable that the Carpenters had nicknamed her as a 'well-spring of delight.' In the beginning, Anandi was their delightful pen-friend; then she had become one of their family members. Being highly impressed by her, once Uncle Ben sent a message to Gopal, via Anandi, that the Carpenters were fortunate to gain what he had lost and they thanked the Almighty for this happy gain. Anandi had made them very happy. Now their 'well-spring of delight' had grown feeble. So, from Uncle Ben to little Helena, everybody in the house, tried their best to make her happy and cheerful. Aunt Theo said, "At no time did any of the 'gloom' of sickroom attend her. Everything was done to make those precious days as bright and cheerful as possible"[14]

References:

1. *The Life of Dr. Anandabai Joshee* - Caroline Healey Dall. 1888p 152
2. Ibid, pp 153,154,155
3. Source: The Nancy Cobb Stone collection of letters.
4. Ibid
5. Ibid
6. Ibid

7. Ibid
8. Ibid
9. *The Life of Dr. Anandabai Joshee – Caroline Healey Dall. 1888. p 161*
10. *The letters and correspondence of Pandita Ramabai – compiled by Sister Geraldine / Edited by A. B. Shah / 1977 / p 165*
11. *The Life of Dr. Anandabai Joshee* - Caroline Healey Dall. 1888 p 105
12. Ibid, p 163
13. Ibid, p 171
14. Ibid, p 169
15. Ibid, p 169

29

The Homeward Journey of Anandi

Anandi-Gopal were to start their homeward journey on Sunday, 9th October 1886 by the ship 'Etruria' which would have taken them up to London, where they were to change the ship. Roselle was such a small town then, that people knew each other very well. Hence, Anandi was also well-acquainted with many of them. Since all her friends wanted to bid farewell to her, the Carpenters had ordered a carriage well in advance of the train, so that before leaving, Anandi could take a round in the town and say goodbye to everybody. The parting was very sad and Anandi's mind was heavy with memories of those beautiful days that she had spent in Roselle. While answering a question in the album of Aunt Theo where she would have preferred to live, Anandi had written, "In Roselle now, hereafter in Heaven." [1] Roselle was her Heaven on earth.

Many of the 19th century railway stations in America still exist, but they are not in use, Roselle being one of them. While researching on Anandi's life in America, I was desperately trying to find out the old Roselle station, which I had located on the map but which I could not find anywhere. The railway track was visible up to a certain point, after which it disappeared behind a long wall and there was no way to go near it. After a while, I could see the track again but not the station. But, after carefully going over the place twice or thrice, the puzzle was solved. The old Roselle station was perfectly hidden behind a gas station and a parking lot. I was thrilled to see that old, deserted, single-storeyed building of the Roselle station and the platform which was fenced from all sides with iron wires. Only the railway track was outside the fence where I was standing. In the 19th century, many of the small railway stations consisted of only one platform and the other side was open; and the old Roselle station was designed in the same way. I could locate the ticket window from where I was standing. I felt that the station was a silent eyewitness to Anandi's farewell.

On that same spot, Anandi's friends had gathered on 9th October 1886, to make their adieus. Being at a loss of words, their tearful eyes, strong handshakes and flowers might have performed the job of words. Anandi's heart was bowed with grief, but she accepted the flowers with a smiling face. Along with the Carpenters, Ramabai and Govind Sathe were also going up to the New York Port, to see them off. When the train moved, waving hands, craning necks and eager faces slowly turned into small spots which vanished into nothingness as the train speeded up. Feeling weary, Anandi leaned on the shoulder of Aunt Theo. Those last moments of togetherness were very precious for both of them. A carriage took them to the New York Port where they were to embark on the ship. "She was very weak", wrote Aunt Theo to Caroline Dall, "but sat firmly in her seat as we drove, looking as bright as the flowers she carried. She was glad to lie down as soon as we reached the steamer. Not for a moment did she give up."[2] Once Anandi was comfortably settled in her cabin, her friends rushed to meet the agent of the line, the doctor, and the authorities. All of them were requested to take utmost care of Anandi who was in no condition to go on such a long voyage. Accordingly, the agent instructed the purser and steward to take special care of Anandi's diet. The doctor in charge also kindly agreed to take every care of the patient's health. The painful moment of separation was signalled by the loud siren of the steamer. Trying to control their tears, Aunt Theo, Uncle Ben and others bade goodbye to Anandi for the last time and left her in charge of Gopal.

On 'Etruria', Anandi-Gopal were well-cared for and special attention was paid to their food, as promised by the agent. Remembering that they were vegetarians, the chief steward made it a point to provide them with a sufficient quantity of grapes, apples, pears, peaches besides vegetable soups, baked apples, tomatoes, ice creams and puddings. But Anandi was not comfortable because the weather was very rough. Gopal also suffered from the common cold. Anandi was so ill that she could not leave her bed. Dr. Gald visited her twice a day. As she was suffering from vomiting and stomach ache, the small fund of energy was almost spent. On the night of 12th October, gusty winds were roaring on the sea. Anandi was badly coughing all night. The frightfully vigorous motions of the ship made her feel that she was thrown up and down in her bed. Thinking that she was at the death's door, Anandi's heart sank in the endless darkness of the stormy night. She urged Gopal to tell Aunt Theo, that she remembered her in her last hour. While the doctor gave her some brandy with hot water and a sleeping pill, lone Gopal helplessly watched her with dismay. Once again storm brewed on 14th October, which according to the sailors, was the most frightening one that they had ever encountered. Had not 'Etruria' been a strong and sturdy ship, the storm might have broken it into pieces.

During the voyage, the traditional roles of husband and wife were reversed. Traditionally, a husband enjoyed the supreme position in the hierarchy and the wife was placed at the lowest position. So, husband and wife were never treated as equals. The wife was supposed to serve her husband all her life, as he was her God. But in the voyage, his wife being an invalid, Gopal had to look after her. Not being accustomed to doing the job of nursing, he found it difficult. Caroline observed, "Gopal was much exhausted by the unusual labours of a nurse, labours from which oddly enough, if we look at it from a religious point of view, every high caste male Hindu is taught to shrink."[3]

No doubt Gopal was exhausted, but it would be unjust to include him in the general category of the 'high caste male Hindu.' Neither was he feeling below dignity to serve his wife, nor did his male ego made him shrink from the job. Till her last day, it was Gopal who took care of his wife without feeling degraded. The only thing was that being all alone on the ship and a complete novice as a nurse, he was afraid that he would make a mess of the job. He himself had described his confusion when he combed Anandi's long hair: "For days I have not combed her hair, because I am afraid. I cannot wear them properly in a braid. I am afraid to comb her thick and long hair which get entangled." He had maintained a diary in the voyage which depicts his troubled mind. The overwhelming fear of Anandi's death during the voyage, forced him to vent his righteous wrath on God.

When Anandi-Gopal reached London on 18th October, they had no idea of what was in store for them. Thomas Cook and Son had booked their tickets from New York to Bombay and had secured by telegraph a berth in the British Steamer [F1]Hergoda. On their arrival in London,

F1 According to Kashibai Kanitkar, the name of the British steamer was not Hergoda but Henazab.

their luggage was immediately transferred at a heavy charge to Hergoda. After settling Anandi comfortably in a hotel, Gopal went to the office of Thomas Cook to enquire about the departure of Hergoda. But being unable to give him any details, the person in charge sent him to the office of the 'British India Steamer Ship Co.' Knowing that the two passengers were Indians, tickets were denied to him on the ground that the passage money was not paid and they refused to accept money from Gopal. Their luggage was immediately removed from the steamer. The whole experience was so unexpected and shocking that Gopal did not know what to do. Boiling with rage, he tried to argue with the authorities, but in vain. So, he had to return to the hotel, without tickets.

Caroline Dall who thought this to be another tale woven by Gopal's fertile imagination, had expressed her doubts in the biography. "It is impossible to understand this story as Gopal tells it. Hindu passengers and European passengers of every rank are constantly making the passage from India to England and back in the same vessel and there is nothing in the public opinion of England to sustain the outrage here described."[4] Caroline had seen Gopal's letter in which he had informed how the arrogant attitude of the 'British India Steamer Ship' Company's people provoked him. "I was all wrath and indignation. I burst as is my wont, into bitter exclamations. I abused the English right and left and said that their houses in India should be blown up and every insult retaliated by bloodshed."[5] After reading this, Caroline felt that Gopal was to blame for the denial of the tickets because, "Such words as these and the far worse words that followed, could hardly have availed to secure the accommodation that he wanted."[6] Having experienced how irritating Gopal could be, it was but natural that Caroline passed such remarks but the question still remained, whether it was a fictitious tale or a true story and Caroline could not arrive at any conclusion in the biography.

After the above incident, Gopal went back to the hotel where two ladies had called on Anandi. Gopal narrated the whole story which the English ladies could not believe. Gopal wrote in his letter that the ladies went to the office of Thomas Cook to make sure what they had heard was true and found that Gopal was absolutely right. Then Anandi-Gopal were helped by one of the ladies, Mrs. Pattison and her husband. The couple took the initiative and immediately made arrangements for

Anandi-Gopal's voyage to India. Their tickets were booked for the P & O Steamer which was to sail on 21st October. Gopal further wrote that Mr. Pattison handed him a check for 80 or 90 pounds, because he had no money. This statement was also instrumental in creating doubt in Caroline's mind. "Why there should have been any 'lack of funds' it is difficult to understand. The Dewan of Kolhapur was to pay all the expenses of the new superintendent of the Albert Edwards Wards, and the large amount of money known to have passed into Mr. Johee's hands, makes it impossible to understand why he could not pay his own passage."[7]

With the purpose to insult Anandi's American friends, Gopal deliberately commented, "Her [Pattison] words at parting were more consoling and redeeming than all the dollars Mrs. Joshee received as present from her American friends in pomp."[8] It was just not possible for Caroline to overlook those arrogant words. Therefore, she rebuked, "These words are printed and I cannot pass them by. Not only did Dr. Joshee receive many gifts from the ladies of Philadelphia, but many benefactions were also offered to her husband for her sake and with a delicacy which hid from every 'left hand' what the 'right hand' did."[9] Moreover, Gopal had made it a point to send the information to The *Index* which was printed on 23rd December 1886. Therefore, it was but natural that Caroline was annoyed by his ungratefulness. This kind of behaviour is one more example of his perversity and sadist nature. Hence Caroline was right in doubting his information. She had to depend on Gopal's account of the voyage to India. So, she was very cautious. Since Gopal had shrouded Pattisons in mystery, Caroline was not able to ascertain who were Pattisons; how did they know Anandi-Gopal; why did they help the unknown Indian couple; exactly how many pounds were offered and was the money given as a gift or as a loan?

While researching, I discovered two letters that enabled me to fill in the gaps in the above account.

1. The expense statement prepared by Anandi for the perusal of the State of Kolhapur.

2. A letter from Ramabai to her British friend Dorothy Beal.

These valuable documents provided me all the missing links. Gopal's letter in *The Index* was a bolt from the blue to Ramabai and she was disturbed to know that Anandi-Gopal received very insulting treatment in England, from certain British racists. Being unable to take this news passively, she let her British friend Dorothy Beal know how Anandi-Gopal were ill-treated in London. "I would not have been surprised at it, if the incident had occurred on Indian soil, for it is one of the daily occurrences there; but to think it took place in England is really remarkable, for whatever may be said of the English in India, I have almost in all cases found them very polite and kind to strangers at home."[10] Dorothy was also shocked to hear this, but she asked if Ramabai had any proof. At that moment, Ramabai had no other proof than Gopal's letter. But in December 1887, just by chance, she came across the proof and it was immediately sent to Dorothy Beal. Ramabai's letter of 19th December 1887 presents a clear-cut account of the incident in London. Accidently Ramabai met a certain 'Miss Borden' in a meeting at Boston, who was Anandi's friend. She told Ramabai that she knew the incident to be true, because she had heard of it from the very woman who had helped Anandi in London. Things became very clear when Borden said that she herself had written a letter to her British friend 'Mrs. S. P. Pattison' about Anandi. She had given Anandi's London address and had requested Mrs. Pattison to meet Anandi. Mrs. Pattison called on Anandi accordingly and found her to be ill and alone in the hotel, coughing fearfully. After knowing all these details, Ramabai wrote to Dorothy Beal, "Soon after Mr. Joshee came in and informed his wife and the lady that the British India Liner Steamship's agents had refused to give passage on board . . . and that it would be impossible for them to sail home, because the special S. S. Line (P & O Line) that was open for Hindus and all the rest, cost eighteen guineas more than they had in their hands. The kind-hearted lady . . . went to her husband and told him of it and they decided to send a messenger to the Steamship Company's office to find out whether Mr. Joshee's story was true. Unfortunately, enough they found it all a plain fact. The gentleman then took in the situation at once. He could plainly see. ...that it was quite impossible for her to sail without a little more money. He risked the eighteen pounds, took a paper signed by Dr. and Mr. Joshee agreeing to return the money to him as soon as possible and in two days the sick woman and her husband (who got a third class passage because he had not money enough to procure for himself a first class berth) were on their way home."[11] Further Ramabai gave Dorothy the address of the Pattisons, in case she wanted to check the story. When Anandi reached India, she sent the [F2]expense statement to the Diwan of Kolhapur and requested him to send the money to Pattison and accordingly the money was sent.

That means the calamity was not Gopal's fancy but plane reality. Yet Gopal failed to win the sympathy of his American friends like Caroline because his description was flavoured with acrimony, sarcasm and exaggeration. There was no need to say 'Eighty or Ninety pounds' when the amount he received from Pattisons was just 'Eighteen pounds.' At last, on 21st October, Anandi-Gopal embarked on the steamer named 'Peshawar' that took them to their homeland. Anandi was feeling much better when they left London and was able to walk without assistance. The next day, she went on the deck and sat there reading. But this enthusiasm was not to last for long, because once again, her illness raised its head. Anandi took a cold and she was confined to her bed. Here again Gopal created a tale about himself. He told Anandi's American friends that as he didn't have sufficient money, he bought a low-class ticket. Moreover, just out of curiosity, to see what would happen, he declared that he was Anandi's servant. He told Kashibai Kanitkar the Marathi biographer of Anandi that by doing so, he tried to save his money for his mother. Neither Caroline Dall nor Kashibai Kanitkar believed in these fake stories. But now, being a servant, he had to stay away from her, till sent for. Caroline who could imagine how this foolishness might have disheartened Anandi, reacted sharply, "If by 'curiosity' is meant a desire to see how much irritation and ill-will he could excite by his own violence and perversity, we cannot deny that his experiment succeeded."[12] In the voyage, the ship had to weather a storm in the Bay of Biscay. When they reached Gibraltar, Anandi was in a critical state, so throwing away the disguise of a servant, Gopal remained with his wife day and night. The unending health problems were ruining her hope to get well soon.

Caroline Dall had mentioned in the biography that from Gibraltar Gopal had sent a letter to Aunt Theo that "in this letter came a few lines from Anandabai to Mrs. Carpenter, the last she ever wrote."[13] Here Caroline Dall is guilty of falsehood and of tampering with the original letter. It is not at all true that Anandi wrote 'a few lines.' On the contrary, she had written a full-length letter, which was condensed into 'a few lines'

F2 For this letter see: Appendix no. 4.

by Caroline Dall herself, for no reason. It is just not understandable as to why Caroline shrank the letter and presented it as the original. I could obtain the real letter of Anandi from the Nancy Cobb Stone collection. This rare letter, runs as follows:

"Gibraltar

October 26 1886

My dear aunt,

I am not able to write a long letter but I did want to say to you something about my health. I think I am a good deal stronger though my cough is very bad yet and my Bronchitis somewhat worse.

I was exceedingly surprised to read Mr. Joshee's letter! What object could he have in saying that I did my best in exhausting myself to death? He writes I was trying to paste the cards which I never dreamed of as there is not a single card packed with the scrap book (in the tin box). This I discovered the day before I went up on the deck (where I sat in hot sun until I felt the least cold) while looking for a notepaper for him.

I pity his position very much as I know he must get very weary of me, for he never can stand the presence of a sick person, but if he is really weary, he should say so and not make out that I was disobedient or a fool; for one certainly must be a fool who tries her best to be ill.

I am just getting over my sea sickness which has prevented me from getting proper nourishment or exercise.

I am still in bed, have poultices on all day. The Dr. comes to see me twice daily.

I am writing this in bed while lying down.

Shall write more next time.

With love to all.

There has not been a day since the 9th when I did not miss your precious company.

Very affect.

Yr. niece,

Anandibai Joshee."[14]

When I compared the original letters of Anandi with those in the biography written by Caroline Dall, I found that in some of the letters, Caroline had changed the original words and constructions, while she quoted. Instead of truthfully repeating the matter, in quotations, as per the basic rule that a researcher or a biographer must follow, she had reconstructed them. If something is omitted from the original text, it has to be indicated with 3 dots and the additional words have to be put in square brackets. But she had taken full liberty to change the original matter, in whichever fashion she pleased. This attitude ultimately culminated into shrinking the whole letter of Anandi into 'a few lines.' If she did not wish to give the complete letter, she could have quoted those words of Anandi which she found to be important. But the way she tampered with the letter is simply disgusting. She condensed the above letter as follows. "I am stronger' she says. 'Cough better, throat worse. I shall improve when I am able to eat. There has not been an hour since I left New York when I have not missed your precious self. I am writing in bed and see my Doctor twice a day."[15] And this Caroline presented as a quotation. Anandi's letter shows that even when troubles were brewing from all sides and Anandi's life was at stake, Gopal could dare to ruin her peace of mind by his habitual backbiting and whims. Here his perversity touched the level of madness and the graph of his self-destruction reached the climax.

'Peshawar' halted at Malta for a few hours to take in water, fruits and vegetables. On 3rd November, the ship entered the Suez Canal. Then crossing the Red Sea, where it was extremely hot as usual, it arrived at Eden on 9th November. Impatiently waiting to see with her own eyes, the shore of her country, Anandi passed her days enthusiastically planning her future programme. At last, the tiresome journey ended on the morning of 16th November 1886 when 'Peshawar' reached Bombay.

Anandi dressed herself in a black brocaded silk sari which she wore after the traditional Maharashtrian style. Her costume was complete when she put on the jewelled ear tops, a nose ring and a pair of boots with stockings. On the port of Bombay, a large crowd had gathered to receive her. People were waiting jubilantly for her arrival. When she disembarked, her excited friends and well-wishers showered flowers on her and gave a heartiest welcome to the first Indian woman doctor,

Dr. Anandibai Joshee. In Indian mythology, Gods shower flowers on great men who perform magnificent deeds for mankind, which is called, 'Pushpa-Wrushti.' By following this myth, her countrymen expressed their profound respect for The Pioneer.

References:

1. *The Life of Dr. Anandabai Joshee* - Caroline Healey Dall. 1888. p xii
2. Ibid, p 170
3. Ibid, p 172
4. Ibid, p 175
5. Ibid, p 174, 175
6. Ibid, p 175
7. Ibid, p 176
8. Ibid, p 175
9. Ibid, p 175, 176
10. *The letters and correspondence of Pandita Ramabai* – compiled by Sister Geraldine, Edited by A. B. Shah / 1977 / p
11. Ibid, p 180
12. *The Life of Dr. Anandabai Joshee* – Caroline Healey Dall. 1888. p 176
13. Ibid, p 177
14. Source- The Nancy Cob Stone Collection of letters.
15. *The Life of Dr. Anandabai Josh*ee – Caroline Healey Dall. 1888. p 178

30

Shadows of Uncertainty

When Anandi Gopal returned to India, it was a great relief for them to see that the attitude of their countrymen was changed. Forgetting their threat to excommunicate them, people from various strata were rejoicing over Anandi's success. In the same city of Bombay where once she was abused and stoned, people showered flowers on her. Feeling proud of her, they sent telegrams and wrote letters of congratulations. People visited the house where she was staying, just to have a look at the great lady. She had become a person of national importance.

Anandi's college life was over and soon she was to join the 'Albert Edward Hospital' at Kolhapur. But before that, she badly needed some rest. A strong hope was kindled in her mind that the change of climate and food would improve her health and she would gain sufficient strength to work. The State authorities of Kolhapur, who were ahead of others in appointing a lady doctor, were eager to welcome her. Shahu Maharaj, the King of Kolhapur, Meherji Kooverji, his Diwan and Lee Warner, the Political Agent were in Bombay when Anandi arrived. They had come to attend the grand ceremony of welcoming the Viceroy which was to take place on 17th November 1886, in the Government House at Malabar Hill. In the list of the States which were to greet the Viceroy in the Royal Court, the State of Kolhapur was honoured by the British Government, by placing it at the Top. It is most likely that the State authorities paid a visit to their foreign-returned lady doctor when they were in Bombay. On 17th November, Meherji Kooverji wrote a letter to the State executive of Kolhapur and enquired if the doctor's bungalow was ready. On 20th November, he requested Lee Warner to let Anandi work in two major hospitals in Bombay, so that she would gain practical knowledge. "The Council of Administration considers it desirable that she should, before proceeding to Kolhapur attend the Hospital in Bombay for two months in order to acquire practical knowledge. She will attend either Cama or J. J. Hospital or both. I therefore request that you will be good enough to obtain the permission of Government for the same."[1] Anandi was also to get a stipend for this work. Gopal being unemployed, they had no definite source of income. Hence Anandi needed to start her work, but first she had to get well.

In Bombay Anandi, Gopal and their relatives who had come to Bombay to receive Anandi, resided in the house of Bhaskar Date, a maternal cousin brother of Anandi. The small house was so much crowded that it was just not possible for Anandi to get quietude. The house was also so damp that it was unsuitable for a patient like her. Mama Parmanand, a friend of the Joshis, who had once settled them in Bhuj, promptly came to their rescue. He requested his wealthy friend, Seth Madhavdas Raghunathdas to invite Anandi and her family to his house. Willing to help her out, Seth Madhavdas and his wife Dhanakoovarbai warmly welcomed Anandi, Gopal, her mother, grandmother, brother and sister, in their large bungalow at Girgaum near the famous building of Prarthana Samaj. Seth Madhavdas was an affluent merchant of silk and also an active reformist who had advanced the movement of widow marriage by himself marrying a widow. He had sheltered many helpless widows in his house, and had initiated marriages of 50 widows. Naturally, such a benevolent person was glad to help Anandi in the time of her difficulty. The house of Seth Madhavdas was comfortable and quiet, but there was no improvement in the patient. On the contrary, her cough and fever had become severe. Here Anandi stayed for 15 days.

Unless Anandi was well enough to take up her job, there was no other go but to take shelter in a house of a friend or a relative. This was the bittermost fruit of Gopal's hasty decision to resign from his job. Had he retained it, Anandi did not have to depend in her illness on the goodness of others. A self-respecting woman like her had no house of her own because her husband was unemployed. Being in great need of money, she requested the State of Kolhapur to send her Rs. 250 as an advance on her salary and the request was kindly granted. In all,

Anandi stayed in Bombay for three weeks, of which two were spent in the house of Madhavdas, and a week in the other three houses. It is unthinkable how they moved from one place to the other, with Anandi's luggage of 11 trunks and the crowd of her relatives accompanying them. Many European doctors were consulted in Bombay and they had declared that it was the last stage of tuberculosis which was incurable. Anandi intensely wished to go to Pune and consult a well-known native doctor Bapusaheb Mehendale who she felt for sure would cure the incurable disease. In the beginning, her doctors had not given her permission to go to Pune, because the climatic conditions would not have suited her. But seeing that it could have hardly made any difference whether she was in Bombay or Pune, her wish was respected and she was allowed to go to Pune. Anandi longed to have the treatment of Bapusaheb Mehendale, whom she trusted, because he was her father's doctor.

On 9th December, Anandi and her family took the train to Pune at 2.00 p.m. in which two tickets in the first-class compartment were booked for Anandi and her mother and the rest of the family was put in the third-class compartment to minimise the expenses. In those days, the electrification of the trains was not done. The travellers had to pass the weary hours after sunset in the flickering light of oil lamps. When the train reached Pune at about 7.00 p.m., it was pitch-dark. The Pune newspapers were quick enough to take notice of Anandi's arrival. On 10th December, the *Poona Observer* reported, "Dr. Anandibai Joshee arrived in Poona by a Mail train, last night. She is not in good health and is putting up in city." In Pune also, the problem of housing Anandi in a good place remained the same. For the first few days, the Joshis lived in a small house, not suitable for the patient. But a wealthy reformist, Raobahadur Vishnu Moreshwar Bhide came to their aid and shifted them to his large mansion. A few days before, Bhide's elder daughter Chingootai had given birth to a son. The wife of Raobahadur was fully occupied with her daughter and the newborn grandson. Hence, the responsibility of additional guests and a serious patient was another burden on her shoulders. But the large-hearted couple cared so much for Anandi's well-being that they were glad to put out a welcome mat. Anandi's own elder sister

Umabai Omkar also had a huge house of her own in Pune, but it seems that Anandi was not invited there. This one thing alone proves the greatness of the Bhides, who had thoroughly understood the problem of the Joshis and being free from prejudices, took pleasure in helping a woman like Anandi.

Like Seth Madhavdas of Bombay, Raobahadur Bhide was a staunch supporter of widow marriage and had openly encouraged the first widow marriage that took place in 1869. He was one of the founders of the 'High school for the Indian Girls' where he had sent his widowed youngest daughter Awdabai. They were threatened for this with dire consequences but neither the daughter nor the father wavered. Awdabai had developed a keen interest in learning and she always stood first in her class. The polite, well-bred girl who was equally good at various subjects like English, Mathematics and Drawing, was selected by her teachers as the 'Ideal Student.' Having profound respect for Anandi, Awdabai felt highly honoured by her presence in their house. She had maintained a diary in that period, in which she jotted down the ups and downs in Anandi's condition, along with many other things in her own life. She was facing similar obstacles in her day-to-day life, which once Anandi had faced. Therefore, she knew what courage, determination and mental strength were required to swim against the current.

In that period, Awdabai's mind was putting out the tender sprouts of fascinating dreams. In a letter to her teacher, Sorabji, she wrote, "You asked me what I should like to do…I should like to study all my life, if I could… I should like to be an artist if I could… It should be delightful to go abroad into the world and see many countries." Having grasped the social relevance of Anandi's achievement, Awdabai wrote a letter to Lady Dufferin on 7th September 1887, which is a few months after Anandi's death. There she urged, "It would be a very great blessing to have lady doctors because women are too shy to tell their diseases to men . . . So many of them die and suffer intense agony for want of proper care and attendance. So, it would be a great boon to have lady doctors among us." In short, Anandi was an idol of Awdabai and she was pleased that Anandi was staying with them. Along with Anandi-

Gopal, Anandi's mother and younger sister Sundari were also staying in the Bhides' house and the Bhides were very hospitable to all of them. Till 18th January 1887, they stayed there, after which Anandi was shifted to the mansion of Vaidya Balshastri Mate, the maternal uncle of her mother. This was the place where Anandi was born.

The Joshis had gone to Pune specially for consulting the native doctor, Vaidya Bapusaheb Mehendale. Therefore, after reaching there, Gopal immediately met him and requested him to treat Anandi. But according to Kashibai Kanitkar, this doctor, on whom Anandi had centred all her hopes, refused to see her on the ground of her Medical education in America. Vaidya Mehendale was urged by many well-known persons, said Kashibai, to change his decision, but without success. If the story was true, what was the reason behind Mehendale's outright refusal to treat her? If it were not true, how did the rumour flare? Was Mehendale so orthodox that he did not wish to see the foreign-returned woman doctor? Or was Gopal instrumental in spreading the rumour? Did the doctor have some personal problem? Answers to these questions are not found in the biography written by Kashibai because she had not probed into the matter, to find out the truth.

Secondly, there were some native doctors who looked at Anandi as a sinner and insisted that she should offer atonement to God, but Anandi took a firm stand that as she had not done anything wrong, she would never yield to such an unjust demand. Caroline Dall had mentioned that many doctors refused to treat her. "The Mahratta papers had warned the physicians not to allow their professional jealousy to interfere with duty to a patient in whom all India felt a national concern."[2] It is to be noted that Caroline Dall had used the plural form of the word 'Physician.' Then why did history record the refusal of Bapusaheb Mehendale alone? Why no other doctor's reaction was noted by Kashibai?

To reach the truth, it is essential to look into the life and character of Bapusaheb Mehendale. It would be interesting to know how he took to this profession. Once his niece was seriously ill. He went to a physician and requested him to come with him to see the patient, but the physician straightaway refused. Bapusaheb, who was shocked by his carelessness towards a patient, instantly vowed that he himself would learn Medicine and be so outstanding a doctor that the pompous doctor would be belittled by his success. Within a short time, he really learned Medicine and established himself as an eminent doctor who was highly respected by people. Would such a doctor deny his services to a patient? And if at all he denied, there might be some strong reasons.

The argument that he was anti-women's education would not stand since he had taken a keen interest in his daughter's education and had decided to entrust the heritage of his Medical knowledge in her hands. One cannot say that he despised European medicine because, having realised its importance, he had learnt to dissect the human body after the European method, for acquiring practical knowledge. He was not ill-disposed towards the Europeans, on the contrary, some of his patients were the Europeans. Hence, such arguments would fail to explain his refusal to treat Anandi. Gopal wrote a letter to Aunt Theo, on 16th December where he said, "We are now in the place [Pune] where Dr. Joshee was born. As we came up into hill, she brightened up. At first her cough was better. We sent for one native doctor in whom we have full confidence and whose remedies were very gentle, but collapse followed."[3] Gopal had not mentioned the doctor's name, but it is unlikely that he would have gone to someone else when they had shifted to Pune, just for the sake of Mehendale. Secondly, Gopal had specifically written in the letter that they had sent for the doctor, in whom they had 'full confidence.' Who else could it be but Mehendale whose treatment Anandi desired the most? But it seems that the medicines did not work and the collapse followed.

Then how it was rumoured that Bapusaheb Mehendale refused to examine Anandi? The above quoted letter gives a clue. When it was confirmed in Bombay that Anandi had reached the last stage of tuberculosis which was incurable, Gopal was shaken. Now Mehendale's treatment was his only hope. But finding that even it did not work, he might have lost heart and once again consulted someone else, perhaps a European doctor. His impatience might have angered the hot-tempered doctor who then might have decided not to take the case in his hands. Gopal did not mean to insult the learned doctor, but, then nothing could be more important to him than his wife's life. Vacillating between hope and fear, he was expediting his efforts to save Anandi.

The deeper study of the personality of the doctor brings into light some more facts. Govind Krishna Tilak, his biographer, has depicted Bapusaheb Mehendale as the most intelligent doctor whose knowledge and skills were beyond questions. He would cure any disease that was within the scope of the Medical science of his time. But if, after his examination, he found the disease to be incurable, he would never keep his patient in the dark or would never rouse his false hope. He preferred to tell frankly that he had no medicine on the particular disease. Thus, his refusal was the final indication, the red signal of incurability. He had set an ethical rule for himself that if a patient died, he would not accept money from the dead person's relatives. Therefore, if at all he had refused to treat Anandi, it was because he thought the case to be hopeless. In this fashion, he had refused not only Anandi, but many other patients. The only thing was that Anandi being a well-known person, this particular refusal gained excessive publicity.

In short, the prospect of Anandi's life had faded. She was enduring whatever hardships and agony were in store for her, and knew that her days were numbered. Though even Gopal was aware of this fact, he was trying his best to save Anandi. In a letter to his friend Mama Parmanand, written on 5th January 1887, he said, "My wife is not worse.... She is not yet strong, but the fever is little abated. It will take some time before marked change is produced. It is a neglected case and pronounced to be hopeless by European doctors. If she recovers which I hope she will, it will be a victory of the native drugs." It is really praiseworthy that even when Gopal was under tremendous mental tension, he did not cease to think about the wider application of Anandi's recovery by Indian drugs.

In this last phase of Anandi's life, Gopal's tenderness and true love for her, dormant so far, surged up, leaving behind his jealousy and perversity. He was sincerely trying to make her happy though it was too late. He requested Aunt Theo, "I write to you but you do reply to her, that she may feel as if the letter were her own. A word from you is a tonic."[4] Had he shown such understanding and sensitivity when Anandi badly needed it, his love would have augmented her strength. Though now Gopal was with her all the time, they had little privacy; as men and women constantly visited them. "Some come from curiosity, some from sympathy and affection. Those who scarcely ever leave their houses come to see her, the good among the orthodox and the superstitious, forgetting that we have been to America. Dr. Joshee's illness is the concern of all. Siva is our God of Death. To appease him, water is gently trickled over his head for hours daily. The people are doing it now. Every day the Brahmins put ashes on Dr. Joshee's forehead, and she touches a bit with her mouth. Columns are printed in the newspapers about her condition."[5]

On 18th January 1887, Anandi and her family went to the house of Vaidya Bal Shastri Mate. Bal Shastri was seized with an impulsive idea that Anandi would be saved from the clutches of death in the house where she was born. Though a rationalist, Gopal was now ready to perform any sacrament that he was told to, and was ready to fall on his knees before any deity to save his wife. He would many a time leave Anandi with her mother and go to various temples to offer sacrifices and prayers to Gods and her guardian planets so that their anger and her death might be averted. At the same time, he was grateful for people's cooperation and sympathy, who were once their opponents. The public anger had turned into admiration and most of the relatives were treating them with love and respect. "A few days ago," he told Aunt Theo, "the 'pacification of waters' was performed for her. Brahmins were seated at dinner and her old uncle sent for me that I might sprinkle water on the banana leaves, on which the food was served. Did they consider me as an outcast when they asked me to do this? Even the reformers are astonished at the manner in which we have been treated by the most orthodox Hindus. We have conquered every enemy but Death."[6] Though Gopal had not given up, day by day the hope of Anandi's recovery was diminishing. The month of February was the hardest one when the tension increased due to the pecuniary problems. Anandi had requested the State of Kolhapur to extend her half-pay leave, but it was not possible for them to grant further concession. Hence, the only source of money was also closed. Realising their acute need, Bal Gangadhar Tilak and Gopal Ganesh Agarkar, great patriots and the editors of *Kesari-Maratha* newspapers and Lady Ray came forward to offer monetary help.

In the month of February, Awdabai Bhide visited Anandi four times, though warned by Miss Herford, the superintendent of the girls' high school, that if she would go there, she might catch the infection. In her diary, Awdabai had described at length the pathetic condition of Anandi, which is the only available eyewitness account of Anandi's last days. The original matter was in Marathi, the translation of which would be as follows:

February13,1887 Sunday.

All the doors of Anandibai's room being closed, it was suffocating inside. I perspired profusely when I went in. Anandibai was very serious. Gopal sat on the bed, leaning against a thick pillow and Anandi had rested her head on his chest. For last two three days her stomach was swollen.

Repeatedly she panted for breath. Last night her hands and feet turned cold. [I] do not think she would live long. I was there for some time. Then Miss Herford came in. ...She was saying something to Gopal and I was standing near her when I suddenly felt dizzy. While I asked for some water I fainted and fell down but did not realize what happened. I was given some water and then I regained consciousness. Miss Herford had her buggy and she dropped me off near my house. She warned that if I would go there, I would fall ill." Miss Herford, a prominent figure in the field of woman's education was pining to save Anandi's life. On 14th February, she called on Dr. Cook, who was attached to the 'Sassoon Hospital' and took him to examine Anandi at her own expense. Dr. Cook requested Anandi to move forward, as she was sleeping on the backside of her bed, but she was too weak to make even the slightest movement. Therefore, Dr. Cook climbed on the bed to examine her. Her relatives and well-wishers still had a hope that some method, medicine or the mercy of God would do a miracle and she would be brought back from the death's door. Although Anandi suffered beyond measures, not a word of complaint escaped her lips. Gopal felt proud of his wife when he wrote, "She suppressed her groans that others might not suffer. When conscious she was grave and thoughtful. She never showed the slightest irritability."[7]

When every other medicine was proved to be of no use, as the last measure, it was decided to try the strong remedy known as 'milk medicine.' But it required to follow a strict regime of diet. During the treatment, a patient was not allowed to have a single drop of water. If thirst was unbearable, cow's milk had to be consumed. Gopal prepared Anandi's mind to try this medicine and immediately a native doctor began the treatment, yet the collapse was unstoppable. On the contrary, the medicine increased her agonies, as the thirst and the burning sensation in the throat were unbearable. Her piteous cry for water brought tears to people's eyes. Twelve hours passed without water, but then Gopal was afraid that the medicine would sap her remaining energy. Thinking that the poor soul should not at least die thirsty, Gopal gave her water which calmed her down and the medicine was stopped. Now it was obvious that her end was near. On the deathly night of 25th February, no one in the house could sleep and Gopal kept a watchful eye on Anandi, who breathed so heavily that he was afraid. The next morning, a native doctor gave her opium which reduced her coughing. In the late afternoon, her family gathered around her and turn by turn they told her amusing stories to divert her attention from her pain. Awdabai who visited Anandi that evening wrote in her diary, "I had been to Anandibai's house. She is very serious. Her feet looked swollen."

After sunset, the house sank into the gloomy darkness. The flickering light of a small oil lamp cast mysterious shadows on the walls. Anandi had a chill and fever but her breathing was better than the night before and had no cough. At 8 p.m. Gopal gave her some food and a dose of medicine but she vomited out everything. After some time, he spooned some milk into her mouth and gave medicine at 10 which she retained. Having spent many a sleepless night, Gopal was deadly tired. After entrusting Anandi with her mother,

Gopal went with Vinayak, the younger brother of Anandi, on the first floor, where beds were prepared for men and soon, he was fast asleep. A lone oil lamp was burning in the patient's room like the thinnest hope. Anandi was asleep, therefore her mother stretched herself on her bed. At midnight, a shrill cry went cutting through the silent house. The startled mother jumped out of her bed and took Anandi in her arms who had gone into a violent convulsion. Before she passed away, Anandi muttered hopelessly, "I have done all that I could." Embracing the dead form of her daughter, her mother screamed, "She is gone."

The long struggle for survival came to an end in the calm of the night of 26th February 1887. Gopal who had witnessed the development of Anandi's unmatched mind and the ruin of her body, was now alone and beaten. Gloom poured through his pen when he wrote to Aunt Theo, "The family then bathed the body and decked it with bright garments and ornaments, according to our Hindu custom. There was no time to spread the sad news throughout the city, but all who had heard of it, followed her remains to the cremation ground, on the following Sunday, thus showing their respectful affection. Some of us had feared that the priests might object to cremating the body with the sacred fire, according to the Hindu rites, but our fears were groundless. When I offered sacrifices to avert her death, they had gladly officiated, showing a generous liberty." [8]

As Gopal stood before the funeral pile, silently watching the flames devouring the body of his wife, he did not forget Anandi's last wish to send her ashes to Aunt Theo, since she intensely desired to remain near her aunt, even after her death. The next day, Gopal returned to the cremation ground, in order to collect the bones, which were to be deposited on the 10th day in a sacred river. He also gathered her ashes in a vessel or Raksha kalash which he was to send to Theodosia Carpenter in America, regardless of the objections strongly raised by his relatives. Anandi's last wish was the holiest order for him which he would not have disobeyed at any cost. Before removing the corpse out of the house, two photographs were taken; one was that of the dead body alone whereas in the other photograph, Gopal is seen holding Anandi close to him. The eyes which hold back tears, stand out on the grief-stricken face and his fixed gaze is very pathetic.

My longing to understand the American side of Anandi's life had drawn me to the U.S.A. I studied in the archives of Anandi's college, which is now known as the 'Medical College of Pennsylvania' instead of the 'Woman's Medical College of Pennsylvania,' because now men are allowed here. There I could carry out a thorough study of Anandi's college life as well as the struggle of the 19th century women doctors. I wandered in the town of Roselle; saw the old railway station and had a feel of the places where Anandi once lived. The small winding roads and many of the houses that belong to the 19th century, helped me picturise before my mind's eye, the old town of Roselle. Yet I had a feeling that I could not return to India unless I found out Anandi's grave where her ashes were supposed to be buried.

Caroline Dall had mentioned in the introduction to Anandi's biography, "With some difficulty and against the wishes of his people, but doubtless with a strong desire to bear witness to Anandabai's devotion to this country, Gopal gathered the ashes of his wife together and they are on their way to America. The box which contains them will be buried in the Eighmie lot in the cemetery at Poughkeepsie, where a suitable stone will tell the story of Anandabai's life."[9] The biography had been published in 1888. (The month is not mentioned in the book.) The vessel or Raksha kalash was not buried till then, because Caroline had written, '*The box...will be buried."* Anandi had died on 26th February 1887. If Gopal had sent the box of ashes to America, why did it not reach till 1888? What might have happened in between? Kashibai Kanitkar too had mentioned in the biography that the box was sent. But since Caroline Dall's book was published before the burial and Kashibai had never been to America, these proofs were not sufficient to affirm that the box was buried. Did the box reach America? Could the Carpenters procure permission to bury the ashes of a Hindu woman in a Christian cemetery? Why was it buried in the cemetery at Poughkeepsie which is far away from Roselle?

The only way to answer these questions was to find out if the grave really existed. My relatives Ashok and Manisha Gore, with whom I stayed in the U.S.A., had requested their friend, Viraj Sardesai who lived in Poughkeepsie, to enquire about it in various cemeteries at Poughkeepsie. I was waiting impatiently as I had limited days at hand

and I was to return to India soon. At last, one night at 11.00 p.m. when I was about to sleep, the phone rang urgently. It was Viraj on the line who poured out the great news that Anandi's grave existed in the 'Rural Cemetery of Poughkeepsie.' All of us went into raptures over this news and fixed up the day for visiting the grave. We started at the daybreak from the town of Holland towards Poughkeepsie. It was only a three hours' drive but those last moments of waiting were simply unbearable. In order to resist my excitement, I closed my eyes and sat quietly, but various events in Anandi's life, passed before my mental eye.

When Dr. Muilage died, Anandi had asked, "Is she taken away from those who love her dearly and needed her so badly? How true that our deepest sorrows flow from our deepest affections. What an instrument of… torture one's own heart is?" Aunt Theo and her family might have felt the same when they had received the box of Anandi's ashes. Aunt Theo preserved her remains in the Eighmie Lot, in the 'Rural Cemetery of Poughkeepsie.'

In the office of this cemetery, a lady put two papers in my hand, one of them being the map of Eighmie Lot. On the same paper, a list of persons buried there was written, Anandi's name being the 17th one. It was the private lot of the Eighmies and I was surprised to see that even after a century it carried the name of Geromye Eighmie, who was the father of Aunt Theo, as the caretaker of the lot. I was told that for decades no one had visited the Eighmie lot and the office did not know who could take place of Geromye Eighmie. Adventitiously a few months after my visit, Nancy Cobb-Stone, the great-granddaughter of Theodosia Carpenter, who was out of U.S.A. for many years, visited the cemetery. She told me that in that period, she had felt an inner urge to go to Poughkeepsie. After her visit, she was made the caretaker of the Eighmie Lot.

The other paper that was given to me carried Anandi's name and it was meant to be the personal record of the buried person. But I could see that many of the columns under various headings were empty. Place of death: Not stated. Cause of death: Not stated. Married: Not stated. It is obvious that when the office of the cemetery had begun to update the records of the buried persons, there was nobody who could provide them with the information about Anandi. With the permission of the authorities, I was glad to fill up all those columns. With zeal, they told me that they wished to gather as much information as possible, about the persons buried over there. I was impressed by their archival interest and the sense of preservation, reflecting through their eager enquiries.

We stepped out of the office building to enter the silent city of the dead people, with a map of the cemetery in my hand and according to the instructions, we marched towards the Eighmie Lot. The clement September morning was turning into a mild afternoon, with cool breezes flowing through trees that shaded verdant green hillocks and small paths running throughout the cemetery. I had plucked roses from the garden of Viraj, remembering that Anandi liked roses. We climbed the hillock in the Eighmie Lot and began to search for Anandi's gravestone, among other gravestones scattered over the place. Viraj was the one who located Anandi's grave and we rushed there in great excitement.

There I see myself, standing before the grave of Dr. Anandibai Joshee, looking at it with tearful eyes, touching it with my fingers, perceiving the beautiful moment of discovery, with deep satisfaction. The grave stood erect, resisting hundreds of snowfalls, storms and rainfalls; only the letters on it looked weather-bitten and had lost their sharpness. I wanted to make sure that it was Anandi's grave. So, I read the letters in a different way. Suddenly when I put my finger in the engraved letters and read by touching them, like the Brail script, I felt I was touching not the name but the person.

In the neighbourhood a tall squarish stonework with a tapering column looked conspicuous. This represents the Carpenter clan, on one side of which are carved names of Theodosia Carpenter and her children who were buried there. Around this structure there are the actual graves of Aunt Theo's children. All of them had died very young, so the gravestones are small. Her eldest daughter Viola was born on 27th April 1866 who died on 31st January 1872. Sirena, the second daughter was born on August 22nd, 1868 and died 20 days before Viola, which was on 11th January 1872. Eighmie was born in 1871 who died of Tuberculosis in 1899. Roselyn, who was born after Eighmie, died as a suckling. Otis, the only son of Theodosia and Benjamin was born in 1877. He died in 1878. Helena was the youngest child who had survived. When Anandi went there, Eighmie and Helena were the only two children in the Carpenter family. Theodosia died in 1920 whose grave is near Anandi's grave. After the death of his wife, Benjamin Carpenter went to California and died there in 1927. Therefore, his grave was not there in the Eighmie Lot.

Though Anandi and Aunt Theo were highly devoted to their respective religions, neither of them was a bigot, because they valued humanity the most. A strong bond so developed between them, that they loved each other like a real mother and daughter and it made no difference to them that they did not belong to the same nation, religion, race or language. That is why neither was Aunt Theo filled with remorse for giving a place to her non-Christian, Indian daughter in her Christian graveyard, nor did Anandi feel guilty for her yearning to rest among the dead children of Aunt Theo. In essence, the grave or the 'Samadhi' of Anandi is the symbol of the union of their minds, the union of East and West. More than a century ago, the Carpenters and other friends of Anandi, Caroline Dall and Dean Bodley might have gathered here for the last offices. Cloaked in the shroud of gloom, the mourners might have interred the box of Anandi's ashes with prayers quivering on their lips. Strewing the grave with flowers, they might have returned, silently travelling down memory lane, where Anandi was alive.

The bright afternoon had faded into evening. It was time to go back. As we started walking down the hillock, I paused to look back at Anandi's grave. On the backdrop of clouds, imbued with the glory of the setting Sun, Anandi's grave looked so lonely that I felt like a mourner. And yet that was a turning point and a moment of inspiration for me. At that moment, I thought of making a short film on the struggle story of Anandi's life. The dream changed my life forever and I became a filmmaker.

Anandi's story does not end at the point of her death. Though she died very young, she continued living in the minds of people. Many women who were sailing in the same boat, drew inspiration from her. Hence, it is essential to take note of what happened after her death.

Though she could not work as a doctor, due to her untimely death, she was the person who opened the doors of knowledge to Indian women. We are because she was.

References:

1. Source: The Government's archives, Kolhapur, Maharashtra State, India
2. *The Life of Dr. Anandabai Joshee* – Caroline Healey Dall. 1888. p. 184
3. Ibid, p 181
4. Ibid, p. 182
5. Ibid, p. 181, 182
6. Ibid, p. 184
7. Ibid, p. 183
8. Ibid, p. 185, 186
9. Ibid, ix preface

31

The Door Opened

Anandibai Joshi is the pioneer Indian woman doctor who went abroad to learn Medicine when women's education was a disputable question and girls' schools were almost non-existent. On 11th March 1886, the degree of M. D. (Doctor of Medicine) was conferred upon her in a special ceremony. The fact that Anandibai was the first Asian student of the 'Woman's Medical College of Pennsylvania,' speaks a lot about the grandeur of her success on the international level. She was instrumental in opening the door to higher education for women. Her struggle story inspired other women to pursue their own dreams. In India, common people had no inclination to educate their daughters, but Indian activists, social workers, reformers and intellectuals had acutely felt the injustice done to women. They had also realised the value of women's education in changing the future of their people. Hence, taking the help of the British government whenever needed, they were working hard for the emancipation of women.

Since 1875, the 'Madras University' had opened its gates for women who wanted to become a doctor. But it had offered only a partial Medical course for them. In 1884, the 'Bombay University' decided to allow women to learn Medicine and a full-fledged course was given to them. The Madras University followed its golden step and did the same. Though European women were learning Medicine from the Madras University since 1875, it took some time for native women of South India to take advantage of this opportunity. Sagunabai Khisty, a Maharashtrian Christian was the first woman to take admission to the Madras Medical College. But due to her sickness, she could not complete the course. Abala Bose, a Bengali woman to whom the Bengal Medical College didn't give admission, had entered the Madras Medical College. In 1888, three native women Abala Bose, Rose Govindrajulu and Gurdia Singh completed the Medical course of this college. Muthulakshmi Reddy who was from the princely State of Pudukkotti in the Madras Presidency, entered the Madras Medical College in 1907. Wining many prizes and gold medals, she graduated in 1912 and became the first M.B.B.S. of South India. She worked as a house surgeon in the Government Maternity and Ophthalmic Hospital.

When in 1884, the Bombay University announced that women would be admitted to Medical Colleges, 12 women enrolled their names in the Grant Medical College. To name a few, Motibai Kapadia, Ratanbai Malabari, Manakbai Tarkhadkar, Miss Dosabhai and Anni Jagannath Walker belonged to this first batch and were graduated in 1887. Manakbai was a daughter of Dr. Atmaram Tarkhadkar who belonged to the first batch of native doctors of the Grant Medical College which was founded in 1845. It was a unique coincidence in that period, that both father and daughter learnt medicine from the same institute and they belonged to their respective first batches. In those days, the degree of 'Bachelor of Medicine and Bachelor of Surgery' (M.B.B.S.) was not conferred on [F1]Indian doctors. It was kept reserved only for the Westerners. The Indians received the diplomas, 'L.M.' (Licentiate to Medicine), 'L. M. P.' (Licentiate to Medical Practice) or 'L M. S.' (Licentiate to Medicine and Surgery). These diplomas had no value outside India, as it was just permission to practise Medicine and did not indicate the quality. This underlines the fact that Anandibai Joshi who was graduated abroad in 1886, was the first person to receive the Medical degree, 'Doctor of Medicine.'

The first batch of women doctors of the Grant Medical College graduated in 1887; after which Motibai Kapadia went to Edinburgh for acquiring more knowledge. Successfully completing two courses, Motibai received degrees - 'L.R.C.P. & S.' (Licentiate to Royal College of Physicians and Surgeons.) and 'F. R. C.S. I.' (Fellow of Royal College of Surgeons of Ireland). She returned to India in 1889 and built up her career as a doctor. In the same year, a benevolent Gujarati industrialist Ranchhodlal Chhotalal had founded the 'Victoria Jubilee hospital' for women in Ahmedabad and he invited Dr. Motibai to take charge of it. Dr. Motibai Kapadia was the First Gujarati woman doctor. She devotedly worked in the Victoria Jubilee hospital for almost 40 years

---

F1 For more details, see Chapter no 1 - Heartbeats of the 19th Century

and for many years she was the only woman doctor in the city. Later, two more women doctors Dhanbai Wadia and Gulbanu Medora joined her and they all worked together. Motibai advised Chinubhai Baronet, Ranchhodlal's grandson to launch a nursing college for women. To appreciate Dr. Motibai's good work, the British government conferred on her the 'Kaiser-e-Hind' title. Dr. Manakbai Tarkhadkar also gained fame as an efficient doctor. In 1902, Bombay was in the grip of the Plague epidemic and the death toll was very high. In those difficult days, without caring for her own life, Manakbai worked herself very hard and saved many lives. To appreciate her great humanitarian work, she was felicitated by Sir Jamshetji with a silver cup. Dr. Anni Jagannath Walker, a classmate of Dr. Motibai Kapadia also went to England for acquiring more knowledge before starting to work as a doctor. After she returned to India from Edinburgh in 1892, she was appointed as the House Surgeon in the Cama Hospital at Bombay. She worked there for some months. But within a year, she succumbed due to Tuberculosis.

When Indian universities started admitting women to Medical Colleges; girls belonging to progressive communities like Parsi, Christian, Anglo-Indian or Brahmo were ahead of others in taking advantage of this opportunity. The story of a Bengali woman Kadambini Ganguly runs parallel to Anandi's story. She was born on 18th July 1861 in Bhagalpur, Bihar in a Brahmo family. Being a champion of women's education and a headmaster by profession, her father Brajakishor Basu was determined to give good education to his daughter Kadambini. He had founded an organisation, the 'Bhagalpur Mahila Samaj,' for the emancipation of women. In the beginning, Kadambini's name was enrolled in the 'Banga Mahila Vidyalay' which later merged with the Bethune School. While at Bethune school, she cleared the entrance examination of the 'University of Calcutta' in 1878. It is said that to encourage Kadambini, the Bethune College introduced the Arts course for women. Kadambini and her friend Chandramukhi Basu became the first Indian graduate women in 1883. The same year, Kadambini married her teacher Dwarkanath Ganguli who was a prominent Brahmo Samaj leader. Like Gopal Joshi, he was also a widower and 17 years older than Kadambini. Dwarkanath proved to be a pillar of strength for his wife. After her graduation from the Arts faculty, Kadambini applied to the Medical College of Bengal. She was refused the admission because she was a woman. But Kadambini was lucky to have the firm support of her husband Dwarkanath, who was not a person to accept the refusal meekly. The couple challenged the authorities of the college by sending them a legal notice. Ultimately in 1884, she was accepted as a Medical student and was awarded a scholarship of Rs. 20 per month. In 1886, she received the degree of GBMC. (Graduate of Bengal Medical College). After Dr. Kadambini Ganguli, Bidhumukhi Bose and Virginia Mary Mitra graduated in 1890. Whereas Bindubhashini Bose, a sister of Bidhumukhi Bose, graduated in 1891. They were the earliest women graduates of the Medical College of Bengal.

Both Anandi and Kadambini graduated in the same year 1886 and became eligible to practise Western Medicine. The only difference was that Anandi was a foreign-returned woman doctor having the degree of an American college and the course Anandi completed was more extensive. It is said that Kadambini worked for some time in the Dufferin hospital where she had to face strong opposition from her colleagues and administrative staff. Even as a homemaker, Kadambini's job was challenging. She had to shoulder the responsibility of eight children, including her stepchildren. But nothing could deter her from pursuing her goal. She decided to go abroad for further studies and sailed to England in 1892. She opted for the triple diploma and studied very hard. She returned to India with the prestigious qualifications of L.R.C.P (Licentiate of the College of Physicians, Edinburgh), L.R.C.S (Licentiate of the College of Surgeons Glasgow) and L.F.P.S (Licentiate of the Faculty of Physicians and Surgeons Dublin). She was the only woman candidate among the 14 successful students. After returning to India, she developed her own practice and worked till her death.

Gurubai Karmarkar and Rakhmabai Raut were two women from the Bombay Presidency who decided to learn Medicine in foreign universities, though the Bombay University permitted women candidates. Like Dr. Anandibai Joshi, Gurubai Karmarkar also took admission to the 'Woman's Medical College of Pennsylvania.' She was the wife of a converted Christian Rev. Sumant Karmarkar from Vasai. On 5th May 1892, Gurubai Karmarkar received the degree of Doctor of Medicine (M.D.) in the 40th Graduation function of the College. In 1890, Rakhmabai Raut took admission to the 'London School of Medicine for

Women.' In those days, the British were so orthodox that they didn't allow women to appear for the final examination of Medicine. Hence, like the other women, Rakhmabai also went to Scotland for her final examination which was conducted by the 'Conjoint Board of Colleges of Physician and Surgeons of Edinburgh and Glasgow.' Rakhmabai received the degree of L. R. C. P. S. in 1894. She returned to India in December 1895 and was appointed soon as the House Surgeon in the Cama Hospital. After 6 months, Rakhmabai went to Surat, a town in Gujarat and till 1917 worked in the Malvi Hospital as a medical officer. From 1918 to 1935, she worked in the 'Rasulkalji Zenana Hospital' at Rajkot.

In the biography of Dr. Rakhmabai, *Rakhmabai: Ek Arta*, written in Marathi by Mohini Varde, the author claims that Rakhmabai was the first Indian woman doctor who practised Medicine. But that is not true. Dr. Kadambini Ganguli graduated in 1886 and worked in the Dufferin Hospital before going to England. The name of Dr. Bidhumukhi Bose who graduated in 1890, was mentioned in the journal of 'Association of Medical women in India' as a practising doctor. The women like Dr. Motibai Kapadia and Dr. Manakbai Tarkhadkar who belonged to the first batch of Bombay University, had started practising Medicine years before Rakhmabai. When they began their work, Rakhmabai Raut was learning Medicine. Dr. Motibai Kapadia started her Medical practice in 1889 which is just two years after Anandibai's death whereas Rakhmabai got her medical degree in 1894. No doubt, each one of those women had struggled hard against various odds for becoming a doctor and had done pioneering work in the Medical field. But it is a fact that other women had started practising Medicine long before Rakhmabai.

After completing their Medical courses some women doctors worked in hospitals whereas some developed their own private practices. On the map of the city of Bombay, dispensaries of women doctors looked conspicuous, because they were symbols of the changing time and the flags of educated women. Manakbai Dadina at Andheri, Nagutai Joshi at Girgaum, Manakbai Tarkhadkar at Malabar Hill, Kashibai Navrange at Cathedral Street and Meherbai at Khareghat enthusiastically established their dispensaries and made their services available for sick women. The benevolent work of these women doctors proved their worth and usefulness. Over the period of time, people even forgot that once upon a time, they believed that a woman's place was inside her house and they didn't want learned women among them.

While all these delightful changes were taking place, the post at the 'Albert Edward Hospital' at Kolhapur which was offered to Dr. Anandibai Joshi had remained vacant, even after 14 years. Her unrealised dream was ultimately realised by Krushnabai Kelavkar, a young woman from Kolhapur State itself. She was the daughter of Krushnaji Kelavkar who was a well-known doctor. Her mother Rakhmabai was the first native lady superintendent of the Education Department of Kolhapur State. Dr. Kelavkar had put his two daughters — Krushnabai and Dwarkabai — in the 'Highschool for Native Girls' at Pune. In the future, both the sisters became doctors. In 1899, Krushnabai Kelavkar passed the matriculation exam with flying colours. Her father requested Gopal Krushna Gokhale to give admission to Krushnabai in the 'Ferguson College' at Pune. Gopal Krushna Gokhale, who was a famous freedom fighter and the Guru of Mahatma Gandhi, was on the staff of the Ferguson College. Some professors were against admitting a young girl to their college. But Krushnabai had scored such good marks that they could not neglect the request. Krushnabai and her friend Godubai Deshpande were the first women students of the college.

In 1875, it had been difficult for Anandi to go to a primary school and in 1894, it was possible for women to get admission to a college. Within two decades, the Indian society had advanced a lot on the path to progress. A special sitting arrangement was made for these two girls, near the table of their professors. As an additional measure, a screen of split bamboo was dropped to hide them from boys. Plus, a separate staircase was kept reserved for the two girls. But it was creditable that the boys never misbehaved with them. After a few months the screen was removed because Dr. Krushnaji Kelavkar objected to it. After two years, Krushnabai came to Bombay and enrolled her name in the Grant Medical College, where her father had studied. This bold decision of Dr. Kelavkar disturbed even the leader like Gopal Krushna Gokhale. He requested Dr. Krushnaji not to send his daughter to a Medical College. According to him, the social conditions were not favourable for Medical women. Though a well-known intellectual like him wavered, Dr. Krushnaji was firm on his decision. He had decided to make his daughter a doctor. His decision was backed by the Kolhapur State. The only condition was that after becoming a doctor, Krushnabai should work in the 'Albert Edward Hospital' at least for 5 years. In 1901, Krushnabai passed in the first class and became a doctor. She was awarded the Charles Moorhead Gold Medal. She returned to Kolhapur and joined the Albert Edward Hospital.

In 1887, Dr. Anandibai Joshi was to come there as the first lady doctor of the Hospital. After 14 long years, women of the Kolhapur could get a lady doctor with whom they could talk freely about their physical problems. When Dr. Krushnabai was a young girl, she had read Anandibai's biography written by Kashibai Kanitkar which had left a deep impression on her mind. On her 74th birthday, that is on the 26th April 1952, she wrote down her memories. There she wrote that she wished to read Anandi's biography once again but could not get the book anywhere. Krushnabai's life began where Anandi's life ended. Hence, she could not forget Anandi.

Dr. Anandibai Joshi was like a candle in the wind which flickered but did not extinguish from the public memory. Even today in the 21st century, she is alive in the minds of people and has not stopped inspiring them. Her story has taken various shapes in different mediums like novels, biography, drama, short film, and feature film. It seems that Dr. Anandibai Joshi who was the shining light of her century has become an icon of women's struggle for their human rights.

Appendices

Appendix 1

Dr. Anna Thorburn's letter to Dr. Rachel Bodley

46, Dhurramtolla St.
Calcutta
Nov. 27 1882

My dear Prof. Bodley,

It seems a long time since I said good-bye to you – for so many things have come into my life since then. I feel as if I had lived years, instead of *months* in India. My home is a very happy one, my work is very precious to me, and I thank God for placing me here. I am so thankful for my knowledge of medicine. I find it an excellent means of *getting* at people.

Some of my patients have been very interesting – and their lives would read well in story books if anyone had time to write.

I little thought, for the first time I should write to you, it would be to make application for a *Hindoo Woman* – to enter the college. I am amazed myself and I am sure you will be.

A gentleman of whom my husband had never heard, wrote to him a few weeks ago, to know if he knew of any family going to America, who would be willing to take charge of a lady who wished to go to a medical college. In this way it came about that the lady herself came to me for information and of course I turned her thoughts *Philadelphia-wards*.

The lady is a Brahmo,[π] 18 years of age, and has been married a number of years. Her only child died so that she has no family to care for and her husband heartily sympathises with her in all her plans – and seems very glad to have her taken up this work.

π This information was wrong. Anandi was not Brahmo.

Some Presbyterian Missionary lady has encouraged Mrs. Joshee – and I think will help to provide means to meet her expenses. I judge from the letters she writes her, that she knows the little woman well, and she seems to be a woman capable of judging wisely. (I mean the Missionary lady.)

Mrs. Joshee is willing to board in an American family, and to take our style of dress. I have been buying clothing for her, and am having it made. I fitted the first dress on her, that ever she had fitted. The religion of Brahmos is not very unlike that of Unitarians. We know of two Missionary families who are going to America in Feb'y. Mrs. J will probably go with one of them; and if so, will reach Phila[π] for the beginning of the Spring Session.

She will be a real curiosity. No doubt the first Hindoo woman who has ever set foot on American soil. I trust my native land will deal kindly with her. There will hardly be time for an answer before she must set sail – possibly there may be however – but if not, I shall take it for granted that my candidate is accepted and send her along.

She is a bright little woman – speaks English fairly well – and writes it better than I do. Her husband says that she has some knowledge of medicine already. She will no doubt appear dull at first as she will get on well after a time.

With love to your good mother, if she is with you still, and kind remembrances to all the friends,

I am sincerely yours,

Anna J. Thorburn.

My husband sends kind regards.

π Phila- Philadelphia

Appendix 2

Anandibai Joshi's speech at Shrirampur

Ladies and Gentlemen, – I stand here to fail, as I am not likely to succeed. I am however exceedingly thankful to you for the trouble you have taken to attend this meeting. You may have gathered here anxiously to hear of some interesting subject, but I am afraid you will be disappointed to hear me talking of an uninteresting one. But what should I do? There is no remedy. Had it been in my power to give you a pleasing address, I would have done so. The only attempt I have ever made to speak in public is this. I have studied but a little while and the language which I intend to speak in, is not only foreign but thoroughly out of command, and entirely unused. I am therefore liable to make thousands of blunders even in grammar. Many of those who are present here, are mere school boys who will rejoice to find that I am not equal to themselves; the young will laugh and the old will pity my ignorance.

I wish I had better knowledge of the language to attract the attention of you all. Pardon me for the disappointment you will have to suffer. I do not wish to tire you by a long preface, and as I want your unfatigued attention to a long narration, I beg to discontinue it.

I wish to thank the college authorities for allowing me to stand here, more especially the Rev. Mr. Summers for presiding.

Our subject today is, "My future visit to America, and public inquiries regarding it."

I am asked hundreds of questions about my going to America. I take this opportunity to answer some of them.

Why I go to America?

Are there no means to study in India?

Why do I go alone?

Shall I not be excommunicated on my return?

What shall I do if misfortune befall me?

Why should I do what is not done by any of my sex?

1. I go to America because I wish to study Medicine. I now address the ladies present here, who will be the better judges of the importance of female medical assistance in India. I never consider this subject without being surprised that none of those societies so laudably established in India for the promotion of sciences and female education have ever thought of sending one of their female members into the most civilised parts of the world to procure thorough Medical knowledge, in order to open here a college for the instruction of women in Medicine. There is probably no country so barbarous as India that would not disclose all her wants and try to stand on her own feet. The want of female physicians in India is keenly felt in every quarter. Ladies both European and native are naturally averse to expose themselves in cases of emergency to treatment by doctors of the other sex. There are some female doctors in India from Europe and America, who being foreigners and different in manners, customs and language have not been of such use to our women as they might. As it is very natural that Hindu ladies who love their own country and people should not feel at home with the natives of other countries, we Indian women absolutely derive no benefit from these foreign ladies.

They indeed have the appearance of supplying our need, but the appearance is delusive. In my humble opinion there is growing need for Hindu lady doctors in India, and I volunteer to qualify myself for one.

2. Are there no means to study in India?

No. I do not mean to say there are *no* means, but the difficulties are many and great. There is one college at Madras, and midwifery classes are opened in all the Presidencies; but the education imparted is defective and not sufficient, as the instructors who teach the classes are conservative and to some extent jealous. I do not find fault with them. That is the characteristic of the male sex. We must put up with this inconvenience until we have a class of educated ladies to relieve these men.

I am neither a Christian nor a Brahmo. To continue to live as a Hindu and go to school in any part of India is very difficult. A convert who wears an English dress is not so much stared at. Native Christian ladies are free from the opposition or public scandal which Hindu ladies like myself have to meet within and without the *zenana*. If I go alone by train or in the street some people come near to stare and ask impertinent questions to annoy me. Example is better than precept. Some few years ago, when I was in Bombay, I used to go to school. When people saw me going with my books in my hands, they had the goodness to put their heads out of the window just to have a look at me. Some stopped their carriages for the purpose. Others walking in the streets stood laughing, and crying out so that I could hear:

"What is this? Who is this lady who is going to school with boots and stockings on?"

"Does not this show that the Kali Uga has stamped its character on the minds of people?"

Ladies and gentlemen, you can easily imagine what effect questions like these would have on your minds if you had been in my place!

Once it happened that I was obliged to stay in school for some time, and go twice a day for my meals to the house of a relation.

Passers-by, whenever they saw me going, gathered round me. Some of them made fun, and were convulsed with laughter. Others, sitting respectably in their verandahs, made ridiculous remarks, and did not feel ashamed to throw pebbles at me. The shopkeepers and vendors spat at the sight of me, and made gestures too indecent to describe. I leave it to you to imagine what was my condition at such a time, and how I could gladly have burst through the crowd to make my home nearer!

Yet the boldness of my Bengali brethren cannot be exceeded, and is still more serious to contemplate than the instances I have given from Bombay. Surely it deserves pity! If I go to take a walk on the strand, Englishmen are not so bold as to look at me. Even the soldiers are never troublesome; but the Babus lay bare their levity by making fun of everything. "Who are you?", "What caste do you belong to?", "Whence do you come?", "Where do you go?" are, in my opinion, questions that should not be asked by strangers. There are some educated native Christians here in Serampore who are suspicious; they are still wondering whether I am married or a widow; a woman of bad character or excommunicated! Dear audience, does it become my native and Christian brethren to be so uncharitable? Certainly not. I place these unpleasant things before you, that those whom they concern most may rectify them, and those who have never thought of the difficulties may see that I am not going to America through any whim or caprice.

3. Why do I go alone?

It was at first the intention of my husband and myself to go together, but we were forced to abandon this thought. We have not sufficient funds; but that is not the only reason. There are others still more important and convincing. My husband has his aged parent and younger brothers and sisters to support. You will see that his departure would throw those dependent upon him into the arena of life, penniless and alone. How cruel and inhuman it would be for him to take care of one soul and reduce so many to starvation! Therefore, I go alone.

4. Shall I not be excommunicated when I return to India?

Do you think I should be filled with consternation at this threat? I do not fear it in the least. Why should I be cast out when I have determined to live there exactly as I do here? I propose to myself to make no change in my customs and manner, food or dress. I will go as a Hindu, and come back here to live as a Hindu. I will not increase my wants, but be as plain and simple as my forefathers, and as I am now. If my countrymen wish to excommunicate me, why do they not do it now? They are at liberty to do so. I have come to Bengal and to a place where there is not a single Maharashtrian. Nobody here knows whether I behave according to my customs and manners, or not. Let us therefore cease to consider what may never happen, and what, when it may happen, will defy human speculation.

5. What will I do if misfortune befall me?

Some persons fall into the error of exaggerated declamation, by producing in their talk examples of national calamities and scenes of extensive misery which are found in books rather than in the world, and which, as they are horrid, are ordained to be rare. A man or a woman who *wishes to act* does not look at that dark side which others easily foresee. On necessary and inevitable evils which crush him or her to dust, all dispute is vain. When they happen, they must be endured, but it is evident they are oftener dreaded than experienced. Whether perpetual happiness can be obtained in any way, this world will never give us an opportunity to decide. But this we may say, we do not always find visible happiness in proportion to visible means. It is not a thing which may be divided among a certain number of men. It depends upon feeling. If Death be only miserable why should some rejoice at it, while others lament? On the other hand, Death and Misery come alike to good and bad, virtuous and vicious, rich and poor, travellers and housekeepers; all are confounded in the misery of famine, and not greatly distinguished in the fury of faction. No man is able to prevent any catastrophe. Misery and Death are always near, and should be expected. When the result of any hazardous work is good, we praise the enterprise which undertook it; when it is evil, we blame the imprudence. The world is always ready to call enterprise imprudence when fortune changes.

Some say that those who stay at home are happy, but where does their happiness lie? Happiness is not a readymade thing to be enjoyed because one desires it. Some minds are so fond of variety that pleasure if permanent would be insupportable, and they solicit happiness by courting distress. To go to foreign countries is not bad, but in some respects better than to stay in one place. The study of people and places is not to be neglected. Ignorance when voluntary is criminal. In going to foreign countries, we may enlarge our comprehension, perfect our knowledge, or recover lost arts. Everyone must do what he thinks right. Every man has owed much to others. His effort ought to be to repay what he has received. Let us follow the advice of Goldsmith who says: "Learn to pursue virtue of a man who is blind, who never takes a step without first examining the ground with his staff." I take my Almighty Father for my staff, who will examine the path before He leads me further. I can find no better staff than He.

And last you ask me, why I should do what is not done by any of my sex? To this I can only say, that society has a right to our work as individuals.

It is very difficult to decide the duties of individuals. It is enough that the good of one must be the good of all. If anything seems best for all mankind, each one of us must try to bring it about. According to Manu, the desertion of duty is an unpardonable sin. So, I am surprised to hear that I should not do this, because it has not been done by others. Our ancestors whose names have become immortal had no such notions in their heads. I ask my Christian friends, "Do you think you would have been saved from your sins, if Jesus Christ, according to your notions, had not sacrificed his life for you all?" Did *he* shrink at the extreme penalty that he bore while doing good? No, I am sure you will never admit that he shrank! Neither did our ancient kings *"Shibi"* and *"Mayuradhwaj"*. To desist from duty because we fear failure or suffering is not just. *We must try*. Never mind whether we are victors or victims. Manu has divided people into three classes. The meanest are those who never attempt anything for fear of failure. Those who begin, and are disheartened by the first obstacles, come next; but those who begin, and preserve through failure and obstacle, are those who win.

The greater the difficulty, the greater our courage. Never let us desist from what we once began.

I have done. I am afraid I have exhausted your patience for which I beg to be excused.

Appendix 3

Anandibai Joshi's Thesis

Obstetrics
Among the Aryan Hindoos
SUBMITTED TO THE FACULTY
- OF THE –
Woman's Medical College of Pennsylvania
FOR THE DEGREE
- OF –
Doctor of Medicine,
Anandibai Joshee
- CLASS OF 1886 –
VM. H. HOSKINS, PRINTER, 918 ARCH ST. PHILAD'A. π

Obstetrics
Among the Aryan Hindoos

As the importance of Obstetrics can be measured only by the value of life and health, and both being of paramount consequence it is deserving of most careful study. When we realise how difficult and vast the subject is, it is not surprising to find so many great minds thoroughly absorbed in its magnitude, from the time immortal. Since our study naturally embraces the cause and effect, race, habits, climate, influences and means of assisting nature in her operations, we must not entirely overlook the history of past ages and consider the superior minds which laboured, with marked success, in the same field of investigation, under promptings of the same motives, as far back as 15th century B.C. They may enable us to the better appreciation of the science and pay due respect to the discoveries, thesis and

π Only the first page was printed. The thesis is in Anandibai's hand writing.

mode of application of remedies of minds of different nations at different times. I therefore need not apologise for choosing the subject.

The Hindoos divide these signs into those of conception and of pregnancy. "The signs of conception if carefully observed are, the woman feels languid, fatigued, thirsty, with weakness of the thighs, irritable with throbbing in the vagina. Fecundation not uncommonly sets in with febrile reaction in which case high temperature, full, quick and sounding pulse, anorexia, headache and thirst are very marked. Fever may set in with a sense of chilliness or may be nervous in character. Duration from a few days to 2 weeks."

"**Signs of Pregnancy** are cessation of menses, headache, insalivation, nausea, vomiting, variation in appetite, as a rule anorexia, general lassitude and 'bearing down' pains. Nausea and emesis are especially marked in the morning but may last all day. Later the cuticle around the nipple is deepened in colour and raised which often simulate the appearance of 'little nipples.' The enlargement of the mammae is sudden and marked. Skin become tense over the glands, lacerates with edges torn quite asunder. They have a thin, watery but greasy secretion appearing at the expiration of the third month. Vertigo, frequent micturition, change in disposition, irritability, peculiar and often unnatural cravings become prominent. There is another very important sign which the midwife should always look for. This is the Divine Writing which almost invariably means but one condition which is pregnancy. This extends from umbilicus to pubic. After five months have elapsed, irritability of bladder and rectum to some extent that of the mind are relieved. At this period a marked change is observed in the gait of the woman on account of the enlargement of the womb in the abdomen. About the seventh month her face presents peculiar lustre which is termed the 'lustre of pregnancy.' When this is reversed, the condition is very much feared." On account of the religious regularity of habits constipation is as unknown as it is injurious and if ever incurred, it is regarded as a disease and every effort is made to banish it. Foetal movements may begin at any time after the fourth month of pregnancy, but they generally begin about the 18th week and last throughout the entire period. They are always appreciated by the mother and often by the examiner's hands and eyes. Ballottement is considered as a valuable sign of pregnancy and presence of living child in uterus. No mention whatever is made in regards the foetal pulse by the ancient authors while on the other hand mother's pulse is considered as one of the most reliable sigs of pregnancy. To this the following characteristics are given. "It is full, strong, slow, normal and non-irritable." Their accuracy in regards to it is as great as their dependence on it. I have known at least two native physicians positively decide pregnancy from the pulse alone while in one case of my personal acquaintance, there was no other sign present.

The following good rules are laid down by Manu the great Aryan Legislator, Susruta and other physiologists. They say, "transgressing them means committing sin."

"**Hygiene of pregnancy**: Woman from the time of conception should be kept pure and happy. She should avoid sexual intercourse. She should not fast, retch, drag or lift heavy things, ride on horseback, sleep during the day and wake at night. She should avoid eating or drinking intemperately or indigestible foods, taking purgatives and emetics. She should avoid stretching, violent exercise, grief, fear and anger. She must not be frightened, nor hit at even in joke, as it will either produce abortion or leave an unerasable mark on the person of the baby. She must not be blistered. She will avoid all disagreeable sights and excitement and everything that will produce a shock. She should take no medicine if possible, nor without the advice of a skillful physician. She should not eat stale food or anything that is warmed over. Her bed should be moderately soft, low and comfortable. Her dress should never be heavy, tight or dragging. Let her wear white and a few ornaments. She should not take more than one full bath a day which should be according to rules in the morning. She must avoid taking cold after it. She must take some exercise in order to store up strength for a safe and natural delivery." The whole household unites and cooperates to fulfil the laws prescribed and friends and relatives take a great interest in her happiness and well-being especially do they endearer in case of a primipara. A primipara is invited to parties where young women, especially those in the similar condition, are invited. Garden parties, moonlight parties and candle-light parties have no end. Singing, playing, gentle dancing (strictly among women) constitute chief amusement. A variety of other amusements are invented. She is daily asked by friends and relatives as to her desire for certain things, food or drink. She at least receives three new light-coloured dresses. One at the end of the third month, one at the end of the fifth month and the third during the seventh month of pregnancy. "All these rules", says Susruta, "must be observed in order to avoid any catastrophe and disaster such as making the foetus congenitally deaf, dumb, blind or deformed, marking its body as by a hit or blister (on mother) interfering with its perfect development as by bad living, causing abortion as by shocks, fear or grief. If the mother is emotional, selfish or generous so will be the child. Prayers should often be repeated by the woman. All these should be borne in mind in connection with the child's futurity for its physical, mental, moral and psychical cultures, nay its very existence is dependent on its environment and the mother's condition."

A number of theories and long discussions exist on the development of ovum and foetes but as they will necessarily take up a great deal of time and space, I am obliged to omit them entirely.

Pathology: If there is any derangement of bile, wind or phlegm, discomfort or sign of abortion, leucorrhea or hemorrhage a physician of the following description should be sent for, at once. "The physician should be of a good family, of a healthy body, young, (or old experienced one when a family physician) handsome, pure, vigorous, modest, discreet, patient, firm and intelligent. He should keep his nails short and body clean, should be well acquainted with the shastra (his profession), should be studious and ready to do everything. He should be dignified in his department and correct in his manners and habits, gentle, kind, amiable, cheerful, collected and self-confident. His language must be mild, candid and encouraging like that of a friend. His heart pure and charitable. He should possess a character for strict voracity and chastity. He should be a man of sense and benevolence and his constant thought should be how he could do good. Such a person alone should be permitted to study this grand science of Medicine." He will note the following circumstances, observe the dress, manners and speech of the messenger, the planets and then his own impressions. He will next examine the patient with five physical senses and two higher ones. (I) Touch: will learn the condition of skin, temperature, dryness or moisture, roughness or smoothness, softness or hardness, regularity or irregularity of surface or of organs. (II) Hearing: will defect the condition of the Lungs, Heart, respiration, voice and disease of wind. (III) Vision: change in colour, tongue, eyes, urine are learned by vision. (IV) Taste: will decide the constituents of the urinary secretion as the red ants are found to be very fond of sugar. (V) Smell: will teach us about the reaction of secretion and excretion and discharge and also breath. (VI) Speech: will find out more than any other yet mentioned if judiciously employed. Histology, sex, time of invasion, habits, cause, strength, appetite, degree of pain, examination etc. The physician will treat disease here as in any other condition but more mildly and cautiously. Medicine and instruments should always be on hand and in best condition. Let the physician make a thorough examination, wait for a reasonable length of time, consult if necessary and use the seventh sense which has not been mentioned, the common sense or the inner sense in diagnosis & decision, on the kind of treatment he is to administer to his patient. Treat as early as possible while every condition is favourable. If there is pain, great turgescence and laceration of the mammae and abdomen inunctions of Sesame oil with gentle friction should be applied before daily bath and if necessary, a comfortable bandage to the abdomen should be fitted on. If insomnia exists give simple anodyne. For excessive emesis rest in bed and something to allay the irritability of stomach. Black mustard plaster may be applied over the area of the stomach. Physician should have free access to his patient. Soothing drinks do good. If abortion is threatened following symptoms will present themselves: Severe pain in the uterus, loins, groins, Bladder, Rectum with profuse white or bloody discharge from the womb. In such a case put the patient to bed and in perfect quiescence of body and mind with her hips raised above her head. Effusion of cold water or hot sitz bath are useful. Ice should be given internally. Pieces of cloths dipped in cold water and laid over the abdomen will do good. Prayers should be recited. If pain be very severe give Asafoetida and prepare Orris-root in milk. Another way of preparing Asafoetida is, take a piece of the green asafoetida of about the size of a small pea. Pop it well until it becomes 2-3 times its original size, pulverise it, mix with sugar and give in divided doses, within one hour. Repeat this until effect is produced. This is good for insomnia and intestinal colic. Give opium in small doses or Cannabis Indica in very small doses. If there is general feebleness, give 'Loha' or Iron and other tonics and spirits. Give broth of wild animal." This last thing is not resorted to by the higher classes. "If haemorrhage is excessive, astringent application, ice, hot water is good but never a canaling here." Gentle friction over the abdomen will often stop. Tampon the vagina if these fail… For this purpose, use cotton with all its seeds removed & cleaned. "The shastras advise not to use any medicinal treatment during gestation. Unless it is forced to be the only saviour of your patient. Hygienic treatment is best at times."

"**Duty of the patient**: A patient rejecting a physician will be punished here and hereafter. The deceased person, if not too ill, should recollect carefully the directions of her physician and follow them with exactness, not being afraid of the result of medicine that is ordered. She will expect to be visited by her physician every morning. She is to occupy a clean and pure part of the house, convenient both to the patient and doctor. She must have confidence in her doctor in order to effect cure."

Causes of abortion: Disease of the vagina, misplacement of the uterus, syphilis, gonorrhea, excessive coitus, fever, shocks and violent exercise. Age and criminal attempts are important." In spite of their limited knowledge of the physiological action of drug, experience, had no doubt befitted them to combat with diseases like syphilis and gonorrhea with some simple but valuable means as injection of water with certain salts as copper sulph, zinc sulph, Iron sulph, or common salt, decoctions of certain bark and mercury with comparatively good success. They also recommend leeches for the early stage. "A primipara" says Dhanwantaree, "should be instructed to think it very modest to inform her elder women in the house, in case she should experience pain whether false or true and that in spite of all desires to micturate or defecate, she must not go the privy after that, as delivery may take place and prove fatal to both the mother and the child. Such a sensation is caused by pressure of the womb on Bladder and Rectum. If pain subside after treatment for Intestinal Colic, they are false. The false pains are irregular and are reduced in intensity and frequency by time and healing. They are "generally confined to the front. The true pains commence in the back and traverse towards the front.They are regular and increase in intensity. While the pains are moderate and everything else normal the patient should walk about in the room, in order that the foetus may adopt itself to the parturient canal. But as the pain becomes more and more severe, the patient should be put to bed and kept quiet, calm, cheerful and composed. Her back should be supported by someone. Her mother or whoever takes her place should change her dress and rub her back with oil and bathe her in order to divert the attention of the suffering woman. She should be put to bed so that the membrane may not rupture prematurely."

Preparation for lying in: The preparation for lying in consist of, a comparatively dark room is to be put in order. The ancients say, "A hut should be temporarily built for this purpose and is to be destroyed as soon as the lying-in period is over." But this is out of practice. Now every house has in it a room built for this purpose, with windows opening towards Eastern South, as described by Charak Susruta and others. "This should be kept clean, neat, dry, aerated and sunny." It is fixed with a cot, a bed, a fireplace, with a few medicines, baby clothes, scissors (dull), bobbin, oil of sesamum, Indica, finely pulverised turmeric, soft muslin napkins both for the mother and the baby. Those for the mother are folded into may folds (about 7-10 in) and between each two surfaces (excepting the two upper most layers) are put very finely sifted wood ashes. These are believed to prevent putrefactive changes in the lochia. They are placed under the patient. Two bandages, one for the mother which is from 4 to 6 yards long and the other one for the baby which is half its length. These should be made of soft and strong material. A little honey, a chamber vessel for the placenta. "There should always be hot water in the house after the seventh month of pregnancy and religiously so if there is any suspicion or warning that the labour had commenced. If the labour is found to be in labour panic, a skillful midwife and two other elderly women with calm and non-excitable disposition with short nails and clean person be sent for." These persons and a midwife are always engaged beforehand. "These should not include mother of the parturient woman." The midwife will make a thorough examination and decide the position of the patient according to the position of the foetus in uterus. Thus, she may put the woman on her back (which is by far the commonest position in India), semi prone or even easy chair position. Let the midwife watch the progress of labour carefully and note the position of the foetus. One word to the midwife or the physician "Let the surgeon or obstetrician," says Manu, "bear in mind that they are but second hands to Nature and that any effort on their part should be simply to assist Nature in her wise work and method of operation. She can do her work more simply and prudently than they can with all their knowledge and interference. This is daily seen in the lower animals and for this reason never interfere unless nature calls for it. The patient should be told that her infant, like the extraneous substance must be expelled and must assist by her methodical efforts. No one but the assistants and the elderly women in the home should know anything about the condition of the woman. No one but the assistants should be allowed to enter the room. Men and children should be kept ignorant of it." The superstitious believers think it will increase the suffering on part of the patient to have men and children know of it.

Accident of labour: If the breach presents it will be born readily but the after coming of the head will call for some interference. If the foetus is transverse it must be verted. The lower part is to be pushed down and the upper upwards in order to bring about version. To accomplish this an assistant is required for external manipulation, while the midwife with her hands inside will turn the child. The hand outside will retain what is gained by the operation. If knee presents bring down the leg either one or both and it will simply be a breach presentation. If there is prolepsis of hands or feet and cannot be reduced, knife must be used; but this should seldom take place while the foetus is alive. If the child is dead and is not expelled, crematory should be performed. Some time is necessary to remove limbs and trunk in sections. There are certain conditions under which cutting into the uterus is necessary, through vagina such as atresia and certain disease of the Cervix Uteri. This is a dangerous operation, being on an internal organ, it is like working in darkness. After the contents are removed put sutures in and treat the case as you would a serious wound. If the pelvic is so deformed that the presenting part is beyond pelvic cavity this operation is justifiable. If the presenting part cannot descend and is beyond your reach and the pelvic so small that it would not admit of any operation through the vagina there is but one thing to be done. This is cutting into the abdomen and uterus. The woman is to be considered in great danger. The child may endanger its own life by changing the position. Her protector, whether father, mother, husband or king should be informed without delay of her condition. The surgeon should next do his operation formidable and perilous as it is by cutting into the lima alba after the intestines are pushed out of the way, cutting the uterine walls in the same line. Extracting the foetus and the placenta gently. After this wash the organ out next with certain waters as prescribed and close the wound with sutures of silver or gold wire or silk, put compress on. The wound must be fumigated three times daily for the first few days by burning the resins and other substances in a chaffing dish while the patient lies on an open cane cot. This is a formidable operation but has saved both the lives when they could not be saved by anything else. The operation is fully described by Susruta, "There are three causes that may impede delivery. These are deformity of the pelvic, preternatural presentation and deformity of the child's head." Order of presentation according to Charak, Vertex, Breach, Footing, Back, Face and Knee. Each of these have a sub-division which I cannot here give on account of rarity of space. "If the foetus is alive manipulation and prayers should be tried before any operative measures."

After the foetus is expelled, wait for ½ an hour for the placenta and if it is delayed for a long; wash your hands clean and introduce it into the uterus. Carefully place your fingers all around against the walls of the uterus and gently remove all the membranes and the placenta.

Resuscitation: If the baby was asphyxiated and did [not] cry or show any sign of life it must be attended at once while the assistant will attend to the woman as will be told afterwards. Gently rub the back of the child and stroke its chest. Remove all the mucus from its throat by your little finger.Hoop out everything that may lodge in throat. Small pieces of clothes dipped in cold water should be laid over the chest suddenly and changed instantly by placing another one in its place. Move the arms of the child up and down or extend and flex them alternately. If this will not be sufficient, place the child in warm water, place the placenta as far from it as the cord will allow you to do with safety. A few shreds of cotton should be next placed over the placenta at short distance and set fire to them. As they ignite, the blood will be warmed and remove the difficulty if it be caused by the infant's being chilled after birth. I was informed of this by an elderly lady who herself tried this method in two instances of apparently dead babies, with decided success. One of these two infant died many years after that and the other is a man of twenty-three years of age.

"The umbilical cord should be tied with a string six fingers breadth from the navel and divided. Warp up the baby in warm clothes and put it in an oblong basket which is designed for it and attend to the woman.

After the woman is delivered of the placenta in whole, she should be made comfortable by placing her on her back if she is not so already. The womb should be pressed upon until bandage is applied. The vagina and labia should be well smeared with sesame oil and turmeric powder in warm milk and washed or injected thoroughly with hot water. Bandage is next to be applied. This makes the woman comfortable by caressing pressure on parts that have been subjected to it and of which they are suddenly deprived. It also compresses the uterus. A napkin should be next placed under her and is to be removed from time to time. From this time the patient is to lie on her back for ten days. This period is sufficiently long enough to affect the inoculation of the uterus. If a woman neglects and does not follow these directions, she will suffer from subinvolution, pain in back, displacement and many such troubles probably all her life. Hot bath is given every morning after the sixth day after delivery and on every other day before that. Oleaginous friction massage and daily injections are given. The person of the patient must be kept very clean. Massage and injections are kept up for four or at least three months after parturition. The room should be thoroughly disinfected twice daily by burning certain resinous substances." There are some special resins that are burned in a chaffing dish and the person of the patient is fumigated twice a day for the first 4 or 5 days. And once only for a few days after that. She lays on an open cane cot while she is being fumigated. Her food should be simple and nutritious kind, consisting of wheat-bread and a large number of other articles. Milk she can take plentifully. She cannot take either water or milk that has not been boiled previously, nor can she take them if they have been mixed with water unboiled in order to cool. "Water can be easily cooled in the khujas in these days." The ancients strongly believed that, "the atmosphere is densely populated by germs of infinite variety and minuteness and can never be seen by human eye." These can be destroyed by heat and fumes of certain resins hence the boiling process. Susruta says, "give her the following mixture. Long pepper and its root, dry ginger, asafoetida, Iris Germania, Amreona[?] Squamosa, Dolichos Senensis[?], Cicer Ainanturmn[?] as a decoction in the first few days." This formula is greatly modified and used with some more pleasant and palatable drugs. We can easily see why this modification was necessary. Milk, linctus and wines are given. I tried to procure some of the formulae of present days but was disappointed not to get them in time. There are many things, even the names of which I do not know, that are used in puerperal fever etc. Female visitors may be allowed to see her after the first 48 hours but they are not to ask her any questions for 4 to 5 days and only a few after that. They should never enter the room without washing their hands and feet in certain disinfectant waters prepared for this purpose and sprinkle their clothes with them. They should stay at a distance, for they are not to touch the woman nor her baby. No one but the nurse and midwife and perhaps one other person are allowed to touch her or the new born for ten days, unless they are willing [to] go through the process of bathing, washing their hair and changing their clothes. She does not resume her full diet for nearly a week. On the eleventh day, she is bathed early in the morning, wrapped up in warm clothes and removed in a warm room where she makes her more permanent abode (for four months). On the twelfth day is the naming ceremony where friends and relatives are gathered to celebrate it. Musicians sing their gentle melodies from beginning up to this day. Male visitors can see the patient after four days.

"After the second day (after parturition) the woman feels pain in her breasts. These glands are exquisitely sensitive to touch and greatly enlarged. There is rise of temperature, headache and general discomfort for 24 hours after which milk appears." After about two weeks she is not at all required to stay in bed, nor in one place. "She may take sufficient exercise inside her own room by taking care of her child." But she is not to expose herself to change of weather or of clothes. She is not to sit up all day for many weeks yet. (Period of lying in lasts for 40 days.) She must not do any manual work, fetch or draw water or lift heavy things for these months. She should avoid fatigue and over exertion of any kind. These are almost the causes of prolapses uteri so should be borne in mind. She must avoid intemperance in eating and dressing and anger.Sexual intercourse is religiously prohibited for four months after delivery. Avoid excess of sour, pungent or sweet thing. "Germ Acacia is popped and coarsely powdered, a certain proportion of sugar is made into syrup and a large number of other drugs in fixed proportion, such as Cinnamomum, Pimento Caryophyllids, Myristica, Cardamom, Zingiber, Pepper, Nigreum (?) etc. mixed together in the syrup and made into little balls of about the eye of the English walnut and this is taken every morning. Ginger cake with number of ingredients that exceed some scores are taken every morning for two to three months." Her dress should be warm and simple. "The sleeves of her bodice which otherwise only reach her elbow are now made to reach her wrist. Unlike the usual custom she also wears a cape in order to protect her head from catching cold.Thus, high neck, long sleeves and a cape are to be worn for four months. She must not walk about without shoes. She should not bathe her hands or feet in cold water. Change in food, dress and exercise (outdoor) must be gradual one. She must nurse her own child. She must keep her breast clean and in good condition. "She must avoid anger, for anger has killed babies by poisoning through milk."

After the Cord has been tied and divided, the new-born should be smeared all over with sesame oil and gently rubbed. While doing this the nurse should examine the child's body and note that there is no imperfection anywhere. She must anoint the little finger and carefully pass it in the anus if she can. This will decide that there is no imperforate anus. Let her next pass her another little finger under the tongue and see that the Phrenum[?] does not extend too far. Then pass the same finger further on and hook out all that may lodge in the throat. Examine other parts of the body at the same time. If there is imperforate anus or tongue tie, opening in the former and tearing in the latter case is necessary, and should be resorted at once. Finger nail as a rule will answer every purpose. This will take but a moment for an experienced and skillful nurse and require little skill at this period of life but will save many an hour of suffering. Give a brief bath to the child and dry it well especially under the arms, in the groins, neck, ears, between the toes and fingers because at these points, friction will give rise to eczema. Take a piece of muslin as large as the palm of the hand, burn a hole in it large enough to admit the cord through. It is better to leave as much of the charred surface on as possible.The cord should be thoroughly cleaned and covered with the piece of cloth with a drop of oil in it. Put a small pad of soft muslin on it and bandage the abdomen. Bandage should not be too tight nor should it be loose enough to easily be displaced. A soft muslin napkin is next applied. The dress of the infant should be warm enough to retain the animal heat and long enough to cover its feet. The child is to be moved about gently and any exposure to loud noises is to be avoided. Avoid heavy dress. Baby is not to be suddenly awoke nor to be moved or handled roughly. It is not to be held sitting up long, nor to be lifted up by the arms, as these careless manners will make the child lump back or dislocate its limbs. A good healthy child ought to creep and walk before it is nine months old. Avoid exposure to cold, sun, wind, lightning. The bed of the child should be properly made. The new-born should be placed on its back until it is able to assume its own position. Soon after it is all dressed up it should be given a little honey, about as much as would come on the tip of your index finger. This acts a laxative and helps Nature to remove meconium as mother's milk does not usually appear on the first day, especially in a primipara. Feed the baby after this. If mother's milk is not sufficient for the first few days, goat's or cow's milk should be substituted for it. The former is better borne by the young infant than the latter. This should be boiled twice and skimmed after cooling the same each time before administration. The infant should be fed every hour for the first two months in small quantities, every two hours until it is six months old, every three hours until it is weaned after which you will manage according to the circumstances. Child should not be weaned until it is a year old under ordinary conditions. Infant should be bathed every day in the morning, dressed, fed and put to bed in a cradle. The time of feeding should be regulated. The baby should be kept clean. It is very important that the milk the child drinks should be well-boiled and skimmed at least once before administration." The marked acidity of child's stomach and the extreme heat of our summers cause curding of cream which the unboiled milk naturally possesses. This forms a precipitate which sometimes, indeed quite commonly becomes a source of great suffering on the part of the child. These cheesy masses are very small in the beginning of about the size of lima beans, but soon become coated and constitute what we call 'Watak' or Stomach Calculi. When small, they are expelled during the act of Emesis which is so common with babies. When large, as I said before they become the source of great alarm and uneasiness. They often reach the size of about one inch in diameter and 2 to 4 inch in length. They occlude the oesophagus or pharynx and cause death by strangulation. I have seen three children suffering from suffocation and one death after a number of attacks. These Calculi when within reach, are extracted with difficulty. They are hard, tough, long masses of creamy white colour and broken with difficulty. If discovered early enough they can be broken up into smaller particles which can be vomited off. The tongue is coated while coating being heavy and not easily removed. This symptom and vomiting with the cheesy masses as described above give rise to strong suspicion and a careful mother puts herself on the guard. For this the child is given to such some alkalis several times a day, such as a little chalk (or sometimes in milk), Bismuth in very small doses and some other earthly matters. Emesis is induced by ticking the fauces and thus rid the stomach of these masses.

"The child should be fed with a pointed or conical spoon made of gold or silver which is next to mother's nipple." Hindoos never use a bottle for feeding the baby. After the child has thus lived for six months on milk alone, it may take a small quantity of rice, well boiled and made almost into gruel, in milk with little salt into it. Bread boiled in milk, barley or other digestible substances can be given. The diet of a child should be simple, nutritious and more or less liquid in consistency. Honey and sugar have done much harm. They are the origin of any infantile diseases, so should be used with due caution. If the mother is angry, pregnant, fatigued, in grief, is feverish or anaemic, has intemperate sexual appetite or has mammary disease, the milk is rendered unhealthy to the child. So, it should have a wet-nurse or be fed on cow's milk. If the child is sick, medicines are to be given to the mother or a nurse. But medicines should not be resorted to until the child is a year old, if possible.

"Wet-nurse: The wet-nurse should be of the same caste or class as the child. She should have a perfect body, good complexion and loving nature. She should be of medium height, middle age (not old) and in good health, devoid of chronic diseases and non-covetous. She should be of a good temper, of a staid, cheerful disposition and have natural fondness for children. Her milk should be good quality and flow easily. The nipple neither too short nor too long, nor too small with pendulous breasts. She should present a good family history. She should be clean in person and clothes and regular in diet and sleep. She should not nurse more than one child."

When it is found to be absolutely necessary to have a wet-nurse these preconditions are religiously observed and a careful inquiry is made into her family history, health, occupation, etc., unless she is known to have nursed any children before. They are careful for they sincerely and correctly believe that feeding on her milk, the child will naturally inherit her good or bad qualities, health or disease say nothing of the influence she exerts on the baby, both moral and intellectual by her association and be as they say, "As is the soil and seed, so will be the tree that bear the fruit."

Diseases of infancy: are too numerous to describe and treat here, but I will select a few only out of the long array as given by Charak which come directly under care of the Obstetric Cases.

Marasmus Causes: Malnutrition, nursing a sick or pregnant woman or one who have little milk, sore nipples or breasts. May be a defective intra uterine development, a premature birth.

Symptoms: The child is thin, peevish, sallow, restless and presenting appearances of extreme age.

Treatment: Healthy mother's milk or cow's milk, a wet-nurse's milk, most important. Cow's milk is nutritious, sweet and easily digestible. Buffalo's (Egyptian) milk is sweeter and heavier and adopted for older people. Goat's milk is sweet and excellent, especially for infants.Ewe's milk is saltish and disagreeable, not easily digested. Mare's milk is saltish, acidulous and easily digested. Ass's milk is very fresh, easily digestible and very good in extreme debility. Must be taken as soon as it is drawn. Out of these, choose for your patient according to the case. All milk except human milk (and I believe Ass's milk, for I have seen it prescribed in one case about 10 years ago) must be boiled before taking. Give plenty of milk, massage and daily bath. Carefully filtered or strained through a thick cloth, cow's milk can be used as a stimulant and food. Give it three times daily. If the bones of the child are soft and the fontanelle not closed in time, give hartshorn in small quantity twice daily or more. (This is the antler of the deer, incinerated in closed vessels. This burnt hartshorn leaves 57.5 per cent Phosphate of Calcium.) Nutritious foods must be combined with this.

Diarrhea: Caused by too often feeding and excess of cow's milk. Artificial feeding causes it.

Treatment: Change in diet. Get a good wet-nurse if mother is not able to nurse baby.If there is much pain give very minute quantity of Opium. Certain medicinal leaves are used for poulticing the abdomen. Take fresh ginger, pare it, crush or macerate it and squeeze out the juice and strain it. Make syrup of a definite proportion of sugar, mix and boil them a little while. This makes very nice ginger syrup. Give a little of it to the baby from time to time. Sodium Phosphates are given.

Persistent hiccough: Give ¼ gr. of Kamarupu musk in milk 2-3 times a day. Nepal and other musks are not so good.

Convulsions: **Asafoetida** in milk, preparation of garlic, baths and sudden dash of water.

Seat worms: **Cause**: Malnutrition, too many sweet things, candies, sugar, etc.

Treatment: I cannot give all the preparations, but I will simply mention the names of some of the drugs. Pornica granatum, Careca papaya, Sulphur (most commonly given, after Mangifera Indica), Vernonia Anthelmentica, etc. and Castor oil which takes a high rank. Cathartics are recommended for the unpleasant escape of gas. Cardamom with husk on, burnt in charcoal fire pulverised and given in honey.

I have not mentioned those principles, theories and treatments, in this paper, which are entirely out of practice in India, though there are many valuable things with perhaps as many ridiculous ones in our ancient Medical and Surgical literature (concerning obstetrics) that are not in practice. I have said too little to do justice to what is taught and practiced among the Brahmins, but on account of the rarity of valuable time and space, I am obliged to say no more.

Anandibai Joshee

Appendix 4

Statement of extra expense at London, sent by Dr. Anandibai Joshi to the Diwan of Kolhapur

Bombay

Dated 20th Nov. 86

To,

Dear Diwan Saheb

A first-class passage from London to Bombay was secured through the Agents of Thomas Cook & Sons in New York by J. J. Harzada of British J. S. N Company, but on arrival in London and just before the date of starting, I was refused it; in consequence of which I was put to more expenses than that at first estimated. I had no sufficient funds at my disposal. I therefore, obtained a loan of £18 from Mr. Pattison of London, being the difference passage money between B. J. S. N and P & O Company's steamers, I shall have to remit the sum to that gentlemen [in] London. His address is

"Mr. Pattison
5 Lyndhurst Road
Hampstead
London."

The estimate that I had sent to you [from] America was as follows: -

New York to London	\$ 100 or £ 20
London to Bombay	\$ 250 or £ 50
Outgoings etc.	\$ 150 or £ 30

	\$ 500 or £ 100

The expenses incurred are detailed here. Before I came to London I had no [idea] as to the Hotel and Boarding charges there, which by far exceeded my original bill.

New York to London	$ 100 or £ 20
London to Bombay	$ 340 or £ 68
Sundry expenses up to the date of landing in Bombay	$ 200 or £ 40

	$ 640 or £128

I have not included in this my expenses since arrived in Bombay. Please therefore advance me Rs. 250 just to meet my current expenses.

Yours very truly,

Anandibai Joshi (MD)

The List of English Reference Books

1. *The Life of Dr. Anandabai Joshee* – Caroline Healey Dall, 1888
2. The Letters and Correspondence of Pandita Ramabai – Compiled by Sister Geraldine, Edited by A. B. Shah, 1977
3. The Reprint of *The High Caste Hindu Woman* – Pandita Ramabai, February 1981
4. *Builders of Modern India* – Pandita Ramabai,1930
5. *Pandita Ramabai Saraswati: Her Life and Work* – Padmini Sengupta, 1970
6. *My Indian Friends* – F. Max Muller 1899
7. *Saguna: A Story of Native Christian Life* – Krupabai Satthianandhan, 1895
8. *Kamala* – Krupabai Satthianandhan, 1894
9. *Women Gain a Place in Medicine* – Edythe Lutzker,1969
10. *Lone Woman – The Story of Elizabeth Blackwell: The First Woman Doctor* – Dorothy Clarke Wilson, 1970
11. *Storming the Citadel: The Rise of The Woman Doctor* – E. Moberly Bell, 1953
12. *Women Doctors in America (1835-1920)* – Edited by- Ruth J. Abram, 1985
13. *Women in White* – Geoffrey Marks and William K. Beatty, 1972
14. *A Woman's Quest: The Life of Marie E. Zakrzewska* – Edited by Agnes C. Victor, 1972
15 *Doctors Wanted: No Woman Need Apply: Sexual Barriers in Medical Profession (1835-1975)* – Mary Roth Walsh, 1977
16. *Glances and Glimpses* – Harriot K. Hunt, 1856
17. *Women Doctors of The World* – Esther Pehle Lovejoy, 1957
18. *A History of Women in Medicine* – Kate Campbell, Hurd Mead, 1938

19. *Great Women of Medicine* – Ruth Fox Hume

20. *A Practical Illustration of Women's Right to Labor or A Letter from Marie E. Zakrzewska* – Caroline H. Dall, 1860

21. *An Introduction to History of Medicine* – Feilding H. Garrison, 1961

22. *Woman and Medicine* – Beatrice Levin, 1988

23. *The Cloister's Pale: A Biography of The University of Bombay* – Aroon Tikekar, 1984

About the Author

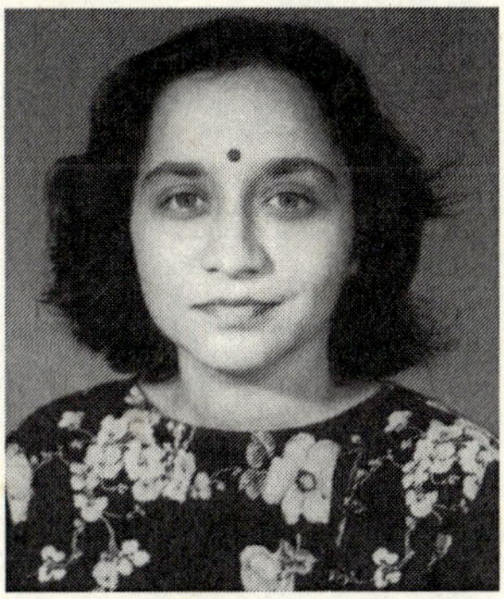

Anjali Kirtane researched on 'The Impact of Molière on Marathi Drama' and received her Ph.D. from Mumbai University in 1983. She worked as a co-editor of the 'Encyclopaedia of Marathi Literature: Volume 4: Criticism' under the able guidance of two stalwart writers late Prof. W.L. Kulkarni and late Prof. M. V. Dhond. Later on, she worked in Popular Prakashan as an Editor and Manager of the Marathi Division. Anjali is a versatile and creative writer who expresses herself in various literary forms like short story, poem, essay, novel, biography, drama and screenplay. She has written the biographies of the pioneer Indian woman doctor, Dr. Anandibai Joshi, renowned author Durga Bhagwat and a sweet voiced classical singer of the Gwalior Gharana, Pt. D. V. Paluskar.

She produces and directs research-oriented short films. Her first film on Dr. Anandibai Joshi was made in 1993. It won the 'Best Documentary Award' from the state of Maharashtra. She has written books as well as made films on various subjects like Dr. Anandibai Joshi, famous author Durga Bhagwat, the Golden era of Classical Hindustani Music and Pandit D. V. Paluskar. She makes her research films like feature film, using locations and actors. Her films are well appreciated in America and England as well. For reaching a wider audience the two films on classical music are made in Marathi, Hindi and English. Presently she is researching on the life and work of a great grammarian of Hindustani Music Pandit Vishnu Narayan Bhatkhande.